Key to map of Calcutta
1. House of Mr Petruse
2. Writers' Buildings (where students were housed)
3. No. 31 Bow Bazar – Lall Bazar Chapel
4. No. 34 Bow Bazar – Carey's rented rooms
5. College of Fort William
6. Government House

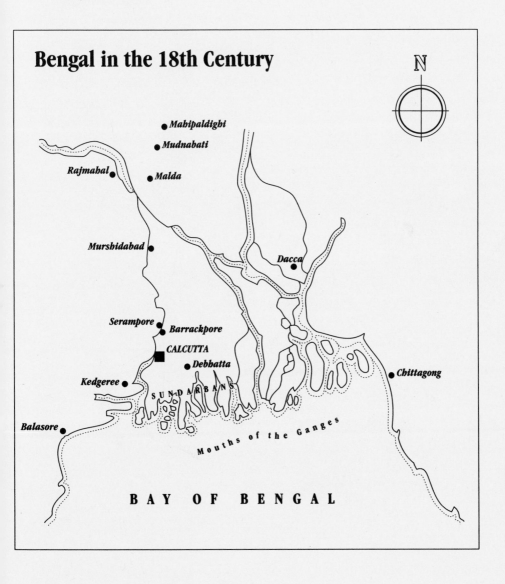

Bengal in the 18th Century

N

- Mahipaldighi
- Mudnabati
- Rajmahal
- Malda
- Murshidabad
- Dacca
- Serampore
- Barrackpore
- CALCUTTA
- Debhatta
- Chittagong
- Kedgeree
- SUNDARBANS
- Balasore
- Mouths of the Ganges

BAY OF BENGAL

WILLIAM CAREY

William Carey and his Pundit, by Robert Home of Calcutta, 1812, courtesy of Regent's Park College, Oxford

WILLIAM CAREY

S. PEARCE CAREY

'The father of modern missions'

THE WAKEMAN TRUST * LONDON

THE WAKEMAN TRUST
(UK Registered Charity)
5 Templar Street
London SE5 9JB

WILLIAM CAREY

© Copyright 1923, S. Pearce Carey (1862–1953)
First published by Hodder & Stoughton Ltd, London, 1923
Revised and enlarged eighth edition published by the Carey Press,
London, 1934
This copyright edition, edited by Peter Masters, published under licence
with world rights by the Wakeman Trust, London, 1993

ISBN 1 870855 14 0

Jacket design and endpaper illustrations by Andrew Sides

Printed in Great Britain by Butler and Tanner, Frome, Somerset

Contents

Illustrations

Foreword

S. PEARCE CAREY surpassed all other biographers in the unfolding of the extraordinary story of his great-grandfather –'the
father of modern missions'. This volume, to borrow a phrase,
'towers like an o'ertopping alp' above the other records, admirable as
they are.

The author was a distinguished Baptist minister and missionary
statesman of the first half of this century, but he became famous in the
Christian world as a writer. His acclaimed and best-selling life of Carey
appeared in 1923, and passed through eight editions by the time it was
extensively revised in 1934.

An accomplished historian and prodigious researcher, S. Pearce
Carey was a master of the biographical craft. Armed with a charming
and compelling style, he structured his life of Carey around the
remarkable providences by which God led the missionary band to
undreamed-of achievements. Pearce Carey's work breathes the atmosphere of places and events as no other history of these events does.

It was essential that such a major biography be reissued for the
bicentenary of Carey's sailing to India, for the story of how a self-
educated, country shoe-maker summoned into life the modern
missionary movement is far too significant to be left to short sketches.

By the mighty power of God, Carey cut through the formidable theological, legal and social prejudices of his day to become the most productive missionary church planter *and* Bible translator of all time. By his accomplishments (and deportment) over many years he overcame the implacable hostility of the British Government toward missionaries. Eventually, the man who was forbidden to preach became consulted and employed by the Government, and one of the most frequent guests at the Governor-General's table.

The tireless evangelism of Carey and his colleagues led to more than 600 baptisms within nineteen years of the establishment of their Serampore headquarters, though their care in accepting professions of faith was considerable. The translation and printing achievement of Serampore was phenomenal. In a thirty-year period 212,000 items (Bibles, Testaments, Gospels, books and tracts) were printed in forty languages. Indeed, the Serampore missionaries translated the Scriptures into so many languages (including non-Indian tongues such as Chinese) that their home detractors charged them with inventing the names of languages, then claiming to have mastered them and translated the Scriptures into them.

Carey's work, more than any other influence, led to the birth and rapid growth of the missionary efforts of all Christian denominations. Suddenly, long years of indifference and resistance gave way to a deep concern for the evangelisation of the heathen, so that within four decades of Carey's sailing, thirteen new missionary societies were formed in Britain alone, and a tidal wave of missionaries left European and American shores for distant peoples.

On the mission field, Carey was far ahead of his time in terms of his *spiritual* non-colonialism. Dedicated to a policy of teaching Indian people the Gospel in their own languages, he quickly trained Indian converts as evangelists and ministers to win Indians to the faith. At his Serampore headquarters he established equality of Indians with Europeans, also calling upon Indian converts to renounce their caste.

As convinced Calvinists, Carey and his colleagues embraced and loved the 'doctrines of grace', holding to the Reformation and Puritan view of human depravity, God's predestinating love, and the necessity of an irresistible work of the Holy Spirit to bring lost sinners to salvation. These same doctrines, to their mind, required them to publish the call of the Gospel with utmost zeal in every corner of the world.

Always, their greatest inspiration and comfort in times of difficulty was the conviction that God's saving will was irresistible, and therefore people would be moved to seek the Lord no matter how antagonistic their hearts might initially seem to be.

The great theological battle of Carey's day concerned the use of 'means'. Would God use the efforts of Christians to spread the Gospel, or would He save the lost in a direct manner, using great catastrophes and awakenings? Carey answered – God would work by the missionary efforts of His people. He was proved right, and once again in our day we need to learn the absolute necessity of evangelistic activism on the part of Christ's churches.

How greatly this narrative of God's power is needed today! At a time when Christians are tempted to garnish the Gospel with 'worldly' attractions and entertainments in order to make its message more attractive or palatable, this history of pioneer missionary labour gloriously exhibits the great power of the Gospel unaided by human gimmickry.

In connection with Carey's unflagging activity, it is striking to note that he was never strictly a full-time minister or missionary. Despite his enormous translation output, and the ever-expanding schemes which he pursued, he always worked for his living, whether mending shoes or keeping school in his early days, or cultivating indigo or lecturing Sanskrit and its vernaculars in later years. Always, too, there was some vital purpose served by these secular labours. The challenge of such a life may be intimidating, but in Carey we have an example of mighty spiritual achievement set by one who was really never *wholly* set free to the service of the Lord.

A substantial work such as this is bound to give attention to the trials of the missionaries, especially the long period of antagonism from home Baptists who should have been their keenest supporters. The chief and subtle cause of this tragic episode was a severe bout of 'establishmentitis' – the institutional form of *pride*. A vociferous party within English Baptist churches wanted to possess and control the missionaries, and so create a missionary empire of which they could be proud. When the missionaries resisted, they were remorselessly vilified. While S. Pearce Carey recoils from providing a judicial review, he describes the effect upon the missionaries, and their remarkable response to severe testing. In such distressing portions the author's record is replete with implicit lessons for the servants of God in every age.

This new (1993) edition of *William Carey* has been edited with a view to literary improvement only. The facts and conclusions remain as the author presented them in the 1934 edition. The aim of editing has been to remove certain literary idiosyncrasies together with peculiarities of the 1920s, and to update the punctuation. Some excessive detail has been removed, especially where this related to quite incidental matters, or to the subsequent history of causes only slightly connected with the Carey story. One entire chapter providing examples of Indian humour and wisdom has been omitted, and the author's unusual survey of Carey's botanical exploits has been turned into an appendix, where it no longer disturbs the flow of the book. Indian terms, which appeared in profusion in earlier editions, have either been explained or replaced by English terms. Where letters are quoted, the original spelling and grammar has been left intact, however quaint.

The author's original quotations prefacing each chapter (omitted from the 1934 revision) have been largely restored, with additional material – mainly significant statements from other major biographers, or quotations from primary sources.

In all editing the greatest care has been taken not to damage the author's graphic, moving and gracious style.

May this modern classic of Christian biography seize the minds and hearts of a new generation of Christians, showing how much can be done by the power of the Spirit, when the old truths are really put to the test! May the testimony of Carey and his dedicated colleagues speak again!

PETER MASTERS

Metropolitan Tabernacle,
London,
January, 1993

Preface

THIS DOES NOT attempt to be an exhaustive record of the origin of Carey's *Particular Baptist Society for the Propagation of the Gospel amongst the Heathen,* nor of its first forty Indian years. Certainly, I agree with Sir John W. Kaye that 'the son of Marshman has done this work with such authority and with such ability that this great chapter of evangelical history can never need further illustration.'

My aim is personal – the disclosure of a man.

In the days when Eustace Carey wrote his uncle's *Life,* Christian biographers stressed their heroes' pieties and blurred their human frailties. The modern way is almost the reverse. We take the pieties more for granted: our interest is in the human aspects. My aim has been to recover and display *the man* – to make him familiar.

Spurgeon thanked Dr George Smith for having rescued Carey from the lumber which had so long overlain him – for making him more knowable than Eustace had left him. But even he frequently lost the man in the movement. His pages disclosed the movement's magnitude and might, and the force of Carey's contribution, yet Carey himself was often out of focus. This was in great part due to Dr Smith's abandonment of chronological order in more than half his story, so that we found ourselves thrust to and fro, back and forth, hither and thither, through most of the Indian chapters, to our inevitable confusion. The development of the man – of his faith, endeavour, and achievement was not distinctly enough manifested.

I set myself to write Carey's *whole story* – to gather and to garner truthfully and livingly *all* that deserved enduring remembrance. This all-embracing purpose has claimed from me my ten gladly-devoted years.

Of course, the Baptist Mission House in Furnival Street, London, has been my richest field for gleaning, where are scores and scores, not just of excerpts from Carey's and Marshman's and Ward's letters, but of their whole originals, along with folios of Fuller's letters to India, and of Marshman's from Serampore, the complete diary of Ward for many years, and the Society's first minute-books and accounts. There are also invaluable contemporary reference books, Fuller's day-book, and the letters of Felix Carey to his father, etc, etc.

The Bristol and Regent's Park College libraries; the Northampton and Leicester reference libraries; the Church Missionary Society library, the Moravian Church library and the British Museum newspaper library in London; the parish registers of Paulerspury, Piddington and Moulton; the Baptist Church vestries of Fuller at Kettering, of Belvoir Street at Leicester, and of College Street at Northampton, have been richly rewarding, especially the last, where I found documents undreamed of lying forgotten in a cupboard, which gave me the whole Association background of Carey's deathless sermon, and also set Harvey Lane's relationship to him in a new and winsome light.

Then interested folk, from many parts of the kingdom and beyond, sent me data or loaned me letters, either of Carey's, or about him, which have been of great value. One correspondent typed and sent most of Mrs Marshman's diary, thus admitting me into many privacies of Serampore's domestic life. A few made themselves my tireless helpers and even co-investigators, especially Mr Frank Bates of Northampton, who gleaned for me much country lore, and discovered the incident of 'the runaway apprentice'.

Then, four years ago, came a rare windfall – a large bundle of copied Carey letters, sent to Dr Shakespeare during the war. One third was entirely new to me, and one letter was simply priceless, disclosing the hitherto never-published name of the fellow apprentice who had led Carey to the Saviour, and putting me on the track of this whole vital beginning.

My crowning mercy, of course, has been that for two recent years I have had the chance of inbreathing India, and of feeling the pulse of her quick life. I have sojourned in every place Carey dwelt in, and talked with some whose fathers knew him in the flesh. My brother William gave me the free use of his abundant Carey data accumulated through forty years of Indian missionary service.

Calcutta's libraries, too, were my fortune. In that of the Board of Examiners, for example, I found eighteen thick folios of the copied minutes and correspondence of Fort William College through all the three decades of Carey's professional service: folios which, the librarian told me, they had a short while previously been tempted to destroy. They contained scores of Carey's letters and memoranda, which set me in the living midst of his tutorial conditions, till all his students and pundits and class methods became disclosed and familiar.

In the Imperial Library I found his *Book of Indian Wisdom and Humour*; in the Upper Circular Road Indian Library all the first years' files of Serampore's pioneer newspapers; and in the Horticultural Society's and in the Botanic's I unearthed exciting new evidence of the length, breadth and depth of his botanic science and service. The Government's Records Offices, too, yielded me documents beyond my hopes. And Serampore, besides constant aidings and inspirings, supplied me with a considerable packet of never-published letters, which threw a flood of light upon Carey's last years.

Indian friends, too, laid themselves out to aid my quest. I would like to mention many, but I must name three – Dr Dinesh Chandra Sen and his brilliant son Kiran, and, beyond all others, the Rev B. A. Nag.

On my return from Calcutta, two fresh *piles* of letters and documents, discovered in Furnival Street cellars (by the Rev J. L. Forfeitt, missionary in the Congo) awaited examination, and behold, the larger pile consisted of letters from Carey's sons and invalid sister and other relatives, revealing the fine fidelities of his home circle life! And, more recently still, Principal Robinson found in a box behind a Regent's Park College bookshelf the many letters of Carey to his Amboyna and Ajmere missionary-son Jabez.

Moreover, two fresh letter loans reached me just in time for inclusion – one, Carey's first to Vanderkemp, from the London Missionary Society's office, and the other, a Yorkshire Baptist's account of Carey's last Leicester Sunday, written red-hot from the events, a letter such as would have warmed the heart of a Carlyle.

I have also had the advantage of valuable books on Carey published since Smith's *Biography* – notably Mornay Williams' *The Serampore Letters,* and Professor Susil Kumar De's *History of the Bengali Language and Literature from 1800–1825.* The former reveals the early co-operation of America's Baptists and others with Carey; the latter, devoting to him and to his influence three chapters, gives him the primal place in India's modern literary development.

I have been especially keen to trace what British missionary activity was current in Carey's age, and to claim for him only that measure of primacy and pioneership consonant with these. He was distinctly *not* the first British missionary, though he did exert the most stimulating influence.

I have most rejoiced to rescue the name of the mother of all his children from the cruel wrongs which have been done her. Biographers without exception have echoed her dispraise. Now that the facts will be known, feeling will rebound in her favour. She will be unanimously defended in her first-felt inability to accompany Carey to Bengal, and will be acclaimed for *her eventual going at a single day's notice,* and will then be deeply compassionated for the price she tragically paid. Carey would wish me to lay this wreath upon her grave.

I am more than ever conscious that he was greater than I have had power to tell: but, at least, I have spared neither time, toil nor money to ascertain the facts and to present their story.

S. P. C.

Sandown,
30 July, 1923

From the Preface to the Revised Edition of 1934

Ever since the first issue of this book I have maintained the quest for Carey-treasure, and have been fortunate to discover considerable fresh material. I have been permitted to see a diary of Carey's own for his first two Indian years, of whose survival I had no reason to be aware. Also, to see the four *private* manuscript volumes of Ward's Serampore diary till 1811, which proved often fuller and more intimate than its folio form, which was all I previously knew. I have also ascertained that the whole series of the original letters of Carey to Ryland, preserved in College Street vestry, Northampton, is more extensive than their typed copies in London, with which I had hitherto worked.

Then, by the good offices of the Rev F. G. Hastings of Aberystwyth, I have learned of and explored the valuable *Isaac Mann Collection* of letters of Carey and his English and Indian colleagues, now in the possession of the National Library of Wales. Moreover, by the grace of descendants of the Marshmans, I have now seen *all* that is believed to survive of Mrs Marshman's diary, whereas before I had only been privileged to receive extracts; also, seventy letters of Mrs and of Dr Marshman; and their daughter Rachel's interesting *Memoir of the Mission.* Then the letters of Fountain, Brunsdon, Chamberlain, Robinson and Rowe, in the archives of the Baptist Missionary Society, which I had unaccountably overlooked before, have yielded not a little fresh detail and colour.

The Gough papers, also, in the Aylesbury Reference Library, have proved worth examining; and Deaville Walker's *Carey* and Maurice Hewett's (unpublished) *Sutcliff* and Ernest Payne's *Clipston* have all been informing and suggestive.

Then a recent severe judgement on Felix Carey, which had wide circulation in Burma, and, still more, the offensive caricatures of him and his wife and home in a biographical Judson novel, which had a large sale on both sides of the Atlantic, have called for a fuller record of the facts concerning this first-born son of Carey.

S. P. C.

Gurrow Point,
Dittisham, Devon,
31 December, 1933

Part I

Carey's Thirty-Two English Years

The story of how God laid on him,
and through him on modern Christendom,
the constraint of world missions

1. The Times

It is no exaggeration to call Carey one of the greatest of God's Englishmen. He broke the way for us all into Asia, and gave his life, without an interval, for its people.

SIR GEORGE ADAM SMITH

The record of the work done by the Serampore missionaries reads like an Eastern romance. They created a prose vernacular literature for Bengal; they established the modern method of popular education; they founded the present Protestant North Indian Church. They gave the first impulse to the native press. They set up the first steam-engine in India: with its help they introduced the modern manufacture of paper on a large scale. They translated and printed the Bible, or parts thereof into thirty-one *[correctly thirty-five]* languages, earning the main part of their funds with their own hands. They built a college, which still ranks amongst the most splendid educational edifices in India. As one contemplates its magnificent pillared façade, overlooking the broad Hooghly, or mounts its staircase, one is lost in admiration of the faith of the three men, who dared to build on such a scale.

SIR WILLIAM W. HUNTER, before the Society of Arts, 1888.

The man who did so much for India, in agriculture, horticulture and education: who, as professor, helped to train some of our noblest administrators, and, as translator of Scripture, removed more difficulties out of the way of his successors than any other man of modern times; who led the Protestant nations into the heathen world, and anticipated and successfully adopted all missionary methods; this man, whose varied greatness as philanthropist, scholar, missionary and saint is likely to become conspicuous in proportion as his age recedes, died as humble as a little child, having all his life conceived and steadily pursued aims far greater than Alexander, and probably as varied and beneficent as the aims of any man of whom we read in modern times.

SAMUEL VINCENT

1. The Times
1761–1793

CAREY WAS FORTUNATE in the period in which his English years were cast. Many movements were stirring. Seeds were germinating. A breath of spring was in the air.

Children of ordinary people were beginning to get the chance of school, not yet by the nation's will, nor at its expense, nor by any concerted system, but here and there, by the benevolence of the few. Even in English villages charity schools were being founded. The fare was severely frugal, but at least it broke the fast. Carey was especially linked with this beginning, for his grandfather was the first schoolmaster of his village, and his father at thirty-two succeeded to the same mastership.

William passed his second seven years with the schoolhouse as his home, and entered beyond most village lads into this educational opportunity. In adult years he often mourned its limitations. Except for his initiative and determination it would not have taken him far. Still, it was something in those days to come of a father and grandfather of studious calling and spirit, and to have a measure of food provided for his unusually hungry mind.

Carey was fortunate, too, to be the child of a pleasant village with a forest at its door. Nature and he were sister and brother. The wonderland of trees, flowers, insects, and birds became to him an open book. To watch things grow was always his fond recreation. The spirit which was to yield us our naturalists was his in rich measure.

He came, moreover, at the height of the events in India and America, when Britain passed from grave forebodings into supremacy and strength. The rivals for colonial power – Britain and France – had been so matched that Britain's double and decisive victory was an infinite relief to her. Plassey and Pondicherry broke France's Indian expectations, and clinched a hold on both Bengal and the Carnatic. Then Wolfe's scaling of Quebec, Montreal's surrender, and Spain's exchange of Florida for Cuba, left Britain as mistress of Canada, and of America from the Mississippi to the sea. This twofold 'dominion of the palm and pine' added cubits to the nation's stature, and brought the consciousness of a larger responsibility in the world.

Carey was born just then, when the young were seeing visions, and the old dreaming dreams. From infancy it touched him, through the home talk about his Canadian uncle, and then even more when the emigrant returned after years of pioneering. He had been out West during the French and British wrestlings for the possession of Canada, and could make vivid the victory of Wolfe. Uncle and lad became inseparable companions, and he poured into the boy something of his own spirit.

Conquests other than those of the sword also stretched people's thinking and filled their conversation. Captain Cook was discovering Pacific isles and mapping New Zealand and the east coast of New Holland. The world was growing! Even before Carey read Cook's log-books to find them more thrilling than all romance, the news of the discoveries fired his mind and warmed his spirit. Novels and plays seemed dull beside this world of fact.

Then he saw Britain stripped of her chief Western inheritance, the major portion of her colonial estate. He was twelve when the news reached his home of the Boston tea riots. By the time he was twenty-three, after much bloodshed, the forfeiture of the thirteen states was sealed. It was, of course, the chief topic of conversation in his workshop, in the village gatherings, and with his uncle at his home goings. J. C. Ryland, the rugged preacher of Northampton, defended the resisting states, declaring –

Were I General Washington, I would call together all my brother officers. I would bare my arm, and bid every man bare his, that a portion of
blood might be extracted and mingled in one bowl. Then I would bid
every man draw his sword, and dip it in the bowl, and swear by Him
that sitteth upon the throne and liveth for ever and ever, not to sheathe
the consecrated blade till the freedom of his country was achieved.

Such were the outbursts that Carey heard from his non-pacifist senior. That he caught their spirit is proved by his own unyielding fight
for freedom through many difficult years at Serampore.

There were other contests for freedom within Britain. Pitt maintained against the King the prerogatives of ministers and Parliaments.
Parliaments upheld constituencies in their election of representatives,
even when their choice was a Jack Wilkes. The press insisted on their
right to publish Parliamentary debates, and to discuss public policy.
Catholics claimed protection from the riots of Lord Gordon, and Ireland scored the triumph of her Grattan Parliament. The decade of
1780–1790 saw 'the coming of the platform to its place of political
power'. This struggle of Britain for more self-determination made
young Carey a Radical.

His choice of Nonconformity, within a few weeks of his spiritual
new birth (against his home bias), and then his enlistment with the
Baptists (Froude's 'most thoroughgoing of Protestants') evinced his
independence. Nonconformists were still smarting under the Test and
Corporation Acts. Only Church of England communicants were
appointed to paid offices of State. Likewise, only Anglicans could be
masters in public schools, and officers in the army or navy. Only these
could graduate in the university, or collect the nation's taxes. Nonconformists lived and moved and had their being under suspicions and
exclusions. Their representatives demanded equality in vain, efforts to
overthrow such restrictions being continually defeated in the House of
Commons, though by waning majorities.

Fox in 1790 supported the Nonconformists with much power, but
Burke and Pitt, alarmed at the French upheaval, rallied the traditional-
ists, and the reform was defeated by three to one. Carey was then in
Leicester. Its borough council had declared that 'to admit Dissenters to
any civil office was to give them perpetual opportunity of injuring the
State.' Leicester's leading vicar had invited the Nonconformist ministers of the country to his breakfast table only to chide them for their

political ambitions. In such an environment, Carey readily agreed to serve as secretary of the town's Dissenters' committee!

Not even the French Revolution shook Carey's sympathy with political reform, nor Leicester's 'revolutionary' unrest in 1790, when a mob ransacked the borough offices and trampled its torn documents in the streets. He watched France's awesome drama with sympathy, hoping that it would prove to be 'a movement towards a completer humanity'. He declared it 'God's answer to the recent concerted prayings of His people', 'a glorious door opened, and likely to be opened much wider, for the Gospel, by the spread of civil and religious liberty, and by the diminution of the papal power.'

Andrew Fuller recorded that 'Carey's mind was much engaged in these things.' Convinced of 'the common and equal rights' of all people, Carey yearned to share with all his rich inheritance in Christ.

Under the same impulse he was wholeheartedly for the emancipation of slaves. The slave-trade had reached disgraceful proportions, Britain having developed what Portugal and Spain had begun. In Carey's time, London papers openly advertised children for sale. Two million negroes were shipped to the colonies in a century. Just under two hundred vessels full of slaves left British ports in 1790 for the West, and half their living cargoes perished on the way through brutality, starvation, and disease. The ships were described as 'floating hells'. Britain's sins were scarlet. Her crimes cried out to God. Yet public feeling was silent. Even religious opinion stirred little. The Quakers were the first to protest, then the Baptists.

Carey from the time of his conversion was fiercely against this shame. His sisters never heard him pray without reference to this traffic 'so inhuman and accursed'. Under the influence of Cowper he watched the collaboration of Clarkson, Wilberforce, Macaulay, and Sharp. He saw the Commons faced with the question, Fox's stand for abolition, Wilberforce's superb effort in the House of Commons in 1789, and the subsequent mitigation of the transport atrocities. Then, in 1791, at a time of Parliamentary reaction to the turbulence of France, he was jarred by the horrific triumph of the slave-trade, in spite of Wesley's dying entreaty. His own response was to abandon the use of sugar, that he might wash his hands of blood.

Britain was at this time also beginning to repent of two other inhumanities – namely her treatment of prisoners and the insane. Two intimate friends of Carey's threw their strength into these crusades, one (a Leicester manufacturer) was a prison reformer, and the other (a local physician) was the founder of Leicester's first hospital for the rational treatment of the insane.

Meanwhile, the public conscience was challenged over British behaviour in India by the impeachment of Warren Hastings, which signalled that the East India Company must henceforth expect the searchlight of Parliament and of public opinion to be upon its activities. Britain's rule over her great dependency would, in future, need to be humane. The long occupation of the public mind with the Hastings trial no doubt prepared British Christians for Carey's Indian appeals.

In the year of Carey's birth, William Law, the eighteenth-century mystic (also from Northamptonshire) died. Ten years after his *Serious Call* stirred the Wesleys, William Law came so much under the spell of Boehme that he withdrew to his native King's Cliffe, where he gave himself to philanthropy, meditation, and prayer. He (together with an aunt of Gibbon's) spent each year a fortune in personal social service. Not till he had distributed milk to the poor from door to door each morning, did Law retire into his 'snuggery' to 'prostrate himself for hours in abysmal silence before the central throne of the divine revelation'.

Carey was early touched and drawn by Law's intensity and devoutness. What restrained him from following that path was Law's trust of intuition beyond the written Word, for Carey was convinced that God could only be reliably known by the understanding and obedient appropriation of the Truth. For his part he resolved to master what was written, and to make himself a man of the Book. None the less, the studiousness, simplicity and philanthropy of Law deeply impressed him, and such virtues were later reproduced in Serampore.

It was Carey's greatest benefit to be alive when the tidal wave of spiritual awakening still swept the land. Almost to the end of Carey's English years (and for a score before his birth) the movement of the Spirit associated with George Whitefield and the Wesley brothers turned countless souls to the Lord.

In that century when reason clipped faith's wings, and religion was 'icily regular', and when Hume was the oracle, Voltaire the idol, and 'all people of discernment had discovered Christianity to be fictitious' – Britain's soul was saved by three evangelists. Heaven's rains, through these apostles, refreshed and fertilized the earth. Their viewpoints differed; their phrasings often clashed; but alike they published God's rich grace in Jesus Christ, and the people heard them gladly, and thousands were reborn.

For thirty of Carey's English years John Wesley rode everywhere for his many daily preachings, 'paying more turnpikes than any other in the land'. Carey, as a lad of twelve, may have seen him at seventy in Towcester; or more likely a few years later in Northampton and Leicester. Certainly he met many who described to him the preacher's dignity, courage, intensity, and power. Over the length and breadth of Britain Wesley demonstrated through fifty years the force of the preached Gospel. Carey's zeal to evangelise heathendom was all the stronger for his having lived in the blaze of Wesley's achievement.

The revival had awakened Christian song, an outburst certainly anticipated by Watts, and whose endorsing chorus included the hymns of Doddridge, Steele, Beddome, Williams, Newton, Cowper, Toplady, Fawcett, Ryland and Pearce. Carey was linked with all these. Doddridge was a household name in his county. Anne Steele dwelt in the village of his friend Steadman. Beddome desired Carey as his pastoral successor. Williams' hymn *O'er the gloomy hills of darkness* became Carey's and the Mission's 'Marseillaise'. Newton gave him his blessing before he left London for Bengal. Sutcliff told him so much about Cowper, and his poems were his joy. Toplady was the bosom friend of his county's chief Baptist preacher. Fawcett was Carey's personal ally, and lit the Mission's first beacon in the North. Ryland and Pearce were also his own yokefellows.

Carey certainly dwelt amongst the poetic prophets of Christ's kingdom. Harps were unhung from the willows to be tuned and played anew. Then came the yearning to proclaim the Gospel to all mankind.

The pulpit doctrine of Carey's denomination was often extravagantly hyper-Calvinistic. God's sovereignty was stressed until all human responsibility vanished. They left entirely to God the ingathering of His guests. Robert Hall of Arnesby, and then Andrew Fuller, defied this error – an old man and a young one. Hall published his views first, and then Fuller issued *The Gospel worthy of all acceptation*. Their tournament with the 'old guard' was long, and the clash of the lances fierce, till Carey's fellows began to accept that Christ's Church was bound to proclaim the Gospel to all.

It helped Carey's purposes, too, that the Baptist churches with which he was linked were becoming grouped into associations. His own association, the 'Northampton', stretching from St Albans to Lincoln, was one of the youngest, but also one of the most vigorous, and its leaders (the elder Hall, the Rylands, Sutcliff, and Fuller) were exceptionally able. Carey could scarcely have found a finer group of colleagues.

From this Northampton Association the call to prayer sounded forth in 1784. Scottish ministers, roused by Whitefield, had first issued it in the 1740s. Jonathan Edwards had resounded it through the States. Now, a quarter of a century after his death, it was republished in mid-England, and evoked an encouraging response. Churches, distressed at their barrenness, welcomed the summons to special monthly intercessions. They climbed the slopes of Carmel, and cried to God for His rain. They little guessed into what consequences these pleadings would lead them, and how God would take them at their word, and challenge them through Carey to the task of world missions. Where prayer flourished, the soil was most ready for the growth of missionary zeal.

The first inventions of modern machinery, the inauguration of the chemical and electrical sciences, the harnessing of the driving force of steam, all belong to this period, and they revolutionised the toil, outlook, and interrelation of the world. Carey little guessed, with all his scientific spirit, what developments awaited his father's weaving trade, his mother's lace-making, or his own shoemaking. Nor could he have foreseen that his England of forests, villages and small towns would become the world's factory and market, covered by industrial zones. He could never have expected that the streets of Leicester (only just furnished with oil-lamps) would eventually be electrically lit, or that Leicester would be brought within two instead of twenty hours of London, or that the Calcutta he was to reach in five months would be made easily accessible by aeroplane. Nevertheless, by the initiative of the Lord, as the first stirrings of world change were taking place, Carey summoned the people of Christ to fresh vision and advance.

Adam Smith, the student-statesman of the future 'economy', was the earliest to recognise that the business world had outgrown its restricting conventions, and that the motto of the future must be 'mutualism'. Each nation, he insisted, could only thrive through the prosperity of all, and free interdependence must be the watchword of wise trade. In the very decade in which Smith bade his fellow-countrymen remove the barriers to world commerce, Carey universalised their spiritual outlook, exhorting them to find their true wealth in sharing with all lands their Christian treasure, and to purchase their own progress by the glad service of the world.

Nor was he alone in the British recognition of this missionary obligation. John Montgomery (the father of the hymnwriter) was with six other Englishmen (and their wives) in the Moravian mission to the West Indies, and James Rhodes and William Turner were in the Moravian mission to Labrador. Thomas Thompson, of British birth and university, after five years' ministry in New Jersey, had given brief service to Africa's Gold Coast. Wilberforce was planning to make the freed isle of Sierra Leone a modern Iona. Thomas Coke was urging Methodism towards Eastern or African missions. Samuel Pearce was yearning to get to Botany Bay as the convicts' friend for Christ, and thence to the Maoris. Rector Haweis was enlisting young Welsh volunteers for Cook's South Seas, but could not get them commissioned. Director Grant of the East India Company was pleading for a mission party for Bengal. Thus a few British souls had missionary vision and passion, though churches and denominations were on the whole either listless or afraid. The period's lack of *collective* missionary achievement indicates the measure of the mountains of obstruction which Carey cast into the sea.

Carey had to *make* the conditions in which his Society could be born. He could not merely apply the match to the tinder, for the tinder itself had to be prepared. When he woke to the missionary vision, he found to his amazement that most of his fellow Christians were fast asleep. He had to create the very desire which at length created the Mission; to provoke the demand which he himself would then supply. For ten years he resisted his contemporaries' inertia and fought their disbelief to conquer 'by the stubborn minority of one' – 'going at length against every dictate of common sense, every calculation of prudence, and all but universal opinion, because in the solitary sanctuary of his brooding soul an entreaty kept sounding from destitute heathendom.'

Nevertheless, Carey was raised up at an ideal time. Education was arriving for the children of the poor. Colonial expansion enlarged international outlook and responsibility, opening up trade and travel.

Captain Cook was charting the isle-strewn Pacific, and outlining south coasts. Sons of the Pilgrim Fathers were buying new freedoms with their blood. Home campaigns for freedom were being won for the people, Parliament, and press. Free Churchmen were challenging statutes that denied them fair citizenship. France was in the birth-pangs of a juster day. Britain was blushing for her slave-trade. Compassion was waking for the imprisoned and the insane. Westminster was stirring to protect India from British greed. The Methodist Awakening had proved again the power of the preached Gospel. Redeemed people were quickened to poetry and praise. Hyper-Calvinism was yielding to the persuasions of the offered Gospel. Churches were beginning to co-operate. Collective prayer was becoming a valued habit. Industrial, commercial, and social change was at the doors. Britain's business world was being reasoned into an opening of closed gates. The unevangelised peoples of the world were burdening at least a few British consciences, and constraining them toward the path of missionary toil.

This was the environment of Carey's English years. To borrow from Paul, the period might be described as a 'fulness of the times'. At such a time, God raised up a humble yet wonderfully dedicated soul to seize and speed its converging forces. Had not God's *man* been ready, the times would have yielded scant result.

2. The Boy

Thank God! a man can grow!
He is not bound
With earthward gaze to creep along the ground:
Though his beginnings be but poor and low,
Thank God! a man can grow!

With little teaching, he became learned; poor himself, he made millions rich; by birth obscure, he rose to unsought eminence; and seeking only to follow the Lord's leading, he led forward the Lord's host.

A. T. PIERSON

The village was not then a moribund society, nor was it a society hoping to revive by the backwash of life returning to it from the town. It was the country's most *characteristic* unit. It embraced the chief daily concern of the majority of Englishmen. It was the principal nursery of the national character.

G. M. TREVELYAN

Like his schoolfellows he seemed born to the English labourer's fate of five shillings a week and the poor-house in sickness and old age. From this, in the first instance, he was saved by disease which affected his face and hands most painfully whenever he was long exposed to the sun.

DR GEORGE SMITH

2. The Boy
Paulerspury, 17 August, 1761–1775

NORTHAMPTONSHIRE is England's central county, the very heart of the Midlands. No other is so girdled – nine counties touch its borders. Its rivers, the Nene, Welland, Avon, and Ouse, are 'natives', to use Thomas Fuller's expression. They all rise within Northamptonshire's watershed, and it gives them to its neighbouring counties. In this core of England Carey was appropriately born, for the movement he impelled flowed from the heart of English Christendom.

Carey was born in the south-east of the county, in the village of Paulerspury, where, at a thrust of the river Tove, Northamptonshire bulges into Buckinghamshire. The ancient Roman road Watling Street, from Dover and London to Chester, passes behind the village, bringing it into touch with the life of the country.

Carey's grandfather, Peter Carey, was not a native of the village, but arrived there in early manhood, Carey says 'from near Yelvertoft' where, like many others in that north corner of the county, he had been a weaver of 'tammy', a calico-coloured worsted. In August 1722, he married in Paulerspury Ann Flecknoe, who, like himself, was not born there.

In coming to Paulerspury he was possibly returning to a home of his fathers, for a James Carey was its curate from 1624 to 1629, a clergyman with good handwriting. One named James Carey – perhaps the same – was buried there on 7 April, 1661, an Elizabeth Carey in 1665, and a John in 1676 – perhaps the curate's wife and son. If Peter Carey descended from these, then William came of distant parentage of some culture. But he may have sprung from another John Carey, and in that case from the very poor. For this John was buried there on 6 October, 1680, 'in a coffin only'; whereas the other seventeen who died that year were buried in woollens, as the law required. John Carey's shroudlessness was his poverty's stigma.

Olney, ten miles from Paulerspury, was possibly associated with Carey's more immediate family, for the Carey name was familiar there through the century before his birth. Sixty Carey entries appear in its register between 1669 and 1771.

Amongst Paulerspury's chief families were the Marriotts. William Marriott first endowed the Towcester grammar school, and then in 1720 arranged funds to pay for the schooling of six boys in his village. Thomas Nicholl, a London citizen with lands near Paulerspury, six years later also sponsored the education of six village boys. So, before national schools were heard of, and even while village charity schools were rare, Paulerspury had its school, with a dozen free places.

Peter Carey was its first master. He must have been capable beyond the rest of the village or, as a newly-arrived weaver, he would not have been promoted to be its teacher, nor to the allied role of parish clerkship. A county historian described his signature as 'particularly free and elegant', and found therein a token of his fair education. It certainly was the penmanship of no rustic.

That two of Peter Carey's three sons became good teachers, further suggests his studiousness. For eighteen years he honourably discharged his dual office as schoolmaster and clerk, then died when only in his forties, heart-broken over the loss of his first-born, William (a promising teacher in Towcester), who was laid at twenty in the grave. In less than a fortnight the grave at the church porch was reopened. The entries succeed each other in the Pury register:

William Carey, buried 26 July, 1743.
Peter Carey, buried 7 August, 1743.

'Much people' shared Ann Carey's double overwhelming grief. A few months before she had been as blest as any, with an honoured husband, and gifted sons. Now she was stripped of all but one – Edmund. Another, named Peter (after his father), had gone to far and unfamiliar Canada, and no word having reached her, she filled the void with imagined catastrophe. Edmund, a child of seven, seemed all she had left. As she returned from the twice-filled grave to the school-house, she remembered the old widow-story of the Book of *Ruth*, and from that day called herself not Ann, but Naomi.

The village took her to its heart, and enabled her to remain and make a living. It paid for the stone over the twice-dug grave, and granted Edmund one of the twelve free school places. As soon as the lad could understand his mother's loneliness, he sought his happiness in hers. He learned the tammy weaving of his father, and worked with such a will that when, at twenty-four, he married Elizabeth Wells in Towcester, he made their thatched home his mother's haven as well.

They dwelt together 'in sweetest harmony and beauty', a very Ruth and Naomi. 'Linked with the mother's delicate habit of body was a remarkable tenderness of soul. She was as distinguished for her meek-ness and gentleness as for her loving spirit, united with a true refinement of manners.' The grief, which had overwhelmed her husband, wrought in her a spirit of sweetness and calm.

Edmund Carey was poor, yet felt rich as he worked at his hand-loom and glanced out at his little garden and at the daisied hill on which the church was set, and as he read on winter nights his few choice books. On 17 August, 1761, a child was born to him whom he named William, to his mother's delight, in memory of her first-born.

His grandmother made the child 'her especial care'; her light at eventide. When two years later Ann was born (named after herself) she was indeed Naomi, to whom the Lord had been bountiful. Then, before a further year had elapsed, she left this present life.

Her son Peter had not perished in Canada. When about thirty-five, he returned to settle in the village, but whether in time to close his mother's eyes is not known. Childless, but a child-lover, he drew his nephew William to him, telling him tales of ships and the sea, of Canada's Indians and French people, of its woods and winters, of rivers, falls and lakes, beasts and birds, trees and flowers; casting the spell of the New World about him.

Paulerspury parish church – much as seen from Carey's boyhood home

Peter had been in Canada through the life and death struggle of Britain and France. He could thrill his nephew with the glory of Wolfe and Quebec; and better, could reveal to him what he himself had discovered after his long exile – the sweet beauty of England. Expert gardener as he was, on his return he awoke to the loveliness of his native woods and hedgerows, and poured his enthusiasm into the lad's receptive soul.

In 1767 the schoolmastership and parish-clerkship again fell vacant, and the new rector was pressed to offer them to Edmund Carey, for his father's sake and for his own. Paulerspury had watched his devotion to his mother, his integrity and industry, and his love of books. So, when William was six, the home was removed from Pury End to the schoolhouse on the hill, an elevation in both geographical and social terms. Thus the weaver was called to be schoolmaster in the school of his boyhood. The low thatched building had no desks: its benches were rough tree planks. But Edmund Carey was better suited for his task than many schoolmasters of his day. He was a lover of children and of books, and a man of good penmanship. He taught arithmetic in both Towcester and Paulerspury. And to the drill of the Catechism he at least brought a reverent mind.

The small schoolhouse seemed large after the Pury End cottage. Two wide-spreading plane trees grew in front, while at the back were an orchard and a garden, to the joy of the children. Between these and the rectory's large grounds stretched a moat full of water, a glorious habitat of sticklebacks and tadpoles, and well worth a lad's netting for larger spoil. Five hundred yards or so from the school could be seen the great coaches on Watling Street. Like Mark Rutherford, Carey would 'love the very signposts pointing to London'. He soon helped to fetch water from the spring down the lane across the highway, and to gather firewood from the Whittlebury forest, which then bordered the village.

'Our father,' says Carey's youngest sister Mary, 'discovered no partiality for the abilities of his own children, but rather went sometimes too far the other way, which tended to discourage them a little.' William's only special aptitude, according to his father, was steady attentiveness and industry, plus a good capacity for quick mental arithmetic. The boy's mother often heard him counting when he should have been asleep. His own preference was for science and travel books.

Of Columbus he read and talked so much that the boys gave him that name. Nor could they have christened him better.

The story of Columbus entranced him more than the fiction of Crusoe, though that gave him pleasure, and may have instilled into his mind an unconscious interest in missions, for which Defoe exhibited a strong concern. *Reality* was to Carey the best romance. He craved to learn of lands and peoples overseas. This was the spring of his interest in languages, which revealed itself so early. He memorised at twelve the sixty pages of Dyche's *Vocabularium*, though its first samples included such Horatian uncommon nouns as *lanista, lixa, rabula* and *scurra*. It was a red-letter day when he could translate the romantic Latin inscription adjacent to the parish church's unique, alabaster tomb.

Not that he was just a bookworm. Mary says he was 'most active in all the amusements and recreations'. The favourite game of the village boys was 'stagastagaroney', in which one chased the many, till, with the help of each captive, he chased and captured all. It was the perfect game for Carey, and he played it in later life in deadly earnest.

Dearer than the playground, however, were the hedgerows and meadows, the rectory moat and the Whittlebury forest (the traces of whose ridings survive in the lanes' anemones and wild hyacinths). These were the haunts of the life he loved. In catching and killing he took no pleasure, but he possessed the scientist's instinct for finding and observing. His bedroom, by his mother's wise concession, was stocked with these companions. He even learned to draw and paint them, love bringing him skill. Among his peers he became the recognised authority on natural history. Of any unusual flower, bird, or insect, they would say, 'Tek it to Bill Carey; he'll tell you all about it.'

His sister Mary's sketch of him is remarkable:

> Of birds and all manner of insects he had numbers. When he was from home, the birds were committed to my care . . . Being more than five years younger, I was indulged by him in all his enjoyments. Though I often killed them by kindness, yet, when he saw my grief, he always permitted me the pleasure of serving them again; and often took me over the dirtiest roads to get at a plant or an insect. He never walked out, when quite a boy, without making observation on the hedges as he passed; and when he took up a plant of any kind, he always examined it with care.

His brother Tom, seven years his junior, gives a similar testimony:

I was often carried in his arms on many of his walks, and he would show me with delight the beauties in the growth of plants.

William enriched the schoolhouse plot and orchard from his far-ranging rambles, though the county was not the best of plant-hunting grounds, being mostly pasture and wheat land. 'No mosses, mears, fells, heaths, such as fill many shires with emptiness,' boasts Thomas Fuller. 'It is an apple without core or rind.' Boy-botanist Carey would have welcomed more 'rind'.

Short of stature (5 feet 4 inches by adulthood), he climbed the most difficult of trees to watch a bird and win an egg. Once, falling, he was stunned and badly hurt, costing him days of confinement. But at his first chance of freedom he conquered the tree with pride.

His was a happy boyhood. Awakened early by his birds, he was up to greet them, to clean out their cages, and the homes of his other pets, to get their food from the lanes and forest, and the fresh water for his water-creatures. He would welcome each surprise, each new butterfly and moth; and then carefully weed and till his garden. Nothing was too commonplace for his observation. He loved to see into what marvel each could grow.

He had a fourth companion besides his sisters and brother – a Paulerspury orphan whom Carey's parents helped. Mindful of Paulerspury's kindness to his mother, Edmund Carey and his wife gave the child a home. The food in the school cottage was frugal, with income small and seven round the table.

Religious books, so-called, Carey did not greatly care for. *Pilgrim's Progress* won him as adventure, but he read it 'to no spiritual profit'. The only Scriptures that interested him were the historical books, for they were the most akin to tales of travel. Later he thanked God for the daily parental Bible drill, 'that installation of his mind,' as Ruskin would have termed it, and also for the strict church attendance in which he was nurtured. 'My mind was furnished with themes, which afterwards were often influential on my heart.'

His musical training, too, as a Pury choirboy, was a lifelong enrichment. Not that choir membership meant godliness. Many of the choir, he recalled, like the bell-ringers, were rough-tongued and blasphemous. Yet he liked to be with them, and also with his fellow footballers at Inwood's smithy, and he fell into their coarse and godless talk, 'though with many stirrings of conscience'.

However, his hunger and thirst for knowledge set him apart. 'Whatever he began, he finished,' Mary said. 'Difficulties never discouraged him. As he grew, his passion for knowledge increased.' His brother Tom said of him: 'From a boy he was studious, deeply and fully bent on learning all he could, and determined never to give up a particle of anything on which his mind was set, till he had arrived at a clear knowledge and sense of his subject. He was never diverted by allurements, nor driven from its search by ridicule or threats.'

Carey himself said years later to his nephew Eustace, disclaiming all other talents, 'I can plod and persevere. That is my only genius. I can persevere in any definite pursuit. To this I owe everything.'

And yet he was thwarted in his first attempt to make his way in the world. Upon leaving school at twelve he wished to be field-tiller or gardener, like his hero uncle. But scurvy-like irritation of his hands and face so worsened under exposure to the sun that at night his inflamed skin banished sleep. Do what he would, he could not allay 'the very painful trouble', and after two years' struggle he was forced to give in. He who was to endure forty years of Bengal heat was turned out of his first chosen path by the distress of English sunshine. But God was thrusting him upon an unplanned path.

One thing, however, he says he learned in those open air days, which came often into his mind, was the rule that for straight ploughing the eyes must be set upon a definite mark.

Paulerspury, the home of his first fourteen years, made good soil for his growth – with its setting in woodland beauty, its grandparental and parental love, its inherited studiousness, its field and forest companionships, and the larger horizons of his uncle's conversation, inspiring empathy with the wider world.

3. The Beginnings

Therefore if any man be in Christ, he is a new creature: old things are passed away; behold, all things are become new. And all things are of God, who hath reconciled us to himself by Jesus Christ, and hath given to us the ministry of reconciliation.

THE APOSTLE PAUL, *2 Corinthians 5.17-18.*

Before this, with respect to religion, he was at enmity with God, and in many things ridiculed His people. I well remember our wondering at the change. This was evident in his conduct and conversation. For some time he stood alone in his father's house. Like Gideon, he wished to throw down the altars of Baal in one night. I often wished he would not bring his religion home. Often have I seen him sigh as if his heart were overwhelmed. He asked leave to pray in the family. He always mentioned the words – 'all our righteousnesses are as filthy rags.' That used to touch my pride and raise my indignation.

MARY CAREY, William's younger sister.

A gentleman who lived in the neighbourhood, and who had observed the signs of promise in the boy, informed the family that 'never a youth promised fairer to make a great man, had he not turned a cushion thumper.'

DR JAMES CULROSS

3. The Beginnings
Piddington and Hackleton, 1775–1785

WHEN CAREY WAS THRUST from the fields and gardens, his father did not select for him his own familiar weaving (now threatened by new machinery), but the shoemaking which was becoming the chief craft of the county, and which held the promise of the future day. He could, however, barely provide the premium for his seven years' apprenticeship. He searched carefully for a master into whose home to entrust him, and was led to Clarke Nichols of Piddington.

There had been much talk of this Clarke Nichols in the two Pury villages, for, one Sunday morning in September 1772, one of his apprentices, a Potterspury youth of seventeen, had run away, and Nichols had advertised in the *Northampton Mercury* for him to be detained, or for information about him to be forwarded. His 'blue coat, buff-coloured waistcoat, leather breeches joined in the thighs, speckled stockings, and scuttle hat' were all cited in the advertisement, and suggest that he was still wearing some of the clothes of his former charity school. Another Potterspury lad – John Warr by name – soon took the runaway's place. Then Edmund Carey selected Clarke Nichols as the master and trainer of his son. Nichols was more than a repairer of shoes. He was a craftsman trained to make them throughout – sole, vamp, and uppers. His repute as a strict Churchman also commended him to Edmund Carey.

It did not take William Carey long to form his own judgement about the deserter, and to admire his initiative in bolting from his master's hot temper and rough tongue (especially following his Saturday night drinking-bouts), and from his Sunday morning hard errands – the long distances he sent him to his customers with the week's bag of made and mended boots.

Certainly the books on Nichols' shelves suggested religious sympathies and interests – among them works by Jeremy Taylor, Northamptonian Nathaniel Spinckes, and a New Testament commentary. They were little to Carey's taste, however, and hardly commended by his master's drunkenness and severity. Indeed, the lad soon sickened of all that savoured of religion, and began to choose irreligious companions. Piddington, though smaller than Paulerspury, and only some eight miles away, might easily have become his 'far country'. He was saved from this slide into godlessness by his older fellow apprentice.

John Warr came from Yardley Gobion, the hamlet of Potterspury, the neighbouring village to Carey's. He and Carey may well have known each other before they met in Piddington. It broke Carey's loneliness to share workshop and attic with this youth from his own district, for they could obviously talk about many familiar things. Warr helped him, too, in the shoemaking craft, being three years older, and familiar with the trade from infancy. There was much more that Warr could teach Carey, for his grandfather had been a co-founder of Potterspury's Independent church. There, under an exceptionally fervent ministry, and of course in his own home, John Warr drank in biblical Christianity, with its answers to the deep questions of the soul. He was not yet himself a conscious and assured believer when joined by Carey in Nichols' workshop, but he was deeply affected, and often led their conversation to the themes of Christianity and conversion.

Carey, at this time, disdained Dissenters. Their children had been excluded from the Paulerspury school. Furthermore his father and grandfather had been parish clerks, official 'pillars' of the Anglican and village establishment. He was bigoted and bitter. Indeed, he would readily have destroyed the meeting-house in Hackleton (hamlet of Piddington) which John Warr was attending.

Of his 'discussions' with John Warr, Carey wrote:

I had, moreover, pride sufficient for a thousand times my knowledge.
So I always scorned to have the worst in discussion, and the last word
was assuredly mine. I always made up in positive assertion what was
lacking in my reasoning, and generally came off with triumph. But I was
often afterwards convinced that, though I had the last word, my fellow
apprentice had the better of the argument, and I felt a growing uneasiness and stings of conscience gradually increasing, but had no idea that
nothing but a complete change of heart could do me any good.

Meanwhile, John Warr sought God for himself with all his strength,
till Christ became his conscious Saviour and his living Lord. He
learned what it was to be reborn from above. Then was he vastly rich;
only a shoe-maker's apprentice, but one who had discovered the treasure of the field. God's pearl was his, and in his hand. God's peace was
in his soul. Desire to share his secret soon possessed him. He talked of
Christ to Carey and his master, not now for discussion, but to win
them for his Lord. Says Carey:

He became *importunate* with me, lending me books which gradually
wrought a change in my thinking, and my inward uneasiness increased.

Warr's changed and better life, too, was as impressive as his per-
suasive speech, and he soon won Carey into attending the Hackleton
prayer-meetings, where there was a fervour foreign to the cold correctness of the parish churches, and a closer hold upon God. Carey felt the
spell of a different spiritual world and yearned to explore it. He bal-
anced, however, these timid associations with the Nonconformists by
threefold Sunday attendance at the parish church, seeking through
these increased religious exercises to lift the burden of his soul.

I also *[he says]* determined to leave off lying, swearing, and other sins to
which I was addicted; and sometimes, when alone, I tried to pray.

He needed to be humbled and convicted of sin before he could be
saved. 'The wood had to be charred, ere God could limn with it.' He
writes:

I had been to Northampton, where I had made some purchases for myself, which amounted to about a shilling more than I was worth. But I
had a counterfeit shilling, which Mr Hall, the ironmonger, had given
me as a Christmas-box. I knew it to be a bad shilling, but I was strongly

inclined to assert to my master that it belonged to other money with which he had entrusted me to purchase things for him, as this would clear my private account. I recollect the struggle I had all the way home, and I prayed to God to excuse my dishonesty and lying for this once; I would never repeat such action, but would break off with sin thenceforth. My wickedness prevailed, and I told the falsehood, and was detected by my master. A gracious God *did not* get me safe through. I soon concluded that my theft was known to the whole village. I concealed myself from all, as much as I could, and was so overwhelmed with shame that it was a considerable time before I went out.

Carey expected dismissal, a cancelled apprenticeship, a forfeited premium, and his father angry and distressed – for to Clarke Nichols the blackest of sins was a lie. But his master relented – won to mercy, perhaps, by the Frances Howes he had married only that year. Carey all his life recalled this Christmas with horror and with gratitude – horror at his deceit and blasphemy; gratitude that it had forced him to realise his deep need of a Saviour. When seventeen and a half he exchanged the Pharisee's righteousness for the publican's meekness, and flung his helpless, sin-stained soul upon the mercy and kindness of Christ. In the Saviour Who both died and offered up His righteousness for sinners, he found ransom and peace. Ever after he was a redeemed, transformed and dedicated child of God.

Thus John Warr was the Andrew who first led this Peter to Christ. A youth of Potterspury did this immeasurable service for the youth of Paulerspury, naturally unaware that in urging his fellow apprentice to the Lord, he would help to add India's jewel to the diadem of Christ, so 'annexing for Him a continent'.

Then was Carey happy to have been thrust from the Paulerspury gardens into the Piddington workshop to make life's supreme discovery – the saving experience of Jesus Christ. Now his feet were shod with the 'preparation of the gospel of peace'.

Without this experience of shame of sin, true repentance, and spiritual transformation, he could have rendered no special service to God's kingdom. As a botanist or linguist he might have succeeded and excelled, backed as these natural gifts were by an iron will. Yet even in these realms he would have missed his full mental unfolding. Christ brought his powers and gifts to fruition.

Some of these powers were already in evidence before his

conversion. In the New Testament commentary on his master's shelves he had been attracted by words and sentences in an unknown script! Of course, his master could not decipher them, so he copied the letters and took them on his next home visit to Tom Jones, a Paulerspury weaver, who had received a Kidderminster grammar school education, but had, through folly, lost his chance of a better profession. From Jones he learned that the unknown script was Greek. Jones rubbed up his scholarship and obtained for the lad a Greek glossary and grammar. Then he guided him at each home-coming. The pupil soon left his teacher far behind.

William Carey could never date precisely the day and hour of his new birth, but just when and where he became a Nonconformist, he could precisely remember. Alarmed at Britain's reverses in America, the King had proclaimed Sunday, 10 February, 1779, a day of national fasting and prayer. John Warr persuaded Carey to spend the day with the fellowship at the little Hackleton meeting-house. He had never shared till then their Sunday worship. During the day a Thomas Chater spoke, a beginner in lay preaching. He pleaded for out-and-out abandonment to Christ, clinching his words with 'Let us go forth therefore unto him without the camp, bearing his reproach' – a scripture which pierced Carey to the heart. His own sharpest 'crucifixion' and 'reproach', he knew, would be to follow the judgement of his conscience and attach himself to these despised Christians of the meeting, through whose fervour he had been helped to a personal and saving knowledge of Christ. Less than two years before, he had had enough hostility in his heart to desire the destruction of this place of worship, but now he felt impelled to join its ranks. In villages where the conduct of each was the gossip of all, it meant the running of a gauntlet. But from this step, once taken, he never looked back.

Four years later that lay preacher Thomas Chater planned a Gospel mission to Olney, of which even gentle Cowper wrote thus derisively to Newton:

> Because we have nobody to preach the Gospel in Olney, Mr Chater waits only for a barn at present occupied by a strolling company. The moment they quit, he begins. He is disposed to think the dissatisfied of all denominations may be united under his standard; and that the great work of forming a more extensive and established interest than any of them is reserved for him.

The man, whom even Cowper was to scorn, was used to make a Dissenter of Carey, and soon would urge him to attempt lay preaching.

The September of this 1779 brought Carey a big shock. His master lay dying after only two years of marriage. Yet the sorrow was sanctified by his being led by his two apprentices to a personal trust in Christ. His death-chamber was changed into a soul's birthplace. He told all who saw him of his new sure anchorage, and bade each 'look to Jesus as the sinner's Friend'.

A day or two after his burial on 5 October Carey passed into the service of Thomas Old of Hackleton, a relative of Nichols. Within a week he met there Thomas Scott, a young clergyman from near Olney, who was to deeply affect him. Scott had a happy story to tell of how he had led an aunt of Thomas Old's into Christian assurance. Scott had so presented to her the Gospel as to win her instant response, and lead her into blessing. Scott marked, as he spoke of this, Carey's intentness, and his apt and modestly put questions.

Carey's mind being scientific, he sought to shape into rational order his Christian experience, and to chart his new mental and spiritual world. With the help of a few books he formulated what he supposed was a consistent and secure creed. To its defence he was soon called.

There lived at Quinton, not a mile off, a group of mystics, disciples of William Law, whose leader invited Carey to a spiritual discussion. He readily responded, confident that even in theological discussion he would be capable of keeping his footing. The mystic was much his senior (a parish clerk, like Carey's father) and reputedly 'of violent temper'. However, Carey found that he pleaded with him as a friend – 'even unto tears' – to advance from his present views. Not content with challenging Carey's Calvinistic doctrine, he reproved his way of life, and convinced him that he was far short of real spiritual light and feeling.

> I could neither believe his system nor defend my own. The conversation filled me with anxiety, which increased when I was alone.

It cost him three years of wilderness struggle to regain his assurance. Hackleton saints had befriended him, like those who blessed Bunyan at his conversion. 'They frequently took me by the hand,' he says, 'and communicated to me their experience, which much encouraged me.' But learning of his fellowship with heretical mystics, and that he was reading their books, they looked at him anxiously and disapprovingly, and for a long time drew away from him, which he felt keenly. From the preaching of John Luck, the elder at Hackleton, no relief reached his spirit, nor release from his doubtings. In truth, the elder belonged too much to the hyper-Calvinistic school. So, on Sundays, Carey tramped to Roade or Ravenstone or Northampton or elsewhere, for preaching which might meet the hunger of his soul. One judgement which he soon reached, was that human speculations were too unreliable for trust. This was his growing quarrel with the mystics. He wanted rock underfoot. So he resolved to search the Scriptures to discover as exactly as possible the message of God. He 'pressed God's lamp close to his breast'.

Thomas Scott most helped him – the clergyman who was destined to become such an illustrious commentator. Scott was well fitted to guide him. Like Carey, he had taught himself Latin, Hebrew, and Greek. But ahead of Carey he had been led out of deism's dreariness into evangelical joy, and had published the story of his spiritual struggle in a most impressive piece of autobiography. Carey now endeavoured to hear Scott whenever he could, and had many opportunities for personal conversation with him. Scott, for his part, was struck by the youth's developing mind, and said to several 'he would prove no ordinary man.' He dubbed the Hackleton shoe-maker's workshop 'Carey's College', and, forty years later, was surprised and blessed to hear that Carey had written the following comment about him:

> If there be anything of the work of God in my soul, I owe much of it to Mr Scott's preaching, when I first set out in the ways of the Lord.

Another messenger of God to Carey was the new minister of the Baptist meeting at Towcester, Devon-born Thomas Skinner. He lent Carey a copy of a book by the elder Robert Hall – *Help to Zion's Travellers.* Carey was overjoyed to find that his own timorous conclusions were Hall's confident pronouncements. His reading of Scripture was corroborated by this strong and saintly mind. Even where Carey had felt compelled to break from hyper-Calvinism, Hall was with him, insisting on the duty of the individual soul to receive the Gospel of Christ. To many the book was 'rank poison'; to Carey 'sweetest wine'. 'He never read a book with such rapture. He drank it eagerly to the bottom of the cup.' (His own annotated copy is in the Bristol College library.)

By 1783 Carey had fought his doubts and laid them to rest. Scripture's infallibility and sufficiency had conquered and satisfied his mind. His intense experience at this time of Scripture's truthfulness and worth made him its lifelong servant and disciple. He was an omnivorous reader, and, together with his Indian colleagues, the founder of a great Western and Eastern library; yet he was the man of one Book, and beyond his contemporaries he strove to put that Book into the hands of many peoples.

Although in the realm of the spiritual Carey proved thorough and efficient, he is often accused of having been slow, inept in his trade – 'never a competent workman', and, 'never able to make a decent pair of shoes', and so on. These legends have two sources – an *a priori* assumption, and Carey's own words. It is taken for granted that his mind, instead of being on his trade, was absorbed in his books, dreams, and visions, that his thoughts were roaming to the extremities of the earth. Yet, it was not until after he had been a journeyman for some years, that he began to think of being a minister, still less a missionary. Indeed, he was not a Christian till his apprenticeship's fourth year. But, did he not himself imply that he had never progressed far in his shoemaking? True, but in its right setting what he said yields quite a different sense. A young British staff-officer sitting next to Carey in India at the Governor-General's table – and in the hearing of others – rudely and disdainfully asked him if he had not once been a shoe-maker. 'No,' Carey replied. Then to the surprised and incredulous questioner he added, 'Not even a shoe-maker, sir: just a cobbler.' He belittled his past as a response to snobbery, not to confess incompetence.

In fact, Carey tells us that 'he was accounted a very good workman,' 'a skilful and honest workman', and that shoes of his making were often set in his firm's window as samples of the best it could produce. At Nichols' death, he was instantly accepted by Thomas Old as a journeyman, and he earned enough before he was twenty to marry a sister of his new master's wife.

William Carey and Dorothy Plackett took love's oath in Piddington church on Sunday, 10 June, 1781. He was five years younger than his bride, as his father had been before him. Neither she nor Lucy, her bridesmaid sister, could sign their names: for the village was without a school. Even the officiating curate was of limited education, if we may judge from his bizarre spelling of names – 'Lusie', 'Dority', 'Katran' and 'Sharlot'.

Illiterate Dorothy may have been, but she was not ill-chosen. Her father was a chief leader of the Hackleton Meeting. Her oldest sister was the wife of godly Thomas Old. Another sister married a deacon of the Meeting, another joined its membership, and of Catharine, the youngest, there will be a noble tale to tell. The home was puritan, in every best sense, and the sisters all earnest believers and lovable. Carey could rejoice on that wedding Sunday in his Dorothy, the 'gift of God'.

Happy were their first two years. Carey dwelt in his cottage thankful for home after six years' boarding. He loved his wife, stitched his leather, studied his books, progressed in his Latin and Greek, dressed and kept his own first garden, worshipped with the village saints, and exulted in their first-born, naming her 'Ann' (after his grandmother and sister). The next year both he and Ann were down with fever, from which, alas, she died, to the anguish of her parents and of her Aunt Mary, who even forty years later wrote to Carey, 'How I did love that child!' Then, for eighteen months, severe fever distressed him, making him bald at twenty-two.

Thomas Old died unexpectedly before he was forty, on the last day of 1783. Carey now had to shoulder the business and accept much of the care of his wife's widowed sister and four orphans. A customer, taking advantage of this death, countermanded a large nearly-finished order, which was left on Carey's hands. The winter was one of mid-England's severest, and all trade was almost paralysed through Britain's American humiliation and defeat. Carey had to tramp far in the snow soliciting orders, even buying and mending for resale old second-hand boots – as his well-known signboard testifies. Small wonder that he lost his temper with boy Parker, flicking him sharply with his leather apron for letting the wax boil over! To eke out his income he opened an evening school in the village, concealing his privations from his neighbours (and even from his mother until she was there to be his nurse). As soon as his only brother heard of his troubles, though only fifteen, he sold his few treasures, added his savings, and with the help of Paulerspury neighbours, overwhelmed him with a goodly gift.

Soon after his conversion in 1779, Carey had been pressed into

Carey's signboard, now in Regent's Park College, Oxford

taking part in the Hackleton 'Sabbath evening conferences'. 'When he did, they, being ignorant, sometimes applauded, to my great injury,' he said. A month before his marriage he joined with his father-in-law and brother-in-law, William Manning (a shopmate) and Thomas Chater and a few others, in forming the informal meeting-house fellowship into Hackleton dissenting church. Though so young, his signature stood third, his zeal having much to do with this step.

Carey's first experience of an 'Association Day' – a gathering together of many churches in the county – was an event to be remembered. No leader knew him or gave him a thought. He was one of the least of the concourse thronging the Olney meeting-house and graveyard, where the people gathered. From an improvised pulpit under a removed window the three preachers were heard without and within. 'Be not children in understanding,' was young Andrew Fuller's fiery text and message. Carey had never seen him before and wanted to thank him. He had never witnessed such a day's religious zeal. With not a penny in his pocket he could buy no food, and, except for a glass of wine at a friend of Chater's, he fasted. But his mind and spirit had a feast.

At Chater's instigation in that same June of 1782, the Earls Barton Baptist Meeting persuaded him to join their lay preachers' scheme. Carey insisted that he had no aptitude for preaching, but subsequent pressure extracted the promise of one visit, which ended in his serving them each fortnight for three and a half years. Earls Barton is famed amongst English villages for the Saxon tower of its moated church – an architectural glory. Across the road from this church the Baptist meeting-house was a paltry thatched cottage. Scorn dubbed it 'the mat shop', in derision of the poor weavers (who made rush mats from the reeds of the marshes) who worshipped there. But Carey tramped twelve miles to serve them, braving the abominable tracks in all weathers, though he was still suffering a fever, and though 'they could not pay him enough to cover the cost of the shoes and clothes he wore out in their service.' Their internal disunion was his one grief.

When Pury End Dissenters heard of his Earls Barton visits, they claimed him also for themselves, and he joyfully consented to go, partly for the sake of the monthly home visits their pulpit afforded. After his first Pury End service, the mother of another lay preacher visited Carey's mother to tell her how he had fared.

'And will my boy make a preacher?' asked Carey's mother. 'Yes, and a great one, if God spares him,' was the reply – the fever accounting for the 'if'. In his parents' home, also, Carey bore witness. Mary says, 'he stood alone there for some years, very jealous for God, his soul like Gideon's.' Sometimes, in more zeal than discretion, he seemed for 'throwing down all Baal's altars in one night'. His sisters thought him 'righteous overmuch' when he burned his playing-cards. He begged and was given the opportunity to lead home worship. Mary used to be very disturbed to hear him pray that he and they might be 'stripped of the rags of self-righteousness', though it was his own fight with pride that prompted the prayer. His parish clerk father once joined the Dissenters' service to hear his son preach, hiding himself from notice, and went home thoughtfully, content, though not yet moved to seek.

Carey came into personal Baptist light after hearing a paedo-baptist sermon from John Horsey, a successor of Doddridge – a sermon which unsettled listening Carey. At that time his own Hackleton Meeting was following a liberal line on baptism, and not requiring submission to the ordinance for membership. Carey reinvestigated the New Testament, and was led to the conviction that the ordinance of baptism was appointed for those of *conscious faith and consecration*.

Accordingly, at six o'clock on the first Sunday morning of October 1783, in his twenty-third year, he was baptised in the Nene at Northampton by John Ryland. For his five miles' walk there he left home at early dawn, extremely happy. Very few met on the castle slope for that service; for he was the only 'candidate', and just a village shoe-maker, and anyway he was not joining the Northampton church, because he was already in the Hackleton membership. For Carey's baptism only a handful gathered with the pastor and the three deacons. Years after, at the Missionary Society's twentieth anniversary, Ryland said:

> 5 October, 1783, I baptised in the Nene, just beyond Doddridge's meeting-house, a poor journeyman-shoe-maker, little thinking that before nine years elapsed he would prove the first instrument of forming a society for sending missionaries from England to the heathen world, and much less that later he would become professor of languages in an Oriental college, and the translator of the Scriptures into eleven different tongues. *[As at 1812.]*

Ryland's text at the later preaching service that morning has always seemed strangely predictive: 'Many that are first shall be last; and the

Carey's Piddington cottage

last first.' Not that the preacher had the least inkling of its prophetic significance: he re-preached it in Kettering the next Sunday. Still less aware was Carey, who never expected to be anything more than shoe-maker and lay preacher.

At this stage Carey's soul was only just awakening to the pitiful state of heathendom. In that same autumn of his baptism he was fortunate to borrow some books he greatly coveted, the expensive folios or quartos of *Captain Cook's Voyages,* with their fascinating engravings. Here were travel records after his heart – accounts of exploration, astronomy, art, botany, seamanship, statesmanship, and peaceful world conquest. These records were recent, too, and the achievement of an Englishman. Carey eagerly devoured them. The old village sexton noted his rush lights burning till all hours.

Then, for Carey, the log-books changed into something deeper – a revelation of the sin and sorrow, the immorality, cruelty and misery of unevangelised peoples; a drama of the world's tragic ignorance of Christ, a door opening into hell. The peoples of these South Seas and of the coasts of New Zealand, though so likeable, were also so barbarian. War was their chief sport, and their victories often cannibal celebrations. All was scorched deeply into his soul, and his compassion aroused to an inextinguishable degree. The South Seas began to lure him. He dreamed of ships other than Cook's *Endeavour* and *Resolution* speeding on an even nobler errand, ships chartered for the heralds of saving grace. Captain Cook's log-books were the match that lit the torch in Carey's heart, and made him yearn to be a missionary.

Not that Captain Cook ever conceived of such a result. Quite the contrary. Within the period of his second South Sea voyage explorers from Peru had visited Tahiti and had erected a wood cross there over a comrade's grave, but without explaining the symbol. This set Cook speculating on the chances of a Christian mission to the isles. However, so poor was the impression that the church of his day made upon him, that the following was his matter-of-fact but damning judgement:

> It is very unlikely that any measure of this kind should ever be seriously thought of, as it can neither serve the purpose of public ambition nor private avarice; and, without such inducements, I may pronounce that it will *never* be undertaken.

Carey longed to prove this prophecy wrong, and to cancel Cook's 'never'. Of cancelling it himself he could indulge no hope. He could only think, read, and pray. Thereafter, none heard him pray without making intercession for Cook's islands.

While he had no valid hope of going to the South Seas as an ambassador of Christ, he could do what lay nearest. He could try to lead his own sisters to Christ, especially Mary, his childhood's companion, over whom he yearned particularly anxiously because her spine was threatened with disease and her days seemed destined to be short. He sought to introduce her to true Christianity, and happily, before his Hackleton years ended, she and Ann both turned to the Lord in repentance and faith. By 1783 they had been baptised in the river Tove by Carey's Towcester friend, Thomas Skinner. Mary's conversion had this added sweetness, that in the end it was the fruit of Scott's preaching, to whom Carey was so indebted. Both she and Ann, however, always insisted that they owed their discipleship to the insistent pleadings of William.

They became truly noble Christians: Ann, a Martha; Mary, true to her ardent and meditative biblical namesake. Ann won her farmer-husband William Hobson to Christ. He then opened his Cottesbrooke farmhouse for the preaching of the Gospel, to the never-abating wrath of Sir James Langham his baronet landlord, who refused to allow the smallest departure from the established Church of England. At Mr Hobson's early death he promptly evicted his widow. 'I certainly shall never feel disposed,' he wrote, 'to surrender my farms and houses to those who oppose my wishes in matters which I consider of the utmost importance. Besides, yours is a conspicuous family, and of much influence in the neighbourhood.' 'I wish we may be more conspicuous for God,' wrote Mary to Carey. 'Although we are so poor and harassed, sister chooses to fall into the hands of God. We have proved His faithfulness, but Sir James' we have not. His tender mercies are cruel, but our refuge is in God.' Carey blessed them for their faithfulness.

Notwithstanding their quiverful of seven, the Hobsons made room for invalid Mary; and even after her own widowhood in 1816, Ann still mothered her to the end of her long helplessness, with Carey's faithful monetary aid. By twenty-five she was paralysed. Then for fifty years she was confined to her sick-room, a grievous imprisonment for one who, like her brother, so loved the fields and woods. For eleven years she could not speak, nor even whisper: then, strangely enough, after smallpox, she whispered a sentence or two with much pain; then was again soundless for twenty years. Her right arm was her only unparalysed limb. Yet her face shone, radiant from within, a wonder and blessing to all who knew her.

They used to say that 'patience had in her its perfect work.' Loved by her sister's many children, she drew them to Christ. With a slate as her only tongue, she led for years a Boxmoor Bible Class in the pretty 'Moor End' cottage by the stream. Although to write a letter caused her great physical distress, she loved to write propped up in bed in one position, to her whole scattered family circle. Her pen was her soul's one outlet. She called it 'conversing', and so it was. 'I forget my weakness, whilst I am conversing with you. It seems to remove the distance and to bring you near. What a mercy I can write!' 'I think you will never have patience to read all this through, but you'll excuse me. I can't leave off. I want to converse by any means with those so dear, though it costs me much pain.'

Many of her close-written folio sheets to Carey have survived. She tells him every scrap of the family news, and she pours out her Christian heart to him. She was one of the Mission's 'chief priests' – the

The Hackleton Dissenters' meeting-house

incense of whose ceaseless intercession was fragrant to God. Eustace
Carey learned his best missionary passion in her sanctuary.

'Aunt's sufferings,' wrote her niece in 1828, 'were a few weeks ago
distressing; yet we could not give her up. We do all love her so dearly:
to part with her would tear us asunder. Her late affliction was enough
to kill a person in good health. She is merely skin and bone, and not
much of that, and so weak as to be hardly able to sit pillowed up in her
chair, while her bed is made. Yet she continues the same sweet-
tempered, humble Christian she ever was, feeling for others more than
for herself, and always fearful lest mother should debar herself anything for her comfort.'

She lived to be seventy-four. Dr Gotch, her later pastor, used to say:
'Her work in her affliction, in its way, was as great as that which her
great brother wrought.'

The Lord crowded many formative experiences into Carey's ten
years in the village and hamlet of his beginnings. He learned his trade,

was initiated into Greek, discovered his sins and his Saviour, accepted the reproach of Nonconformity, hammered out his Christian faith and doctrines (making sound shoes for his pilgrimage), and tasted the joys of marriage, the ecstasy of fatherhood, the anguish of child bereavement, and the ordeal of poverty. In these years he first laboured at teaching, bore his first Christian witness, took his first vows of church membership, preached his first sermon, rendered baptismal obedience, caught the heart-rending condition of lost heathendom, and led his sisters into grace and the lifelong service of his own Lord.

4. The Village Pastorate

Carey felt the word *world*.

R. H. LOVELL

The map of the world hung in Carey's work-room; but it only hung on his wall, because it already hung in his heart.

F. W. BOREHAM

William Carey was a shoe-maker, one of the common people; but he was not content to remain a common man. It was not an uneducated and untrained ministry that led the first great attack in Christ's name on the ancient religions and superstitions of Bengal; but a man who by consecrated energy and capacity, as well as by devotion to the cause, was an instrument prepared for the great work to which he was called.

SIR ANDREW FRASER

I knew Carey when he made shoes for the maintenance of his family; yet even then his heart burned incessantly with desire for the salvation of the heathen . . . even then he had drawn out a map of the world with sheets of paper pasted together, besmeared with shoe-maker's wax, and the moral state of every nation depicted with his pen. Even then he was constantly talking with his brethren on the practicability of introducing the Gospel in all nations.

ANDREW FULLER, minister at Kettering and
founding secretary of the Mission.

4. The Village Pastorate
Moulton, 25 March, 1785–1789

CAREY REMOVED TO MOULTON on 25 March, 1785, his 'certificate of settlement' there being published in the *Northampton Mercury* in the following September. This certificate affords a glimpse into social conditions of the time, and the working of the Poor Law. It is signed by three overseers of Paulerspury, and delivered to those of Moulton. Carey's father and another attest it, while two magistrates allow it under this certificate. William Carey and Dorothy his wife are permitted to reside at Moulton, upon the acknowledgement that he really belongs to Paulerspury, so that in the event of his becoming a pauper or requiring relief, he would at once be returned there by the constable, where Paulerspury overseers would be answerable for him and his issue, and provide for them out of the rates. Not that Moulton had any reason to fear his becoming a pauper, though the wolf had often been at his door; but such a certificate was required of all people who settled in a new parish if their rental was under £10.

Carey went to Moulton to start a school, having learned that William Chown, the schoolmaster, had left the village after his father's death. Carey still meant to follow his trade to supplement his income from school fees. His cottage, built for a shoe-maker, with a stone trough in the porch for soaking the leather, stood at the far end of the village. He cleared away the rubbish of a ruined barn, and made a garden, the waste area soon blossoming as the rose. Across the road on a green stood a public house, whose Sunday revelry both saddened and angered his soul.

Schoolroom discipline was at first a problem to him. He confessed 'When I kept school, the school kept me.' Yet for teaching he was born. He thirsted for knowledge, and 'absorbed it as by instinct'. He could retain and convey it. History, geography, travel, and science were his unwearied enthusiasms. His self-drawn and coloured world map, covering a wall of his cottage, and the leather globe which he stitched himself, with the lands made vivid in different coloured leathers, witnessed to his ardour. No doubt his boys would have loved to have put the globe to other use upon the green, but through eyegate, eargate, and handgate he strove to capture their young minds.

Unfortunately the former schoolmaster soon returned to Moulton, reopened his school, and regained many of his pupils, for he was a native of the village and the Moulton poet. He was Church of England too, while Carey was Baptist; and his school centrally situated, while Carey's was out of the way. Still, refusing to be defeated, Carey maintained his own school throughout his Moulton years.

To the Baptists of the village, Carey's coming was a godsend. Their church stretched back to Bunyan's days, and their founders were similar heroes. Now, however, their lamp was almost quenched. Pastorless for many years, their services had become occasional, and their message had also lost its power. For months at a time their meeting was closed, and the building had fallen into dilapidation and dishonour.

At Carey's presence these believers took heart, and he gave them his spare Sundays. By his preaching he drew them into a warm covenant with one another and with Christ. Conversions of the young brought them a joy not experienced for many years, and they pleaded with him to be their minister, the captain of a ship so stranded and forlorn. Earls Barton also begged him to be their leader.

Unexpectedly led towards pastoral responsibility, Carey sought the counsel of wise Sutcliff of Olney, and presently sought and received admission into the Olney Baptist Meeting, agreeing to submit the question of his fitness for the ministry to the judgement of that church.

The Moulton Baptist meeting-house

To this end he preached there one summer Sunday of 1785. The wide-galleried meeting-house, seating seven hundred, was much the largest in which the young shoe-maker had led worship, and its listeners the most demanding. The town's chief tradesfolk attended, and companions of Cowper (barber Wilson, for example, to whom the poet sent the ink-wet stanzas of *John Gilpin*). Overawed at this ordeal, and perhaps at the presence of the dignified pastor, Carey made a poor impression. The church felt unable to commend him, and advised him to continue lay preaching, and to resubmit later for the retesting of his gifts.

The next summer they heard him preach again. This second message was 'as weak and crude as anything ever called a sermon', but it appealed to them, and they warmly approved him. Preachers are not always the best judges of their work. 'They commissioned him to preach, *wherever God in His providence might call him,*' which was their usual form of words for recognising preaching gifts. Ryland, after twice

The Olney Baptist meeting-house, before modern alterations

hearing him that year, wrote in his diary, 'I would I had a like deep sense of Truth.'

Carey undertook the Moulton pastorate after two months' hesitation. The offered stipend was merely £10 a year, less than the current pay of local farm-labourers, and much less than that of roadmen. London's Particular Baptist Fund added five guineas yearly, and just once gave another five for books. But Carey knew out of what poverty the Moulton membership gave. Their little pewter communion cup reveals their economic plight, as does their Poor Fund, which was often disbursed in sixpences. The very walls of the meeting-house were unsafe. The church secretary (whose spelling is here retained) recorded: 'Whe met in peas and parted in younity.' The whole scene at Moulton was of the humblest.

Carey turned the more steadfastly to his lapstone and leather. Though now a pastor, he was not ashamed to be still a workman. Rather than be his own employer, he hired himself to Thomas Gotch, Kettering's brightest man of business. Every fortnight Carey carried there his bag of finished boots and brought back uppers and leather. The ague had now left him, and he loved the walk. Furthermore his thoughts made good company, especially thoughts of his young converts, whose constancy, he told Sutcliff, was his 'glory and crown'.

When the joy of these conversions spread around, the folk so gathered that the meeting-house had to be enlarged. In Moulton's letter to the Association in May 1788, they reported that 'the increase of their congregation and the ruinous state of the building had compelled them to pull it down, and to rebuild and enlarge it.' They also reported that 'the new meeting is well filled out . . . a spirit of attention manifest' and that 'many from neighbouring villages' assembled with them.

At Carey's ordination at Moulton in August 1787, twenty brother ministers assembled. A Miss Tressler of the village begged the money which bought him his suit of black. A minister who was a direct descendant of the founders of the church came to enact the laying on of hands. Ryland, Sutcliff, and Fuller, though in no way foreseeing their lifelong association with him, took the leading parts. His 'confession of faith' was judged 'sound and sensible'. His one grief was the absence of his mother, who had just died of a throat abscess.

He held 'the pastoral office, the highest honour upon earth'. To a brother minister he wrote: 'Preaching, though a great part, is not all of our employ. We must maintain the character of teacher, bishop, overlooker in the chimney-corner as well as in the pulpit.' His tender faithfulness in his own chimney-corner was seen in his wife's baptism in the following October. He was also faithful as a shepherd of the flock, not forbearing to discipline more than once Elizabeth Britten for 'talebearing and tattling'; Edward Smith for throwing himself on the parish, when he had means of his own; and even deacon Law and his wife, the workhouse master and matron, for unkindness to the poor!

He saw very dark days come to Moulton. Smallpox struck in 1788, scourging the village, followed by 'a very bad and malignant fever', which, to quote Vicar Stanton, 'carried off a great number of the poorer, owing, as a gentleman of the Faculty said, chiefly to their want of necessaries and their lack of cleanliness.' What a glimpse into the social conditions of Carey's first pastorate – lack of sanitation, poverty, numerous deaths and many other tensions! They went meatless for weeks in his own cottage. He must often have been deeply anxious for his wife and two boys.

His most constant distress was the perceived meagreness of his own education. 'I was so rusticated as a lad that I could never recover myself.' He persisted, however, in his Latin and Greek, and never rested until Hebrew was added. From Latin he passed to Italian. French he unravelled from Ditton's long treatise 'The Resurrection', and Dutch from an old quarto – without dictionary or grammar! Ryland happened to catch him when he began to struggle with this quarto, chiding this wasting of his limited spare time, but he was soon thankful to secure from him the translation of an important Dutch thesis (Carey's noble rendering of which survives).

On his first visit to him in Moulton, Fuller discovered his linguistic zeal and perseverance, and mentioned them to Carey's employer, who happened to be one of his own younger deacons. The result was of immense blessing to Carey. One day when he brought to Thomas Gotch his fortnight's labour, Gotch said, 'Let me see, Mr Carey, how much do you earn a week by your shoemaking?' 'About nine or ten shillings, sir.' Gotch, with enthusiasm in his eyes, announced: 'Well now, I've a secret for you. I don't mean you *to spoil any more of my leather,* but get on as fast as you can with your Latin, Hebrew, and Greek, and I'll allow you from my private purse weekly ten shillings.'

This has sometimes been cited as proof of his poor craftsmanship, but nine or ten shillings a week could not in those days have been earned by an incompetent workman in oddments of time snatched from school-keeping, a pastorate, and the preparation of four weekly messages! Possibly behind the teasing lay some remembered mishap. But to infer Carey's incompetence is unjust and undiscerning. On the contrary, the very fact that Thomas Gotch – who was soon to be Kettering's first banker and first army and navy boot-contractor – should give £26 a year indefinitely to an obscure pastor, whose future fame was then undreamed of, showed his high regard for him in every respect. Carey went home 'glad and lightsome'. He had lost a great burden. The next Saturday, walking the twenty-two miles to Arnesby to preach for his pulpit hero, the elder Robert Hall, he called half-way on deacon John Haddon of Clipston. 'I suppose you still work at your trade,' said Mr Haddon. 'No, indeed,' answered Carey, and reported his master's kindness.

Though his reputation as a preacher was growing, not a few scented heresy in his progressive and challenging utterances. Ryland was ashamed and angered that even at College Lane, Northampton, several members refused to attend if Carey were conducting the service. It was reported that they found in him 'a strange spirit', and called him an

Arminian. 'Lord! pity us,' Ryland wrote in his diary. 'I am almost worn out with grief at these foolish cavils against some of the best of my brethren – men of God who are only hated because of their zeal for holiness.' Of Fuller's enthusiasm for Carey let C. M. Birrell tell:

> Carey had preached, and there came pushing his way to him a man of thirty-three, robust and broad-shouldered, with the lines of thought cut sharply in his face, but with an almost feminine tenderness trembling in the eyes, under the shadow of the dark eyebrows. Seizing the hand of the preacher, who had given utterance to sentiments, which had for some time been struggling for room in his own heart, Fuller said to Carey what became true – 'We must know more of each other.'

Carey's pastorate admitted him to the ministers' fraternal of the Northampton Association. The elder Ryland insisted that he and the other new member should propose themes for discussion. The pastor of Clipston suggested a vexed text of *2 Peter*, and was bluntly referred to the venerated Dr Gill. Then Carey, when pressed, proposed (in careful terms from long thought) that they should consider 'whether the command given to the apostles to teach all nations was not binding on all succeeding ministers to the end of the world, seeing that the accompanying promise was of equal extent.'

John Ryland later contradicted the story that gained wide currency that his father brushed Carey's topic aside with a rough, 'Young man, sit down, sit down! You're an enthusiast. When God pleases to convert the heathen, He'll do it without consulting you or me. Besides, there must first be another pentecostal gift of tongues!'

But Thomas Wright of Olney, chief authority on Ryland, regards the outburst as extremely likely from the gruff old hyper-Calvinist. Carey himself, at different times, told his nephew Eustace and Marshman that he had received an abashing rebuke, and that the subject was dismissed.

But it was not dismissed from his own mind. For four years already it had burned in his bones. He *felt* the world's darkness. Nightly he kept adding to his own world map, from ethnographer Guthrie and others – the map which surprised Fuller on the wall of his workshop. He amassed his data and accumulated arguments in support of the proposition – that God uses means in the salvation of the lost, and that His servants must preach to all nations.

One of Thomas Gotch's sons never forgot a question cropping up at a ministers' gathering held in his father's home, about a small East Indian isle. 'Neither Hall nor Ryland, Sutcliff nor Fuller, could supply the needed information. Presently, from a back corner, with much reticence, Carey reported its location, length, breadth, and nature, and the number and religious character of its people, to the amazement of the rest, who as good as said, "How do you know?" '

He had schooled himself to detailed research in order that he might make an accurate survey of the church's task, and present his Lord's pressing commission. His globe was his other Bible, as with Robert Arthington later – a voice of loud appeal. His pupils saw sometimes a strange sight, when their master would be moved to tears over a geography lesson. As he pointed to continents, islands, and peoples, he would cry, 'And these are pagans, pagans!' The village of Moulton was his Troas, where he ceaselessly heard Macedonia's entreaty. From his cottage windows he seemed to look out unto the uttermost parts of the earth. His sister-in-law, Catharine, says that more than once she saw him stand motionless for an hour and more in his little garden, absorbed in his tense thoughts and prayers, till his neighbours judged him beside himself .

He read the lives of John Eliot and David Brainerd. He learned how the one had toiled with a scholar's patience and an apostle's grace for nearly sixty years amongst America's Indians, and had been the first to translate the whole Bible into a pagan tongue. The other, in three seraphic years, had burned himself out for those Indians and the Lord. These two, with Paul, were henceforward his heroes and models.

The Bible, too, now throbbed with new meaning. He saw it as the progressive unfolding of God's world-missionary purpose. The Old Testament, especially the later portion of *Isaiah,* shone to his renewed sight with missionary prophecy, as the New shone with missionary exploits and achievements.

Church history also became his fascination, though also his poignant pain, as he realised how far from its heroic periods was the listless church of his own day.

A chief glory of the Moulton parish church, the largest in its deanery, and dedicated both to St Peter and St Paul, was its peal of bells. The village loved to hear 'the five' set swinging in the wakened tower. Carey yearned to hear a strident peal from God's Word which would rouse Christ's church to catch again the missionary spirit of Peter and of Paul. He himself, though he knew it not, was to ring that peal.

To others more capable Carey looked for the effective lead. He looked, for example, to Fuller, who knew better than some of his brethren the dimensions of God's love, and who had already in pulpit and print challenged the hyper-Calvinism which had so paralysed the churches. He hoped, perhaps, that Sutcliff might lead the way, for in 1784 he had sounded the reveille for the monthly prayer-meetings. Carey laid the burden of his soul on all his brother ministers, especially on those of his own age, as likeliest to listen. Surely, he thought, they would see the imperative of world missions.

'They mostly regarded it,' says Fuller, 'as a wild impracticable scheme, and gave him no encouragement. Yet he would not give it up, but talked with us *one by one,* till he had made some impression.' Fuller was as little custom-bound as any, yet even he was tempted to say, 'If the Lord should make windows in Heaven, could such a thing be?'

Since 1784 the Association had been praying for 'the great offensive' of Christ's forces, yet could not see that the Christian conquest of the world would not be accomplished by prayer alone, but through the active efforts of God's people. Carey proposed that they should get up and go forth, and enable God to respect and answer their pleadings.

Meanwhile, he did not fail to be an evangelist near home. Subsequent pastors of Moulton repeatedly encountered the fruit of his service in the surrounding villages. So busy this district preaching kept him, that a friend expostulated with him for neglecting his business, his shoemaking. He replied, 'Neglecting my business! My business, sir, is to extend the kingdom of Christ. I only make and mend shoes to help pay expenses.'

In 1788 he went to Birmingham in the interests of his meeting-house enlargement fund, and there met a young deacon from the Cannon Street Baptist Meeting, businessman Thomas Potts (later a co-founder of Birmingham's first general hospital).

As a youth, and before America's secession, he had traded amongst the Indians of New Orleans, winning such favour that they offered him land measuring a mile deep from the river bank by the length of the cutlery he should lay there and give them. This offer would have been formally ratified, had he not worshipped on the Sunday with the negroes, and treated them as Christian brothers. Upon hearing of this,

Thomas Gotch's house at Kettering

their enraged masters threatened his life, and he had to flee from their fury.

With such a man Carey soon plunged into talk of world missions. The merchant begged him to write a pamphlet to inform and arouse the churches. Carey replied that he had tried, but was utterly dissatisfied. Besides, he could not afford to print, even could he write, the needed message. Potts answered, 'If you can't do it as you wish, do it as you can, and I'll give you £10 towards its printing.' With this encouragement Carey promised to try again, unless he could prevail on someone else more competent. Meeting next evening Ryland, Sutcliff, and Fuller together, he appealed to one or all of these to shape the great appeal. All excused themselves and insisted that he should do it, with, perhaps, their revisional help. So he was compelled to face up to the task.

Although diffident about writing a pamphlet, he would gladly have faced the danger of going overseas. Young artist Medley (son of preacher Medley of Liverpool) never forgot hearing Carey say at the home of trader Potts that, if a few friends would send him and support him for a year from his landing, he would go wherever God might open the door, his own preference being for the South Seas and Tahiti. Cook's full-page engravings of this island haunted his memory. When reminded that so many of these isles were fiercely cannibalistic, he replied that he knew it well, but would still go.

Carey returned from Birmingham with more than money for his meeting-house rebuilding fund. He stood committed to the writing of a challenge for the stirring of the churches to the task of overseas mission. He was more thankful than ever for Thomas Gotch's weekly ten shillings, and for the time this brought him for study and reflection.

In the midst of this new undertaking came the removal to Leicester.

5. The Town Pastorate

In 1789, Carey had left Moulton for Leicester, whither he was summoned to build up a congregation ruined by antinomianism, in the mean brick chapel of the obscure quarter of Harvey Lane. In an equally humble home opposite the chapel the poverty of the pastor compelled him to keep a school from nine in the morning till four in winter and five in summer. Between this and the hours for sleep and food he found little leisure. In a letter to his father we have this division of his leisure: Monday, the learned languages; Tuesday, the study of science, history, composition, etc; Wednesday, I preach a lecture and have been for more than twelve months on the book of *Revelation*; Thursday, I visit; Friday and Saturday, preparing for the Lord's Day.

DR GEORGE SMITH

Under the varnish of two doors of Harvey Lane sanctuary this request is still traceable, 'Please to take off your *pattens.*' I always feel that I ought to take off my shoes from my feet as I enter, in remembrance of its sacred traditions.

DR WILLIAM YOUNG FULLERTON (in 1920).

5. The Town Pastorate
Harvey Lane, Leicester, 1789–1793

CAREY FIRST SAW 'Harvey Lane' in what proved a sad week. The Association was meeting there in 1787 under the moderatorship of the elder Robert Hall, and the welcoming church was found in a shamefully lawless condition. The delegates, shocked by all they learned on the spot, would not leave without expressing a solemn remonstration against the wrongs. This strengthened the hands of the church's worthier section, and the next year they excluded two deacons and some other members for drinking. The pastor who had let things drift so disgracefully agreed to resign. The following January even his membership was cancelled. The next month (February 1789) the church asked Carey to be their probationary pastor – a task to dismay anyone.

The church's letter to the Association, cautiously hinting at this call, is a rare spelling feat, and a curio in capitals. It provides a vivid glimpse of those whom Carey was solicited to serve.

Dearly beloved in the Lord,

It is with a Degree of Pleasure we Inform you That in the Genneral we are at Peace amongst our Selves; we also earnestly pray the Same Blessing may rest upon every Community who Desire to worship the

Lord in the Beauties of Holyness. With respect to our Present Sittuation
as we Believe most of you are in Some measure Aquainted with it, we
need not Say anything By way of Informing you that we are without an
Under Shepard to go in and out Before us.

Yet we Aacknolage ourselves greatly indepted to Divine Goodness
which has Inclined the hearts of So many of the Lord's Sarvants to Supply us in these times. We have in Less than a Year Been Visited with
Twenty Three Ministers; which has given us an opportunity of
Disearning a Diversity of Gifts. But all by the Same Divine Spirit; we
Trust it is our Prayer that these Labours may not be In-Vain amongst
us. And we take this opportunity, to Return our very sincear thanks to
all and every one of the Lord's Sarvants for their Kind Assistance to us
in our Low Estate. But we Belive a Stated Minister to be a Peculear
Blessing: we have taken we hope some Prudent steps to Bring a Bout
that Desirable Ende.

We need not Dear Breethren in form you of the Person we meditate
upon to Supply us for three months, But Shall only add that we Request
an intrest in your Prayers and also your frendly advise in our futer
Preceedings; and if the Lord should smile upon our Attempts we shall
Rejoyce – on the other hand if he fusterates our Designs we wish to
submit and waite his time

We conclude the a Bove and Join the Apostle; with what is ritten in 2
Th.2.16,17.

Signed May 31st 1789 By us in Behalf of the Church

JOHN PURSER

FRANCES PICK, *Deacons*

and nine members

N.B. – We have appointed Bro. Yates for our Messenger.

In the days of Charles II these Leicester Baptists used to walk eight
miles on Sundays to meet their co-worshippers of the county at
Sutton-in-the-Elms, under the protection of the Five Mile Act. When
at length they met in Harvey Lane, it was in a barn; but from 1760 they
had a new meeting-house, with Christopher Hall, the uncle of famed
Robert, as the first pastor. But then, through six successive ministries,
they fell into rifts and dishonour. Three pastors came and went within
three years. The church had become a scandal by the time Carey was
asked to take pastoral charge.

He consulted his father and requested his prayers – prayer having
by this time become real to Edmund Carey. He himself confessed that

if he only regarded worldly considerations, he would go without hesitation, the meeting-house and its membership, the stipend and the future opportunities all being larger than those afforded at Moulton. But, reflecting on the Harvey Lane problems, and on the bond and the blessings which held him to the work in Moulton, he was hesitant. For five weeks he weighed the pros and cons, setting them before trusted counsellors.

At the end of March he consulted his relations while at Ann's wedding. On 2 April, he told the people of Moulton what was transpiring, and they began to meet on Mondays for pleading prayer. To their distress, though scarcely their surprise, they learned what until then had been nobly hidden, that 'their pastor had been in considerable straits for want of maintenance.' A month later he accepted the Harvey Lane call. The next Tuesday Ryland comforted the Moulton flock from *Daniel 9.17* – 'Now therefore, O our God, hear the prayer of thy servant, and his supplications, and cause thy face to shine upon thy sanctuary that is desolate, for the Lord's sake.'

Thus it came to pass that the one who was yearning for the distant service of preaching to heathen lands was called to cleanse and save a mid-England church. Moulton had tested his courage; Harvey Lane would tax and strengthen his wisdom and endurance still more. To resavour its salt as a church would cost Carey toil and tears without measure, for though the Association's remonstration had rid them of the worst transgressors, relatives remained, and these were bent on inflicting misery and mischief.

At first matters sped forward as though all was well. The call to Carey was unanimous. The membership rallied to his lead. All girded their loins and trimmed their lamps. 'Their hearers were so increased by the first quarter-end that they had not room to sit conveniently,' and a front gallery was agreed on (at a cost of £98), for them a most daring venture involving strict economies for six years. The work was finished by the spring – Carey's second such programme of church enlargement. He was full of expectation.

Then, suddenly, all was ruined from within. Several members again fell into sin, laying themselves open to the challenge of the rest. Soon bitter strife made havoc, the fellowship was shattered, the spiritual atmosphere was ruined, the blessing was quenched, the unsavoury news got abroad, the people ceased to gather, conversions became impossible, the leaders lost their joy, and the pastor was heart-broken. He told Fuller that 'he was distressed beyond measure at the trials of his situation.'

The church sent miserable tidings to the Association at Olney:

> We have the Word preached amongst us in its purety, and we hope that it is pleasant to the souls of many of us. But far from enjoying harmony and peace, we are divided three against two, and two against three. Nor can we boast that meetings of prayer are well attended, though the monthly prayer meetings for the spread of the Gospel are better attended than the weekly. The number of our members is two less than last year.

All of this was wormwood for Carey after his first year's labour, and especially after the auspicious promise of the early months. It was hard that the news should go to Olney, the church which had sponsored him! Sutcliff, learning all the facts from him at the meetings, told Mary 'that the Harvey Lane difficulties would have daunted any other'. Carey often wished himself back in poor, kind (even though fever-stricken) Moulton, and they wished for him, bemoaning their loss at the Association meetings. But having set his hand to the plough he would not look back, and he continued to plod through the unyielding ground.

For nearly two years the destroyers of the church resisted his every effort to win them to a Christian spirit, till they drove him at length, in September 1790, to propose the church's dissolution, and its re-formation on the basis of a solemn covenant, which would 'bind them to a strict and faithful New Testament discipline, let it affect whom it might'. This was approved by the majority and done. The refractory element, holding back, were declared no longer in membership after two months, whereupon they hardened into Carey's bitter personal foes and threatened to destroy the solemnity and peace of his day of ordination. The remainder drew nearer to their pastor and to God, spending much of the week after the adoption of the solemn covenant in fasting and prayer. From this moment on they filled that fellowship with faithful love. Thorns, briars and nettles gave way to the flowers and fruits of the Spirit – a fragrance for Leicester and a victory for God.

In the spring of 1791, the church brought Carey's long probation to an end, and he was formally ordained to the pastorate, with Ryland, Sutcliff, and Fuller again participating in the service, and Pearce preaching in the evening on 'Glorying in the Cross' – the most intense message Carey had ever heard. It was his first encounter with Pearce – 'the seraphic'. He reports the day 'as one of pleasure and profit to the greater part of the assembly'. He could not say 'to all', for the dissidents were still sullen, though none dared, as they had threatened, to break the meeting's decorum. (Of a noteworthy happening of that night the next chapter tells.)

Leicester was Carey's first *town*. The change was great from the villages of Paulerspury, Piddington and Moulton, though the population of Leicester was a mere fraction of today's, being almost totally confined by its walls and river. Only a section of Gallowtree had a double pavement, and only the High Street had the distinction of oil-lamps. All coal came in on the backs of horses, until the canal was completed in the midst of Carey's four-year pastorate. The first spinning-machines had alarmed and enraged local labour. The mail took twenty hours by coach from London. The town's Nonconformist churches could be counted on one hand.

Harvey Lane, the location of Carey's church, really was a lane, not even cobbled. Carey's cottage looked out on fields and gardens that sloped down to the river. New and standing alone, with its roof of Swithland slates, its bit of back garden, and the Soar in sight beyond, it was truly pleasant. Its brick-floored living-room, lean-to kitchen, rude stairs, one bedroom and attic, all breathed the simplicity with which Carey was wholly familiar.

It cut him to the quick in his second year to lay his infant Lucy in the meeting-house graveyard opposite his cottage. 'He used to mention her death in every letter,' said Mary, 'and we knew he had been touched at a very tender point.' Dearly loving his own sisters, he had wanted his three boys to have a sister too.

When Carey joined Harvey Lane it was a simple whitewashed meeting-house, seating from two to three hundred. Carey's stipend was better than at Moulton, but rather less than £40 per year, the membership being only sixty strong and the ill-willed giving little. Furthermore foods were at high war-prices (driving the townspeople to riot). Carey turned once again, therefore, to his school-keeping, from nine to five in the summer, and until four in the winter. Also, he was obliged to turn again to his shoe-craft, despite being now pastor in a proud, important town. Gardiner's sketch of him is vivid:

I well recollect Carey's coming to Leicester in 1789. He was chosen to preside over a small congregation in Harvey Lane. He lived in a very small house just opposite the meeting, which may now be distinguished from the rest by its ancient appearance; at that time it was the only one on that side of the street. I have seen him at work in his leathern apron, his books beside him, and his beautiful flowers in the windows.

On Mondays the classics were 'beside him'; on Tuesdays textbooks of science, history, and composition. On the other days his Hebrew Bible and Greek Testament, with the developing notes for his mid-week and Sunday expositions, were his companions. To what effect and in what manner he studied, his essay on the *Psalms* proves. He discusses the literary character, authorship, and titles of the *Psalms* after the manner of Lowth, Michaelis, and Sir William Jones, of whose judgements he takes special notice. He shows what force a familiarity with Bible geography lends to the understanding of Hebrew poetry. He glories in the *Psalms'* ethical and religious superiority to the best ancient pagan literature and achievement. For a millennium before David, he argues, arts flourished on the Euphrates. Three centuries before him, the Indian Vedas were being shaped. Two centuries before him, India was calculating eclipses, Phoenicia was traversing the seas, Greece was emerging (though Homer had not yet sung), Egypt was in her splendour and Ephesus architecturally magnificent. Nevertheless, in her *Psalms*, ie: in the spheres of ethics and religion, Israel as far surpassed Chaldea and Persia, Egypt and Hindustan, as these surpassed Israel in the *lesser* kingdoms of knowledge. Carey finds here sure proof of God's especial indwelling of Israel, and of His unique illumination of the minds of her prophets. He closes with counsel which he faithfully followed: 'We should let few days pass without reading in the Hebrew one of these poems. The more they are studied, the more will they delight. None ever repented such labour, though many its neglect.'

Grand old Robert Hall was his honorary tutor. 'It was one of my chief privileges,' Carey wrote to his Leicester successor, 'to be favoured with the kind advice and kinder criticism of men of the greatest eminence, and their friendship was a jewel I could not too highly prize.' Hall criticised his sermons as too matter of fact. They lacked windows. 'There are not enough *likes* in them, whereas the Master was always saying, "The kingdom is *like* seed or treasure or leaven."'

After the departure of its dissidents, the Leicester church learned that there was a prophet in its midst. The people again gathered. Conversions made them glad. Vicar Robinson of St Mary's (whose ministry, Robert Hall said, 'formed an epoch in Leicester's religious history') remarked that Carey was attracting his hearers. The young Baptist pastor answered – 'I would rather win to Christ the poorest scavengers in Leicester than draw off to Harvey Lane the richest members of your flock.' His care for the town's least-accounted-of gave his message added power.

Outwardly, Carey had nothing in his favour as a preacher. He was short, impoverished, and lacked a college education. His hands were seamed and stained by leather stitching. His appearance and manner were that of a peasant, and his wig was 'odious and stiff'. Yet the people gathered as to one whose lips had been touched by a hot coal from the altar. Not that he coaxed them with easy themes. For more than a year he cut his mid-weekly way through the forest of the Apocalypse, thrusting himself on this task for his own mental discipline.

Nor was he content to preach seven times a fortnight in Harvey Lane. As few other pastors of the period, save for General Baptists and Methodists, he went out to the villages and laid the foundations of churches in Thurmaston, Syston, Sileby, Blaby, and Desford. In Thurmaston there were many conversions. More than a hundred folk would gather there for his services. His first Indian letter to Harvey Lane is full of concern for these villages.

He had been in Leicester only six months when he was pressed into the secretariat of its Nonconformist committee, which thrust him into the thick of the contest for the repeal of the Test and Corporation Acts, just when the reactionaries were strengthened by the violence occurring in France. It was this secretariat that brought him in touch with Dr Thomas Arnold and Robert Brewin, the doctor being the committee's chairman, and the wealthy spinner its treasurer. With these men he bore the weight of Leicester's Free Church witness and protest in those combative days.

These colleagues led him also into other social sympathies. Brewin stimulated his compassion for Leicester's brutally-treated prisoners, and Dr Arnold his indignation at the current cruelty to those suffering mental disorders. In their loathing of the slave-trade they rivalled one another. Dr Arnold and Brewin had long lifted their voices against this infamy. In Carey they found an informed and fervent ally. Years later a Leicester deacon told Marshman's son that he never heard Carey pray without remembering the slaves.

Fetters on people's intellects were as hateful to Carey as fetters on limbs or liberty. He was all for the unbounded freedom of human inquiry. This drew him quickly into the coterie of the town's zealous scientists, despite the fact that in their theological outlook these men differed widely. They gathered in the library and lounge which young Richard Phillips had opened. For ten years Phillips had been the fearless leader of Leicester's intellectual life, having founded its Philosophical Institute. He had brought there reformers like Howard, together with scientific discoverers and lecturers like Priestley. The Institute was full of telescopes, planetaria, and electrical apparatus. Phillips had set up Leicester's first lightning-conductor – to the people a thing as impious as dangerous! There is little doubt that in this library and Institute Carey first met rich young Gardiner, and perhaps heard there his papers on 'Gravitation' and 'Comets'.

The discussions of public questions held at the Institute were so outspoken and radical that the municipal authorities intervened and declared their displeasure. Phillips, their leader, was repeatedly threatened with prosecution for the boldness of his newspaper – the town's first – and his manifest sympathy with the Revolution across the Channel. For selling Paine's *Rights of Man* he was thrust into prison. But he lived to be honoured as a knighted sheriff of London.

Carey was republican himself, but suppressed his youthful political sympathies for his work's sake.

Both Brewin and Arnold gave him the freedom of their libraries, and Brewin loved to have him in his extensive garden to show him its rare plants, and the pomegranates in the sheltered places, and his prize auriculas.

The master interest of Carey's Leicester life, however, was still the evangelisation of the world. Nothing could cool this passion – not the business of his crowded days, nor the widening range of his town ministry, and not even the urgencies of English programmes of reform. In Leicester, as in little Moulton, the cry of the heathen continents and islands haunted his spirit. Indeed, Leicester's thirteen thousand made more vivid and poignant the distress of the world's hundreds of millions.

Carey's Leicester cottage

6. The Enquiry

This, as nearly as I can obtain information, is the state of the world; though in many countries, as Turkey, Arabia, Great Tartary, Africa and America except the United States, and most of the Asiatic Islands, we have no accounts of the number of inhabitants that can be relied on. I have therefore only calculated the extent, and counted a certain number on an average upon a square mile . . .

The inhabitants of the world, according to this calculation, amount to about 731 millions: 420 millions of whom are still in pagan darkness; 130 millions the followers of Mahomet; 100 millions Catholics; 44 millions Protestants; 30 millions of the Greek and Armenian churches, and perhaps 7 millions of Jews. It must undoubtedly strike every considerate mind what a vast proportion of the sons of Adam there are who yet remain in the most deplorable state of heathen darkness . . . utterly destitute of the knowledge of the Gospel of Christ, or of any means of obtaining it.

WILLIAM CAREY, *An Enquiry into the Obligation of Christians to use Means for the Conversion of the Heathen*, 1792.

How then shall they call on him in whom they have not believed? and how shall they believe in him of whom they have not heard? and how shall they hear without a preacher? and how shall they preach, except they be sent? as it is written, How beautiful are the feet of them that preach the gospel of peace, and bring glad tidings of good things!

THE APOSTLE PAUL, *Romans 10.14-15.*

6. The Enquiry
Leicester, 1792

THE CALL OF GOD came to Northamptonshire Baptists at Clipston in 1791, at the Association's Easter gathering in the meeting-house on the hill. Of all the Association's young leaders none exercised a weightier influence than John Sutcliff of Olney, and he was one of the preachers for that day. On two previous occasions he had called the Association to earnest prayer for the conversion of the heathen. On this day at Clipston he preached on 'Jealousy for God', a message which became warmly missionary, as he pleaded for 'hearts which embrace a globe and every habitable shore'. Then followed Andrew Fuller's striking sermon on 'The Disaster of Delay'. The text was *Haggai 1.2* – 'Thus speaketh the Lord of hosts, saying, This people say, The time is not come, the time that the Lord's house should be built.' This clarion call to world mission could scarcely have been clearer.

'An unusual degree of attention was excited. I know not,' says Ryland, 'under which I felt the most. The mind of every one was possessed by a solemn conviction of our need of more zeal, and of the sin of negligence.'

Even at the ministers' dinner in one of the village inns 'scarcely an idle word was spoken.' 'Every heart was subdued,' writes Webster Morris, Clipston's pastor, 'Such deep solemnity has seldom been witnessed.'

Then Carey appealed for action, striking while the iron was hot. He called for *impression* to be turned to *expression*, sentiment to service. He pleaded with them on Christ's behalf to become His ambassadors to the world, and to venture forward to begin an overseas mission. To his warm mind it seemed that the child for which Christ had long travailed was coming to the birth, and that this Association Day gathering was to be his manger. Had Clipston obeyed, it would have set its church upon a hill never to be hid. To its everlasting loss, the 'wise and prudent' prevailed, who counselled the people to be non-committal and who would not take any initiative. Not even the two preachers of the day stood with Carey! They had not anticipated such a hasty response and drew back from Carey's literal application of their urgings. 'Feeling the difficulty,' says Fuller, 'of setting out on such an unbeaten path, their minds *[including his own]* revolted at the idea of attempting it. It seemed too much like grasping at an object utterly beyond their reach.'

They would not rise and build, but merely advised the speedy publication of Carey's pamphlet (the *Enquiry*). Let him present the case to all the churches. They could then gauge the churches' response.

That night Carey and others stayed at the manse. Until beyond midnight Carey kept them talking of an overseas mission. Supper had been eaten, but at one o'clock Fuller was again hungry. 'Morris,' he asked, 'have you any more meat?' 'Yes,' answered Morris. 'Then roast it here before this fire,' and Fuller bored the mantelpiece, and hung by a cord from the gimlet the beef for their nocturnal second repast. As portions were ready, slices were cut and served round. One can imagine the pleasantry, as Carey continued to press his case. But the discussion ended with no change of mind by the ministers, yet the double supper with its improvised spit was never forgotten, nor the insistent pleadings of Carey. When in later years the Clipston church acquired a new manse, the pierced mantelpiece was taken and installed there for the memory of that night.

The next month came Carey's induction at Leicester. After the public proceedings ended, at the request of Samuel Pearce, Carey read to a little group the part of his pamphlet so far written.

The scene is worth visualising. Scholarly Ryland, cautious Sutcliff, dynamic Fuller, earnest Pearce, and others – with Carey pouring his zeal into their hearts. His life had been more handicapped than theirs, and his chances more limited, yet here he tracked for them God's missionary path through biblical and wider history, and bade them hear the call of their dying century and of their ever-living Lord. 'It added fuel to my zeal,' said Pearce.

Carey's best reading and thinking for the previous eight years was invested in this 'piece', as he called it, of eighty-seven pages.

The pith of its *Introduction* is this. Not by deluge nor other such judgement will God deal with the world's sin. God now calls people by the grace of Christ's Cross. The apostles published it near and far, as their Lord had bidden them. Cultured and barbarian peoples alike received it and were blessed. Zealous Christians of later centuries also published it – sometimes with great response, but never in vain. Now only a few seem to care and obey. It is time for Christian people to awake from the love of money and ease.

The *Enquiry* consists of argument, review, survey, challenge, and programme, and the *Argument* sets out the chief criticisms Carey had long encountered in his advocacy of missions – with his answers. For instance, to the question, 'Was not Christ's charge to evangelise the nations addressed to the apostles, rather than meant for us?' Carey replies: 'Then why do we baptise? If baptism concerns us, world missions must no less. The two were bidden in one breath; were part and parcel of each other. Besides,' he adds, 'we claim our share in His promise: "Lo! I am with you." We have no right to the promise unless we observe the command. The one conditions the other. To neglect His commission is to forfeit His benediction.'

Objection: 'But how do we know that this command is still valid? Not even divine injunctions abide for ever. They have their periods and pass, like the Levitical law.'

Reply: 'Nay,' responds Carey, 'divine injunctions abide till they have fulfilled their function. Who can think this commission exhausted, with the vast majority of mankind not yet acquainted with Christ's name?'

Objection: 'But were there not God-set limits to the execution of the commission even in apostolic days? Was not Paul forbidden to go to pagan Bithynia?'

Reply: 'Yes, because the divine purpose needed him then more elsewhere. But he was ceaselessly missionary, as we must be ever.'

Objection: 'But Christ's command could scarcely have been absolute, even for the apostles, seeing that they never heard of vast parts of the globe – the South Seas for example – nor could these be reached. Neither can we think it absolute today, with very large regions still unknown and unopened.'

Reply: 'Maybe: but, as they were responsible for going according to their strength into all their accessible world, we are in duty bound to speed into our much enlarged world. Indeed, we ought to be keen to get everywhere for Christ, till all closed doors are opened.

'Papists brave all peril. Moravians have not turned back from Abyssinia's heat nor Greenland's cold, from difficult tongues nor savage manners. British traders press into the East Indies and Persia, into China and Greenland. Cursed slave-raiders dare deep into Africa. Should we Christians be less resolved and adventurous than these?'

Objection: 'But is there not a secret God's time for such a world movement, which we can neither hasten nor delay, whose arrival and appearing we must just await?'

Reply: 'In that case it is also vain to *pray* for the speeding of Christ's kingdom; and who will dare say that?'

Objection: 'But must not a second miraculous Pentecost precede and permit successful world missions?'

Reply: 'This logic comes too late. Its theory collides with fact. Wherever the Christ has been lovingly offered to men, some, and often many, have accepted the gift with joy. God's power has been proven.'

Objection: 'But if God purposes to save the heathen, will He not take steps to effect it Himself?'

Reply: 'God's one deliberate method is to work through consecrated men.'

Objection: 'But have we not task enough to engage us with the heathen at home?'

Reply: 'Forsooth, there are thousands of our fellow-countrymen living as far from God as possible. We ought to be tenfold more eager than we are to win them to the Christ. But the news is at least within their hearing, and in almost every part of the land there *are* faithful ministers. If the home church wakened, the home heathen could be won. But pagan lands have neither true Bible nor true ministers.

Multitudes have neither a written language, nor decent government, nor any of our chief blessings. Pity, not less than Christianity, should constrain our instant help.'

The *Review* portion of the pamphlet describes very fully the activity of the apostles, and then briefly recalls the Christian conquest of the Roman Empire and the preaching of Christ's name even beyond its borders, by such as Frumentius, James of Nisibis, 'Hermit Moses', Palladius, Patrick, Finian and Columba. Then it tells of the winning of wild Europe by Augustine, Paulinus, Birinus, Felix, Columban, Gall, Wilfrid, Kilian, Boniface, Willibrod, Anskar, Gaudibert, Methodius, Cyril, and others; then of the compulsive missions of corrupt Rome, followed by the mercy of the Reformation; and, finally, of the re-emergence of true missions under Eliot and Brainerd, and under the Danish and Dutch, the Moravians and Methodists.

This was the first modern attempt at a roll of world missionaries. The facts were not readily to hand, for no one else was then studying this aspect of history. Yet almost all the names which modern mission-ary research discloses are here enshrined.

The *Survey* part of the pamphlet describes the world as Carey knew it: the message of the map. This he made the substance of his plea. Flower growing and map making were his hobbies. The one known decoration of his cottage was his handmade Mercator world map; while close to his bench was positioned his own stitched globe of leather, with its lands in various colours. The *Survey* is his atlas, world census, and world directory. And his facts and figures agree with the best maps and reckonings of the time.

Sweep of purpose is here combined with wealth of detail. The minute precision of information is almost extravagant. Islands but two or three miles across are not too trivial for his attention. The Friendlies, he says, number twenty, the Sandwich seven, the Society six, the Kurile twenty-five, the Madeiras three, and the Virgin twelve. 'The Ladrones are inhabited by the most uncivilised pagans.' 'Two thousand out of the 40,000 folk of Dominica are Caribbs.' In Amboyna the Dutch have twenty-five churches.

He knows the religious complexion of each Swiss canton, of each Aegean and East Indian isle. Like his contemporary geographers, he has to estimate the populations of Turkey, Asia, Africa, and all but the European settlements of America, but he does so by no rule of thumb.

He has studied their conditions, and his estimates are careful and considered.

His statistics were his griefs. To have to write 'Pagan' ninety-nine times against vast and populous regions, and 'Mohammedan' fifty-three times moved him to deep sorrow. He cared for people everywhere – not just in the South Seas of Cook, nor in the India of impeached Warren Hastings, nor the wronged negroes of the West. 'The ebb and flow of all men's hearts went through him.' As far as his map was concerned, even pin-point dottings on the oceans were precious in his sight. His interest in islands is most marked. Two hundred he names either as individuals or clusters, partly out of exactness, and partly because his own hope was to make his missionary home on some strategic one of them. His feet and hands moved in Leicester; his heart was in Tahiti.

His statistical findings were tragic. Of the world's seven hundred and thirty-one millions, more than a fifth were Mohammedans, and more than half pagans – seven-ninths in all being either Mohammedan or pagan. Half of Asia, most of Africa, most of America, and all but the coast of South America were 'as wanting in civilisation as in true religion', with peoples sometimes cannibal.

Arabian Mohammedanism had bled Africa to death through the slave-trade, of which Christian nations shared the guilt. Jesuits through their political intrigues had deeply prejudiced the Far East against Christianity. European traders had corrupted the Indies. Greek Church peoples were illiterate and superstitious. Papists had only a dim knowledge of divine things. Even in privileged Britain the Established and the Free Churches alike embraced many errors and much looseness of life, and the Gospel was fiercely hated and attacked by many people.

Yet Carey avoided no issue. He faced the worst and believed the best. 'All these things are loud calls to Christians, especially to ministers, to exert themselves to the utmost.' He took it sublimely for granted that Christ would bless the world, if His people would be faithful. In Christ's name he defied all the power of the enemy.

Carey's pamphlet moved to its *Challenge* confronting every obstacle of distance, barbarism, death, hunger, and language. The mariner's compass, he said, had made the Pacific as navigable as the Mediterranean. Trade was not intimidated by distance, but ceaselessly pressed into the unknown, each advance freshly revealing the ignorance, cruelty, and misery of the unevangelised world. The barbarism of peoples had never deterred apostles, or their like-minded successors, not the wildness of Germany and Gaul, nor of 'more barbarous Britain'! *Their* watchword was not 'Civilisation first and then Christianity', but 'Christianity the royal road to a worthy civilisation'. Tertullian had boasted that 'those parts of Britain which were proof against Roman armies, were conquered by Christ.'

Eliot and Brainerd transformed America's Indians through the power of the Gospel as no European civilisation ever could have done. Barbarism baffled no traders. Even to distant Alaska they ventured just for otters. If we Christians loved men as merchants love money, no fierceness of peoples would keep us from their midst. Their very barbarism would evoke our swifter help. Eliot and Brainerd, by the grace of the Gospel, both subdued and uplifted men. We cannot afford to leave even the most dehumanised races without Christ.

Even if service of barbarian races should involve death, no true Christian should grudge it. Hunger will be less serious than we think. Native food, if not inviting, will suffice. A servant of Christ will be ready for hardship, forgoing crowded churches, kind friends, a civilised country, legal protection, and affluence, and be prepared for rejection, hatred, false friends, imprisonment, torture, the company of barbarians of uncouth speech, miserable housing, hunger and thirst, weariness and painfulness, hard work and little encouragement.

If lay workers are also sent with ordained missionaries, whose knowledge of farming, fishing, and fowling shall supply the mission's creaturely necessities, the initial outlay will often be the only and the whole expense.

Traders learn the language: so can we. A year, or at the most two, should enable us 'even with no very extraordinary talents to communicate with any foreign people'.

Choose 'men of piety, prudence, courage, and forbearance'; men of sound knowledge of the Word and the Gospel; men prepared to forgo comforts and endure hardships. Let them mingle with the people, always presenting the kindly nature of their errand, resenting no injury, assuming no airs, and grudging no service. Let them above all be instant in prayer, and they will not fail, especially if they be quick to discern and develop the faculties of their converts, who, with their in-born understanding of the people, must always be a country's chief evangelists, endorsing and adorning their message with their changed lives.

Carey's pamphlet closes with the *Programme* which Christians must surely pursue. We must pray, for without the Spirit all is vain. No ruler's help and authority, and no orator's eloquence, or human genius can establish Christ's kingdom, as Portuguese and Spanish missions tragically prove. 'Not by might, nor by power, but by my spirit, saith the Lord of hosts,' shall the great work be accomplished. Prayer, according to *Zechariah 12* and *13*, is the beginning of all blessing and victory, the first link in the divine chain, the key to Heaven's treasury.

Since the churches of the Northamptonshire Association commenced monthly prayer for the world, new opportunities of evangelism have arisen, argues Carey. France has begun to break Rome's fetters; the slave-trade has been challenged; Sierra Leone looks likely to become a base for African freedom, commerce and Christian advance. These are large encouragements. Had such prayer been more general and intense, we might have seen by this time Daniel's prophecy fulfilled – not only gates opened for the Gospel, but many news bearers running through, and the knowledge of the Truth far increased. Prayer is basic for the spread of the Gospel. All, even the poor and illiterate, can swell its force.

However, we must *plan* and *plod* as well as pray, or else the children of this generation will again shame the children of light. When traders form a company and win a charter, they go to the limit of their secured concessions and prerogatives, choosing stocks, ships, men, routes, everything, in accordance with their purpose. They strain every nerve, run every risk, dare every danger, watch every vessel, mourn every delay, and never rest 'till the rich returns are safe in port'. We Christians must be equally earnest in the business of our Lord. For the present, each denomination of Christians must form its own missionary society, though in friendliest communication with the rest.

Then we must *pay* as well as pray and plan. Let the rich embark a generous portion of their God-entrusted wealth; it will yield them liberal returns. Let those of more moderate income devote a proportion, say a tenth, of their annual increases to God, after the pattern of patriarchs, the precepts of Moses, and the practice of many Puritans. Such giving will supply at once the needed funds for the home ministry and for home and world missions. Let the members of our congregations give a penny *or more* a week according to their power. Preachers could then be sent into our little-evangelised English villages, and a good surplus would remain for overseas missions. Let part, or even all, of what we spend on luxuries, *and even on necessary items, where these are bound up with social wrongs*, be given to the Gospel. 'Many of late have left off the use of West Indian sugar, on account of the iniquitous manner in which it is obtained. These families have not only cleansed their hands of blood, but have made a saving.' (Carey had done this himself.)

'We have only to keep the end in view and have our hearts thoroughly engaged in its pursuit, and means will not be very difficult.' His programme was comprehensive, and heroic. His pulling together of the home ministry, home missions, and overseas missions as one enterprise was as right as it was novel and daring. The term 'foreign missions' he never uses. All, whether at home or abroad, were one.

He closes with the reminder that bold giving to the kingdom is the one investment of the Lord's sanction. It is the Saviour Who commands us to lay up treasure beyond the reach of thief and moth and rust. This is sowing for the most satisfying returns. 'What a treasure, what a harvest must await such as Paul and John Eliot and David Brainerd *[his three models]*, and others, who have given themselves wholly to God's work! What a heaven to see the myriads of the heathen, of Britons among the rest, who by their labours have been brought into the knowledge of God! Surely such a crown of rejoicing deserves our aspiration! Surely it is worthwhile to lay ourselves out with all our might in promoting Christ's kingdom!'

7. The Deathless Sermon

Then he said, Who shall order the battle?
And he answered, Thou.

1 Kings 20.14

The pulpit was ceded to Mr Carey, and he preached that sermon which was long remembered as having laid the foundation of the Missionary Society. He took for his text 'Enlarge the place of thy tent, and let them stretch forth the curtains of thine habitations: spare not, lengthen thy cords, and strengthen thy stakes.' From this text he deduced and enforced the two principles which were embodied in the motto of the Mission, 'Expect great things; attempt great things.' Into this discourse he poured the accumulated energy of those feelings which had been gathering strength ever since he read Cook's voyages, and determined on the establishment of a mission.

JOHN CLARK MARSHMAN, son of Joshua Marshman.

I call that sermon of Carey's wonderful, because there has, perhaps, been no sermon preached in modern days, which has had so distinct and traceable an effect on Protestant Christianity throughout the world.

DR F. W. GOTCH

Why the 'deathless sermon'? It has been pointed out that no other sermon since Bible times has won such an enduring place as Carey's in the memory of the Church. Very few Christians can quote anything from the sermons of the great preaching worthies, such as Luther, Calvin, Whitefield and Spurgeon. But Carey's Nottingham watchword, 'Expect great things; attempt great things,' is famous throughout the Christian world. Is it not fitting that the sermon which triggered the age of missions should have been given such a distinguishing honour? 'He hath exalted them of low degree!'

EDITOR

7. The Deathless Sermon
Nottingham, 30 and 31 May, 1792

NOTTINGHAM WAS THE farthest north the Northampton Association of 'Particular Baptist' churches had ever ventured. For some ministers and messengers it meant a horseback ride of from sixty to seventy miles. In 1792, seventeen ministers from the twenty-four associated churches assembled to take part. Other silent ones were also, perhaps, present. Messengers from the churches were few by reason of the distance. Even the College Lane congregation at Northampton excused itself for sending only its pastor.

They put up at 'The Angel', the largest inn of the town's wide market-place. 'It was good,' says A. G. Fuller, 'to witness the arrival of worthy farmers of the old school, on their stout and stalwart steeds, unaddicted to hunting, or driving their better halves and daughters in capacious vehicles; pedestrians covered with dust and perspiration, the product of many a weary mile of travel; a goodly array of black coats (for such wear was then sacred to mourners and ministers) exchanging hearty greetings, and acknowledging that through mercy they had arrived safe and well.'

Their talk that May was of France, and of Burke's forebodings; of

Warren Hastings; of the anti-slavery debate and defeat in the Commons; of glorious Wilberforce; and (among the more literary) of Boswell's *Johnson* and of Cowper's *Task*.

Their meeting place was the town's one Baptist chapel in Friar Lane, a simple white building, seating not more than two hundred and thirty.

On the Tuesday evening John Ryland was called to the chair, and the churches' letters were read. College Lane, Northampton, bemoaned a year of dissension and distress. Moulton was in deep depression. Oakham lamented its feebleness; Braunston its lethargy. On the other hand, Foxton was full of hope, and Bottesford was thriving. Arnesby was comforted after the death of Robert Hall by a prospective new pastor, while Roade wrote of enlargement and Gretton of wakened interest. Clipston spoke of quickening after days of fasting and prayer, and Walgrave of arousal. Harvey Lane could say, 'The Lord has smiled on us and healed our dissensions,' while Nottingham had just used its baptistery for five (and the year before for nineteen), and Guilsborough said it had 'never enjoyed so much of God before . . . Not many days pass now in our village but some seek the way of salvation.' Kettering had 'never such a spirit of prayer', and had just been gladdened by the baptism of ten. Ryland could truthfully sum up and say that 'most of the church news was encouraging' – the fruit of their increased prayer, and that 'circumstances were conspiring towards the fulfilment of great prophecies.' He was thinking of France and of her troubled awakening, which several of the church letters had hailed. God's rain cloud, already bigger than a man's hand, could be seen on the horizon.

On the Wednesday they met at 6 am for prayer, and at 10 am for the first sermon, with Carey in the pulpit. *Isaiah 54* was his scripture. He knew its song by heart, having so often read it in the original Hebrew, his one regret being that its rich Hebrew assonances were not echoed in the English rendering. With Isaiah's faith his soul was all aglow. When presently he made verses 2 and 3 his message, his intimates knew that into that hour the passion of eight years was to be poured. He rang the great challenge out:

Enlarge the place of thy tent, and let them stretch forth the curtains of thine habitations: spare not, lengthen thy cords, and strengthen thy stakes; for thou shalt break forth on the right hand and on the left; and thy seed shall inherit the Gentiles, and make the desolate cities to be inhabited. Fear not.

Dr Whitley says that 'Cowper's lines:

> *Behold at Thy commanding word,*
> *We stretch the curtain and the cord;*

gave Carey the idea for this sermon.' They may have done so. (These lines occur in the original version of *Jesus where'er Thy people meet*.) But it is more likely that Sutcliff's report of the sermon to Cowper gave the poet the idea for his couplet.

The text itself was a treasure trove. There could be no more inspiring missionary message, yet it had lain in the grave unrealised and forgotten until it woke for Carey, and held him with its power. Isaiah (especially in his later chapters) had been for years to Carey *the* regal prophet. Now, with his words he lit a beacon that was to blaze for years to come. One has called it 'a burning bush of missionary revelation'.

First, as was always his habit in exposition, he set forth the historical context of the words. Chaldea had destroyed Jerusalem, devastated Judea, deported the Jewish people, and driven them into long exile, hardship, and despair. Judah seemed like a woman once loved of her divine Husband, and blessed by her children, but now disowned and left to perish.

Nevertheless, the prophet brought her cheer. Things were not all they seemed. Divine pity and love atoned for her sins – according to the infinite Gospel of the preceding chapter. Her heavenly Husband forgave and designed to bless her. Not for ever was she disowned; only disciplined, to cleanse her from her sins. By no choice nor will of His should she remain disgraced, barren, wretched. He bade her fling away her worse than widow's weeds, and become once again a cherished wife and a mother of happy children. God called her to a new and splendid destiny. The shabby wind-blown tent, in which she found poor shelter, was to become a pavilion, indeed, an ever-multiplying family of tents, strong and beautiful. 'Get up,' God said. 'Find larger canvas, stouter and taller poles, and stronger tent-pegs. Catch wider visions. Venture on bolder programmes. Dwell in a larger world. Thy Maker is thy Husband. He is Lord of all the earth.'

Then in the prophet's picture of widowed Israel, the preacher found

a mirror of the Church of his own day, with its defeatedness and dishonour, its dearth and decay. He knew the facts in village and in town,
in the Established Church and in the ranks of Nonconformists. He had
seen them at close quarters in Paulerspury and Piddington, in Moulton
and Earls Barton, and in growing Leicester. He had felt the lifelessness
of Anglicanism, except under such preachers as John Newton and
Thomas Scott.

In Nonconformity he was familiar with the low enthusiasm, the barren and bitter arguments, and the smallness of vision and of life. He
had only to recall how decayed he had found the Baptist cause and
building in Moulton, how weak and strife-torn the fellowship in Earls
Barton, and what disgrace Harvey Lane, Leicester had suffered with its
drinking pastor and deacons. Or he could remind them of the previous
evening's confessions of Braunston, Oakham, and College Lane.

Carey was not content to mourn this dearth as unusual. He breathed
no soft excuse. He scourged it as the people's sin. His words were half-
battles. The Church's disobedience had destroyed her just as Judea's
sins had flung her into Chaldea's clutches. He charged the churches,
yet with tenderness and grief. Said Ryland, 'Had all the people lifted up
their voice and wept, as the children of Israel did at Bochim, I should
not have wondered, so clearly did he prove the *criminality* of our
supineness in the cause of God.'

All this was, however, but the austere preparation for the gladness of
his news. The time past was to suffice for disobedience and dearth. God
loudly called them to a different and brilliant future – to leave the
lone, drear, ragged tents of their cramped feebleness, and to pitch and
stretch mother-tents in accordance with the amplitude of His purpose
and the splendour of His will.

Carey believed, as he had indicated in the *Enquiry* (which was on
sale there), that in the closing decade of the eighteenth century the
nation and the Church were on the eve of great developments, whose
omens were many and clear. Examples were obvious in Britain's widening commerce, Captain Cook's great discoveries, the established
Empire in India and Canada, the fight with the slave-trade, the French
Revolution, and the new interest in prayer. As Isaiah had hailed the
emergence of Cyrus as the signal for Israel's deliverance, so Carey
heard in these contemporary events the auspicious appeal of his Lord.

He packed his message into two brief urgings – 'two plain, practical, pungent, quotable watchwords' – *Expect great things from God. Attempt great things for God.*

For seventeen years he had been making things in his workshop in pairs, and this sermon fell under the unconscious power of the same habit. His pair of 'biddings' – the right and left-foot shoes for every pilgrim and soldier of the Lord – rang with homely brevity and unorthodox audacity. By contrast with the multi-headed, many-jointed sermons of the period (and in particular of Association sermons) he dared to be simple and direct. His words were not for display but for persuasion; not to secure personal pulpit success, but to win a case, a very battle, for his Lord.

The burden of his message was that the divine way out from failure and disgrace was a wider vision and a bolder programme. He led them back to Galilee's mountain of the forgotten commission, and laid its obligation on their consciences and hearts.

The order of Carey's watchwords is often misquoted, and has sometimes been criticised, as if our *attemptings* should precede our *expectings.* Carey's order was the true and reverent sequence – Christian enterprise the fruit of Christian faith. Anything else, as Principal Culross said, would be the cart before the horse.

He worked his message to an imperative issue and demand. Like Peter at Pentecost, he pleaded for committal; for action. The prayer-call had gone forth from Nottingham eight years earlier. Now Carey urged them to wait no longer, but to go forward.

Fuller, in a letter to Fawcett, called it 'a noble sermon'. Its effect on Ryland we have already recalled.

The next morning, after a sunrise experience meeting, in which, Fuller said, 'they yearned to feel each other's spirits,' the private business session of the ministers and messengers was held. They made grants to two infant home mission causes. They gave half a guinea towards the fares of each of their four poorest ministers. They voted five guineas to the fight with the 'inhuman and ungodly trade in the persons of men'; a handsome contribution bearing in mind that the Association's whole income was only £21. Then they found themselves up against the issue of Carey's sermon with its closing appeal. This time they could not escape, as previously at Clipston, by requesting the publication of his pamphlet. His *Enquiry* was on sale and in their hands, loudly sustaining the challenge. Yet, as J. C. Marshman tells us,

'When they came to deliberate, the old feelings of doubt and hesitation predominated, and they were about to separate without any decisive result, till Carey was in an agony of distress.' He could not believe that his brother ministers and fellow delegates, after responsible deliberation, would once again have no faith to do anything, and that like the scouts returning to Kadesh they would see only the Anakim and the impossibilities. As once more his colleagues quenched the Spirit, and made the great refusal, all the disappointments of God surged through him:

> *Desperate tides of the whole world's anguish*
> *Forced through the channels of a single heart.*

Turning to Fuller, that 'square-built athlete', as Brock termed him, that 'man with so large a quantity of being', and gripping his arm, Carey cried, 'Is there nothing again going to be done, sir?' This proved a creative moment in the history of evangelistic endeavour. Deep called unto deep. Fuller trembled an instant under that desperate, heartbroken gesture, and then his own soul was stabbed awake, and the Holy Ghost flooded his spirit. *He* also heard God's sigh at the need of the lost. Often had he sympathised with Carey's propaganda, though too timorous for committal. Now, in a moment, he became convert and colleague, the first of Carey's captives, the first of Christ's 'expectant attempters'. He crossed his Rubicon. He put both hands to the plough, and then never once looked back. He stood from that instant as Caleb with Joshua. They became two men with one soul and found, in the words of Ibsen, that – *No precipice is too steep for two.*

Once Fuller threw his inspired strength into the cause with Carey, things changed and men yielded. Carey alone was merely an enthusiast; the man with a 'bee in his bonnet'. Him they could elude, but Carey *and* Fuller could not be ignored. When Fuller pleaded for the reopening of the shelved business, they could not refuse him. He took the kingdom by violence. Under his insistence, even at that twelfth hour, they repented and turned their faces towards the light. Before they dispersed that Thursday noon, Carey saw this motion passed, on Fuller's proposition:

> Resolved, that a plan be prepared against the next ministers' meeting at Kettering, for forming a Baptist Society for propagating the Gospel among the Heathens.

It sounds little, and indeed has been represented as only another polite postponement, but it registered a change from the former inactivity. The shut door was at last being opened, compelling a further consideration of the question. The motion authorised and commissioned the preparation of a definite proposal. The 'pamphlet' was now to be followed by a 'plan'.

Carey's spirit of heaviness was transformed into a robe of praise. Then, in the faith that the Society would certainly be born, he moved to be its first contributor. Money would be needed, and he decided to give all the proceeds of the *Enquiry* to its funds. With the cost of printing virtually covered by the gift of Thomas Potts, and the interest in its message now so increased, these were sure to be healthy. He gloried to lay them on the altar.

Naturally, of all these things the town of Nottingham knew nothing nor cared. The Association meeting had not so much as rippled its surface. Carey's message found no place in the town's *Journal* of that week. It was filled with the sound and fury of the Revolution, then reaching its height. It contained a long letter from tumultuous Paris, and told of war between Austria and France, of Birmingham riots, of Newgate executions, and of the Tories' wrath at the Whigs' mildness with Tom Paine.

For 'earthquake, wind, and fire' it had eyes and ears, room and welcome. But God's 'still small voice' in Friar Lane it could neither catch nor interpret. Yet what was said and done that week in the humble meeting-house of the town's Baptists had profounder issues for God and man than anything else in the columns of the *Journal*. 'The foolishness of God is wiser than men.'

8. The Society's Birth

It was a spark dropped from Heaven.

JAMES MONTGOMERY

When we began in 1792 there was little or no respectability amongst us, not so much as a squire to take the chair. Hence good Dr Stennett advised the London ministers to stand aloof and not commit themselves.

ANDREW FULLER

The Congregationalists made no sign. The Presbyterians, with a few exceptions like Dr Erskine, denounced such movements as revolutionary. The Church of England kept haughtily aloof, although king and archbishop were pressed to send a mission. One man in India had striven to rouse the Church to its duty. Charles Grant had in 1787 written from Malda to Charles Simeon and Wilberforce for eight missionaries, but not one clergyman could be found to go. Thirty years later, when Chairman of the East India Company, Grant wrote: 'I had formed the design of a mission to Bengal. Providence reserved that honour for the Baptists.'

DR GEORGE SMITH

Am I wrong in suggesting that the solution of the money problem of missions rests with the ministry? I recall always, and with increasing interest, that the £13 2s 6d, the first collection of our Society, was a ministers' collection – ministers with small incomes but large hearts.

HERBERT ANDERSON

8. The Society's Birth
Kettering, 2 October, 1792

KETTERING MIGHT WELL have been the cradle of modern missions fifty years before 1792, because Philip Doddridge, the town's Independent minister, had then been deeply burdened for the evangelisation of the world. He poured forth his yearning to East Anglian ministers in 1741, and propounded a scheme.

Following preliminary resolutions, Doddridge delivered his soul to the 'Great Meeting' in October of that year, and a conference followed. But the project was stillborn. He could not persuade them to take action. The initiative of Doddridge was half a century before its time.

Fifty-one years later to the very month, Kettering became the gathering place of another conference, this time Baptist, to face precisely the same problem. The 'Little Meeting' (the Baptist chapel's name) proved braver than the 'Great'.

It was fitting that Kettering, Fuller's home town, should be the mother town of modern British missions. More than anyone else he had rescued the churches from the fatalism which had smothered all Christian sense of obligation to carry the Gospel to the unreached world. *His* sledge-hammer had broken the cold reasoning of hyper-Calvinism. He had saved the day, too, at Nottingham, and was to prove

the unrivalled home captain of the missionary cause. His capable hand
is seen in all the arrangements for the proceedings of 2 October.

The preparatory meeting of the leaders was held in the home of
Thomas Gotch, who was the most ready of Fuller's deacons for enterprise, who had already substantially helped Carey, and who doubtless
spurred them all forward. The morning preacher was Ryland. Fuller
rejoiced when Ryland ran his flag to the mast-head, and committed
himself to the contemplated venture. His text announced his course –
'I will work, and who shall let it?' *(Isaiah 43.13.)* Pearce preached in the
afternoon, having been brought from outside the Association's borders, to cast love's fire into their hearts.

In a letter of William Cowper's of that very date (from the same
district) we read of 'a bad night, succeeded by an east wind, and a sky
all sables', and the evident approach of winter. Yet on that sombre day,
the heroic step was taken.

For the evening fellowship and business the ministers were welcomed, as so often before, into the hospitable home of Mrs Wallis, the
home that they called 'Gospel Inn', so many preachers having been
guests there through the twenty years of its standing. Deacon Beeby
Wallis had died not long before, but his widow gathered them to her
table, having arranged, it would seem with Joseph Timms, a wool-
stapler, who had just been elected to fill her husband's place on the
Kettering diaconate, to act in her stead as the nominal host. After this
hospitality they adjourned for the day's chief business into the cosy,
lean-to back parlour. Only twelve feet by ten, it was a tight pack for the
twelve ministers, a student from Bristol, and young Deacon Timms.

When the preliminary items of business had been dealt with, they
were called to consider the shaping of *The Plan,* according to the Nottingham instruction. But most of them were still unready to commit
themselves to the *idea* of a missionary society, still less to discuss its
plan. Only a minority of them had been present at Nottingham to hear
Carey's sermon, or Fuller's twelfth-hour prevailing appeal. Furthermore, some who had, had since grown apprehensive. They felt
themselves so helpless. Theirs were such little flocks, and their folk
were illiterate and poor, and could neither be expected to grasp nor
support such a vast undertaking. In any case, they lacked experience or
precedent to guide them. Overall they seemed – to themselves – to be
too inland and isolated to direct an overseas effort. The greater centres

Widow Wallis' house at Kettering – the 'Gospel Inn'

and churches, they said, must surely take the initiative and shoulder the burden.

None of this should surprise us. In human terms they really were nobodies from nowhere, with no influence beyond their village bounds. Indeed, their villages were so obscure that a mid-Englander would have never heard of them! Braybrooke, Cottesbrooke, Foxton, Thrapston, Arnesby, and Roade were unknown place-names.

The Thrapston Baptists were too few to constitute a credible church. In Roade and Foxton they numbered less than twenty-five. As Fuller said years later, 'there was little or no respectability amongst us, not so much as a squire to take the chair.' They were justly apprehensive.

Then Carey, who had been a close student of Moravian missions and a long-standing reader of their *Periodical Accounts*, produced their latest issue, and reported its contents – the record of a veteran missionary's prosperous last voyage amongst the West Indies; a Christian triumphal march of Brainerd's successor, Kirkland, with Indian

Christian warriors and chiefs; hundreds of adult negro baptisms; three missionaries bound for the Cape; three others just arrived at Tranquebar; and notice of a hundred and thirty-five on the missionary roll of the Brotherhood.

'See,' said he, 'what Moravians are daring, and some of them British like ourselves, and many only artisan and poor! Cannot we Baptists at least attempt *something* in fealty to the same Lord?' Under the constraint of this challenge, they eventually overcame their fears and acquiesced. How they trembled, but yet they decided to press ahead. It was only faith like a grain of mustard seed but, ever after, they had witness borne to them that they were well-pleasing to God.

The faith of the five – Carey, Fuller, Pearce, Ryland, and Sutcliff – in founding a missionary society with such humble and feeble backing was entirely new in modern British history. The Puritans had looked to Parliament as patron and treasurer of missions. Cromwell had planned a department of Commonwealth service. Rector Castell, of Carey's own county, had petitioned the House of Commons, to stir *them* to action. Bishop Berkeley built all his elusive hopes of West Indian missions on a Parliament bounty. Brainerd had been the agent of the strong Scottish Society for the Propagation of Christian Knowledge. Wesley had been sent to Georgia by the new colony's trustees. Even the Moravians had behind them their wealthy and consecrated Count, as well as a centrally governed and united denomination. But the five had only these seven fearful pastors of obscure little village causes! The overwhelming majority of their British churches knew nothing of their ideas. The other five Baptist Associations in England stood wholly unaware and uninvolved. The London churches, naturally, could only be critical of a movement so provincial and rural. There was no national denominational organisation.

The resolution, to which they all committed themselves, ran as follows:

> Humbly desirous of making an effort for the propagation of the Gospel amongst the Heathen, according to the recommendations of Carey's *Enquiry*, we unanimously resolve to act in Society together for this purpose; and, as in the divided state of Christendom each denomination, by exerting itself separately, seems likeliest to accomplish the great end, we name this the Particular Baptist Society for the Propagation of the Gospel amongst the Heathen.

The name assumed by them echoed the ninety-year-old *Society for the Propagation of the Gospel* which the Anglicans had formed. But the added words 'amongst the Heathen' marked a vastly greater and far more courageous objective. The aim of the older Anglican Society, as its own charter defined it, was 'for the spiritual benefit of our loving subjects', with just an added bonus of blessing for their heathen neighbours. It was a colonial enterprise, while the Baptist Society was a missionary one.

They seem to have agreed that half a guinea should be the minimum subscription for membership, and each was asked to set down on paper what he was able and willing to give. The papers were collected in Fuller's store snuff-box (emptied, perhaps, during the day by his brother ministers and visitors). The promises were these:

	£	s	d
John Ryland, Northampton	2	2	0
Reynold Hogg, Thrapston	2	2	0
John Sutcliff, Olney	1	1	0
Andrew Fuller, Kettering	1	1	0
Abraham Greenwood, Oakham	1	1	0
Edward Sharman, Cottesbrooke	1	1	0
Samuel Pearce, Birmingham	1	1	0
Joseph Timms, Kettering	1	1	0
Joshua Burton, Foxton	0	10	6
Thomas Blundel, Arnesby	0	10	6
William Heighton, Roade	0	10	6
John Ayres, Braybrooke	0	10	6
Anon	0	10	6

The total was £13 2s 6d, plus the proceeds of Carey's *Enquiry*, which amounted to £1 from the sales in Kettering alone.

The tradition that the £13 2s 6d was contributed in cash on the spot is legend, as the Society's early accounts show, and a moment's reflection establishes. Such poor pastors could not have suddenly produced this sum. The subscriptions were promises, most of which were paid at the month-end at the Society's next meeting. Three of the poorest needed a few months' grace, and one a full year.

The snuff-box seems a strange receptacle for the first gifts to modern British missions, yet this one had a sanctity and fitness all its own, a representation of Paul's conversion being finely impressed on its lid.

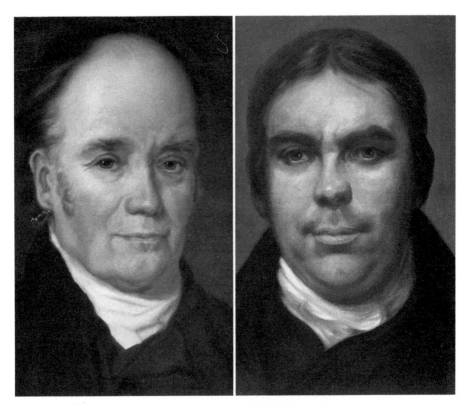

John Ryland and Andrew Fuller, courtesy of Regent's Park College, Oxford

A caustic reviewer, years later, poked fun at the launching of a world mission on £13 2s 6d. But there is nothing here for ridicule; rather everything for respect. The sum was small but of great significance. It was one of the heroic subscription lists in Christian history. Ryland's wife had to keep school to stretch his small income, yet he promised two guineas. Pearce was only the visiting preacher for the day, and from outside the Association. His income was only £100 a year, yet he joined in giving a guinea. Sharman was just taking the Moulton pastorate at 7s 6d a week; Greenwood was in grave anxieties in Oakham; Fuller was only pastor of the 'Little Meeting'; Burton had to be schoolmaster as well as preacher; Blundel was just settling at Arnesby with wife and five children; Heighton was getting 13s a week at Roade, and Ayres 11s 6d at Braybrooke. The 'Anon' was student William Staughton, immensely grateful that he was there, but, true to studentdom, penniless, even after his five Sundays' supplying the College Lane pulpit. He had to borrow to give his half-guinea. In later years he used to say, 'I rejoice over that half-guinea more than over all I have given in my life besides.' Being just a bird of passage he modestly withheld his signature.

The chosen executive numbered five – Fuller, Ryland, Carey, Sutcliff, and Hogg – with the first as the inevitable secretary, and the last as treasurer, not just because of his private means, but in recognition of his wholehearted missionary zeal. From student days Reynold Hogg had gloried in preaching in cottages, workhouses, and barns, on village greens and in busy streets.

The leaders were all comparatively young – Sutcliff 40, Ryland 39, Fuller 38, Carey 31, and Pearce 26. Young men caught the vision. Young men took the initiative. And from that time on they lived for the Mission. Into the rush of its deepening river every interest of their hearts was swept.

Nor were the others – whose story can be traced – forgetful of their covenant. Ayres was a lifelong enthusiast. Burton kept his little church at Foxton missionary-minded until his death. Blundel was a much-sought advocate of the Society, raising in one journey not less than £500. Hogg gave to the work in faithful annual bounties nearly £150, with a further £90 at his death. Staughton became an eloquent preacher in the United States, a college president and a chaplain of Congress. But world missions remained his passion, and he did not rest until a missionary arm was established by American Baptists. He served that arm as secretary, and then as president until his death. 'Hearts of ice,' men said, 'would melt near his. His whole soul was in missionary enterprise.' The fire was lit within him, he always said, in Widow Wallis' back parlour. So American as well as British Baptist missions were in the womb of Kettering that night.

The world, of course, did not take note of the insignificant little company of humble pastors gathered in a lean-to parlour.

Kettering itself had no notion the next dawn that it had immortalised itself during the night. Yet its line was to go out through all the earth, and its influence to the end of the world.

9. The Volunteer

When once the Society was formed, the pillar of fire soon began to move forward.

DR D. L. LEONARD

William Carey, stirred by the reports which Captain Cook had brought back from the Pacific Isles, proposed in his heart to go to Tahiti, if ever he should be permitted to become a missionary of the Cross. He was prevented by the Spirit, and sent to India instead. And could we, if we had had the placing of him, with the light of all subsequent history to guide us, have selected a post more truly strategic, considering the extraordinary genius which he developed as a linguist, and the work he was to do as a pioneer in biblical translation?

A. J. GORDON

9. The Volunteer
Kettering, 9 January, 1793

CAREY COULD ATTEND neither the second nor third meeting of the Society. To the second he sent a Newcastle friend's donation of £20, plus his promise of four guineas yearly, equally cheering as Pearce's £70 from Cannon Street, Birmingham – the first contribution of a church, and a substantial one. Still more significant was the declaration by this church that it had formed an auxiliary society for the support of the Mission.

To the third meeting of the Society Carey sent this note:

I have just received a letter from Mr Thomas, the Bengal missionary, who informs me that he intended being at the Kettering meeting, but forgot the time when it was to be. He tells me that he is trying to establish a fund in London for a mission to Bengal; he earnestly desires a companion, and inquires about the result of our Kettering meeting. The reason for my writing is a thought that his fund for Bengal may interfere with our larger plan; and whether it would not be worthy of the Society to try and make that and ours unite into one fund for the purpose of sending the Gospel to the heathen indefinitely.

This note clearly cost Carey something to write. John Thomas' project could well disarrange, delay, and destroy his own chances for missionary labour. Keen as he undoubtedly was to be the Society's first missionary, he here introduced them to another missionary, and this one an expert, who seemed to have arrived by punctual and dramatic providence. True, this other wished a colleague, and Carey might be offered this post. On the other hand, the Society might well aid Thomas, and only vaguely promise him assistance when fuller funds and surer conditions allowed. In any event, the letter of Thomas offered, at best, second fiddle for Carey, and a probable long postponement of his hope. Moreover, it substituted Bengal for his coveted Tahiti. It dissolved his nine years' dream-world into a scene wholly different – a Leah for his Rachel! Yet, since it seemed God's leading, and he wished to do nothing but that which was worthy, he instantly forwarded Thomas' letter, and advised co-operation.

The Society considered it 'a probable opening in providence', and commissioned Fuller to make personal inquiries in London about the writer, and to interview him if he thought fit.

Who was this John Thomas, who just at this time swam into Carey's and the Society's awareness? Thanks to the data in C. B. Lewis' invaluable *Life* of him, we may make his acquaintance. He had been a great Christian, a great missionary, a great unfortunate, and a great blunderer.

Everyone in Fairford in south-east Gloucester knew about Jack Thomas, the family 'Esau', and the obverse of his brother. As a youth he was into all mischief; kicking against all goads; fishing, bird's-nesting and shooting rather than attending school. He was impatient of discipline; and the despair of his deacon father. He ran away to alluring London; and was captivated there at last by the opportunity of a medical course – something he felt he could 'do with his might'. He then tasted life's thrills and terrors in the navy as a surgeon, but tired of the navy after brain-fever in Haslar. He tried to operate a practice in London; fell in love and married 'a genteel cousin of Squire Thursby'. But then he fell to desperate poverty and was driven to sea once again as an East Indian Fleet surgeon. He sailed to Calcutta where, in the Hooghly, he alone kept his head when fever filled the ship with more dead than the living could bury. Being an excellent shot he revelled in dangerous hunting in the Sundarbans, then travelled home via St Helena – mountain climbing and adventuring at great risk where foot of men had never trod. For love of home and wife, he attempted once again to make a success of a London practice, but again failed, returning to Calcutta as ship-surgeon. There he became the pampered friend and hero of a few highly-placed British Christians, who urged him to a missionary career.

What sort of a Christian was this man? He certainly exulted in the Saviour, confessed Him boldly, wooed others to His saving love and delighted in His Word. Once saved from his wayward youth – at twenty-five – he revelled in Christ. His letters read rather like Rutherford's. 'Mine is a hope worth all the world.' 'Jesus Christ is still the life and briskness of all my joys, worth the name.' 'Very precious is the Saviour to a sinner of my magnitude.' 'I am defiled, nonplussed, and baffled, with sad slips and slides the backward way; but with no thorough turning back yet.' 'My heart is all window to Him.'

As soon as he was converted, Thomas craved baptism, and in spite of the cautioning words of pastors, he soon took this public vow. He gloried in preaching in rural Cambridgeshire and Hertfordshire. He preached on the ships he served as surgeon (though it was unheard of for a ship's doctor). Indeed, he made his cabin a chapel. In Calcutta, instead of entering through society's gilded doors, as he so easily could have done with his professional rank, he rather courted the few friends of the Saviour, and warmed their Christian love. He won young Englishmen in that city for Christ – Richard, the brother of Fanny Burney (of *Evelina* fame) among them, who was just being caught into the current of Calcutta's social round, but whose new earnestness helped to prepare him for headship of its orphan school, and a lifetime of public service.

John Thomas loved God's Word like David the psalmist – as sunshine, honey, and gold *(Psalm 19)*. His letters were shot through with its light. *'Psalm 103* is so woven into the texture of my mind, that it will never be picked out.' He could have said this of whole volumes of Scripture. 'When I am asleep and when I am awake, I am still by a multitude of thoughts led into and all about Thy Word.' 'Sweet, happy day! How I boast in the Lord without measure or limit! My thoughts rise in multitudes, and the comforts of the Holy Ghost delight my soul!' Even under crushing anxieties his spirit could be ecstatic. In his most forlorn Indian years his hut was a Bethel, and he named it 'Bethelpur'. His severest critics agree that he strove to spend himself for both man and God.

It is only just to acknowledge that Thomas was also a great missionary. On his first acquaintance with Calcutta he was moved with compassion for the multitudes as he saw their devastating fevers, and their danger from wild beasts, hurricanes and floods. His soul was stirred within him, like Paul's at Athens, by their idolatry. The converted people among the merchants he discovered there on his second arrival were so moved by his ardour that they believed him capable of reaching all Bengal and Bihar with the Gospel, and pressed him to attempt this. Thomas wrote: 'I think I could do anything for Christ. I would suffer shipwreck and death to glorify Him but a little. But if He should tear me from these Indians, there would be a bleeding; for my soul is set upon them.' No one else in Bengal cared for the multitudes as he did. He was 'the first, whether of English or any other race, who made it his life's business to take the Gospel to the Bengalis'.

Long before he could preach in their tongue, he was treating their sicknesses. He 'never turned aside from man, woman, or child'. 'I am set down here in a house I have made of bamboo, straw, and string. Every morning the river bank is covered with the lame, halt, and blind; every one to be cured gratis, and be given a few *pice [farthings]* for food. My heart aches for their helplessness in body and soul.'

The longer he dwelt with them in their famines and pestilences, wrongs and oppressions, the more completely he was theirs. He saw their *sati* (widow-burning) twice, and his soul blazed like the funeral pile. He made Malda 'a spiritual oasis in the desert of Bengal'. He learned Bengali (as the Swedish missionary Kiernander never had, having devoted himself to the Indo-Europeans in Bengal). After three years he could hold crowds and reason with their teachers. To acquaint himself with Sanskrit he spent time at the Hindu 'Oxford' – Nadia. The people heard him gladly, and hung upon his words. He gloried in telling them that, 'whilst *their* books taught them how the wise and the rich might enter the kingdom, *his* Book showed how the poor, the ignorant and the repenting sinner should be received.'

Thomas translated *Mark* and *Matthew* into Bengali, and grew to be a noted evangelist, a formidable Christian advocate with whom Hindu leaders had to reckon. News of his power reaching Calcutta, the warmth and bounty of his friends revived. Two high-caste Brahmins confessed extraordinary spiritual experiences, and, though but 'halving souls' as he called them, fearful of Christian baptism, they went far towards the embracing of Christianity. His pundit gave him great joy when he composed the first Bengali Christian hymn.

Many of these promising blossoms, of course, failed to bear fruit. To his father he wrote:

> Of your son's success he can say little. Sometimes an inquirer starts up; and sometimes two or three together vanish to the grief of his very soul; but this is a work that requires a length of time *to begin to begin*.

And to his brother he wrote:

> My field of corn, which was very promising in appearance and vigorous in blade, is so infested with rats and mice and other vermin, and so dry for want of rain, and so sickly and feeble, that were it not for a shower now and then to fill up the holes of the rats and mice in dry places, and make it bud a little, I should ere now have given it all over for lost. Many tares, also, have lately appeared, which, whilst young, I took for corn. But, oh, what blessedness to gather in, if it be but a *single stalk* of the first-fruits of the great harvest!

After five years' toil of a kind no other person had yet attempted in India, a lonely, disappointed and homesick Thomas planned to return to his long-missed wife and daughter in England. Yet he never intended to abandon his mission. He set sail with the deliberate and declared intention of returning with British aid and a missionary colleague. Notwithstanding his taste of the grip of caste upon the Indian mind, and the faint-heartedness of 'converts', he was confident of Christ's eventual triumph. We salute him as a great missionary.

However, on the business side of life Thomas was a disaster. Both his attempts at building a London professional practice failed. 'I grew so poor that often pressed for debts I could not pay, after being arrested and for two days imprisoned, I had much difficulty in raising a shilling to meet the expenses of a day. Almost my every valuable was in pledge, and the money all gone. I knew not where to look.' Debt dogged his steps right through. Once he made £600 by trading; but at his next transaction £2,000 worth fetched only £900 and he was hopelessly stranded. His free daily treatment of people cost him poundsworth of drugs. Once a ship's surgeon badly swindled him. Another time an Indian robbed him. He was constantly accident-prone!

Furthermore, it must be said that he was in his own right a woeful blunderer. In money dealings he was almost a fool. He was no rogue, but was stupidly sanguine. Thomas lived in the clouds, never treading the road of reality. He was an exasperating Micawber, dreaming up every possible optimistic idea of how he could extricate himself from difficulty and repay any debt. He planned ventures which would sink him deeper. Owing £1,000, he tried to negotiate the printing of his Bengali *Mark* and *Matthew* for Rs 3,000, sure that the money could be raised by public subscriptions. He even urged his brother and family to come and share his Bengal labours, though he was in great financial need. Finally he fell, along with other esteemed British residents, into the snare of a colossal Calcutta lottery.

In relationships he could also be a great fool. He considered himself called to challenge the devout Master of Chancery, one of his best Calcutta friends, as dangerously Arminian, and wrote him a letter as sarcastic as Toplady's to Wesley. By this act – which was not forgiven – he deeply embarrassed his entire Calcutta Christian circle. He wrote a succession of strictures to his chief sponsor and supporter, letters meant in pastoral faithfulness, but incredibly tactless and extreme. Too late he scourged himself for his 'unmollified, ill-shaped, and hard-carved words'. He thrust his Baptist dogma upon his Presbyterian and Anglican contributors to their sore irritation. He once wrote an 'unanswerable' Baptist pamphlet, whose profits were to be devoted to 'the poor Baptist ministers of Europe'! Too late again, he 'mourned his impulsiveness in this uncharitable walk'. His dissertations – one of eighty-eight pages – were received in Calcutta with increasing dismay, until he became the *enfant terrible* of those who had first supported and encouraged him. Before he returned to England, they had mostly forgiven him and were helping him again, unable to deny his passion for India's redemption, and his devotion to his Lord.

This was the man whose letter Carey introduced to the Society. Carey, of course, knew almost nothing of him at that time. The fact that Thomas had forgotten the Kettering date was typical of his unbusinesslike self. 'He ardently desired a companion' to return with to Bengal, had heard what the Northampton Association was planning, knew of no better hope for assistance, and yet forgot the date of the meeting and failed to turn up!

Fuller made the due London inquiries, especially with the Rev Abraham Booth, with whom Thomas had corresponded from Bengal.

Encouraged, he met Thomas himself, told him much about Carey and of the Kettering meeting, and booked him to meet the Society there on Wednesday, 9 January, at a day of fasting, business, and prayer.

When the day arrived, Fuller was distressed to have neither Ryland nor Sutcliff able to be present; nor indeed Thomas, who had seriously injured his foot. He reported his inquiries and interview, and read some of Thomas' graphic Indian letters to Booth. The Society at length agreed that Bengal appeared to be God's opening door, that union with Thomas was wise, and that, if he concurred, 'they would *endeavour to procure him an assistant, to go out with him in the spring.*' Then they gave themselves to prayer, in which, as Fuller wrote to Ryland, 'they all felt much'.

Carey preached that afternoon from the last chapter of *Revelation*, which he had been steadfastly expounding to Harvey Lane: 'Behold, I come quickly; and my reward is with me, to give every man according as his work shall be.' In the Kettering deliberations and decisions of October and of that day he could hear the Lord testing their alertness, appointing their tasks and giving His blessing. By the close of the service, who should arrive but Thomas? All hearts went out to him for coming, especially with his injured foot much swollen. It was strange that they should make his acquaintance as a brave but limping man, like a Jacob after Jabbok. His injury was a picture of himself, for he always was in some sense a maimed, lame, but committed warrior.

The Society, of course, reconvened, naturally excited that the man of whom they had talked and prayed all day was now with them, to speak to them. Carey watched and listened as one entranced. After nine years' missionary thought and reading, he now looked for the first time on a missionary's face. Thomas recounted his Bengal experience to this eager little company, the like of which he could have found no-where else in Britain. He told of India's piteous need – its poverty, material and spiritual, its pilgrimages and penances, its swingings and *sati*. Then he spoke of its Vedic hymns, and what stepping-stones he had found them to the preaching of the Cross. Then he told of his pundit, Ram Ram Basu, and of two Brahmin inquirers, whose joint letter to the home churches he read, and which to Carey was the very voice of Paul's Macedonian caller – 'Have compassion on us, and send us preachers and such as will forward translation.' Carey could hardly contain himself.

In due course the gathering asked of ways and means, of house rents
and market prices, so that they could plan their budget – not knowing
that Thomas was the last man in the world to consult on such questions. He was incapable of being financially precise, or of giving safe
guidance. His keenness to return did him honour, but it led him unin-
tentionally to romanticise the business facts. 'In Malda,' he told them,
'you could buy fowls for 1d and ducks for 2d, and pigs, sheep, or deer
for 2s 6d, and kids or lambs for 8d. For 18s you could build an excellent house with mud walls and straw roof. *[He had done it, and had
lived therein more comfortably than in England.]* Thousands of native
families covered the cost of everything with 10s a month.'

The rosy picture had truth, but was quite misleading. C. B. Lewis
called it a most incautious assurance of small living costs, pathetically
contradicted by Thomas' own endless money cares. Immeasurable
later tragedy would have been saved had the Society learned at the outset the full measure of the task and its costs.

'Could missionaries support themselves in Bengal?' Thomas was
asked. 'Yes, in large measure, though not, of course, at the first.' It was
at this point that Carey volunteered, for he could now offer himself
with clear conscience. He had long believed, and in his *Enquiry* had
insisted, that the initial outlay in the case of pioneers should normally
be the only and the whole. The moment Thomas declared that this
would apply to Bengal, he laid his life upon the altar of the cause.
Thomas sprang to his feet, forgetful of lameness, and fell on Carey's
neck in tearful joy. Carey was taken aback, but this love-clasp bound
him to his senior, and from that moment they were one.

After that embrace, the Society could hardly pause for shrewd
debate of ways and means. The fountains of the deep were opened, and
they hasted to commit themselves in faith to the support of the two.
Fuller records – 'Knowing Carey's uprightness of character, genuine
piety, sound principles, growing abilities, and great ardour, they could
do no other than accept his disinterested offer. They had long considered him peculiarly fitted for so arduous a work.'

From that moment Carey lived and moved and had his being for
India. Nor did he ever doubt, not even when his road was roughest,
that *God* through John Thomas had redirected him from Tahiti to
Bengal. Though the Indian task was stiffer and more complex than the
South Seas would have been, he could not deny, even with all his

Surgeon-missionary John Thomas, courtesy of Regent's
Park College, Oxford

humility, that by natural and trained inclination and aptitude, he had
been unconsciously prepared for this field. In Thomas, notwithstanding his ungoverned impulsiveness and his appalling business
misadventures, he was to find a great-hearted colleague.

Fuller, amazed at the pace of things, and fearful lest Ryland should
think that in his and Sutcliff's absence developments had been too
rapid, wrote to him: 'You see, events of great consequence are in train;
my heart fears, while it is enlarged, with the weight that lies upon us. It
is a great undertaking; yet surely it is right.'

10. The Missionary Elect

It was very sad that whilst Christian England was waking out of her lethargy to her spiritual opportunities and obligations in India, commercial England threw herself across the path, and denied the right of Christian service for the Christless people of that land.

DR J. P. JONES

§131. Any unlicensed person going to those parts *[East Indies]*, or found therein, liable to fine and imprisonment. §132. Such persons may be arrested, and sent to England for trial, and may be committed. Be it further enacted that if any subject or subjects of His Majesty not being lawfully licensed or authorised shall at any time directly or indirectly go, sail or repair to, or be found in the East Indies . . . all and every such persons are hereby declared to be guilty of a high crime and misdemeanour, and being convicted thereof, shall be liable to such fine or imprisonment or both as the Court shall think fit.

EAST INDIA COMPANY – Powers by Parliament,
Geo III c52 §131–132.

India was a close preserve in the hands of the East India Company. To go there without a licence from the Company was to become a poacher, and to incur the risk of being sent ignominiously home. A man without a covenant was in the Company's estimation a dangerous person; doubly dangerous such an one with a Bible.

SIR JOHN W. KAYE, eminent military historian.

10. The Missionary Elect
9 January – 13 June, 1793

THAT NIGHT and all the way home to Leicester the 'calm, cold, dreadful voice of reason' began its debate in Carey's soul. Ground which had felt firm now trembled beneath him. How would he tell his beloved wife Dorothy that he had undertaken to accompany Thomas to Bengal by the beginning of April? It was out of the question for her to go with him, for just then she would be within a month of motherhood. How could he ask her to face childbirth without him, and later to follow with the children to India's far and foreign land? Dorothy had probably never so much as seen the sea. Born in Hackleton in England's midmost county, and living her first twenty-nine years there, she was home clinging to a marked degree. Her people, as the local registers prove, had for a century at least kept close to one another, sharing all their sunshines and griefs within the bounds of the village. Calcutta, in the thinking of those days, was a million miles from Leicester. The seas were infested with pirates, and no ship sailed except in protective convoy. How could she survive amongst a people of foreign speech, at nearly forty, when she had only learned to write her own language since her marriage?

Carey realised he was in a serious predicament. Faithfulness to his

family was a very marked feature of his character, as his future life
abundantly proved. His mission dream had never weaned him from
devotion to wife, home, and children. It had 'never choked the springs
of warm affection in him'. He would 'oh, so much sooner have fondled
than smitten' his family circle. Like Abraham so long before, he
dreaded the altar building, the wood laying, and the disclosure of the
secret to his loved one.

Dorothy Carey could not be passive as Isaac. Her husband's decision
took her breath away. She resisted, and she rebelled. She would not
agree to his going. Yet he could not surrender. He felt, like Bunyan,
that 'he was pulling down his home on wife, children, and himself; yet
he *had* to do it; he *had* to do it.' 'He that loveth wife or child more than
me is not worthy of me.' He had heard the clear call, and had pledged
his obedience. It would be dishonourable not to tell Harvey Lane the
very next Sunday. He could not bear to have them first learn what had
happened from others. Though it cost such tears, he was bound to
seem ruthless. Oh, the loneliness of these two devoted hearts as –

> *There rolled between them both the sea.*

On the Sunday he told Harvey Lane. So woe-struck was the church,
and so inconsolable his wife, that he had to entreat the mediation of
Fuller. The firmness of his own resolution is seen in his letter to his
father.

LEICESTER
14 January, 1793

Dear and Honoured Father,

The importance of spending our time for God alone is the principal
theme of the Gospel. 'I beseech you,' says Paul, 'by the mercies of God,
that you present your bodies a living sacrifice; holy and acceptable,
which is your reasonable service.' To be devoted like a sacrifice to holy
uses is the great business of a Christian. I, therefore, consider myself
devoted to the sole service of God, and now I am appointed to go to
Bengal in the East Indies, a missionary to the Hindus. I shall have a colleague, who has been there five or six years already, and who
understands their language. They are the most mild and inoffensive
people in the world; but are enveloped in the greatest superstition and
in the grossest ignorance.

My wife and family will stay behind at present, and will have sufficient support in my absence; or should they choose to follow me, their

expenses will be borne. *We are to leave England on the 3rd April next.* I hope, dear father, you may be enabled to surrender me up to the Lord for the most arduous, honourable and important work that ever any of the sons of men were called to engage in. I have many sacrifices to make. I must part with a beloved family, and a number of most affectionate friends. Never did I see such sorrow manifested as reigned through our place of worship last Sunday. But I have set my hand to the plough.

WILLIAM

Carey's father declared that it was 'the folly of one mad'. He could not believe his son would persist. We can sympathise with him, for, as his younger son once said of him, 'though well and strong, he experienced throughout his life every evil in anticipation.' He conjured up every peril. But William had 'set his hand to the plough'.

Fuller took Sutcliff with him on his mission of mediation. But Mrs Carey could not be reconciled. Her husband was not strong; she had seen his long-enduring bouts of malarial fever; he would never be able to endure India's hardships and heat; she was sure she could never follow; they would never meet again.

In Harvey Lane they witnessed another love-struggle, grievings such as Luke relates at Miletus and Caesarea. Carey had led them out of their shameful dishonours and disunions into such love, activity and peace that they were a changed fellowship. A third of the members were his spiritual children. 'They loved him,' as their church book said months afterwards, 'as their own souls.' How could they give him up? Like Dorothy Carey, in their members' meeting they resisted and rebelled, until one member rose and struck a more courageous note. He reminded them how Carey had taught them to care about Christ's kingdom; and how he had stressed the monthly missionary prayer-meetings; and how often he had added extra such meetings on market-days for their country members and neighbours. They had never been so drawn to intercession. 'And now,' said he, 'God is bidding us make the sacrifice which shall prove our prayers' sincereness. Let us rise to His call, and show ourselves worthy. Instead of hindering our pastor, let us not even be content to let him go; *let us send him.*' To this appeal the tearful church responded, and they set themselves to climb the steep mountain track of faithful commitment, sure proof for Carey that he had not toiled in Leicester in vain.

Fuller never forgot that winter night in Harvey Lane – its lamentations and its courage. It became to him the pattern case of a pastor honourably leaving a loving and prospering church for the rendering of greater service. He often recalled it in his correspondence.

Harvey Lane has been charged with extreme indifference to what was transpiring on the strength of this church-meeting minute quoted *exactly* as it appears in the minute-book –

> Sept., Oct., Nov., Dec., Jan. – No business of importance, except that in Jan. our pastor gave us notice that he should leave us in March, having engaged to go on a Mission to Bengall in the East Indies.

Certainly the minute is extraordinary! But the fact is that it must be attributed to a slack, incapable, and tactless secretary rather than to a blind and callous church. This is proved by this letter (original spelling retained) written from Harvey Lane to the next Association Day gathering:

> Dear Brethren,
>
> Last year we observed that the Lord smiled upon us, and Healed our Divisions, and Blessed us. Then we had some Increase. But this year He has shewed himself to Be a God who answers Prayers (Perhaps more than at Former times) to us. We have this year Received 19 members by Baptism and we have Reason to hope that moore are under Concern of soul, our Present Number of Members is 80ty. But in the midst of our Expectations, and our growing Union, we Where Visited with a Blow which we Feel the weight, perhaps moore that You can suppose. Our Dear and Beloved Pastor was Called From us, to go and Preach the Gospel to Heathens. The Shock was great – great indeed to think of Parting with a minister we so dearly Loved – with faithfulness and with efection which he was posest of, Indeared Him to us moore and more. But what can we do? His Heart had been Long set upon it, we had Been Long Praying For the Gospel to Be Sent, and Now Providence opened a way, and we were called to make this Painefull Sacrifice, in answer to Prayers. We know that the Head of the Church can Supply our Wants, and hope we shall Be remembered For good By our Sister Churches.

By request of Fuller and Sutcliff, Carey went north to cast the mission fire into the heart of West Yorkshire's veteran Baptist John Fawcett, who 'entered into the Society's plan with all his soul', became a personal member, and undertook to enlist his people. He also advised immediate communication with William Crabtree. 'Good old

Mr Crabtree of Bradford, though upwards of seventy, could not sleep for joy. He laboured night and day, and obtained more than £40 – going even to the vicar and curate, who each gave cheerfully a guinea.'

Carey seized the occasion of this Yorkshire journey to bid farewell to his younger brother Thomas – wounded ten years before while a serving soldier. Carey was uplifted to find him working, happy, and best of all – worshipping the Lord. The brothers never met again, but, as we shall see, Thomas' two sons, just children at the time, eventually followed their uncle to Bengal.

Samuel Pearce could not let Carey embark without the Cannon Street Church (at Birmingham) hearing him, so he secured him for a week's 'love-visit', and on the Friday Carey 'preached excellently' – so wrote Pearce.

Among the Baptist leaders whose help Fuller solicited for the Mission, was Benjamin Beddome, who for nearly fifty years had been pastor at Bourton. He had written one of the noblest ordination hymns:

> *Father of mercies, bow Thine ear,*
> *Attentive to our earnest prayer;*
> *We plead for those who plead for Thee,*
> *Successful pleaders may they be.*
>
> *How great their work, how vast their charge!*
> *Do Thou their anxious souls enlarge;*
> *To them Thy sacred Truth reveal,*
> *Suppress their fear, inflame their zeal.*
>
> *Let thronging multitudes around*
> *Hear from their lips the joyful sound.*
> *Teach them immortal souls to gain,*
> *Souls that will well reward their pain.*

One would have expected such a hymnist to be as fervent as Fawcett, but this was his reply:

Considering the paucity of well-qualified ministers, I think your scheme hath a very unfavourable aspect with respect to destitute churches at home, where charity ought to begin. I had the pleasure once to see and hear Mr Carey; he struck me as the most suitable person in the kingdom, at least whom I knew, to supply my place, and make up my great deficiencies, when either disabled or removed. A different plan

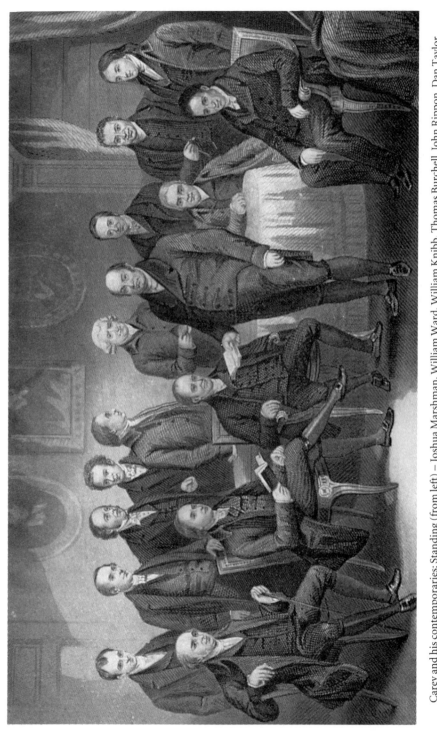

Carey and his contemporaries: Standing (from left) – Joshua Marshman, William Ward, William Knibb, Thomas Burchell, John Rippon, Dan Taylor, Robert Hall, J. G. Pike, William Steadman, Samuel Pearce; Seated – William Carey, Joseph Kinghead, John Ryland, Andrew Fuller, John Foster. (In reality these men were never all present on any one occasion.)

is formed, however, and pursued, and I fear that the great and good man, though influenced by the most excellent motives, will meet with a disappointment. However, God hath His ends, and whoever is disappointed, He cannot be so. My unbelieving heart is ready to suggest that 'the time is not come, the time that the Lord's house should be built.'

London's Baptist leaders were similarly sceptical. By the invitation of the Rev Timothy Thomas, to whom, amongst others, Fuller had written, twenty-three laymen and eight ministers (more than half the whole) met at the Devonshire Square Church. Abraham Booth was absent, unwell. Dr Stennett, from the chair, in nearly an hour's speech, urged much caution. Booth's deacons, Fox and Gutteridge, were definitely hostile. The chairman at length yielded to the suggestion of Dr John Rippon (of Carter Lane, Southwark) that if they wished they should help, as individuals, perhaps even as individual churches, but to form an auxiliary would seem to commit the churches as a whole to the infant movement. Should it end in disappointment, as he feared, they would all be discredited. To this wisdom of Mr Timorous they consented.

> Dr Stennett predicts [wrote Fuller to Carey] that 'the Mission will come to nothing. People may contribute for once in a fit of zeal, but how is it to be continually supported?' For my part, I believe in God, and have little doubt that a matter, begun as this was, will meet His approbation, and that He Who has inclined the hearts of so many hitherto so much beyond our expectations will go on to incline them 'not to lose the things which they have wrought'. I confess I feel sanguine, but my hopes are fixed in God. Instead of failing in the East Indian enterprise, I look to see not only that but many others accomplished.

Carey, blessed in such a colleague, made answer:

> I expected the London people would do just as they have done. But the cause is of God. I feel my heart more and more engaged in the great work, and am so much set upon it, that I would rather undergo all the perils of a journey from Holland to Hindustan, should it be impracticable to obtain a passage by sea [Fuller had written of this difficulty] than not go upon the glorious errand. It is God's work. Yet I have a very severe sensibility of the sacrifices I must make. God sees it best to strip me of those comforts, in which I am inclined to rest too much.

But to his deep solace he could add:

> My wife appears rather more reconciled than she was to my going.

By this time, as we learn from a letter of Fuller's to his friend Thomas Stevens, the minister of Eld Lane, Colchester, it had been definitely agreed that 'in three or four years Carey should return on account of his family', and take them to India, to the home he would by then have made for them. Meanwhile, he had arranged that his wife should live in her native Hackleton in a cottage with her younger sister Catharine, so that she would be surrounded during the years of their separation by her many relatives and friends. First she was to visit other loved ones of her native county in Lamport and in Brixworth. A Harvey Lane deacon, a baker, bought a load of wheat from a Hackleton farmer in order that on the wagon's return it might carry Carey's belongings there at a nominal cost.

A month before leaving Leicester, Carey wrote from there to his sister Mary:

> I am glad you are so resting in God. You express your suspense respecting me: my own suspense is greater. I have not heard whether the Directors of the East India Company have given their consent for us to go in one of their ships, or whether the war will prevent our going or not. My heart is much set upon the undertaking. I much desired to take Felix with me; but it seems the will of God to strip me of all earthly comforts. I find satisfaction, however, in reflecting that I am prompted by a sense of duty, and a desire to God's glory, and that I am in His hands. I have never wavered about the duty itself, but I feel much leaving my family and people.

During the final days Dorothy Carey could not bear to have her husband go utterly alone, so promised him Felix for solace; eight years old, bright and gifted. And in the folds of this tender sacrifice, there is her faith in the Lord to keep them both, and perhaps also a token that she would be ready to follow in due course.

Of Carey's last Leicester Sunday the story shall be given by Thomas Stutterd, a Yorkshire wool dealer, travelling much in mid-England for his trade; and also a chief deacon of the Salendine Nook Baptists, Huddersfield. Stutterd was an enthusiastic and energetic man, who had already stirred his people to raise subscriptions for the Mission. Writing from Leicester to his wife, he says:

> The day I left you was rough, windy and wet. At Penistone I found my breeches very wet, and I had very cold weather from Woodhouse to this place. On Sabbath morning I reached Leicester; went to Baptist

meeting; Mr Carey spoke from *Matthew 28* – Christ's commission to His disciples. Noticed the subjects to be baptised, and the action commanded. Betwixt each of the eight baptisms, a verse was sung. Seven were baptised three weeks ago. *[What joy for Carey!]*

In the afternoon the meeting filled very quickly, and was very full before the service began, with sad countenances and weeping eyes. Mr Carey delivered his farewell to a sorrowful congregation indeed. I never before witnessed such a mournful scene. I could not help being much affected. Loving people were parting with an affectionate minister, who had been made so remarkably useful amongst them, so that the membership is more than double what it was two years ago. Mr Carey left the same evening, perhaps for ever. He leaves a peaceable people, whose hearts are bound to him, a comfortable salary, a wife waiting two months for her time, and two children. One boy goes with him, a voyage of 15,000 miles, to attempt the conversion of the heathen. How greatly must his heart be set upon it! I asked him if he felt his mind comfortable in his proceedings. He answered, 'Yes, I do.' He squeezed my hand to his breast, and said, 'Yes, I do. My family and friends are dear to me. I feel much on account of leaving them. But I am clear that I am called to go. I am perfectly sure that it is the will of Heaven that I must go. Therefore, I am happy in obeying that call!'

For the farewell of Wednesday the 20th, fourteen of Carey's brother Baptist ministers gathered about him, all but one from his own county, and the Society's whole executive together with young student Staughton. It was the first time they had all met since the night of the Society's founding. The morning was given to prayer. Fuller told how Bristol had just contributed £160, a man from Barnstaple twenty guineas, and spoke of how 'the hearts of the little churches in Worcester had never been so opened, their collections far exceeding what the most zealous could have believed.'

The chapel was so thronged in the afternoon to see and hear Britain's solitary Asian missionary, that the service began half an hour before its advertised time. John Thomas wisely attempted no sermon, though announced for such. From the text, 'Their sorrows shall be multiplied that hasten after another god,' he told what he always called his 'tales', the things he had seen of the tragic consequences of India's idolatries.

In the evening Reynold Hogg comforted the bereaved church from *Acts 21.12-14*, and Fuller gave the charge to 'their Barnabas and Paul'.

He was touched to unusual emotion, the springs welling up within his granite constitution. Out of the abundance of the heart he found speech at once impossible and yet irrepressible.

> Every part of this day's solemnities has been affecting [*he said*], but if there be one part more so than the rest, it is this allotted to me. Nevertheless, the hope of your undertakings being crowned with success swallows up all my sorrow. I could, I think, go myself without a tear, and leave all my friends and connections in a cause so glorious.

Then he fixed their thoughts on the risen Lord as their commissioner and pattern, rebreathing on them His 'As my Father hath sent me, even so send I you.'

That night the Society made due provision for Carey's home, in case of his or his wife's death, and pledged every care, as he had asked, for his children's education. Then, somewhere, the *five* contrived to get apart – Ryland, Sutcliff, Fuller, Pearce, and Carey. They talked for the last time together of the task which lay before them, with all its uncertainty and possibility. Carey drew them into a covenant, that, as he went forth in the name of their Master and their Society, 'they should never cease till death to stand by him,' and to this they pledged their troth. And surely, where the two *and* three were gathered together in the name of Christ, there was Christ Himself in the midst.

Later, in Fuller's warm mind, it took imaginative shape, and he would often thus describe it, until his pictorial words became transferred to the original event, and the *rope-holding pledge* became a fixed and consecrated tradition. But the simile was Fuller's, as he once explained to Christopher Anderson.

> Our undertaking to India really appeared at its beginning to me somewhat like a few men, who were deliberating about the importance of penetrating a deep mine which had never before been explored. We had no one to guide us; and, whilst we were thus deliberating, Carey, *as it were,* said, 'Well, I will go down, if you will hold the rope.' But, before he descended, he, *as it seemed to me,* took an oath from each of us at the mouth of the pit, to this effect that 'whilst we lived, we should never let go the rope'.

With entire fidelity, that covenant was kept in every case until broken by death. By Pearce for only six years, by Sutcliff for twenty-one, by Fuller for twenty-two, and by Ryland for thirty-three (Carey himself surprisingly outliving Ryland by a further eight). Pearce became the Mission's home preacher, editor and saint. Sutcliff was its counsellor and tutor of candidates. Fuller served as secretary, statesman, pamphleteer, historian, advocate, and collector, rousing Scotland as well as England, but without a penny payment all his life. His people murmured, 'We never see you.' His wife pleaded – 'you are killing yourself.' 'Yes,' he replied, 'but I can do no other.' Ryland was the chief persuader of students into overseas service (and, after Fuller's death, joint-secretary). These four made Birmingham, Olney, Kettering, and Bristol the focal points of the home base. Like walls they stood about Carey, 'four-square to all the winds that blew'. He could not have been blessed with more devoted and committed comrades.

On the very day of the Leicester farewell Fawcett sent Fuller the promise of £200, as Yorkshire's first gift.

Mr Crabtree [he wrote] has exerted himself to the utmost. He desires me to tell you that the zeal of his heart in this has almost consumed his poor old body. He has gone from house to house, and great respect has been shown him by all ranks of people. I thought I should not be able to raise more than £50; but God has opened the hearts of all denominations. Two thousand 'appeals' have been distributed, which have brought many guineas. My labour and care have not been little, but the kindness of my friends excites my warmest gratitude. My heart is much affected; indeed it is. I am ready to weep for joy. Blessed be God for this call, and that He has given me to see so much regard for His Gospel and for souls. This strikes me most.

Fuller, blessing the veteran, told him of the farewell:

I need not say it was a solemn and affectionate meeting. Thousands of tears of joy have been shed. We love Christ better: we love one another better. A new bond of union subsists between the churches and ministers. How many names will now be embalmed in our remembrance for ever! When we review the shortness of the time and the magnitude of the object, we are 'like them that dream'. It seems too great to be true. We fasted, prayed and trembled, when we set out. We felt we were launching a vessel that needed superior ability to steer. At length we ventured, and hitherto we have succeeded. Surely, the Master hath been our pilot! Perhaps the greatest storms are yet to come! Be it so! Our eyes shall be up unto Him. When Christ was on board, the vessel could not sink, and those who doubted were reproved.

When Carey left Leicester to spend a few last days with his family at Hackleton, William Hinde, one of his Paulerspury childhood playmates, and later the Harvey Lane caretaker, helped him with his baggage. Carey insisted on his receiving a shilling. Poor though he was, Hinde never spent it, but kept it as a sacred token through more than fifty years for love of the pastor to whom both he and his wife owed their conversion. (He showed it to many upon the Mission's jubilee.)

On the Tuesday morning of 26 March, Carey and his wife suffered the anguish of parting. He assured her that in some three years he would return for her, please God, to take her in safety to the Indian home he would prepare for her. That evening he preached at Olney. Young Staughton, fresh from the Leicester gathering, had on the Sunday prepared his way, of which Olney schoolmaster Samuel Teedon records (his own spelling here preserved):

> *Sunday, 24 March, 1793* – I went and heard Mr Storton at Mr Sutcliff's Mtg. give a very affecting acct. of the progress of the Gospel among the hindows under the ministry of Mr Thomas, and that he and Mr Carey were to be here and soon embark for their Mission after a collection.
> *Tuesday, 26 March* – I went to Mr Sutcliff's Mtg. and heard Mr Carey preach the missionary to go to the Hindos with his son about 10 yrs of age *[the intelligent boy looked older than he was]* a collection was made I gave 6d it amounted to £10. The Lord prosper the work.

What was more remembered than even Carey's sermon on *Romans 12*, 'a living sacrifice', was his way of reading the lines of the closing hymn (by Benjamin Beddome):

> *And must I part with all I have,*
> *Jesus, my Lord, for Thee?*
> *This is my joy, since Thou hast done*
> *Much more than this for me.*
>
> *Yes, let it go! one look from Thee*
> *Will more than make amends*
> *For all the losses I sustain*
> *Of credit, riches, friends.*
>
> *Saviour of souls! could I from Thee*
> *A single smile obtain,*
> *Tho' destitute of all things else,*
> *I'd glory in my gain.*

His emphasis on that 'Yes, let it go!' startled the meeting.

Sutcliff had youths living with him preparing for college or the ministry. One of them possessing some artistic capability, pressed Carey for a sitting. The portrait is one that found its way to Regent's Park College. One has said, 'it is a likeness though not a picture.' The wig, which is known to have been 'stiff and odious', is just a smudge, for the student had no skill to render that. (Carey flung that wig overboard on his voyage.) But the *man* is there as he appeared on the eve of his setting forth. He has the face of one of the 'common stock', of a peasant, suggesting an upbringing under unsheltered conditions. The dark brown eager eyes, the strong jawbone, the full, firm lips, reflect energy and resolution. What this man begins, one would expect him to finish.

Inability to get permits filled the last London week with anxiety. Without these the sailing would be illegal and the penalty – enforced return and confiscation of all goods. Yet there had seemed good hope of receiving such licences. When the Company's charter was before Parliament for revision that winter, Wilberforce had persuaded the Commons to affirm that 'measures ought to be adopted for the gradual advancement of the people in useful knowledge and in religious and moral improvement' – to the joy of Company Director Charles Grant, who had urged him to this effort. But, when the law-officers prepared the Bill for its further discussion, and crystallised Wilberforce's general terms into the definite sanctioning of 'schoolmasters and missionaries', Leadenhall Street took alarm, and Westminster lobbies were swept by whirlwinds of protest. The permits for Thomas and Carey were requested at the height of this political uproar. They could not have struck a more impossible hour.

Pearce consulted Mr James Savage of India House – a fervent Baptist of the Eagle Street Meeting – who met the missionaries, 'loved them dearly, would fain voyage with them', yet had to counsel the utmost discretion. To ask leave as missionaries just then would slam and bolt the door. Even Charles Grant (whom Carey approached through the Rev Thomas Scott of Olney) could promise no help. The time was inappropriate, and India House volatile. Besides, Grant was unwilling to encourage the return of eccentric physician John Thomas to Bengal. A most awkward dilemma thus unfolded for Carey and Pearce! They abhorred secrecy, but the path of outright openness was blocked. Yet the urge of Jehovah was *Forward!*

At length, Captain White of the *Earl of Oxford* (whose ship-surgeon Thomas had twice been) agreed to risk taking them to Calcutta without licences. Conscious of their pure and patriotic purpose, they, with Fuller's distressed consent, accepted this offer, and booked their passages.

During this harassing week Carey called on 'good old father Newton', the elder-statesman of the evangelical party in the Church of England, and received his warm blessing. Asked for his counsel in the event of the Company's bundling them home on their arrival in Bengal, Newton replied: 'Conclude that your Lord has nothing there for you to accomplish. If He have, no power on earth can prevent you.' Was Carey quite satisfied, one wonders, with this Gamaliel passiveness?

The week's most influential incident was a meeting between Carey and a young man of twenty-four named William Ward, a printer from Derby, who was visiting city friends. This occurred on 31 March, when Carey preached in Dr John Rippon's pulpit at Carter Lane Chapel, London. Ward waited to speak with him at the close of the service, and they walked almost to the Monument together, and Carey unfolded to him the desire and purpose of his heart respecting biblical translations. Laying his hand on Ward's shoulder as they parted, he said, 'I hope, by God's blessing, to have the Bible translated and ready for the press in four or five years. *[An over-sanguine expectation, for it took him seven.]* You must come and print it for us.' Neither ever forgot this.

Upon removal to Hull the next year, and baptism in the newly-formed George Street Church there, Ward was soon busy with village preaching, and by 1797 was in training for the ministry (under Dr Fawcett), and by 1800 was with Marshman alongside Carey in Serampore. The arrow had reached its mark.

On Thursday, 4 April, the seven embarked, two young Smithfield cousins of Thomas accompanying himself, wife, and daughter. There was no such excitement as three years later attended the sailing of the London Missionary Society's *Duff*. Just Samuel Pearce and a few London enthusiasts bade goodbye at the wharf.

At the Motherbank in the Solent they anchored, waiting for their convoy. Here they were frustrated by a six weeks' delay, but worse, Carey was shocked and humiliated suddenly to discover the many debts of John Thomas – 'creditors hunting him as a partridge'. One summons for £100 compelled him to return to London to disentangle his affairs.

They would have lodged, Carey said, in Portsmouth but for 'the exorbitant expense', so they crossed to the village of Ryde, whose shops were then so primitive and few that he found it 'difficult to buy note-paper'. He preached on two Sundays in Portsea, and in Newport for both the Baptists and the Independents (in the latter case for the Rev John Potticarry, who strangely, later became the first private tutor of Disraeli). Wherever Carey went, he met true friends of Christ, though in Ryde he heard of only a single such household! For the worry and weariness of the six weeks' waiting he was more than compensated by home news, to which this was his response:

RYDE,
ISLE OF WIGHT
6 May, 1793

My dear Dorothy,

I have just received yours, giving me an account of your safe delivery. This is pleasant news indeed to me; surely goodness and mercy follow me all my days. My stay here was very painful and unpleasant, but now I see the goodness of God in it. It was that I might hear the most pleasing accounts that I possibly could hear respecting earthly things. You wish to know in what state my mind is. I answer, it is much as when I left you. If I had all the world, I would freely give it all to have you and my dear children with me, but the sense of duty is so strong as to over-power all other considerations; I could not turn back without guilt on my soul. I find a longing to enjoy more of God; but, now I am among the people of the world [so different from his own home] I think I see more beauties in godliness than ever, and, I hope, enjoy God more in retirement than I have done for some time past.

Yesterday I preached twice at Newport, and once in the country. This place much favours retirement and meditation; the fine woods and hills and sea all conspire to solemnise the mind, and to lift the soul to admire the Creator of all. [The Isle in the incomparable beauty of its springtime, 6 May.] Today I dined with Mrs Clark [once of Harvey Lane] at Newport, and Felix found Teddy Clark one of his old playfellows, which pleased him much. He is a good boy, and gives me much pleasure. He has almost finished his letter, and I intend to add a little to it. He has been a long time about it, and I question whether you can read it, when it comes.

You want to know what Mrs Thomas thinks, and how she likes the voyage. She is very delicate, brought up very genteel, and cousin to Squire Thursby of Abingdon. But she is in good spirits, and the sea agrees with her very well. She sends her love to you, and is glad to hear the good news concerning your delivery. She would rather stay in England than go to India; but thinks it right to go with her husband. *[They had been separated six years.]* A young gentleman and his sister, cousins to Mr Thomas, who have been brought up under the Gospel, go with us.

I shall be glad to hear of you, and how you do, as often as possible. We do not know when we shall go, but expect it will be in a week at farthest. Tell my dear children I love them dearly, and pray for them constantly. Felix sends his love. I look upon this mercy as an answer to prayer indeed. Trust in God. Love to Kitty, brothers, sisters, etc. Be assured I love you most affectionately. Let me know my dear little child's name.

> I am, for ever,
> Your faithful and affectionate husband,
>
> WILLIAM

He added:

My health was never so well. I believe the sea makes Felix and me both as hungry as hunters. I can eat a monstrous meat supper, and drink a couple of glasses of wine after it, without hurting me at all. Farewell.

It touched Carey to learn his new-born boy was 'Jabez'. There were many biblical names in the godly Plackett circle, but no Jabez. Nor was there in Carey's family. The mother had evidently read her Bible's less-known pages, and in her loneliness felt her kinship with that Hebrew mother of *1 Chronicles 4.9* who had named her son Jabez because she 'bore him with sorrow'. But the Hebrew mother's not unworthy ambition was also Dorothy Carey's, that her babe would grow to be 'more honourable even than his brothers, and that God would bless him indeed, and enlarge his coast, and His hand be with him, to keep him from evil,' a desire which was literally and remarkably fulfilled.

While in Ryde, Carey received a farewell letter from Ryland, imploring him and his colleague to exercise the utmost caution and wisdom.

On the Sunday of the week in which the convoy was finally expected, Captain White received an India House letter, signed 'Verax', warning that *one* of his passengers did not have permission of the Court of Directors. To take this person would mean the forfeit of his command. Alarmed, he regretfully told Thomas and Carey and another to prepare to leave his ship. Carey was convinced that the letter was a vexed creditor's of John Thomas, whom if they found and paid, the captain's anxiety could be allayed. John Thomas, confident that through Mr Savage of India House the writer might be traced, and its supposed reference to himself or Carey disproved, rushed off to test this. Unsuccessful, he returned in heaviness of heart, just in time to find the escort fleet in attendance, and 'Carey in tears'. The captain had bidden him to leave the ship that day with his baggage. Mrs and Betsey Thomas and the cousins, having leave permits, might alone go forward; which they did. The baggage was taken out, and 'Carey, with a heart heavier than all, came away' with Felix and John Thomas. The latter rushed once more to London for a last lightning effort, and Carey sent to Fuller the news of their calamity. Up till now he had said nothing in hope of deliverance:

RYDE

21 May, 1793

My very dear Friend,

I have just time to inform you that all our plans are entirely frustrated for the present. On account of the irregular manner of our going out, an information is laid against the captain (I suppose, by one of T.'s creditors) for taking a person on board without an order from the Company. The person not being specified, both he and myself and another passenger are ordered to quit the ship, and I am just going to take all my things out.

Our venture must go, or it will be seized by the custom-house officers *[ie: their stock of goods for Indian sale, for their first year's maintenance]*. Mrs Thomas and her daughter go. I know not how to act, but will write more particularly as soon as I get to some settled place. I leave the island today or tomorrow, and on Thursday the ship sails without us. All I can say in this affair is that, however mysterious the leadings of providence, I have no doubt but they are superintended by an infinitely wise God. I have no time to say more. Mr T. is gone to London again on the business. Adieu.

Yours affectionately,

W. CAREY

On the 23rd, Thomas was back, but again unsuccessful. Thomas, Carey and a bewildered Felix watched from the jetty as the fleet sailed off through the Solent.

Were hopes and aspirations ever so cruelly mocked, that this should be the end of their six weeks' waiting, and of the Society's prayers and arrangements since October? How would they tell the Society and the auxiliaries the outcome of their sacrifice and zeal? Any explanation would reveal their attempt to go without permits, and bolt against them more firmly the doors of India House. How withered Carey's dreams now lay!

Two men were never more depressed or lonely than Carey and Thomas on the Ryde foreshore as the *Oxford* and her escort disappeared from view. The *Oxford* was protected, but the Lord seemed to have left Carey and Thomas alone.

They did not, however, waste their strength in tears over their crushing blow, but hired a boat to Portsmouth, lodged their baggage, and made immediately for London. The leaving of the baggage was as certain an act of faith as 'Joseph's commandment concerning his bones', for they trusted they would be able to leave by some imminent sailing, and refused to believe that the vanished *Oxford* was God's last word. *He* would not mock their hunger with scorpion or stone. It was not the time to stand still, however, for they must take faith's kingdom by a holy violence. Carey proposed an outright demand of permits from the Court of Directors; failing this, *they must take the overland route to Bengal.* This was certainly magnificent and triumphalistic thinking, but hardly a practical course.

John Thomas trod the footpath of reality that week. No fool now, he was galvanised into action. He led things captive to his will, pressed the clay of circumstance, and compelled every resisting adversary to become his friend. Nor was it just his natural resilience, but faith in the living God: faith that uprooted sycamines and tossed mountains into the sea. By faith he subdued problems, obtained promises, out of weakness was made strong, turned to flight armies of hindrances. Walls fell at his challenge. Rivers parted at the touch of his mantle. Chains were slipped and iron gates opened. He moved as one inspired. He rescued them from the catastrophe to which his debts had partly brought them. His outward-bound wife and child, too, compelled him to secure their passage whatever the effect.

What he effected in a week is breath-taking. Not content to make good the loss of their passage, he believed that God had provided for them some better thing than their first expectation. He not only made a way for Carey, Felix, and himself to get to India, but pulled Carey's whole family through as well. He found the ship, constrained the people, raised the money, managed the packing, fetched the baggage, and boarded them all. Carey marvelled.

The coach road to London climbed and stretched through noblest woodland (at its loveliest in May), but even nature-loving Carey had dim eyes for the beeches and chestnuts, until hopes began to wake within him that the day's bitter wind might bring the blessing of his wife and children going with him. Reaching town, he wrote to her to expect him by the next night's coach. Thomas had also done some rapid thinking. The eastward-bound shipping season was nearly closed. No moment must be lost. A British passage was impossible. Some Scandinavian vessel must be sought, even if to reach her they might need to cross to Holland or to France; and then, perhaps, find her bound, not for Calcutta, but for some other East Indian port.

He hurried to a familiar coffee-house on the east side of London, where seamen gathered, and where he knew he could learn the news of the quays. He told his waiter just what information he needed – 'whether any Swedish or Danish ship was expected to sail from Europe to Bengal, or any part of the East Indies, that season'. Presently, to 'the great relief of a bruised heart', the prudent waiter brought these written 'laconic, life-giving words': 'A Danish East Indiaman, No. 10 Cannon St.'

Danish! Then almost certainly bound for Calcutta and the Danish settlement along the Hooghly! Nothing could be better. He hurried to Carey. There were no more tears, he says, that night, but 'their courage revived' and they rushed to 10, Cannon Street, under the shadow of the cathedral, and found it to be the office of 'Smith & Co., Agents'. The sign was laughably uninformative. Next morning they returned to find that 'Smith' was brother of the Danish ship's captain, who had a home in Gower Street, where they went immediately. Yes, his brother's ship was sailing from Copenhagen to Calcutta, was believed already on her way, was daily expected to be signalled if the winds were favourable, and would halt (not anchor) off Dover within five days at the outside. Yes, there were several unoccupied berths. And prices? £100 for adults, £50 for children, £25 for attendants.

On hearing these fares, their soaring hopes were cruelly dashed again, and the Danish vessel seemed to vanish like yesterday's *Oxford*.

All they had was £150, refunded by Captain White. Thomas nobly proposed that Carey and Felix should be booked for the £150. He would take his chance and follow, when God should clear his way. But Carey dismissed the suggestion. Besides, he must see whether his wife would now prefer to go with him, rather than wait for his return in three to four years. He begged Thomas come and add his experienced persuasions to his own. So, that Friday evening at eight o'clock the two took a coach again, the guards armed against bandits with a blunderbuss and a brace of pistols. By five in the morning they reached Northampton, and by breakfast-time had walked to the village of Hackleton and Mrs Carey's home. Must she be condemned for the fact that with her babe not a month old, and her three other boys under nine (if we include Felix) she could not, at *a day's notice*, face the leaving of her relatives, the five months' voyage, and all the hazards and strangeness of Bengal? She could not drink the cup.

Thomas and Carey came away more depressed than on Ryde's foreshore. So desolate was Carey that Thomas could not bear that this should be the end. He urged a further attempt, which Carey forbade, as only the doubling of sorrow for her and for himself. He could not press her. But on the Northampton high road Thomas pulled up. 'I don't care what you say,' he cried, 'I'm going back. I believe I can prevail.' But Carey would not go with him.

Re-entering the cottage, Thomas told of all the sadness in his comrade's soul, and of all the constraints upon his own. 'I simply had to come back,' he said. 'I could not leave things so. For six years I have known the loneliness of sundered family. Don't doom yourselves to such a woe. I did not press you before, but now I feel impelled in love to be severe. If you refuse to go now, you'll repent it as long as you live!' At this remark 'she grew afraid'. Then, at last she cried, 'I'll go, if my sister *[Catharine]* here will go with me.' It is a glimpse into that home circle that Catharine withdrew into her bedroom to pray (as she told Ryland in later years). When she came down, she was willing.

'He maketh my feet like hinds' feet,' Thomas could have said. Before he was near enough for words, Carey saw that he had been successful. Not even in his courtship had he run to her so quickly. She soon knew, through their tears, how much he loved and appreciated her.

The next thing was to report to a responsible member of the executive, and get the needed cash. 'We now,' says Thomas, 'set off for

Northampton like two different men; our steps so much quicker, our hearts so much lighter.' 'The counting of the cost, however, was still enough to damp our hopes. No less than eight fares, besides their necessary outfit; £700 at least: for the four adults £400, and for the four children at least £150. The gear and heavy sundries would cost another £150.' Thomas, however, believed he could strike vastly better terms.

Ryland had that morning received a breathless note. This bombshell had fallen:

KETTERING
Friday, 24 May

My dear Ryland,

Perhaps Carey has written to you – We are all undone – I am grieved – yet, perhaps, 'tis best – Thomas' debts and embranglements damped my pleasure before. Perhaps 'tis best he should not go – I am afraid leave will never be obtained now for Carey, or any other – and the 'adventure' seems to be lost – He says nothing of the £250 for voyage – 'Tis well if that be not lost – committee must be called immediately. You write to [so and so]: I to the rest.

Yours ever,

A. FULLER

Even Fuller's faith had shivered as he concluded the worst. Ryland was summoning the emergency committee when Thomas and Carey were announced.

'Well, I don't know whether I'm glad or sorry to see you,' he said.

'If you are sorry, your sorrow will be turned to joy; for all is proving for the best. We have seen Mrs Carey. She is well recovered, and can accompany her husband, and is willing to do so, if her sister goes with her, and her sister has agreed.'

'But by what ship?'

'There's a Danish ship expected within the next four days, and we can board her off Dover, and there's room for us all. We must all go to London tomorrow. It's the Lord's Day, but it's the Lord's business.'

'But how about money?'

'That's just why we are here. We must have at least another £200.'

'£200! Impossible. I have £13 from Leighton and from Thorn. That's all.'

'But we must have £200.'

'Oh, I just remember, there's a bill for £200 from Fawcett from

Yorkshire; not negotiable yet, but very soon. Go to Kettering, and Fuller will advance it.'

'We've no time for Kettering. We must be back in Hackleton this morning for the packing, and in London tomorrow. There's not a minute to lose.'

Then Ryland, conquered by this firm soul, scribbled notes to London brother ministers, begging them to advance the needed help and promising of early repayment. Then they parted, 'never more to meet on earth'. So Fawcett saved the situation, and Carey's inspiring of him earned its timely reward.

But even with £200 and the refunded £150, how could they meet Smith's business terms? Surely, Thomas was heading for a fresh and worse disappointment. But in this instance he knew the thing to do. Once back in Hackleton he consulted Catharine Plackett telling her the need, and his own secret intention. He would forgo a cabin and be Carey's attendant at the fare of a ship's servant, reducing his cost to £25. Would she 'rough it' in similar manner and be her sister's attendant? She would.

Then Thomas directed them and hustled them so as to be on time. Some of the furniture was sold: the rest was left for Fuller's disposal. And the next morning, albeit Sunday, there were the two filled chaises and the farewell. For the boys, there was the excitement of the ride to London; for the sisters and the home relatives there was the great wrench.

Ryland's chits opened London purses, as Thomas' breathless story opened hearts. Friends advanced £72 more than the £200. In the Mission's emergency the London pastors and leaders proved most generous and prompt. With heavy pockets and light heart, Thomas repaired to 10, Cannon Street once more, astounding Smith by the family he had persuaded to make the voyage. They had sold up home and come, though the usual advantageous business terms were out of the question. Theirs was no business errand, however, but a strange new enterprise for India and Christ. Thomas implored Smith's interest. He could only offer him 300 guineas for the eight; but only two cabins would be needed, he and Miss Plackett going as attendants of the rest, with the fare of ship's servants. Shipping offices are credited with little sentiment, but Smith was so taken by their purpose and Thomas' appeal that without further ado he accepted 'these lowest terms ever heard of'. The Careys, after many purchases, were soon on the packet for Dover, ready for the boarding of the ship.

Thomas once again took a coach to Portsmouth for the baggage, intending to take it round to Dover by boat. But, with the Channel beset with pirates, only one boatman would venture, and he asked twenty guineas, which Thomas dared not agree though he dreaded losing his ship. At length, he bargained for nine, and 'they ran through all the pirates in the dark,' and he reached Dover and the Careys 'with great gladness of heart'.

On the last day of that May Pearce wrote from Birmingham to his wife:

> Prepare, my love, to rejoice and wonder and be grateful! On the evening of the day you left I received a letter from Ryland, and what d'ye think he wrote? Why, Carey *with all his family* are gone to India! When? How? you are ready to ask, and I cheerfully satisfy you.

And he tells her the story, and then adds:

> By this time I suppose they have sailed. O what a wonder-working God is ours! Tell the whole now to others for the honour of our great Redeemer and the encouragement of His people. Three advantages are now secured: (1) the missionaries will go out more honourably, and the enemies of the cause will not be able to reproach the Society with duplicity in transporting them under false pretences; (2) as the Danes are a neutral power, there is no fear of their being captured by the French on their way; and (3) Carey has the satisfaction of his whole family being with him, and the world has lost thereby one objection often raised against his going.

For a whole fortnight, however, the *Krön Princessa Maria* did not arrive, the winds being unfavourable. At last, one morning before three, they were all roused, for the ship and its frigate escort were in the sea lane.

Before getting into the boat that was to ferry them to the vessel Carey made time to pen a last note to his wife's father, who was losing two daughters. The note was kept in the Plackett family through all the years, and still survives. The script is larger than Carey's usual, perhaps, in consideration for an old man's weak eyesight. The poor English and the incorrect date – for it was 13 June – must be attributed to the excitement of that early departure. It runs:

To Mr Daniel Plackett, Hackleton

Dear Father,

We are just going. The boat is just going out, and we are going on board – Thursday morning at five o'clock – 14 June, 1793. We are all well, and in good spirits.

By five o'clock they were on board, but at a cost of three guineas. Thomas scribbled to London friends:

13 June – The ship is here – the signal made – the guns are fired – and we are going with a fine fair wind. Farewell, my dear brothers and sisters. Farewell. May the God of Jacob be ours and yours, by sea and land, for time and eternity! Most affectionately adieu!

As they were borne away from Kent's white cliffs (never, except in Catharine's case, to see them again) they could exultantly say, 'Men never saw their native land with more joy than we left it.' And Carey wrote in his diary that evening:

Thursday, 13 June – This has been a day of gladness to my soul. I was returned, that I might take all my family with me, and enjoy all the blessings which I had surrendered to God. This 'Ebenezer' I raise. I hope to be strengthened by its every remembrance.

Along the track which Carey blazed, other British and English-speaking missionary societies followed in remarkably rapid succession. The London Missionary Society was the first of these, which was sparked by the 'chance' visit of the Rev David Bogue, the noted Congregationalist minister (and historian) to Bristol in the summer of 1794 (the year following Carey's departure). Bogue was invited to join a little group of non-Baptist Bristol people to whom he planned to read Carey's first letters from the mission field. Bogue and the others were so stirred that they convened a much larger non-Baptist group in London, which proposed to form an interdenominational mission on the same lines as Carey's. The response from their churches was electric, and fourteen months later (August 1795) their first missionaries sailed down the Thames in the *Duff*, to the cheering of thousands, bound for Tahiti (Carey's own originally-intended destination), with the missionary party of thirty, singing:

> *Jesus, at Thy command*
> *We launch into the deep.*

Scottish societies came next, in that same year. Two zealous ministers of Edinburgh, Dr Innes and Greville Ewing, hearing of Carey's Bengal initiative in Birmingham, through Samuel Pearce, inspired the churches of Scotland. A missionary society was formed in Edinburgh, Glasgow soon following. Dr Innes lent young Robert Haldane the first volume of the *Baptist Mission's Periodical Accounts*. It so moved him and his brother James that they sold their ancestral Stirlingshire home for £30,000, and with Innes, Ewing, and Bogue, would have hasted to Benares, except for the absolute veto of the East India Company. Thus thwarted they gave themselves to the evangelising of Scotland, and from the Tweed to the Orkneys religion was revived.

Provoked by the forming of the London Missionary Society, the (Anglican) Church Missionary Society was formed in 1799, with Thomas Scott of Olney as its first secretary. Also in 1799 the founders of the London Missionary Society added the Religious Tract Society to their organisation, and five years later the British and Foreign Bible Society.

Meanwhile, America was feeling the new impulse, notwithstanding post-war prejudice against all that was British. The Rev John Williams of New York, and the Rev Thomas Baldwin of Boston corresponded with Carey from as early as 1800, and sent him frequent and generous help. Societies sprang up in both cities and linked themselves with him and the work at Serampore. Leaders like Professor Rogers of Philadelphia and William Staughton of New Jersey (the 'Anon' of Kettering) became impassioned advocates of the cause.

By 1816 the Methodists also committed themselves to Eastern missions, and Dr Coke saw of the long travail of his soul. The General Baptists followed suit in the same year.

By 1834, when Carey finished his earthly course, there were fourteen British missionary societies, besides others Continental and American. As J. G. Greenhough put it, 'The light, which Carey had kindled, spread from hill to hill like beacon fires, till every Christian church in turn recognised the signal, and responded to the call.'

Part II

Carey's Forty Indian Years

The story of how he and his colleagues
established paths which afterward became
high roads of missionary activity

11. The Five Months' Voyage

I have reason to lament over a barrenness of soul, and am sometimes much discouraged, for if I am so dead and stupid, how can I expect to be of any use among the heathen? Yet I have felt of late some very lively desires after the success of our undertaking. If there is anything engages my heart in prayer to God, it is that the heathen may be converted.

WILLIAM CAREY, *Journal of Voyage,*
2 August, 1793.

To disturb and to destroy the religious beliefs, rites, and ceremonies of any people is to make an attack on the sanctuary of the soul, which can only be excused if he who delivers it has the certainty that what he offers is indeed the pearl of great price, to obtain which the surrender of the most sacred possessions cannot be regarded as too high a sacrifice.

A. E. GARVIE

11. The Five Months' Voyage
13 June – 11 November, 1793

CAREY DESCRIBED the captain of the *Krön Princessa Maria* as 'a wide reader, and one of the most polite and accomplished gentlemen that ever bore the name of a sea captain'. He was English born and bred, though naturalised as a Dane after officership in the Danish army or navy. When he gave up his very English name 'J. Smith', he chose to be Captain Christmas, with its suggestions of bounty and goodwill. His half-sister was Lady Langham of Cottesbrooke. He owned the ship he captained, and this was his maiden voyage in the function of command.

Although uninterested in religious matters, he showed the missionaries much respect. In deference to his London brother's commendation he treated them as particularly honourable friends, refusing to hear of Mrs Carey's sister or Thomas ranking as attendants of the others. He gave the Careys the ship's largest cabin, half the stern width, sash-windowed and papered, with a portion partitioned off for Miss Plackett; and to Thomas a first-class cabin. All were welcomed to his own table. He also sent them wine in their early distresses. Twice a day he would check that they had no needs.

The Bay dealt so roughly with them that their mail could not be taken at the return of the convoy – Carey's third day's note running thus, 'Still sick in the Bay of Biscay. Lat. 47°N., Long. 3°W.' – a characteristic entry. Off Spain they were becalmed, and again for a week between the mainland and the Verdes. Wind then drove them near to Brazil, from where the South Atlantic current took them to the Cape.

They met with 'innumerable civilities' from their fellow voyagers. To their morning and evening worship and the Sunday services in their cabin ten or twelve gathered – only one in the ship showing disdain. In these services they formed a 'tolerable choir'. Carey delighted in their racial diverseness – Danes, Norwegians, Holsteins, Flemish, and French.

Mrs Carey and her sister kept well, and 'the children were complete sailors, babe Jabez thriving more than if he had been on land, and becoming a stout fellow.' Between the Tropics, Carey was dangerously ill, yet planned for the far future:

> I am very desirous that my sons may pursue the same work, and intend to bring up one in the study of Sanskrit and another of Persian. May God give them fitting grace for the work!

His chief distress was his own felt 'spiritlessness', the 'inconstancy of his communion', the 'slackness of his warfare', though he spent much of his time in prayer. In all other free hours he studied Bengali, and Thomas said that 'he came on very fast'. Carey aided him in turn in his rendering of *Genesis* into Bengali through his knowledge of Hebrew, Latin, and Greek. 'The goldsmith,' wrote Thomas, 'helped the carpenter, and the carpenter the goldsmith, and the work of God was done.'

To take advantage of the favouring wind, the captain hastened on instead of putting in at the Cape, which was a disappointment for Carey. He had planned to seek out some Dutch minister of the settlement and with what Dutch he knew persuade him to tell British Christendom (and the Kettering Society) of South Africa's spiritual dearth.

Off Africa's southernmost cape a midnight storm almost sank the *Krön Princessa,* which was only of 130 feet keel and 600 tons. From one plunge Carey never supposed she could rally. To his untrained sight the waves seemed 'fifty or sixty yards high!' It took eleven days to repair the damage to the vessel.

Once free of this coast, they ran a straight course into the Bay of

Bengal, and this time through the Tropics Carey kept as fit as the rest; and 'his wife was well satisfied with their undertaking,' looking no longer backward but hopefully forward. In the Bay of Bengal contrary currents pulled them back a month from their almost-reached goal. The captain feared he would be driven into Vizagapatam, but won through at length to Calcutta by 11 November.

The voyage took five months, less two days. It seemed longer because they had entered no harbour and landed no passenger nor mail, though, as Carey said, 'they were in Europe, Africa, South America, and Asia.' They had coasted past many islands, but had never put in. Through their last three months they had sighted no other vessel. The natural history excitements had also been few, even for vigilant Carey; just porpoise herds, mother Carey's chickens, a sperm whale, and flying fish (the wings of one he sent to Fuller).

During the tedious last month the captain sometimes let Carey accompany him on the poop deck. All he observed became a parable of the task before him. He wrote:

> For near a month we have been within two hundred miles of Bengal, but the violence of the currents sets us back from the very door. I hope I have learned the necessity of bearing up in the things of God against wind and tide. We have had our port in view all along, and every attention has been paid to solar and lunar observations, no opportunity being neglected. Oh, that I was as attentive! A ship sails within six points of the wind; if the wind blows from the N., a ship will sail E.N.E., on one tack and W.N.W. on the other; if our course therefore is N., we must go E.N.E. for a considerable time, then W.N.W.; if the wind shifts a point, advantage is immediately taken. Now this is tedious work, and, if the current be against us, we scarcely make any way; nay, sometimes, in spite of all we do, we go backwards. Yet it is absolutely necessary to keep working up, if we mean to arrive at port. So we Christians have to work against wind and currents; and we must, if we are to make our harbour.

The peril he strove most to guard himself and his family against was the ship's spirit towards India's people. Officers and passengers alike talked of them with disdain. He knew that, unless Christ saved them from this pestilence, it would paralyse their power to serve the land of their desire, and against this sin he prayed with all his strength. They mourned that from their Sunday services, though often 'so pleasant and profitable', they knew of no definite conversions, but comforted

Calcutta from the Hooghly at the time Carey arrived, by William Prinsep, courtesy of Spink & Son Ltd.

themselves with what the Spirit said to Ezekiel: 'Surely had I sent thee to people of a strange speech and of a hard language, they would have hearkened.'

Two other divine promises were Carey's peace: 'Lo, I am with you alway, even unto the end of the world,' and 'As thy days, so shall thy strength be.' With this rod and this staff, he felt protected and secure.

A day or two before disembarking he wrote to the Society in these oft-quoted terms:

> I hope you will go on and increase, and that multitudes may hear the glorious words of Truth. Africa is but a little way from England; Madagascar but a little further; South America and all the many and large islands in the Indian and Chinese seas will, I hope, not be forgotten. A large field opens on every side, and millions tormented by ignorance, superstition and idolatry, plead with every heart that loves God. Oh, that many labourers may be thrust into the vineyard, and the Gentiles come to the knowledge of the Truth.

Several of his Bengal letters indicate this sentiment – written in 1825 – that 'when he left England, he meant never to return.' But he little imagined that he would hold the Mission's helm for forty continuous years.

12. The First Ventures

The English came to India first as merchants to gain wealth, then as warriors to gain land. It was only as Carey came that a nobler spirit entered.

A. M. FAIRBAIRN, in India, 1898.

When Carey landed in India, Hinduism was in full vigour – its customs, traditions, institutions and laws all unchanged. The country was practically untouched by any regenerative influence whatever. He had to encounter in its worst forms all the strength of the Hindu system.

SIR WILLIAM W. HUNTER

Although the English in India were emerging from that absolute slough of profligacy and corruption in which they had so long been disgracefully sunk – though knavery and extortion were no longer dominant in their offices, and rioting and drunkenness in their homes – yet there was little Christianity in Calcutta at the end of the eighteenth century.

SIR JOHN W. KAYE

What a contrast was presented by the shy shoe-maker, schoolmaster and Baptist preacher (who found not a place in which to lay his head save a hovel lent to him by a Hindu), to Clive and Hastings – men described by Macaulay as of ancient and illustrious lineage, who had brought into existence an empire more extensive than that of Rome.

DR GEORGE SMITH

12. The First Ventures
9 November, 1793 – 6 February, 1794

THOMAS AND CAREY were the first Englishmen to voyage to India, indeed to Asia, for sheer love of Asia and of Christ. 'Britain's sons,' says Dr Ogilvie, 'had gone to the East in a regular stream as soldiers, sailors, civil merchants, traders, and adventurers; but for nearly two hundred years from the formation of the East India Company no place amongst that crowd of the eastward-bound was found for a Christian missionary.' Company chaplains, of course, went there, but no missionaries. Dutch pastors, although with ebbing zeal, still travelled to their East Indies. Noble apostles had been commissioned by Denmark's king to go to Tranquebar and to Tanjore – the Society for Promoting Christian Knowledge to its credit granting them support. But no British missionary ventured. Thomas and Carey were the first.

By being driven by God to India Carey was thrust on a service more imperial than had ever been envisaged in his South Seas' dreams. Eliot and Brainerd, his enkindlers, had toiled amid primitive faiths and dying races. No living lips now speak the tongue into which Eliot translated the whole Bible. Moravians went, for the most part, to backstream peoples. Carey would cheerfully have done the same in Tahiti or in Africa, but with God's fiery pillar moving to India, he was called, with Thomas, to be the first of British Christians to challenge the East's deep-rooted religions with the Gospel of Jesus Christ. With the help of his later colleagues he was to render the everlasting Word into more Indian and Asian vernaculars than had any of their Dutch or Danish predecessors. Beyond all others he was to be God's lamplighter for the East.

Thus destined, his introduction to India was significant.

As their ship entered the Hooghly, boats drew alongside selling fish. In the midst of their chaffering, the fishers were surprised to be asked by Thomas whether they possessed or had read any Shastras (Hindu sacred writings) – a question they till then had never met. 'Do you think we would catch and sell fish,' they said, 'if we possessed or could read Shastras? They are for the educated and the rich. We're very poor.' Carey's ambition was to bring *God's Shastras* within reach of India's humblest, and so to promote their education, that they would be able and eager to read them.

For the last stage of their passage to Calcutta, and to escape the risk of apprehension by the authorities, as soon as they entered the Hooghly the missionary 'outlaws' took to a native boat, and, until the turn of tide, lay-to near a market in full activity, and Carey heard its hum and hubbub. He heard, too, for the first time his comrade preach to Bengalis.

At events so extraordinary (sahibs, memsahibs, English boys and an English babe) the Bengalis – even the sales folk – forsook their market and listened, amazed at the freedom of the preacher's Bengali, and still more at his concern for their good. No other sahib (European 'superior') had ever addressed them so. For three hours they listened. Carey, while able to follow scarcely a word of the message, was enthused by their interest and filled with hope for a people that could be held so powerfully by the Gospel. Hope grew, as presently they set before them on plantain leaves curry and rice, and invited them to their villages.

The story that Carey lost *all* his money and belongings in the river on his arrival has no foundation, being a confusion on the part of an edition of the *Encyclopaedia Britannica* with the later experience of friends of John Thomas.

We do not know just when and how Thomas found his wife, child,

and cousins; nor where the twelve met, and recounted their
experiences, as the seven had been separated since Ryde. Very soon
they had to bear a sharp disappointment. Ram Ram Basu had fallen
back to the worship of idols. Yet when they heard his story, they pitied
more than they condemned. British Christians, he said, had withheld
themselves from him. His fellows had scorned and shunned him.
When stricken with dysentery, none ministered nor gave to him. At
length a kinsman offered him a home, if he would bow again to idols.
Hushing his conscience by remembering Roman Catholic image worship, he had yielded. So Carey comforted him and engaged him as his
pundit. He could speak English fairly well, though unable to read it.

Carey had never dwelt amidst such swarms of multitudes as in Calcutta – '200,000 Asians,' he said, besides hosts of Europeans. London
itself seemed far less crowded.

The city was pleasant in November's cool brightness, yet it made
him sad. His fellow-countrymen were his sorrow, their Lord's Day
heedlessness filling him with distress, and confirming the proverb that
'they had left their religion at the Cape.'

As soon as Thomas had located a place for them to settle, they
removed a tide's distance north to Bandel, the ancient, famed Portuguese settlement, and there consulted good Swedish Kiernander. His
eighty years had left him nearly blind, but Carey had met none so fervent for India's conversion, though it had never been his practice to
preach in the vernacular language, his whole strength having been
devoted to the Eurasian community. Yet, with all his fervour, he was
very unhopeful of their success.

But the two were young and confident, and began at once to
itinerate, Thomas greatly heartened by Carey's enthusiasm. Daily they
were rowed to fresh villages. That a sahib was preaching, and in fluent
Bengali, with a sahib companion and a consenting pundit, was
unheard-of strangeness. Wherever the three halted, the people flocked.
What they could grasp, too, of the message, deepened their surprise.

> Their attention [says Carey] is astonishing. Every place presents a pleas-
> ing prospect of success. To see people so interested, inquisitive, and
> kind, yet so ignorant, is enough to stir up any with the love of Christ in
> their heart.
>
> Last Sunday Mr Thomas preached to near two hundred in a village.
> They listened with great seriousness, and several followed to make

further inquiries of the heavenly way, and how they should walk therein. The encouragements are very great. I never found more satisfaction than in this undertaking. I hope in a little while to see a church formed for God.

The novice was sanguine. As he began to realise Bengal's dense population and her countless villages, he wrote, 'Ten thousand ministers would find scope for their powers.'

Like Paul at Athens, he was moved by the people's marked religiousness, their morning homage in the sacred river, their 'flowers, shrubs, shrines consecrated to religious uses on every roadside', and more by what pain and cost they would face for the soul's believed profit. 'I have seen two or three already who have swung by the flesh-hooks, with the marks in their backs. One dwells in the house with us.'

Presently, he craved for a centre more purely Indian than Bandel. So they visited Nadia, the birthplace of Chaitanya, Bengal's dearest mystic, where Thomas had once stayed. Carey judged that this home of Eastern learning would be their best school for the needed language studies, and the best base for their campaigning; for 'if this bulwark of Hinduism were once carried, the rest of the country would be laid open to the Truth.' The courteous welcome of the city's scholars made him hopeful of its capture. He planned that in that Bengal 'Oxford' not only should Felix learn Sanskrit, and William Persian, but Peter Chinese – though Felix at the time was stricken, together with his mother, with dysentery, and his life was in grave doubt.

These plans were scarcely formed when they were recalled to Calcutta – Thomas, to resume his medical practice in order to quiet his creditors; Carey, by a sudden dazzling hope. For Captain Christmas, hearing that the superintendency of Calcutta's Botanic was still vacant, interviewed the chief official, showed him a botanical monograph of Carey's, and convinced him of his suitability for the appointment. Then he communicated with Carey, who hasted to Calcutta, but found himself forestalled – Dr Roxburgh of Madras having been selected before him. The disappointment was tempered by the official's pledge of bearing Carey in mind for some later opportunity, and then by the warm friendship of Roxburgh, who had married a missionary's daughter.

Then he applied for a grant of 'waste land' for tillage, as from the first he had intended. Meanwhile, he and his sick family and Ram Ram

Basu were loaned, free of rent, a dilapidated garden house of Nelu
Datta, a money-lender in Manicktolla, today a crowded part of Calcutta, but then a marshy, malarial district to the north, overridden
with armed gangs. Yet he never forgot this mercy, and in after years
well repaid it, when Nelu Datta was in need.

He had never known days so dark as when, as early as in mid-
January, Thomas, the keeper of the purse, reported that their first
year's income of £150 was exhausted, with no more to be looked for
from England till the next autumn's 'venture'. He had pitiably miscal-
culated their first year's expenses. Their resources had been hopelessly
inadequate, and Thomas, hopeless economist as he was (even though
the living expenses for his wife and daughter up to the time of his own
arrival were still unpaid), had rented a commodious city house, and
hired servants, for the resumption of his medical work.

Who can gauge Carey's woe with his family of seven, with his wife
suffering from grave dysentery, and with Felix's recovery still in doubt?
Their only home was a comfortless garden house; they needed money
for their pundit (engaged at Rs 20 monthly), and also seeds and tools
to be bought for the land he awaited. Twelve per cent was the lowest
rate for borrowed money, and no help was forthcoming from England
for ten months. How could he be other than 'much dejected', and
again, 'very much dejected', 'full of perplexity about temporal things',
his 'mind much hurt', and again 'much grieved and dejected', and
again 'very weary'? Even in that loveliest of Bengal's months the 'city of
sunshine and palaces' was bleak and lonely to Carey.

He called on David Brown, Fort William chaplain and friend of
John Newton's. Through his hostility towards Thomas, he was superior and frigid as an iceberg, not even offering Carey hospitality after
his five miles' walk in the sun.

The mental disorder and distress which harrowed Mrs Carey for the
next thirteen years, dates from this misery. Ill with dysentery, her first-
born son still sick, unable to afford even bread, and appalled at their
destitution in the strange and friendless city, her brain began to give
way and her kindly nature suffered change. Who shall lay her melancholy to her charge? And who shall justly blame Carey? He could not
possibly have anticipated nor conceived the conditions which induced
it. Nothing was here for reviling; everything for compassion and tears.
Missionaries' wives paid dearly in these pioneer years: Carey's wife

soonest and heaviest. Yet for him the cup was wormwood. He could not lightly borrow, like Thomas – who little realised his anguish and his shame. Nevertheless, these words stand in his *Journal:*

> *17 January* – Towards evening felt the all-sufficiency of God, and the stability of His promises, which much relieved my mind. As I walked home in the night, was enabled to roll all my cares on Him.
>
> *22 January* – 'In the Mount the Lord is seen.' I wish I had but more of God in my soul, and felt more submission to His will; this would set me above all things.
>
> *23 January* – All my friends are but One, but He is all-sufficient. Why is my soul disquieted within me? Everything is known to God, and He cares for the Mission. I rejoice in having undertaken this work; and I shall, even if I lose my life therein.
>
> *25 January* – Bless God for a day of calm, though I mourn my heart's strange stupidity.
>
> *28 January* – Much relief in rereading Fuller's charge to us in Leicester. *[Fuller must have given him his MS.]* Not being accustomed to much sympathy of late, its affection has overcome my spirits. If I be offered upon the service and sacrifice of the faith, I joy and rejoice.

And in a letter:

> When my soul can drink her fill at God's Word, I forget all.

At last, a few acres of recently, partially redeemed jungle opposite Debhatta in the Sundarbans were offered him, where Ram Ram Basu's uncle had been *zemindar* (landlord), rent free for three years, and then rising to a maximum of eight *annas* a *bigah* in and from the seventh year – on Henckell's scheme for the settling of the Sundarbans. He might also occupy the Salt Department's bungalow at Debhatta, should it happen to be vacant. Though he knew that these forests were infested with cobras and fierce tigers he accepted the allotment, in reliance, he said, on Christ's promise to protect them from their power.

Weary from walking several hours in the sun on his last day in Manicktolla, he refreshed his spirit by talking of Christ to money-changers, who understood a little English, reckoning not even such soil too hard and hostile for the seed.

Ram Ram Basu and he had to be tenderly watchful over ill Felix and his sick mother through the three days of the boat journey through the salt lakes and beyond – especially one night, when none dared to go a hundred yards from their mooring for dread of the tigers. Yet he had 'sweet meditation'. Early on the fourth morning they reached Debhatta, to find the bungalow not vacant. He would have been in sadder plight than ever, without shelter for his family or food beyond that day, had not Mr Charles Short, the Company's Salt Assistant, been the best of Samaritans. Out with his dog and gun, he was astonished at the arrival of the English strangers, hasted to the landing-stage, and invited them to his house. Nor did their missionary errand chill his welcome, though he regarded it as absurd. After breakfast, he installed them as his guests, even the sick mother and Felix, and 'insisted on supplying all their wants'. Then, through the many months of their need he gave them the fullest hospitality and kindness, until, as Carey says, he felt ashamed!

Thus did this bachelor Englishman lift loads from Carey's life. He made no profession of religion, still less of trust in Christ, to Carey's heartfelt pain. But he did walk by the golden rule, and proved neighbour to these stranded ones. Christ was a stranger, once more, in the persons of these His representatives that morning. This young Englishman took Him in. Nor was he permitted to go unrewarded. For him this sixth of February was to be the beginning of romance.

13. The Sundarbans Settler

The Sundarbans are a land of monsters dire. The rivers swarm with hideous alligators, which we often see basking on the shores, or rather embedded in the mud, of which the banks consist; tigers of the fiercest kind pass and repass every night over the ground where the people are at work in the day; and snakes of monstrous size and deadly poison abound. Yesterday a cobra capella, six and a half feet long and of proportionate thickness, crossed our path. We gave him chase. Rabeholm shot him.

JOHN MACK to Christopher Anderson, April 1832.

On landing in Bengal our brethren found themselves surrounded with a population amounting to at least 100 million souls. They heard talk of 330,000,000 gods! Services without end they saw performed in honour of the elements and deified heroes, but heard not one voice tuned to the praise of the one God. They saw this immense population prostrate before the monkey, the serpent, and before idols personifying sin, supposing the world to be under the management of gods ignorant, capricious and wicked. Their three principal deities, the creator, the preserver and the destroyer, had no love of righteousness, nor any settled rules of government, and often quarrelled with each other.

WARD

13. The Sundarbans Settler
Debhatta and Kalutala, 6 February – 15 June, 1794

TO EXCHANGE Manicktolla for Debhatta was for Carey great relief. It was a chief village on the east bank of the Jubuna, whose waters enriched it. The Salt Assistant's bungalow was a fine brick house with semicircular verandah, and was comfort indeed to the Careys after the dilapidated house of Nelu Datta. They were blessed, too, by the beautiful Jubuna and the cool, clean breeze.

No salt works were there (the Jubuna being fresh-watered), only a salt warehouse or *golah*. Carey's allotment was across the river, more than a mile to the north, in Kalutala, whose name preserved the memory of Kalu Dewan, a Mohammedan saint, in reverence of whom the villagers still gather yearly at the great tamarind tree and make their offerings, and the yield of nearby rice fields is distributed amongst the poor.

Identified with village life as he had been for his first twenty-eight years, he was soon more at home in Kalutala than in Calcutta, and was thankful to be a villager again. His leasehold land brought many a dream to fulfilment. He could trust himself to succeed there, for he loved agriculture, the soil was fertile, and the fresh river close at hand. That others had prospered there was proved by the linked mansions of its oldest Hindu residents, who had long made their wealth in Kalutala by cultivation of the land.

Like the many *ryots* (peasants) who were taking up these Sundarban land plots, Carey expected to support his family during the labour and cost of clearing the jungle by the sale of timber, firewood, shell-lime from the innumerable shells (the lime the people chew with the betel-nut and the pân leaf) and wax from the wild beehives. In addition the Jubuna swarmed with excellent fish; and game was plentiful – 'wild hogs, deer, and fowls'. Rice, too, was less than twelve *annas* a *maund*, and goats could be bought for six *annas*. The food problem would be simple.

The chief drawback was insecurity of tenure by reason of the continual challenging of the Government by the local *zemindars* (land-lords), which had almost brought Henckell's scheme to a standstill. Then the *dacoits* (armed robbers), who infested the Sundarbans, were as fearsome as the cobras and pythons, the wild buffaloes, the rhinoceroses and crocodiles, the leopards and the boars. But the tigers were *the* terror. Twenty men had been 'devoured in the Department of Debhatta' in the previous twelve months. Indeed, Kalutala was in large part deserted, so many having fled from this fear. Any coolies and children sleeping out were in particular peril. Carey was no good shot, like Thomas, and could excusably have drawn back, as Mr Short indeed advised him. But where else could he go, without money or friends?

It did not take him long, with coolie help, to make a large enough first clearing – sparing the greater trees: the peepuls and tamarinds, the sundaris (giving the forest its name), banyans, mangoes and cocoa-nuts. Soon he began to rear his bamboo and mat house, and earth-fence a garden, in whose high bank he set the quick-growing plantains for protection and fruit. Then he planted the garden lentils, mustard, onions and peas. 'I never felt myself more happy,' he wrote. He had lost a millstone of worry. Daily he crossed and recrossed the Jubuna with a lightened heart. He enjoyed the open air employment, and the heat was more tolerable than Calcutta's. Besides, rural Bengal was the real Bengal. He felt he would soon win its speech, learn its thought and be its friend. Every day, too, meant newly-observed plants, birds, and insects, whose ways he watched, and whose names he gathered. Best of all, in their new healthful surroundings his wife and

Felix recovered, and his lads could cross the river with him in the dinghy to clear the jungle and help build the huts.

Soon a further great happiness was his. Seeing the sahib's homestead being built, the tiger-scared people took courage to reoccupy theirs, and all the more as Ram Ram Basu assured them that Carey 'would be a father to them all'. Four or five hundred prepared to return. 'We shall soon,' Carey wrote, 'have three or four thousand folk near us.'

He scarcely knew whether to be glad or sorry when, presently, he learned that 'he had been named to Government by one high in office as suitable to send to Assam and Tibet, to make discoveries, which they had much at heart.' It was a botanising quest, most likely, and wholly to his liking. He yearned to go for the sheer adventure, and that 'he might open a door for Western science and for the Gospel into those countries then so remote from the knowledge of Europe.' The hazard to liberty and life, he knew, would often be extreme, especially in Tibet; he might be judged a scout 'towards their subjugation by the English', and his presence within their borders be avenged. But, if needed, he was ready and keen.

Meanwhile, with 'health never better', he toiled as if his future lay all with Bengal. The Jubuna's either bank was lined with villages, not one of which had ever heard the name of Christ. The people were the most approachable, interested and gentle any stranger could desire, and the river with its many dinghies made evangelism simple. He wrote:

> I would not renounce my undertaking for the world. I hope the Society will *keep* its eye towards Africa and Asia. These lands are not like the wilds of America, where long labour will scarcely collect sixty to hear the Word. Here it is almost impossible to go out of the way of hundreds, and preachers are needed a thousand times more than people to preach to. Then there are all the lands of the Mahrattas, and all the Northlands to Kashmir, with *not a soul that thinks of God aright.*

When his bamboo and mat house was well advanced, 1 March brought him a great surprise – not the appointment to Assam and Tibet, but an invitation from Thomas in Malda to join him in positions of importance which had presented themselves. Thomas' best Malda friends were the Udnys, upon whom had come a terrible tragedy in the drowning of young Mr and Mrs Robert Udny at Calcutta from a capsized boat during a night crossing of the Hooghly. Thomas wrote at once to the mother in Malda a letter of tender consolation. Another son, George Udny, was 'Commercial Resident' there. He asked Thomas to revisit them, and soon offered him the management of an indigo outwork he was planting at Mahipaldighi. Thomas at once solicited and won for Carey another such management at Mudnabati. This was the news conveyed to Carey in a letter of contrite affection.

Carey was reluctant to leave his land plot in the Sundarbans, and the people who were returning to Kalutala, but could not doubt that Thomas' invitation was God's opening door. A fixed and liberal salary, association with a Christian employer, reassociation with Thomas, and substance to spare towards the publication of the Scriptures – what a cup running over! He instantly accepted. Yet he could not start immediately as he had to wait for money from Malda towards the three hundred mile river journey. Besides, his wife had to rally again from dysentery, which the severe heat had brought back.

Meanwhile, another surprise touched the 'Salt Sahib's' bungalow. Mr Short loved and won the love of Catharine Plackett. In truth, the place was made for love's awakening. The quiet, the river, the forests, the sunsets did it. Each filled the other's empty heart. They had both been chivalrous. Now they were richly repaid. Carey's congratulations had just one shadow, that he who had been to them so gracious knew not for himself the grace of Christ.

At April's full moon all the Sundarban world flocked to Debhatta in the dinghies and barges, for the Krishna *mêla* (religious fair), the Doljatra, 'the Saturnalia of India'. Not less than ten thousand, Carey says, gathered. For from the days of Gokul Ananda, whose tomb is still hallowed, it had possessed a temple, where Radha and Krishna were worshipped. In this Doljatra the images of Radha and of Krishna are carried into the open, and amidst the shoutings of the people are gently swung in cradled swings at dawn, at noon, at eve – to see which is 'great merit'. Into a bonfire is flung the effigy of a legendary demon. The people scatter handfuls of red powder over one another, and syringe one another with the same in rival groups. Often they abandon themselves to coarse gesture, dance, and song. In their circuit of Debhatta Mr Short allowed their dance upon his lawn, and the crowd thronged the space between the bungalow and the river. But to Carey, especially as it was Sunday, the buffoonery and the din were 'hell'.

That same month he saw for the first time *fakirs* (Hindu begging 'monks') flinging themselves upon spikes from considerable heights, tearing their flesh and bones. Also, he observed the frenzied dancing, and, as a hideous climax, the grotesque hook-swingings, which he thus describes:

> The man who is to swing prostrates himself before a tree, and a person makes a mark with his dusty fingers, where the hooks are to be put. Another immediately gives him a smart clap on one side of the back, and pinches up the skin hard with his thumb and fingers; while another passes the hook through, taking hold of about an inch of the skin; the other hook is in like manner put through the skin of the other side of the back, and the man gets up on his feet. As he rises, water is thrown in his face. He then mounts on a man's back, or on some other eminence, and the strings attached to the hooks are tied to the rope at one end of a horizontal bamboo, and the rope at the other end is held by several men, who, drawing it down, raise up the end on which the man swings, and by their running round with the rope the machine is turned. In swinging, the man describes a circle of about thirty feet diameter, and scatters herbs already offered to Siva, and, perhaps, smokes his hookah *[pipe]*, as he whirls. I saw one swing thus for a quarter of an hour.

These hook-swingings involved only men of the lowest castes – bird catchers, tanners, shoe-makers, and so on, but great crowds thronged to watch.

To Carey it was all so repulsive and pitiful that he pledged his life afresh to give to India the Gospel of Christ. Freed by the Mudnabati prospect from further hut building at Kalutala, he could concentrate on his Bengali. He writes:

> I see that it is a very copious language, and abounding with beauties.

A little later:

> The hope of soon getting the language puts fresh life into my soul. I begin to be something like a traveller, who has been almost beaten out in a violent storm; but who, though with drenched clothes, sees the sky clearing.

Two days after:

> I feel like a long-confined prisoner, whose chains are knocked off.

A stiffer problem than the language was his own froward heart.

Hook-swinging, from James Moffat's *Views of Bengal, between 1805–09*, courtesy of The Oriental & India Office Library, London

My soul is a jungle, when it ought to be a garden.
> I can scarcely tell whether I have the grace of God or no.
> How shall I help India, with so little godliness myself?

Not that his *Journal* was all self-smiting and plaint.

I can say with Habakkuk, 'Though the fig-tree should not blossom, yet in the Lord will I rejoice.'
> I trust I rest nowhere but in the soul's centre, God.
> I feel a burning desire that all the world may know God.
> I have never yet repented any sacrifice I have made for Him.
> Mistook today for the Sabbath. Very glad of the mistake. It has, indeed, refreshed me.
> During the approach of a severe thunderstorm this evening, I walked alone and had sweet communion with God.
> Without, the sky lowering; within, the soul's sunshine.

In rereading Brainerd, he says, he soonest 'caught fire,' though shamed by the 'disparity between them' – 'he so constant, I inconstant as the wind.'

Not all inconstant, however, or how could he have written the following words?

When I left England, my hope of India's conversion was very strong; but, amongst so many obstacles, it would die, unless upheld by God. Well, I have God, and His Word is true. Though the superstitions of the heathen were a thousand times stronger than they are, and the example of the Europeans a thousand times worse; though I were deserted by all and persecuted by all, yet my faith, fixed on that sure Word, would rise above all obstructions and overcome every trial. God's cause will triumph.

And again:

When I reflect on how God has stirred me up to the work, and wrought wonders to prepare my way, I can trust His promises and be at peace.

At last, before dawn on 23 May, they started on their long river voyage – only Catharine (with due chaperon) remaining. She was married there in the following February, 'by Richd. Goodlad, Esq,' the register says, 'no chaplain in holy orders being near the place'.

The travellers were borne by wind and tide, or were rowed, up the Isamuti to Jellinghi and the Ganges; they were towed up the Ganges itself (eight or nine miles wide, though with many shallows) to

Nabobganj, and then up the Mahanada to their goal. It was a tedious river journey of twenty-three days from Debhatta, but it brought better health to Carey's wife. The novel sights and sounds were a continual fascination – the great variety of barges, oared galleys and other boats went on their diverse errands up and down; the dress and faces of very dissimilar peoples; the trees and fruits upon the banks; the birds and flowers; the villages and their markets; the irrigation and crops; the crocodiles sleeping on mud banks; the fishermen and their curious nets; the occasional burnings of the dead; the weird music of the evening hours, and the cries of wildlife in the dark.

Carey had a thousand questions to ask Ram Ram Basu and the boatmen as to the names and meanings of the unfamiliar things. At times the sheer struggle against the stream was a tense excitement. Once in two hard days they only made four miles.

From the beginning, through Thomas' talk of the Udnys, he had wanted to settle near Malda. At Chanduria he made his first attempt to preach, but found himself much at a loss for words. At length, on 15 June, 1794, they landed at Malda, and were welcomed into the Udnys' hospitable and Christian home. For the first Sunday Thomas was also invited from Mahipaldighi, and Carey preached to several Europeans of the district, 'his joy in having his tongue set at liberty again for the Gospel he could hardly describe.'

14. The Planter-Missionary

The first two English missionaries to India seemed to those who sent them forth to have disappeared for ever. For fourteen months, in those days of slow Indiamen and French privateers, no tidings of their welfare reached the poor praying people of the Midlands who had been emboldened to begin the heroic enterprise. The convoy, which had seen the Danish vessel fairly beyond the French coast, had been unable to bring back letters on account of the weather. At last, on 29 June, 1794, Fuller, the secretary; Pearce, Carey's beloved personal friend; Ryland in Bristol; and the congregation at Leicester received the journals of the voyage and letters which told of the first experiences in the Balasore Roads, in Calcutta, Bandel and Nadia, just before Carey knew the worst of their pecuniary position . . . After the first committee met, which heard these tidings, Fuller wrote to India thus:

'We thank the everlasting God for having preserved you from the perils of the sea and having made your ways since prosperous. We feel something of the spirit spoken of in the prophet, "Thine heart shall fear, and be enlarged." We bless you for your assiduity in learning the languages, in translating and in your every labour of love. We cheerfully confide in your wisdom, fidelity and prudence with relation to the seat of your labours, and the means to carry them into effect. If there be one place, however, which strikes us as of more importance than the rest, it is Nadia. But you must follow where the Lord opens a door for you.'

DR GEORGE SMITH

[150]

14. The Planter-Missionary
Mudnabati, 15 June, 1794 – 10 January, 1800

CAREY'S FIRST BUSINESS was to get acquainted with his new industry. He was just in time to learn the art. Mr Udny arranged for him to visit the best indigo concerns of Malda and Goamalti, so that he might see the whole process for himself. For by the end of June the peasants were bringing the indigo to the factories in piled bundles. He watched these steep and ferment in the upper vats, and learned how careful a judgement was needed to know exactly when to let the dark green water run into the vats below. He was amused to see the green water beaten and aerated by coolies standing in the vats flailing paddles until it changed into an ultramarine blue – the coolies as blue as the liquid. He was taught to recognise when this beating sufficed, the liquid should rest, the granulations settle, and the water be eventually drawn off. Then he watched the valuable sediment cleaned, boiled, strained, pressed, slowly dried, cut with much care into cubes, and packed in boxes or casks for Calcutta. To one who had made long and loving study of the practical use of plants the process was of deep interest, and its necessary exactitude congenial to his scientific mind.

The Mahipal and Mudnabati ventures were new outworks of George

Indigo Factory, watercolour by William Simpson, 1863, courtesy of The Oriental & India Office Library, London

Udny's to take advantage of the attractive concessions and prices the Company was offering to its indigo planters in its vigorous attempt to capture the British indigo market from America and Spain. The construction of both outworks was well advanced, the two sahibs' houses, the buttressed reservoirs, and, probably, the vats being almost completed. But the boilers, furnaces, and many warehouses still had to be built, and the water-lifts fixed and set in order. Not an hour could be wasted, for Mr Udny expected output that very season.

The Mahipal works were larger than the Mudnabati, having seven pairs of vats to the latter's five. Its tank, too, was much larger, three-quarters of a mile long, the meritorious work of a maharaja. Though smaller, the pool at Mudnabati was also a clear and beauteous sheet of water. Indeed, Carey's whole landscape at his first settling was a delight, the green young rice as far as the eye could range growing in all-encompassing water broken only by the many palm-fringed tank-banks, bamboo clusters, and raised, tree-sheltered villages, and by white-clothed people darting through the rice in their swift, punted dug-outs.

When on the 3rd and 4th of August Carey brought his family up the Tangan to their first own Indian home, the newly-built, two-storied pukka house, with spacious rooms and Venetian windows, he was a proud and happy father. It was such a haven after the storms; such an advance on Manicktolla and Kalutala! He was happy, too, that several spare acres were included in the factory estate. When the rainy season was over, he planned to make part of them a great garden. With a monthly salary of Rs 200 – worth much at that time – and with the prospect of an additional commission on the produce, he felt a wealthy person. The very next day (5 August) he wrote his glad story to the home committee and added:

> So I now inform the Society that I can subsist without any further monetary assistance from them. I sincerely thank them for the exertions they have made, and hope that what was intended to supply my wants may be appropriated to some other mission. At the same time it will be my glory and joy to stand in the same near relation to the Society, as if I needed supplies from them, and to maintain with them the same correspondence.

He requested that – 'a few instruments of husbandry: scythes, sickles, plough-wheels, etc, should at once be sent to him; and yearly an assortment of all the garden and flowering trees; also of fruit, field, and forest trees, for the lasting advantage of what he now calls his own country. He would regularly remit the cost.' He also asked for *Curtis's Botanical Magazine* and *Parkhurst's Hebrew and Greek Lexicon.* 'A large door,' he says, 'is opened, and I have great hopes. If any lose caste for the Gospel, I can offer them employment.' And in his *Journal* he writes:

> If, after God has so wonderfully made way for us, I should be negligent, the blackest brand of infamy must lie upon my soul.

His employees did not at first grasp his missionary purpose. On the eve of their first indigo making, they asked him to add an offering to their Kali (Kali is the fearsome consort of the Hindu god, Siva), for good luck. He answered that he would rather lose his life than sacrifice to their idol. He was tempted to prohibit theirs, but refrained, knowing that force was no remedy.

His first season proved very unhealthy. So many were ill that he could scarcely carry on business. He himself contracted malarial fever, and in October had an alarming relapse, with paroxysms continuing for 26 hours at a time. Fortunately Mr Udny, though unaware of his illness, brought them a supply of quinine. Then his five-year-old Peter – so gifted that his Bengali was already almost native – fell into a fever even more dangerous than his. Through a fortnight they fought for his life, but he could not recover. Then were they lonely indeed, for, with the people's having such rigid rules concerning contact with the dead, no Hindu or Moslem would offer help for the child's burial. Not even the works' carpenters dared make the coffin; nor would anyone dare to dig the grave.

At last, however, four were persuaded to share its disgrace, digging it on the tank's south side, far away from the village and from the graves of the Moslems. None would carry the body, though they sent seven miles for bearers. They made ready to carry and bury the swathed body themselves, and were only saved from this sorrow at the last moment by an outcaste and their sweeper. The second day afterwards, the village headman outcasted the four diggers. None were allowed to eat, drink nor smoke with them. Though scarcely able to crawl, Carey had to go out and face the fierce contention, which he could only resolve by setting a guard on the headman and by threatening to have him arrested until he had communicated with the European judge at Dinajpur. 'He stuck out,' says Carey, 'till evening, when, being hungry, he thought fit to sign a paper admitting that the four had been innocent.'

How this remained in Carey's memory, and how he related its painfulness to his sons, is shown by a letter of Jabez to his father twenty-five years later, when he lost his own little girl on his river voyage to Ajmere:

> I have for once felt that anguish which you must have felt, my dear Father, when you had to bury my brother at Mudnabati. I was told by the people on board our boat that no one would dig the grave, and I had determined to do it myself, when our cook and bearer came forward and offered to do it, and to carry the little one to burial. I assure you I could not help shedding tears of gratitude for this their kindness towards us. How bitter would it have been to us, if we had had to do everything ourselves! None of the others refused to eat or smoke with them, but all tried every way they could to help us.

The bereavement and its surrounding woes told heavily on Dorothy Carey, and Carey himself was so shaken, even after the fever had left him, that Mr Udny sent him, in the care of Thomas, in his own boat up the winding Tangan to the border of Bhutan. November was ideal for the morning and evening glory of majestic Kinchinjunga. They were much refreshed by their surroundings and also by hunting, Thomas for wild buffaloes and leopards, and Carey for new plants. One night either a tiger or a leopard – chasing a jackal – almost boarded their boat.

The frank and sturdy caste-free Bhutias greatly impressed them. After this trip, they increasingly sought to plant a mission in their midst. The chief drawback, they knew, would be the people's nervous apprehension that Britain designed to subdue them.

On his return, Carey had to spend much of his time in his district to promote the indigo culture for the following season. The peasants were not readily hurried, for, as Heber says, 'the indigo sahibs had done much to sink the English reputation in their eyes.' Only slowly did they discover that this quick-stepping, frankly-spoken, cordial planter-missionary was different from the usual exploiters. However, it was the exploiting that was rife among *the locals themselves* that made Carey's soul blaze with anger – the landholders cheating and fleecing the peasants, the works' foremen systematically robbing the labourers. The overseer clerk, whom he caught swindling every one of the workers out of a twentieth of their pay, he dismissed on the spot. He was sickened at the oppressions of the poorest that he met at every turn.

Being the only Englishman in Mudnabati – Thomas, the nearest, being eighteen miles off – and having hundreds of labourers and craftsmen to manage, made nearly 'a year's difference' in his acquiring the local vernaculars, Bengali and Hindustani. A chief trouble was that the district dialects differed, he said, as much from the standard vernacular as 'Lancashire' does from the King's English.

He was surprised to find his first cold season so wintry. Malarial fever had left him extra-sensitive. 'I wear my greatcoat all day, and yet shiver.' 'Sickness,' he adds, 'is more caused in India by the cold than by the heat.' Early in 1795 his wife fell ill again with serious dysentery, and then all the strain she had lived through reacted upon her, till her brain became the haunted chamber of morbid fancies and tormenting fears. She grew the opposite of all she naturally was. Those whom she most tenderly loved, she turned most against. Her spirit passed into a permanent gloom. It was the price she paid for venturing to India in those unsheltered years. None, knowing the facts, will cast stones. Sympathy is the only fair response.

For Carey, this affliction was blackness of darkness, especially before he knew its full meaning, and could meet it with unhindered compassion.

> This is indeed the Valley of the Shadow of Death to me *[he wrote in his Journal on 3 February, 1795]* except that my soul is much more insensible than Bunyan's Pilgrim. Oh, what would I give for a sympathetic friend, to whom I might open my heart! But God is here, Who not only has compassion, but can save to the uttermost.
> *5 February* – I drown my heaviness of heart by writing to England.
> *7 February* – Oh that this day could be consigned to oblivion!
> *14 March* – Mine is a lonesome life.

Thomas wrote presently: 'You must endeavour to consider it a disease, for the eyes of many are upon you. If you show resentment, they have ears, and others have tongues set on fire. Were I in your case, I should be violent. Blessed be God Who suits our burdens to our backs. Sometimes, I pray earnestly for you, and I always feel for you. Think of Job. Think of Jesus. Only a little while, and all will be over.'

In a few of Carey's letters just at this time, written to intimates such as Fuller, Pearce and Ryland, there were tones and terms of marital rejection and reproach. But this was before the true nature of his wife's illness was apparent. Once this was clear to him, all his marital trials were borne with total, compassionate silence.

He could have borne his loneliness better had home letters reached him. But somehow, though ships had arrived through three seasons, and his friends had been loyal, their communications had all miscarried. The silence for almost two years was as if he had been clean forgotten. From Fuller's 'rope-holders' at the mine-mouth no twitch nor tremor of the rope was felt! This must surely have deepened Dorothy's depression also. At last in May 1795 letters came. Fuller gave news of Carey's father and sisters, and of his brother's regimental promotion; of Mrs Carey's sisters; full tidings of the French Revolution; of his own preaching and collecting for the Mission, the surprising generosity of the churches, London's deepening interest; of the Society's new mission in Sierra Leone; of Pearce's successful ministry at Cannon Street, and of pastoral settlement and baptisms at Harvey Lane. Pearce wrote that Harvey Lane was without exception the most prospering church in the Association, God having so recompensed them. Fifty-eight people had joined the fellowship since Carey had left. Furthermore almost all the churches in the Association professed to have been revived in consequence of the Mission. The letters were living water for parched lips.

Carey's frequent business journeyings over his district through nine months of the year to secure the due cultivation of the indigo, and to settle ever-recurring disputes, gave him an expert's familiarity with rural North Bengal. Every detail of its fauna and flora he mastered. He kept minute records of its animals, fish, and insects, and of its multiplicity of birds, mastering all their local names, and asking thousands of questions. They might have said of him, as Landor of Browning:

> No man hath walked along our roads with step
> So active, so inquiring eye, or tongue
> So varied in discourse.

He says he 'learned every process of local farming, every secret of economy, and every trick of the people', for tricksters abounded, and he had to keep his wits about him. 'Many,' he says, 'never intended to fulfil their contracts with me, and many plausible *ryots [peasants]* belonged even to bands of *dacoits [armed robbers]*.' His daily ledger of current prices and factory happenings, which would have been rare treasure for this chapter, was unfortunately destroyed.

When Carey's letter of 5 August, 1794 reached Fuller, announcing that he and John Thomas were now employed by Mr George Udny, he summoned his committee, and consulted several London supporters of the Mission. Abraham Booth reported that deacons Dore, Giles and Keene ('the triumvirate at Walworth') were 'much aggrieved that Thomas and Carey had entered into such secular employment without obtaining the Society's consent,' and he added that he himself was increasingly of the same judgement. They, Booth and his circle, expressed the view that the Society had now no longer any missionary at all, and they advised that no others should be sent to India, for if Carey, whose heart seemed to be so much fixed on the service of the Mission, had deviated to such a degree, who else could they trust in that part of the world? They had better turn their thoughts towards Africa.

The judgement of the committee was not quite as cynical or severe. They knew Carey better. But even these were much concerned and half displeased, as their treasurer's letter shows: 'They earnestly caution and entreat them not to engage too deeply in the affairs of this life, lest it should damp their ardour, if not divert them from their work.' It touched Carey to the quick. Ever since the *Enquiry* days it had been with him a point of conscience that pioneer missionaries should be self-supporting as quickly as possible. Only on that basis had he volunteered for the work. He replied:

> To vindicate my own spirit or conduct I am very averse, it being a constant maxim with me that, if my conduct will not vindicate itself, it is not worth vindicating. We really thought we were acting in conformity with the Society's wish. True, they did not specify indigo; but trade in timbers was suggested, and cultivation of the ground. Whether 'the spirit of the missionary is swallowed up in the pursuits of the merchant' it becomes me not to say. Our labours will speak for us. I may declare that, after a bare allowance for my family, my whole income, and some months much more, goes for the purposes of the Gospel, in supporting pundits and schoolteachers and the like. The love of money has not prompted me to this indigo business. I am indeed poor, and always

shall be, *till the Bible is published in Bengali and Hindustani,* and the people need no further instruction.

Fuller, through illness, had been absent from the committee which had prescribed the sending of the admonishing letter. His presence would probably have averted the blunder and saved Carey from sharp pain. Had they not been providentially led into business, they would have starved – with the first home supplies always delayed in transit, and even going astray. A case of cutlery which was meant to realise a large sum towards their second year's expenses was despatched by Thomas Potts in August 1794 to a Cripplegate warehouse. But there it lay unshipped by the error of even so friendly an expert as Mr Savage of India House until April 1796. Indeed, it came very near to being sold in London to cover its storage, and when at last it reached Calcutta in June 1797, it fetched far less than it should have done. The Mission would obviously have perished under such conditions, except for the business income.

Carey says that, 'when once the factory buildings were complete *[as they were by September 1795],* no line of life could have afforded him more leisure, nor more opportunity of service.' Only through the three months of the gathering, making, packing and transportation of indigo was he closely engaged at the works. For the rest of the time, the long mornings generally sufficed for business, and the afternoons and evenings were his own. And this was what George Udny had wished. Earnest Christian himself, he did not just *permit* Carey's missionary toil; he advanced it with heart and will. His home was Carey's Bethany; every stay there being a spiritual renewal. It was always open for the Gospel on Carey's visits, the host's courtesy and courage in this winning the interest of many other British civilians. Carey was blessed in such an employer. Although the Company was hostile to the work of missionaries, George Udny, its Commercial Resident in Malda – one of the coveted positions – was the Mission's cordial friend. Thomas, a few years before, had described him thus: 'He is a beautiful copy of Christian temper meltable to divine things: he has an obedient ear, and is as a growing cedar, flourishing in the courts of our God.'

Every Sunday – except in the rains – with the factory closed, and also during two or three evenings a week, Carey would be out in some of the two hundred villages of his own district. With no roads of any kind for miles round Mudnabati, he had to tramp along the ridged narrow paths between the little rice fields. He says he often walked twenty miles a day. November to February was his golden opportunity. On foot or on horseback, he would cover half of his district each winter. 'Preaching the Gospel,' he said, 'is the very element of my soul. Over twenty miles square I have published Christ's name.'

His village was half Hindu and half Moslem, the Hindus worshipping the *Lingam* (the symbol of reproduction), the Siva shrine and basalt images, and the Moslems gathering at a saint's tomb on the east bank of the indigo tank.

By 1795 he could preach for nearly half an hour, and be tolerably well understood, though some hearers would complain that he gave them 'mental trouble', and he knew he was still in the grip of English idiom and sentence construction, and remote from the freedom of Bengali, and from the extreme simplicity of the people's limited speech. Nevertheless, he was encouraged, seeing that as many as five hundred would often gather to Mudnabati on the Sundays, 'coming to him across the fields from every direction, even when the weather was rough and threatening,' asking for systematic instruction, and inviting him to their villages. 'Never was a people,' he says, 'more willing to hear, yet more slow to understand.' They heard of the new way, but followed the old. Custom was king. The past forbade the least change. 'Caste,' he said, 'has cut off all motives to inquiry and exertion, and made stupid contentment the habit of their lives.' Their minds resembled their mud homesteads, destitute of pictures, ornaments, and books. 'Harmless, indifferent, vacant,' he writes, 'they plod on in the path of their forefathers; and even truths in geography, astronomy, or any other science, if out of their beaten track, make no more impression on them than the sublimer truths of religion.'

Yet he pitied more than blamed them. Their superstition and servility, he would often say, came of long subservience, making him the keener to preach to these dull, passive captives. They had been so drilled, he says, to regard Brahmins as 'a sort of half-divinities', that they attributed even the spots on sun and moon and the sea's saltiness to their vexed and potent curses.

> Their ignorance is extreme [*he writes to Dr Arnold*], except with a very few learned men. They know nothing of geography nor astronomy, but are much addicted to astrology; casting nativities and observing lucky and unlucky days, which fill them with fancied troubles.

Oh, my friend *[he cried to Blundel]*, were you with us, you would see every corner full of idols, and at every mile-end the 'high places'. Such are their sacrifices that they would continually excite your compassion and abhorrence. You would feel an increase of affections, and would labour with a new ardency to establish the kingdom of Christ.

And Thomas would write:

Do not send men of compassion here, for you will break their hearts. *Do* send men full of compassion, for many perish with cold, many for lack of bread, and millions for lack of knowledge. The other day I saw the pathway stopped up by sick and wounded people, perishing with hunger in a populous neighbourhood, but none showing mercy – as though they were only *dying weeds, not dying men.* What a luxury it is to see helpless creatures come to your door: despair half fills their countenances, and their bodies seem half dead! But relieve them, and oh, behold their dead bodies spring into motion; down to the earth they fall in a moment, overjoyed with your gift: again they look up at you with tears of joy, and then into their hands again for fear it should be all a dream. I say, this is luxury!

Yet, though the people were grateful for his preaching, and interested, they had not courage to obey. The social cost was too terrible. Thomas and Carey kept hoping the best of one and of another, but nothing ripened unto fruit. 'It is in our *hearts* to follow the new teaching,' the people would say, but from doing it they ever shrank. And the two would make answer:

What would you think now, if we were obliged to go from home, and we bade you let off the water from a vat of indigo within half an hour, explaining to you most earnestly that if you forgot or let it steep longer, it would all be spoiled? We warn you and entreat you to take care, and then take leave. Suppose that in the due time we return and find the vat still steeping, and, of course, utterly lost. What would be the use of your saying, 'Oh sirs, it was in our hearts to do as you bade us. We were faithful servants in our hearts: therefore, excuse our lack of outer obedience'?

But although no Indian was so far baptised, the Mission did get the joy of a baptism at Mudnabati – of young Samuel Powell, Thomas' cousin, who in 1793 had gone out in the *Oxford*. Carey conducted the ordinance, then Thomas, Powell and Carey (with a fourth who soon disgraced them) kept their first Indian communion, and formed Bengal's first Baptist church. It was just a grain of mustard-seed, like the Mission's beginning. At the next month's communion in Mahipal, 'Thomas set Carey's soul on fire' with a new Bengali hymn. Carey himself wrote several such hymns and translated others.

Of India's own sons Carey had hoped that Ram Ram Basu would be the first to desire and dare baptism. Alas! in the summer of 1796 he was shown to be guilty of adultery and of embezzlement. Heart-broken, Carey wrote to Pearce, 'It appeared as if all was sunk and gone.' Through more than nine years this 'writer' had been teacher and colleague, first of Thomas, then of himself; 'a scholar,' said Carey, 'of the very best natural abilities, and a faithful counsellor.' Over none had they so yearned; for none had they so laboured. He had lived beneath their daily influence and knew their very hearts. The first and most frequently sung of their Bengali hymns was his composition:

> Oh who, save Jesus, can deliver us
> From the eternal darkness of sin?

He had enabled Thomas and Carey between them to translate three-fifths of the Pentateuch, and nearly all the New Testament. In a Bengali poem of real power he had satirised the teaching and spirit of the Brahmins over against the Gospel of Christ. Carey said this poem was 'like those thundering addresses against the idle, corrupt and ignorant clergy of the Church of Rome, at the beginning of the Reformation.' Now he dragged the Mission in the dust, and had to be dismissed. Carey was much dejected. With this confidant failing them, of whom could they validly hope? Moreover, vexed at his dismissal, the master of Carey's native school (on which he set much store) went also, and for weeks it was closed down. Yet, after recounting to Fuller this double heaviness of grief, he wrote:

> We can only desert the work with our lives. We are determined to hold on, though our discouragements be a thousand times greater. We have the same ground of hope as you in England – the promise, power and faithfulness of God.

He begged for more helpers. 'Should any come, I should receive them with rapture.' At the beginning of the next cold season one, utterly unexpectedly, arrived.

> One day [he writes – it was 10 October, 1796], as I was sitting with my

pundit *[Ram Ram Basu's successor – 'young, and of very musical ear and voice']* at my desk on the ground floor at Mudnabati, and was searching into venerable Sanskrit, *in bolted a man* with a neighbour of mine, whom he had picked up twelve miles off; and, before I could make inquiries, I found it was a *brother missionary*. This spoiled all my Sanskrit for that day: but it was pleasant.

It was John Fountain, whose story claims special remembrance as the Mission's first recruit. Carey and he found they had much in common. Both of mid-England, of neighbouring counties – Fountain being a Rutlander; both converted in their later teens; both Nonconformists and Baptists by conviction, against the bias of their past; both ex-choristers, understanding and loving music, and capable of singing parts. Even Fountain's voluble republicanism reminded Carey of his own youthful extravagances, long since suppressed for the work's sake. Their happiest link was Mr James Savage, the Society's India House counsellor. Fountain, an eager helper of his social mission in Shoe Lane, off Fleet Street, had so impressed him by his liveliness and versatility, that he offered to send him to India as a lay helper to Carey, to which Fountain eagerly agreed. Alas! it was all frustrated by Mr Savage's sudden death. Upon hearing of his intense disappointment, the Society gave him approval, and help towards his passage. And such was his commitment that he cheerfully went with the servants at the cheapest rate.

He was a refreshment to Carey in those lonely North Bengal years. To Andrew Fuller (distressed at the collapse of the Mission's Sierra Leone work through their missionary's political indiscretions), he was a sore anxiety, because of his strong political ideas, though it was only in home letters he blew off his republican steam; on the field he was more careful. Carey would beg Fuller to make his letters exhorting Fountain 'more tender'. 'You were near to killing him,' he wrote. 'Be assured he is a good man, and fear not to place a proper confidence in him. In a political sense I am as cold as a stone, and Fountain is cooling.' Carey was very drawn to him, as to a true yokefellow.

He took him for his first weekend to see Thomas at Mahipal, where Fountain heard them both preach in Bengali and English – in Carey's case despite a throat abscess, which Thomas lanced. Nearly a hundred were at the services, and unusually attentive. In their Sunday night session of sacred song, Fountain was acclaimed 'the chief musician'. John

Fountain received many a surprise in that first cross-country journey. He had expected to sit in farmers' chimney-corners, as in Rutland, and be given a basin of milk. He found no chimneys in Bengal, was rarely asked into any houses, and when he was, found nothing inside them! In his first home letter he wrote:

> Mr Thomas delights in doing good to men's bodies and souls. He has many qualities which make him the fittest person for a missionary that could anywhere be found. Mr Carey's very being is absorbed in the Mission. His English friends need not fear that riches may alienate his heart. He does not possess them. I am persuaded that there is not a man, who has not learned to deny himself, but would prefer his Leicester situation to that here.

It was Fountain who persuaded Carey to bathe with him in the Tangan every day, to their great health gain. They would swim across to its white beaches.

During 1796 the Mission produced another noble lay worker in Ignatius Fernandez. Born in Portuguese Macao, opposite Hong Kong, he had been trained for the priesthood by an Augustinian monk, and then travelled with him to Bengal. Distressed by Rome's image worship, especially in an idolatrous country, he declined priest's vows. After ten years of Indian clerkship, he settled as a cloth merchant in Dinajpur, and built there a large wax-candle factory. After some time he acquired a Portuguese New Testament, through which he was spiritually awakened. However, it was through contact with John Thomas and his cousin Samuel Powell (the first praying Englishman he had ever met) in 1796 that he was led, aged thirty-eight, into true Christian discipleship. From that time on he was the Mission's ardent friend, devoting his substance to its work, and building in his compound a preaching-hall for Indians and Europeans. He immediately gave Thomas and Carey £40 for books, and Carey sent home for 'works of good philosophy and divinity, not in antiquated language!' In a few years he became an honorary missionary, and made Dinajpur a most active outpost. Through the years he constantly sent the Mission's families money, candles and cloth, and at his death (at seventy-three) left most of his estate to the Serampore Mission.

Carey was specially thankful for his supply of wax candles, for he had often been obliged to pursue his nightly studies with no better light than the people's dim mustard-oil lamps. William Ward used to say of Ignatius, 'I love him beyond all men.' Reporting the conversion of Fernandez to Pearce, Carey longed to be able to send similar Indian tidings; but he felt that greater success could hardly be expected under conditions so adverse.

> Only imagine England to be in the situation of Bengal; *without public roads,* inns, or other convenience for travel; without a post, save for the letters of the nobility; without the boon of printing; and absorbed in the monkish superstition of the eleventh century – that in this situation *two or three men* arrive from Greenland to evangelise the English, and settle at Newcastle – that they are under the necessity to labour for their living, and to spend much time in translating the Scriptures, and you will be able to form some idea of our case.

And Thomas wrote:

> I would fain tell you of our successful labours, of souls converted by thousands. But it may be seven years, and seven added to these, before you hear of what you wish. Remember that when Joseph was sent to save millions, it was seven years before *one* was saved by his mission, and then they *were* saved by the millions.

In the spring of 1797 Carey and Thomas made their second journey to Bhutan. Carey's intriguing account to Fuller, with a few details inwoven from his letters to others, is here slightly compressed.

> The *Zinkaff's* kindness was very conspicuous. He gave us pieces of bacon, a foot long, and so stale as to be smelt at a great distance. The Bhutia tea, mixed with *ghî [melted butter]* and salt, we in vain tried to swallow. The people look like amazing stout English waggoners, very weather-beaten; their dress a sort of waggoner's smock frock. The women, tolerably white, are clad in a petticoat, and a cloth fastened from the shoulders to the waist, so as to form a monstrous pouch over the breasts, in which pocket they keep everything.
>
> Heralded by music, we were escorted to the town of the *Suba,* the Viceroy of the hills – the *Zinkaff* stopping every mile or so, to drink spirits. His restive horse made the procession both amusing and a peril. The townswomen, so different from the secluded Hindu wives, came out to meet us; and, presently, the whole place, two or three thousand strong, joined in. With much courtesy, Sri Naya, the *Suba,* received us in front of his house, giving us white and red scarves in the name of the Grand Lama and himself. Then he led us up into his hall of audience, and we sat with him on the red-covered curtained dais, whilst the

people crowded the benches under the long latticed windows. Shields and helmets hung above these windows; bows, arrows, and matchlocks below them.

His generosity was astonishing. Did we but cast our eyes on any object, he presented us with one at once. Thus he gave us each a sword, shield, and helmet; also a cup of beautiful firwood. He examined with the closest curiosity the compass and mirror we gave him. In eating, he imitated our manners so exactly that he appeared as if he had spent his life with Europeans, though he had never seen any before. We ate his food, though I own the remembrance of the *Zinkaff's* bacon made me sparing. Then we talked long about Bhutan and the Gospel, and he called us 'lamas', teachers of souls.

Next day, in our tent, he gave us further public proof of his friendship. We exchanged Rs 5 and five pieces of betel-nut. Having chewed betel for the first time in our lives, we embraced thrice in the Eastern manner, and then in the English way shook hands. Then he made each of us a gift of a blanket and a cloth richly gold-broidered, which I am sending to Ryland: it might make a pulpit-cushion. But, on return to his house, we had a contrary reception and cross-examination from the pompous and jealous *Vakil*, which so angered the *Suba*, that, but for our entreatings, it would have ended in blows.

They have a written language, and many books of astrology and religion. In their houses is a thumb-size image of the Grand Lama; but regarded only, I think, as a *representative* of God. The *Suba* said, 'there is a greater object of worship seen only by the mind.'

After the scene with the *Vakil*, we were not without cogitations that night, which we quieted by prayer. But we enjoyed our excursion, and glory in having declared Christ's name where before it was never heard. We are full of hope for the near founding of a Bhutan mission. We are each promised a *mûnshi [language teacher]*.

Max Müller used to say that 'the study of Sanskrit and its literature was the best means of making any man who was to spend 25 years of his life in India feel at home among Indians, a fellow worker amongst them, and not an alien among aliens.' From his second Mudnabati year Carey set himself to this language, which Ram Ram Basu extolled as almost divine. It was India's hallmark of culture, the franchise of her real aristocracy; the tongue wherein her scriptures and classics were all enshrined; the speech which unlocked her very soul; the mother and queen of her many languages. To conquer this was to lay open a dozen derivatives; to take this stronghold was to win a multiple domain.

Many caskets of silver lay in this casket of gold. However, the illiterate village of Mudnabati seemed no place for acquiring Sanskrit. Yet Carey met sometimes in the district scholars of the famed culture of ancient Gour, one of whom gave him an introduction to Judge H. T. Colebrooke, magistrate of Mirzapber, near Benares. According to an Oxford Sanskrit professor, Judge Colebrooke had been 'the first to handle the Sanskrit language and literature on scientific principles'. Carey's acquaintance with him ripened into a close friendship and col-laboration – linguistic, collegiate, and even botanic.

To this early grappling with Sanskrit Carey added the study of Hindustani, so that by 1796 he could tell Ryland:

> I have acquired so much of the Hindustani as to converse in it and preach for some time intelligibly. It is the current language of the west from Rajmahal to Delhi and beyond. With this I can be understood nearly all over Hindustan.

He was clearly preparing himself for extensive Indian service.

Into Bengali he completed his translation of the New Testament by the spring of 1797. *Matthew, Mark, Luke (1-10),* and *James* had been the work of Thomas, though with Carey's revising. The rest was all his own. He could tell Fuller that:

> Whereas in any land there are only two obstacles to God's work – the sinfulness of man's heart, and the lack of the Scriptures – this latter God has here begun to remove; for the New Testament is now translated into Bengali. Its treasures will be greater than diamonds.

Throughout, Carey had felt the very great responsibility of such translating – 'mistakes at the fountain-head contaminating all the streams in proportion to their perniciousness'. His method had been this:

> My pundit *[Bengali teacher]* judges of my translation's style and syntax; I of its faithfulness. He reads the translation to me, and I judge by his accent and emphasis whether he fully understands. If he fails, I suspect my rendering – even though it is not easy for an ordinary reader to lay the emphasis properly in reading Bengali, which, except for the full stop, has no punctuation.

But how was he to get the Scriptures *printed* once they were trans-lated? He supposed that the needed punches (for type) must come from England, each at a guinea, and was alarmed at the enormous and prohibitive cost – £4,400 for a ten thousand edition of the New Testament! But in December 1797 he learned that India's first commercial letter-foundry for vernacular types had just been established in Calcutta, and a few months later that a press, recently landed from England, was for sale there for £46. With such enthusiasm did he talk of how this press would serve the Mission, that Mr Udny, always keen for the circulation of the Scriptures, undertook to make it his own gift. So, in the next September it was announced as having arrived at the Mudnabati river landing-place. Excited as they were they 'refrained from fetching it, being Sunday; but they retired and thanked God.' When the people saw it set up, and Carey and Fountain so earnestly busy with it, they innocently called it 'the sahibs' idol'; whereas, in truth, it was meant to disestablish the idols. Until the Scriptures were printed and circulated, the progress of the missionaries could only be slow. Carey wrote:

> We have been labouring here four years in an overgrown wilderness. We have been breaking up the ground, rooting out the rank and most poisonous weeds, and sowing the good seed. Only a little return as yet appeareth, but the wise husbandman waiteth for the precious fruit of the earth, and hath long patience over it.

In case the home folk should deride their scant harvest, he asks:

> What could three ministers do even in England, supposing it now dark and rude as when Caesar discovered it; supposing them, also, to have the language to learn, before they could converse with any; and then to have the Scriptures to translate and write out with their own hands; and this done, to have no other means of making the Scriptures known but by preaching – with printing almost totally unknown, and only here and there one able to write? This, brothers, is our case. May it speed your prompt help. Staying at home is become sinful for many, and will be more so.

Admittedly their hands were pitifully empty, with no reaped Indian sheaf, and with no assured conversions even from among their language teachers and inquirers. One had proved himself a fraud; one was guilty of adultery; one 'of sweet temper, and apt in the expression of his ideas, seemed to have forgotten all of which he had once pleasingly conversed;' and so on. At Mudnabati only two remained as Carey's 'gleams of hope'. It seemed a tiny step for mountainous labour! 'Their inquirers were like grass upon the house-tops, which withereth before it groweth up; wherewith the mower filleth not his hand, nor he that bindeth sheaves his bosom.' Carey owned to Pearce and to Blundel in 1799 his bitter disappointment.

> I am almost grown callous, and am tempted to preach as if their hearts were invulnerable. But this dishonours the grace and power of God, Who has promised to be with His ministers to the end; and it destroys all energy, and makes preaching stupidly formal.

More often he blamed himself:

> Such another dead soul scarcely exists.
>
> My crime is spiritual stupidity.
>
> I am, perhaps, the most phlegmatic, cold, supine creature that ever possessed the grace of Christ.
>
> I have no love. O God, make me a true Christian!
>
> If God uses me, none need despair.
>
> My soul is like the prophet's 'heath of the desert, which withereth ere its beauty appeareth'.
>
> I spoke to Mohammedans today, but I feel to be as bad as they.
>
> I am not one of those who are 'strong and do exploits'. Indeed, I dread lest I may dishonour the Mission.

To John Newton he wrote in December 1799:

> I know God can use weak instruments, but I often question whether it would be for His honour to work by such as me. It might too much sanction guilty sloth, if I were to meet with eminent blessing.

Yet, whether blessing was granted or denied, he was determined to live and die in the work. To Pearce he wrote:

> I would not abandon the Mission for all the fellowships and finest spheres in England. My greatest calamity would be separation from this service. May I be useful in laying the foundations of Christ's Church in India; I desire no greater reward, nor can conceive higher honour. The work, to which God has set His hands, will infallibly prosper. Christ has begun to besiege this ancient and strong fortress, and will assuredly carry it. It is not His way to desert what He has once undertaken.

There was, they felt, 'a moving of the Spirit over the face of the waters, though as yet no particular act of creation'. Carey told Ryland:

> If, like David, I am only to gather materials, and another to build the house, my joy shall not be less.

And to the Society he wrote:

> I hope you will not be discouraged by our little positive success, but
> rather regard it as a call to double exertion, and to send us more men.
> Hindustan *must* be amongst the 'all nations', which shall call Him
> blessed.

The immeasurable vastness of Hindustan's need came home to him
as never before in the spring of 1799, when one evening at Noaserai
(thirty miles from Calcutta) he saw widow-burning with his own eyes.
He had been to the city to see Charles Short, upon whom a grave
illness had fallen. Carey described the appalling spectacle of widow-
sacrifice at length:

> We saw a number of people assembled on the river side. I asked for
> what they were met, and they told me to burn the body of a dead man. I
> inquired if his wife would die with him; they answered yes, and pointed
> to her. She was standing by the pile of large billets of wood, on the top
> of which lay her husband's dead body. Her nearest relative stood by her;
> and near her was a basket of sweetmeats. I asked if this was her choice,
> or if she were brought to it by any improper influence. They answered
> that it was perfectly voluntary. I talked till reasoning was of no use, and
> then began to exclaim with all my might against what they were doing,
> telling them it was shocking murder. They told me it was a great act of
> holiness, and added in a very surly manner, that, if I did not like to see
> it, I might go further off, and desired me to do so. I said I would not go,
> that I was determined to stay and see the murder, against which I
> should certainly bear witness at the tribunal of God.
>
> I exhorted the widow not to throw away her life; to fear nothing, for
> no evil would follow her refusal to be burned. But in the most calm
> manner she mounted the pile, and danced on it with her hands
> extended, as if in the utmost tranquillity of spirit. Previous to this, the
> relative, whose office it was to set fire to the pile, led her six times round
> it – thrice at a time. As she went round, she scattered the sweetmeats
> amongst the people, who ate them as a very holy thing. This being
> ended, she lay down beside the corpse, and put one arm under its neck,
> and the other over it, when a quantity of dry cocoa-leaves and other
> substances were heaped over them to a considerable height, and then
> *ghî* was poured on the top. Two bamboos were then put over them, and
> held fast down, and fire put to the pile, which immediately blazed very
> fiercely, owing to the dry and combustible materials of which it was
> composed. No sooner was the fire kindled than all the people set up a

Widow-burning, oil-painting by James Atkinson, 1831, courtesy of The Oriental & India Office Library, London

great shout of joy, invoking Siva. It was impossible to have heard the woman, had she groaned, or even cried aloud, on account of the shoutings of the people, and again it was impossible for her to stir or struggle, by reason of the bamboos held down on her, like the levers of a press. We made much objection to their use of these, insisting that it was undue force, to prevent her getting up when the fire burned. But they declared it was only to keep the fire from falling down. We could not bear to see more, and left them, exclaiming loudly against the murder, and filled with horror at what we had seen.

Carey's spirit was in anguish in that flame. His brain burned with her body. He vowed, like Lincoln later concerning the auction of slave-women, 'to hit this accursed thing hard, if God should spare him.' Such evil ignorance of God made him sigh for more helpers. His voice seemed mocked in India's wilderness. But a great solace was to be his the following May – a surprise, and a door of hope in his Valley of Achor! It came in a fairly brief letter.

> EWOOD HALL, HALIFAX
> October 1798

Dear Mr Carey,

I know not whether you will remember a young man, a printer, walking with you from Rippon's Chapel one Sunday, and conversing with you on your journey to India. But that person is coming to see you, and writes this letter. His services were accepted by the Society on the 16th. It was a happy meeting. The missionary spirit was all alive. Pearce set the whole meeting in a flame. Had missionaries been needed, we might have had a cargo immediately. Sometime in the spring I hope to embark *with the others*. It is in my heart to live and die with you, to spend and be spent with you.

I trust I shall have your prayers for a safe journey to you, and be refreshed by your presence. May God make me faithful unto death, giving me patience, fortitude and zeal for the great undertaking.

> Yours affectionately,
>
> W. WARD

That same May, Mr Udny decided to abandon Mudnabati at the year-end. The previous season had been a disastrous failure. Writing the previous July, Carey had said:

All my attention is required to repair what I can of the ravages of a very calamitous flood, which has just swept away all this year's hopes. About ten days ago I went all over this neighbourhood, and the prospects were charming. The fields were covered with rice, hemp, indigo, cucumbers, and gourds. On Friday last I went over the same parts in a boat, when not a vestige of anything could be seen. All was a level plain of water from two to twenty feet deep. The rivers have made two large lakes, three miles wide and fifty miles long.

Fountain described it as 'a sea whose bed they could not touch with a ten-foot bamboo'. The prospects for the 1799 season were not much brighter, only this time the curse was drought, which 'burnt the crops and dried up the tanks, and left the people only offensive puddles for their drinking'. Carey says 'the whole district was smitten with such pestilence, as had scarcely ever been known before, six or seven dying weekly in every little village.' Fountain, too, was so sick that they despaired of his life.

Of Carey's five seasons at Mudnabati, three had been ruined by fever, flood and drought. He considered abandoning indigo and moving to Bhutan. But, in order to pursue the employment for which he held licence (with three more years to run), and to provide a business standing to shelter as his partners the new missionaries, and also to establish a mission settlement on Moravian lines, he secured, with the Rs 3,000 he had saved and a loan from Mr Udny, another indigo plant at Khidurpur. This was twelve miles north, and on the other side of the Tangan river. It was on elevated ground, well removed from the area of frequent flooding. Hearing in early November that three, if not four, families were well on their way to him, he hastened his preparations for the reception of them there.

Carey was faced towards the end of August with an ominous future. His allowance from Mr Udny was to come to an end that month. 'We shall be in great distress,' Fountain wrote, 'unless Jehovah appears for us in a way we know not of. But poverty will be no new experience for either of us.'

The Lord did not leave them without encouragement. Hearing of their anxieties, a Mr William Cuninghame, a registrar (deputy magistrate) of the court at Dinajpur, a convert of Carey's, immediately sent them Rs 200, with a letter of exquisite courtesy; and his chief, Judge Parr, suggested their visiting Dinajpur to preach for a final Sunday, which, when it came, enriched them with £30 more.

Word soon arrived that three families had come with William

Ward – the Marshmans, the Brunsdons and the Grants, besides Miss Tidd (Fountain's fiancée). However, although they had landed in an American ship at Danish Serampore, they had been ordered back on board by the British authorities as soon as it was known that they were a missionary party. (They were the first such party these authorities had been formally called to deal with.) A landing clerk's almost amusing mistake had partly caused the trouble. Having no knowledge of *Baptists*, this man had misunderstood their description in the ship's papers, and had listed them as *Papists*, at which the authorities feared they might be emissaries of dangerous France. But, even when the error was corrected, the prohibition of the authorities was maintained.

Colonel Ole Bie, the septuagenarian Governor of Danish Serampore (in response to Denmark's London consul's commendation of them all), fearlessly pledged them asylum and defence, but the British authorities stood firm, leaving the new missionaries stuck in Serampore. They sought Carey's guidance. Committed, as he was, to Khidurpur, by his large plans and expenditure, he begged them to press through to him, sending this message with Fountain, who hastened to meet and marry his bride. He also sent through Fountain letters to his influential friends Roxburgh and Colebrooke, begging them to persuade the authorities, if possible, to allow the newcomers to join him. These did what they could, but in vain.

After five days in Calcutta, Fountain returned to Mudnabati, with Ward, for full consultation with Carey. Of their arrival, after a fast river trip of only seventeen days, Ward's own vivid diary shall tell (with my bracketed comments) –

Sunday, 1 December, 1799, Mudnabati – This morning we left the boat, and walked a mile and a half to Carey's house. I felt very unusual sensations, as I drew near, after a voyage of fifteen thousand miles, and a tedious river passage! If Fuller, Ryland, Morris or Sutcliff had been here! The sight of the house increased my perturbations. At length I saw Carey! He is very little changed from what I recollected, rather stouter than when in England, and, blessed be God, a young man still. He lives in a small village, in a large brick house, two-storied, with Venetian windows and mat doors. Fountain lives in a bungalow *[bamboo and mat]* a quarter of a mile away. Mrs Carey is wholly deranged. Their four boys talk Bengali fluently. Felix is 14 or 15. We arrived in time for the Bengali morning worship. Carey preached at 11.00 in the hall *[a ground-floor room of his house].* I was much moved by the singing. There is a Mission school of about thirty. *[Carey says 'they were of all castes from the highest to the lowest, and of ages from 5 to 20.' At first they had had to give them some little payment for attendance, but later they came freely. Several were orphans, whom Fountain and Carey maintained.]*

Carey was shocked to learn that Grant lay already buried at Serampore from fever, leaving two orphans. He was also stunned to learn that the British authorities still flatly refused to admit the newcomers into the Company's territory, and had again ordered them home despite the mediations of Colebrooke and Roxburgh. The only hope of their remaining in India was through the protection of Colonel Bie, Governor of Serampore. He had long desired to build a Protestant church in the settlement, and was raising a fund for that purpose. He felt that the presence of the Baptist missionaries would hasten this, and wanted them to have it for their ministry. Having been taught by Schwartz (of Tranquebar) the worth of Protestant missions, he had flung wide to them the gates of Serampore – where they could easily rent or buy houses, establish schools, print the Scriptures, get passports into British territory, and preach unchallenged. The haven was attractive, though there would be much to jettison first. The sheer money loss through abandoning Khidurpur would be not less than £500. Carey told Fuller:

> It was all so affecting to my mind that I scarcely remember having felt more on any occasion soever. No one could gauge the conflict of this trial but myself.

Yet the next morning his decision was taken. Ward writes:

Monday, 2 December – Carey has made up his mind to leave all, and follow our Saviour to Serampore. Indeed, whilst He has opened a door there to us, He has shut all others.

Carey immediately began preparations for removal. The divine leading was soon apparent. Almost at once George Udny was promoted to Calcutta. His successor at Malda, strongly hostile to missions, would have fought all their work. Lord Mornington, too, for reasons of State, had just forbidden the use of any printing press in British Bengal beyond Calcutta, a move which would have prevented their printing the Scriptures in Khidurpur.

Printer Ward, in vivid recollection of Carey's words to him on that walk to the Monument, in London, was keen to see what Scriptures were ready for the press. Behold, except for a few Old Testament chapters, *the whole Bible was translated into Bengali,* in Carey's neat penmanship, in thousands of sheets! Fountain had drafted portions of the Old Testament histories, as Thomas had of *Genesis, Matthew, Mark, Luke 1-10,* and *James.* Their revision and the translation of the rest was Carey's own. In his five and a half Mudnabati years he had broken the back of his first major translation work!

The sick people of Mudnabati mourned Carey's going, for he had picked up from Thomas a good deal of first aid. His Mudnabati home, Ward indicated, was a kind of dispensary. 'People came almost daily from miles round for medicine and advice.'

But, while hundreds sought relief for the body, no Indian had let his spiritual message bring salvation of soul. Not even in those days of farewell did anyone show the smallest desire for Christ. He was like a woman craving for child, but knowing no motherhood.

Europeans of the district, whom he had 'pastored', encouraged and revived (including those who owed their conversion to him) had to 'substitute' for Indian converts. He took Ward to see them, to catch their zeal. In Malda there were the Udnys, and 'the church in their house'. Also there, was another indigo planter, John Ellerton, who had been the first to establish a Christian school in North Bengal, and who had preceded Carey in starting a Bengali translation of the New Testament. Then, in Goamalti, on the fringe of ancient Gour, there were two of Britain's noblest civilians, also in indigo, Henry Creighton and William Grant, who had also founded and sustained native schools. Lastly, in Dinajpur, there were four: great-hearted merchant Fernandez; Assistant-Collector Edward Webb; Judge Parr; and his assistant William Cuninghame, whose conversion Carey reckoned 'their greatest event'. Carey knew that this group of Europeans 'would not let the light spread there go out', and he himself also intended at least a yearly revisit.

But what of John Thomas? Unfortunately, before there was any thought of Serampore, he had become deeply discouraged and had abandoned the Mahipal management, to Mr Udny's distress. His relationship even to the Mission became vague. With his wife and daughter he moved hither and thither, never remaining in any one place. Now living in a boat, now in a bamboo hut; now in Nadia, now in Birbhum; now preacher, now sugar-refiner and distiller, and now again indigo venturer! He was ever a rolling stone, possessing a warm heart, but also a wayward judgement and will.

When, with Carey's and Fountain's belongings, the printing press, and a multitude of plants for Dr Roxburgh and for Serampore, the boats were eventually loaded, Carey joined Ward and Powell on a day's sport, though himself gunless. 'He never shoots,' writes Ward. From a boy he watched, rather than took, wildlife. What pleased him more was to cross the Ganges to introduce Ward to the Santals of the Rajmahals, for he had grown very interested in all that he had seen and heard of these sturdy hill tribes, so different from the Aryans of the plains. Without caste or priests, they were animists, and hunted with bows and arrows. They were able to speak Hindustani, and were prepared to welcome a teacher. 'I longed to stay there,' wrote Ward, 'to tell these social and untutored heathen the good news from Heaven. I had a strong persuasion that our Saviour's wounds would melt their hearts.'

However, on the first morning of 1800, after tender farewells, they were obliged to leave Malda for their down-river run to Serampore, which they reached on Friday, 10 January. Carey's missionary apprenticeship was over, and his leadership of a team was about to begin.

15. The Serampore Beginning

In the whole history of missions we know no grander chapter than Serampore.

DR GEORGE SMITH

The Jews might as well forget Jerusalem as the Baptists Serampore ... The three at Serampore were of that type of self-made men so often to be met in English history, men of insatiable appetite for learning, and of practical ability, dismayed by no difficulties, and whose industry and patience knew no bounds. Carey especially was a man of heroic diligence. Each acted as a complement to the others so perfectly and harmoniously that their living together tripled their work-power. They had one household in common in Serampore until death, and stood by one another inseparably in weal and woe, during years of severe trial.

PROFESSOR JULIUS RICHTER, *History of Missions in India.*

The triumvirate of Serampore formed the base of a battle-line for all Asia.

DR H. C. MABIE

Only as our young men are inspired by such examples as your Serampore pioneers, can we hope to realise Seeley's prophecy, that 'England's Indian achievement, whilst her strongest, may also prove her greatest.'

LORD CARMICHAEL, Governor of Bengal,
4 December, 1915.

Thank you, Moravians. If ever I am a missionary worth a straw, I shall owe it, under God, to you.

MARSHMAN

There was a boy who used to carry parcels from a bookseller to his customers. Every day he trudged through the streets heavy-laden. One day, going to the house of a great duke with Clarendon's *History of England,* three folios, his shoulders were so tired that, as he passed through Broad Sanctuary, opposite Westminster Abbey, he laid down his load, and sobbed at the thought that he had nothing more in life to look forward to than being a bookseller's porter. But, looking up at the building which towered above him, he bethought him of the high truths and brave souls there enshrined. Brushing away his tears, he replaced the load on his shoulders, and walked with a light heart, resolved to work his hardest, and to bide his time. His time at last came; for *Joshua Marshman* became one of the noblest and most learned of our English missionaries.

DEAN STANLEY

Unto me, who am less than the least of all our saints, may this grace be given, that I should *print* for the Gentiles, the unsearchable riches of Christ.

WARD'S *Diary,* on the outward voyage.

Don't print too many encomiums *[formal or high-flown expressions of praise]* upon us. The Moravians do not so. I cannot get out of my mind a public show, whilst I read the *Periodical Accounts.* 'Very fine missionaries on view here. Walk in and see.' I cannot think this can excite public confidence, or produce the least good.

WARD to Fuller.

Immediately after the letters announcing the conversion either of Krishna Pal or of the first Brahmin reached Fuller, he was touring Scotland for the Mission, and preached on, 'O sing unto the Lord a new song; for he hath done marvellous things: his right hand, and his holy arm, hath gotten him the victory. The Lord hath made known his salvation: his righteousness hath he openly shewed in the sight of the heathen.' He prefaced his sermon with his news, and the effect was wonderful. The large assembly was overwhelmed with joy to feel that barriers which they had feared might be insuperable had been broken.

DR F. W. GOTCH

15. The Serampore Beginning
10 January, 1800 – 5 March, 1801

I HAVE NOT rushed Carey to Serampore, for a man is most worth watching when he is tackling his first tough problems, and making his apprentice efforts. Accordingly, I have taken time to tell of his early settling in the Sundarbans, and of his five and a half years as a planter-missionary in North Bengal. There he was winning his basic knowledge of rural, real India, asking all his first keen questions, acquiring the vernaculars and Sanskrit, learning to organise and manage men, was laying the foundation of all his translation work and forming the true measure of his task.

The difficulty of writing his life after it became knit with Ward's and Marshman's in Serampore is its embarrassment of riches. From here the story is triple, and the three strands are so plaited that they can scarcely be followed apart. No three men ever had a soul so single. Although Carey had preceded them by six years, they seemed so quickly to catch him up, and make his purposes their own. This now has to be three biographies in one, yet with Carey as the kindling and directive soul. It was salvation for Carey, who was essentially social, that after his lonely years in Mudnabati he should be set in the midst of such co-operative colleagues. Fountain's presence had been a godsend, but, as Carey said, 'we can scarcely vary conversation so much with one person as to keep up its zest.'

Khidurpur, where Carey had planned to move, was completely off the beaten track. But God overruled, and through the hostility of the British authorities, brought the Mission to a place of unforeseen advantages.

Serampore was on a highway, at a mainstream. It was far enough from Calcutta to be secure from those who would have thwarted the work, yet only two hours' travelling distance. The town was 'populous, well ordered, healthful, and beautiful', on the verge of its most prosperous years, under the renewed, wise leadership of Governor Bie. It was Denmark's Bengal port. Its river Hooghly was as wide as the Gravesend Thames, and its channel busy with the ships of Denmark and the world. As many as two hundred big boats in full sail passed by in a single tide. Its residents included Danes, Germans, French, English, Portuguese, Armenians, Greeks, Sikhs, Moslems and Hindus. Across the estuary was Barrackpore, the suburban resort and military station of the British Governor-General of India, whose regal boat came and went for weekends, with its golden eagle and tiger head. Here the Mission found a city of refuge, yet one which gave them an unexpected impact on the world. Its line went out into all the earth. Governor Bie often brought with him to the Mission services visitors from far. With these, and others, even in Serampore's first year, Carey frequently preached to many nations. On 16 November, for example, he spoke to Norwegians, Danes, Americans, Malays, a Malabar, and a Scotsman. The site was strategic. John Fountain said that 'more would hear the Gospel in a week in Serampore than in six months in Mudnabati or in Khidurpur!'

Yet it demanded double courage to plant the Mission there. The district was overwhelmingly Hindu, and Brahmin influence specially dominant. Next to Puri it was the provincial seat of Jagannath, whose festivals were still thronged by multitudes.

Moreover, an attempt had already been made to establish a mission there, but this had been abandoned as a failure. In 1777, loyal to the last plannings and biddings of Count Zinzendorf, Moravian missionaries had settled at Serampore – Karl Friedrich Schmidt and Johannes Grassman. They acquired the Bengali speech, and compiled a Bengali-Moravian vocabulary, but the closer they drew to their mission task, the more formidable they found it. Though the town was under a Danish and Protestant flag, only four families were Protestant, the rest being Hindu, Moslem, Greek Armenian, or Roman Catholic. All were so entrenched in their beliefs, and the Hindus so tenacious of caste, that 'preaching seemed ploughing upon rock.' When, after fifteen years' effort, they could count only one dubious convert, the Moravian effort was abandoned in 1792, the very year that the Particular Baptist Mission was founded in England. So Carey and his colleagues gave battle just where his Moravian heroes had been foiled. He better understood, as his North Bengal years had taught him, how grim the struggle would be.

Nevertheless, he still believed in the Moravian plan of communal settlements for the early years of a mission. This plan he considered would best secure economy, efficiency and fraternity. So he set himself to fuse the families into such a fellowship. Never so happy as with many around him, he welcomed the change from his long northern loneliness, accentuated as it had been by the deep depression of his sick wife. Not that he ignored the strain on human nature of thus living closely together. Even on the newcomers' voyage, made so pleasant by Captain Wickes (son of a Baptist pastor), a father to each and grandfather to the children, there had been friction between the women. Furthermore in Carey's first Serampore week, before the Mission House was bought, two of the men had fallen into a most violent quarrel, and 'in the presence of Bengalis!' Hope of a fused family seemed doomed, especially in the climate of Bengal.

> I tremble [wrote Ward], almost before we begin to live together. So much depends on a man's disinterestedness, forbearance, meekness and self-denial. One man of the wrong temper could make our house a hell. Much wisdom will be necessary. It is but here and there that one makes conscience of strangling thoughts, and of esteeming others better than himself. Only few are fit to live in such a settlement as ours is to be, where selfish passions must be crushed, and the love of Christ swallow up all else.

So great was the missionaries' concern about this, that they asked the home committee to give them local authority to exclude any family which might prove obstinately unwilling to resolve any difficulty.

Yet fellowship was fused and sustained by these first covenanters in every case until death, which, though it claimed Fountain and

Brunsdon within a few months, withheld itself from Ward, Carey, and Marshman for 23, 34, and 37 years. The threefold cord was never broken, though many would have wanted it to be cut or torn it apart.

It helped their early friendship that Ward had seen Carey before, and had been intimate with four of his chief home-base friends – Fawcett, Fuller, Sutcliff and Pearce; and that Marshman had been through five years in association with Ryland, as a member of his Broadmead church, as a master in his Broadmead charity school, and as a private student in the theological academy of which Ryland was principal. All could endlessly talk of their mutual heroes. It helped, too, that they were all on the morning-side of 40: Carey being 39, Marshman and Ward, 32 and 31, and Mrs Marshman, 33. All were ready for the utmost exertion. And their work-power was more than quadrupled by their pulling together.

In the formative months, with Thomas at a distance, Carey was the one experienced missionary. To him they looked: on him they leaned. As they marked his courteous sway, they realised the truth of what they had been told by the Mission's leaders in England – that 'they would find him far from that temper which would make it burdensome to follow his advice.'

In one particular Carey departed from Moravian precedent. Bishop Spangenberg had laid it down in his *Instructions* (the accepted textbook of Moravian missions, published in English in 1788) that 'each settlement should appoint a head or house-father, to whom the rest should in love be subject.' Carey deliberately planned otherwise. Forgoing his own claim to headship or house-fathership, he founded Serampore on equality for each, pre-eminence for none; rule by majority, allocation of function by collective vote; superintendence by each in monthly rotation, the duties including purchase of supplies, presidency of the table, keeping accounts, direction of the servants, the interviewing of callers, and the conduct of the weekly English service. The bold stroke paid off. This democratic basis of the Mission and the family was a secret of its strength. He would have them call no man master, least of all himself. 'One was their Master, even Christ.'

A chief function of Spangenberg's house-father was 'to suppress dissensions, if possible, at their first appearance, or to compose them, should they break out.' This also Carey committed to the Christian wisdom of the five.

We have a meeting every Saturday evening *[he writes]* to regulate family concerns, and settle any difference that may have arisen in the week. Should any be hurt in their minds, and not mention it then, they would meet with little pity afterwards, and, indeed, would be guilty of a crime.

This open treatment so succeeded that towards the second year-end he could declare, 'We have not had a complaint for several months. Should one be made, it is sure to be amicably settled.' He tells us how that from the beginning he solemnly, secretly, bound himself to be never the conscious occasion of friction, and that whatever he suffered, no breach should originate with him. That their fellowship stood the strain of all their lifetimes speaks volumes for the good humour and Christian temper of them all.

The settlement's salvation lay in the mutual forbidding of trading or of labour for personal gain, together with the pooling of all earnings, the apportionment of frugal pay to each family according to its needs, and the consecration of the whole surplus to the Mission's expansion. Here they strictly followed Moravian precedent, smothering all covetous impulse before its birth. In the same spirit they vested all the premises they bought or built in the Society, declaring themselves trustees rather than proprietors.

Allocation of function settled itself. They agreed that publication of the Scriptures was their first objective. Preparation of the clear copy and correction of the proofs were the joint concerns of Carey and Fountain and Carey's son Felix. Expert Ward was to supervise the printing arrangements helped by Brunsdon. To make money towards its heavy cost, Joshua and Mrs Hannah Marshman opened boys' and girls' boarding-schools – soon the best in Bengal – of which wealthy Europeans took thankful advantage. As Colonel Laurie says, 'Everybody sent a son to Serampore.' These boarders and the missionaries' children helped to keep the settlement in lively humanness and moral health. They speedily developed a school roll of over 40 and took over £2,000 in a year. More valuable still, a continuous succession of young lives received the blessing of spiritual understanding. Alongside the 'pay' schools, the missionaries also ran a free school under a Bengali master for the children of India's very poor.

In his colleagues Carey found deep joy.

All have their hearts entirely in the work. Ward is the very man we needed. I have much pleasure in him, and expect much from him.

Marshman is a prodigy of diligence and prudence. Learning the language is mere play to him. He has acquired in four months as much as I did in eight.

Thankful beyond words he was, too, for Hannah Marshman, whose unruffled temper, 'extraordinary prudence', devoutness and zeal made her the settlement's true mother – the Mission's saving health. Her heart was filled with sympathies and her days with deeds of grace. Six times she was called to mourn the loss of infants, but she was too rooted in the trust of God to be morose. Though faced with frequent motherhood, she bore the burden of her own and her husband's boarding-schools with an unruffled temper and a rare sagacity.

It was fortunate and greatly contributed to their efficiency that both Marshman and Ward found Bengal's climate as much to their liking as did Carey.

Rachel Marshman tells us that Carey's Nottingham slogans became the recognised watchwords of the Mission: 'Expect great things from God; attempt great things for God.'

The increasing kindnesses of the Governor were a great cheer. He became a first subscriber to their Bengali Bible, promised Ward his Government printing work, and urged the Danes to send their children to the Marshmans' schools. On 11 March he would have them all dine with him, sending palanquins for the ladies. Hannah Marshman, who sat next to him, found him very 'lively'. She was surprised that throughout the two hours at the tables 'he only ate of two dishes, being very temperate.' He retired at nine, and would wake and walk abroad at five. Though seventy-two, he hoped to live another twenty years. (As a matter of fact, he only lived till the May of 1805.)

From the beginning, by his invitation, the missionaries conducted Sunday morning public worship in the Governor's house, until in 1808 the Danish Church was completed. In all, through fifty years, the Serampore three and their successors made an inestimable contribution to the religious life of the Governor's and of the whole European community, and from first to last without monetary reward. The opportunity itself was their joy. Concerning their preaching to the Bengalis in those first days, Ward's is a graphic sketch:

In this country it is common for a few of the poorest of the people to take up the trade of ballad-singers; for they have no written nor printed books to sell. This morning, Carey, Marshman and I made our stand,

where four roads meet and began singing *our* ballad. People looked out
of their houses; some came, and all seemed astonished to see three
sahibs turned ballad-singers. This evening three of us went one way, and
three another. The people seem anxious to get the hymns which we give
away.

Soon after they moved into the Mission House by the river, John
Thomas came on a visit from Birbhum, completing their circle and
warming their zeal. He and Carey had not met for a couple of years.
The town was thronged for the *Ganga mêla* (religious fair), and the
newcomers could sample their limitless task. 'Under Pearce's Kettering
sermon, and surrounded by Christians, the millennium,' said Ward,
'seemed very near. How far it recedes in the presence of these uncount-
able idolaters!' The crowds were soon vaster, to watch the swingings by
the flesh-hooks – a barbarity and frenzy against which Carey and
Thomas hurled their whole indignant strength.

They kept Thursday, 24 April, 1800, as thanksgiving day for the
completion of their buildings. A sunrise prayer session; a morning
church meeting, with Carey called to the pastorate, and with everyone
describing their conversions; the afternoon given to the preparation of
an address to Governor Bie, and an animated evening sermon by Carey
on 'rejoicing in hope', for hope was still high in him in spite of
Moravian failure and his own six and a half years of Indian disappointment. To perfect the day came home letters, with tidings of
Scotland's enthusiasm for the Mission, and the sale by the Haldane
brothers of 'Airthrey' for £30,000, as a love-gift to their Lord. On the
other hand, they learned to their great sorrow of the capture of the
Duff on its missionary voyage to Tahiti.

Colonel Bie presently wrote to Andrew Fuller: 'I am happy in possessing these – as I shall be, if their numbers increase. This world yields
plenty of mould, whereof earthern vessels are made, but little dust that
gold cometh from.'

Few, however, viewed the missionaries with the same warmth as
Governor Bie. Most Europeans scorned them as mad. 'Many sneer at
us,' wrote Carey, 'but we are preparing materials for God's temple in
this country, and in Him is our confidence.' To keep in vital touch
with Him he made a sanctuary-arbour in the walled garden, which was
called his 'bower'. Here at sunrise and before tea and after supper
(when the moon saved him from fear of snakes) he daily meditated

and prayed, and the Bible which he ceaselessly translated for others, became his own 'hidden manna'.

He counted himself most fortunate, within two months of reaching Serampore, in getting into communication with Panchanan, the skilled old Indian smith, who had learned punch-cutting and type-making in Hugli under Sir Charles Wilkins himself (India's Caxton). Joyfully he engaged Panchanan, and Manohar his nephew, for the Mission. By May, Carey 'ceremonially' actuated the printing of the first page of the Bengali New Testament, and for nine months thenceforward Ward, Brunsdon, Felix, and an Indian compositor set the type and printed the pages of his translation 'on his heels'.

> They pursue me [he said] as hounds a deer. The labour is tenfold what it would be in England – printing, writing, and spelling in Bengali being all such a new thing. We have in a manner to fix the orthography, and my pundit changes his opinion so frequently. Still I venture to say that our MSS. are much correcter than any of their own.

They gloried in their toil. 'Unto me, who am less than the least of all saints,' wrote Ward again, 'is this grace given, that I should *print* for the Gentiles the unsearchable riches of Christ. To give a New Testament to men who never saw one before, who have been reading fictions as God's Word, this is our privilege. Few will know its value immediately; but some time, to many, a leaf, even a verse, will be more precious than a load of hay.'

Carey himself, however, was not just indoors, translating and super-intending the Scripture production, but worked also out in the open, scattering the divine seed. Moravians Grassman and Schmidt had found preaching 'ploughing upon rock': Carey, though, still had faith in its penetrating power. From his first Sunday he was Christ's 'herald on the highway'; often preaching three times in a day, and in the cool months a fourth time. Fridays were soon added to Sundays for these preachings – at the washermen's quarters and in Rishra, and always with the distribution of leaflets.

'Friend, can you read?' he would ask. 'No, sahib,' they would reply. 'Have you any in your family that can?' 'No.' 'Any in your village?' 'Yes, one.' 'Then give him this, and bid him read it to you and your neighbours. It tells you the way of salvation, how your sins can be for-given, and how you can be blest in life and death.' They mostly received these with both astonishment and fear.

Hearers constantly increased, but none dared link themselves with them. 'The Brahmins,' they said, 'must embrace the faith first.' Those Brahmins were surprised at Carey's knowledge of their own Shastras (sacred writings) – Shastras which not one in hundreds of themselves had so much as seen. The Brahmins at first crossed swords with him; but soon they became more careful. Sometimes they invited him to their villages, or met him on the steps of some temple and talked with him till dark. Often they insisted their religion and Carey's were essentially the same, and that all must be saved by the faith of their own race. He would ask whether a rupee and a *pice* (the smallest coin) were the same, and which they would choose if offered. Sometimes they admitted there was no salvation in their gods or *debtahs*, and they would accept a Christian hymn, though not in the presence of the river! Sometimes they protested that the mere reading of a Christian scripture would break their caste, or that it was a sin for them to be taught by an inferior! Often they demanded a sign, to authenticate his message. They would draw off any fellow Brahmins who might be listening, or they would threaten Carey and the people with their curse, saying, 'And, remember, our curses bite home.' Now and then they even hired rowdy youths to mock his preaching and prayers, and to hiss him.

Satire had to be his frequent weapon. 'You think you'll be saved by the incessant naming of your god or *debtah*? A parrot's holiness and yours is one.' Seeing some idol he would ask, 'What is that?' 'Our god,' they would reply. He would then retort: 'Did that make men, or did men make that?' 'The Ganges make you holy? Why, it is infested with thieves! And, see, it flows past Calcutta's jail, which is filled with Brahmins, whom it can neither make honest nor release!' 'You look on the *paita [the sacred thread worn by the three higher castes]*: God looks on the heart.' 'As soon expect mangoes on brambles as holy living from sinful hearts!'

'You say that self-indulgence is only obedience to nature! A doctor orders you medicine in strictly measured doses. You treble the dose and die. Is the doctor responsible?'

A Hindu's begging 'monk' boasted that he had transformed a pitcher of water into milk, and Carey invited him to dinner. 'You need not fear, even should the food be forbidden. A person who can change water into milk can surely change forbidden food into lawful.' Asked why he was rather rough with Brahmins, he would say: 'I am like one finding his neighbour asleep with his house on fire. I fetch him hard thumps to warn him of danger and promote his escape.'

He trusted less, however, to these 'hard thumps' than to the story of Christ's Passion. As early as May 1800, Ward writes:

> Carey and I went to a village this morning. Our congregation was noisy; but, whilst he was relating the sufferings and death of Christ, they were all attention. This is more and more his theme.

Ward sometimes saw even Brahmins weep under this tender message, and Carey himself in tears. 'There *is* a *Ganga* that can take away sin,' he would say, 'but it is not the Ganges.' 'Why did not God strike dead the slayers of His Son? His forbearance is the Gospel's wonder and glory.'

Carey pitied the multitudes who rejected Christ's simplicity for Hinduism's 'hard labour'. 'I hire a boat and bid you take me down to Calcutta. Instead, you pull up the stiff river to Nadia. You toil to no purpose, and against my bidding and will.' 'And what fruit have you for your hard following of your religion? You expect it in another life? From Christ we have fruit now as well as then. Missing it now, how can you ensure it then?' Robert Hall would never now have challenged his preaching as lacking illustration. He had acquired the Oriental mind.

Although, through the months before his colleagues could take their share of the preaching, he sought with such a combination of irony and tenderness to win men to the Truth, there was no sure response. One woman even asked what she should *eat* to be saved. Another ruined his illustration of contrite prayer by saying that 'if *he* petitioned Serampore's governor for pardon, he would look very sorry, but would tell every self-excusing *lie* he could invent.'

Ward speaks for them all on 27 July:

> We are often much disheartened, though we try to keep up each other's spirits. At present it is a dead calm; not one whisper, 'What must I do to be saved?'

'Make us your carpenters or smiths,' said many, 'and we are willing: but your religion we do not want.' In later years Mrs Marshman showed her daughter Rachel a great tree in Serampore, where the missionaries had regularly sung and preached, and from which they would sometimes return with their faces bleeding from the stones hurled at them. Schmidt and Grassman seemed right, 'Preaching at Serampore was ploughing upon rock.' Chaplain Brown bade them conclude that 'God's time for the conversion of Bengal had not yet come.' 'You have lost Grant and Fountain; you have faithfully laboured – with no Indian success. Apostles, rejected in one place, went to another.'

Even the people taunted them – 'If God commissioned you, why are two of you already dead?' Indeed, it was bewildering to the Mission that Grant should have fallen before he had begun to learn the language, and Fountain as soon as he had learned it. Carey's own discouragements are to be seen in an October 1800 letter to John Williams, leading Baptist minister of New York. Perhaps depression made him severe.

> No people can have more surrendered their reason. In business they are not deficient, but in religion they seem without understanding. But a people can hardly be better than their gods. They have made themselves idols after their own hearts. Hindus have not the fierceness of American Indians, but this is abundantly made up for by cunning and deceit. Moral rectitude makes no part of their religious system; no wonder, therefore, they are immersed in impurity.

And to another correspondent Carey wrote:

> Never was such a combination of false principles as here. In other heathen lands conscience may often be appealed to with effect. Here God's law is erased thence, and idolatrous ceremony is engraved in its stead. The multitudes pay a thousandfold more deference to the Brahmins than the people did to the priests in the Papacy's darkest days. And all are bound to their present state by caste, in breaking whose chains a man must endure to be renounced and abhorred by his wife, children, and friends. Every tie that twines the heart of a husband, father, and neighbour must be torn and broken ere a man can give himself to Christ.

And yet, at the same time Carey wrote to John Williams:

> I have no doubt but God will establish His name in this country. Our labours may be only those of pioneers, but Truth will certainly prevail, and this kingdom amongst the others see the salvation of God.

Carey confesses he was – 'often almost dried up by discouragement, and was tempted to go to his work like a soldier expecting defeat'. They would frequently say, as they walked through the streets together, 'Oh, if we had but one Christian Hindu with whom we could freely converse! We cannot be content unless Nineveh shall be brought to repentance. Nothing but the salvation of men can satisfy us.' Their depressions, of course, measured the height of their aim, as Cromwell's dejections were 'the inverted mirror of his greatness'. Had they been satisfied with an indirect Christian influence, they would have escaped their disappointment. It was their agony for conversions which cost them their tears. They looked for nothing short of personal faith, a new birth, and wholehearted consecration.

Fortunately Ward's keenest concern was for Carey's two eldest sons. They worked alongside him in the press, where, as they knew and spoke Bengali and Hindustani like Indians, they were invaluable. But to any *personal* Christian appeal they both seemed insensible. Felix was fifteen, and William not more than twelve, but they seemed uncontrollably self-willed. Felix, according to Marshman, was a very 'tiger'. They had been deprived of a mother's gentle guidance by their mother's mental distress. Ward felt that they could easily break away from all Christian moorings and drift out to the dangerous seas, so (as Brunsdon put it) he gave them 'his peculiar attention', to Carey's everlasting thanks.

Again and again Ward would 'take' them, singly or together, and speak of spiritual matters. With Felix the crowning day was Monday, 20 October – Ward's birthday and his own – which they spent together. The day following, Felix went out into the open and preached. Ward said he never heard a message better fitted for India. Thereafter he was their boy-preacher often to just a few in retired places, sometimes to crowds under Serampore's red cotton tree, or its new pagoda. He also encouraged his brother William to follow in his track.

It changed the face of everything for Carey to have these sons of his so different – lowly and loving and enthusiastic, of one heart and purpose with himself. 'I have more cause for joy,' he wrote, 'than anyone else.' He could be depressed no more. All the clouds and darkness had vanished. For him at any rate the long drought had passed. In the transformation of his sons God was giving him His tenderest blessing and the pledge of his destined success. For the whole Mission to see the hearts of the children joined with that of their father gave the greatest inspiration. They could all hope now that their own sons and daughters would in their turn bring them the same joy, as indeed they

all did. They felt themselves to be in step and moving forward as one
person.

To heighten their happiness John Thomas also was with them again,
a rushing wind, a tongue of fire – with Fakira, a widowed workman
from Birbhum, who for a year had sought the Truth. He had stayed in
Thomas' sugar-refinery at a third of his previous pay, in order to
remain under the sound of the Truth. On Tuesday, 25 November,
before the members of the Mission, he told his experience, confessed
himself Christ's, and requested baptism. 'I have nothing to give to
God,' he said, 'but if a rich man becomes a poor man's surety, he may
trust in him. My trust is in Jesus.' They sprang to their feet and sang
the doxology with new emotion. His baptism was fixed for the Sunday
after his return from the country, where he needed to go to fetch his
child. Tragically, however, he was never seen nor heard of again. Perhaps, his courage collapsed. More likely his relatives detained him by
force, or by some means disabled him. Perhaps the first sincere disciple
was also the first Indian martyr. The cup of joy was dashed from the
Mission's grasp.

On one of those November days Thomas disguised himself as an
Indian, and deceiving his own colleagues, went eavesdropping like
Gideon. Engaging Brahmins in conversation, he asked if any in that
district minded God.

'Yes, a few sahibs have come here.'
'Are they good people?'
'Yes, and they speak of one, Jesus Christ.'
'And Who is He?'
'They call him "Son of God". Some say that after a while Hindus,
Mohammedans, and sahibs will be all of this religion.'

Thomas could assure his comrades that they were building better
than they knew.

Another day, meeting a carpenter, who was also a *guru* (Hindu
teacher), he asked where was the nearest great school of the Brahmins.
On being told, he said, 'Can I get there in an hour?' 'No,' replied the
carpenter, 'it is a long day's journey there' – as Thomas, of course, well
knew. Then the deft evangelist told of Christ's school, and of how
quickly it could be entered, through His costly redemption.

This was not Krishna Pal's first encounter with the Gospel. Years
before he had heard it from one of the Moravians – Johannes

Grassman – for whom he sometimes did carpentry. He had heard it much later from John Fountain in the first month of this very year. But from neither of these did the message reach him with such force. As a youth of nineteen, after a severe illness, he had become a disciple of the Hindu sect of Ram Charan Pal of Ghospara, who had taught him many *mantras* (Hindu hymns). One of these ran – 'O moonbright lord, I breathe, speak, and walk at thy pleasure. Thou art ever with me, bread of my life.' Now, at thirty-five, he was himself a lay teacher, teaching *mantras* to others, yet with little peace, because sin was unremedied. So he desired to know more from these new, Christian teachers.

He needed other help from them soon, for on 25 November, at his morning washing in the river Hooghly, he slipped and fell on the mud bank, and put out his shoulder. Reaching home in dreadful pain he sent to the Mission for the doctor-missionary of whose presence he had now learned. Thomas rushed the half mile to his aid (with Marshman and Carey), and when he recognised the carpenter he had directed to Christ's school, a great hope leapt within him. Against a tree they set his shoulder and then left him to ponder this saying, 'A father chastises a child whom he loves.'

That afternoon Thomas and Marshman returned, and gave Krishna Pal and his neighbours these printed words in rhyming Bengali to be their daily devotional chant (Thomas having explained it 'with unusual enlargement of spirit'):

> Sin confessing, sin forsaking,
> Christ's righteousness embracing,
> The soul is free.

Krishna began to receive these words as more thorough than the *mantras* of Ram Charan Pal. The next morning, as he was still in much pain, he was taken by Carey to the Mission for relief. Soon he was going there daily for spiritual instruction, both Ward and Felix telling him more about the way of salvation. All that he learned he taught Rasamayi his wife and Jaymani her sister. On Sunday, 7 December, 'neighbours listened to Carey's message with great attention, though trembling with the cold.' 'So new and different grew the Mission,' said Ward, 'that the country itself wore a fresh aspect.' None cared for and helped the inquirers more than Felix, out of his own new love for Christ.

At length, on Monday, 22 December, Thomas asked Krishna whether he understood what he had learned. He replied that the Lord Jesus Christ had given His very life for the salvation of sinners, and that he and his friend Gokul did unfeignedly believe this. 'Then you are our brothers,' said Thomas. 'Come, and in love let us eat together' – for Serampore was determined to boldly require every convert to abandon caste. Gokul and Krishna consenting, they sat down with the Mission families and ate with them, having first withdrawn into a quiet place for prayer. In the evening Rasamayi and Jaymani also joined them, and the rapture was complete.

> Thus is the door of faith opened again to the Gentiles *[cried Ward]*. Who shall shut it? Thus is the chain of caste broken. Who shall mend it?

Their testimonies were most assuring. 'Christ's words have blessed our minds. He has removed our sins. He is all to us. The love that died for us is wonderful. Our hearts are nailed to His Cross. Henceforth, a Brahmin's curse or blessing is nothing.' Their baptism was fixed for the next Sunday. Thomas was delirious with wonder. He had waited fifteen years for this joy. Carey himself had almost abandoned its hope.

> Sing, soul, sing *[exclaimed Thomas]*. Sing aloud! Unutterable is my gladness. If thou canst, my soul, sing through thy tears a song of fifteen years. The fifteen years seem fifteen moments now. One poor fox throws down Sanballat's wall. It seems to me the joy will never cease. O angels, see! Oh, this is bliss!

The joy-bells rang in the Mission, though hell's wolves compassed and bayed round Krishna's home. At dawn the people dragged him before a magistrate, who sent him to prison. But at the appeal of Carey and Marshman, the Governor ordered that Krishna be brought before him. The people then shouted: 'This man has eaten with Europeans, and has himself become one.' 'No,' answered the valiant old Governor once he had ascertained the facts, 'he has become a Christian, and not a European, and he has done well. I will answer all demands against him. I forbid you to harm him.'

They withdrew from the Governor's presence, but could not be calmed down. Some had already snatched from Krishna his eldest daughter, who had been contracted months before into marriage with a Hindu neighbour. Hundreds mobbed and mocked him, shouting 'Feringhi!' (Portuguese for foreigner). Carey met Rasamayi frightened and sobbing in the road, and wept with her – which she never forgot, nor the words of his soothing, 'Fidelity to Christ has brought you to this trouble. He'll treasure your tears in His bottle, and will never forsake you.' They would all, however, have been murdered that night had not the Governor learned of the plot and sent a guard to protect them.

Then kinsfolk and neighbours attacked them with pleas, taunts and threats to break their baptismal purpose, until on the Sunday Krishna was the only one still ready to go forward – the rest pleading for more time. Just the one stood intrepid, and in spite of their hissings, 'Krishna, the devil's own; in hell's your throne,' he only smiled and gave the reason for his confidence.

Of the historic baptism, Ward's is the best account. We add a few words in parentheses.

Sunday, 28 December, 1800 – After our English service, at which I preached on baptism, we went to the riverside, immediately opposite our gate *[ie: in front of the present Mission Church]* where the Governor, a number of Europeans and Portuguese, and many Hindus and Mohammedans attended. *[Carey says it was nearly one o'clock, the tide compelling this lateness.]* We sang in Bengali, 'Jesus, and shall it ever be?' Carey then spoke in Bengali, particularly declaring that we did not think the water sacred, but water only, and that the one from amongst them about to be baptised professed by this act to put off all sins and all *debtahs*, and to put on Christ.

After prayer, he went down the bank into the water, taking Felix in his right hand, and baptised him. Then Krishna went down and was baptised, the words in Bengali. All was silence. The Governor could not restrain his tears, and almost everyone seemed struck with the solemnity of this new ordinance. I never saw in the most orderly congregation in England anything more impressive. 'Ye gods of stone and clay, did ye not tremble, when in the triune name one soul shook you from his feet as dust?' When Krishna came from dressing – a quick thing here – a Danish lady took him by the hand, and thanked him from her heart. *[We shall hear much of her.]* Brunsdon was ill, but watched all from a palanquin. Thomas, alas, was confined in the school, raving mad! *[The bruised reed was broken under the stress of the blessedness. Carey's wife, too, had no power to share her son's and husband's joy.]*

In the afternoon we kept the Lord's Supper in Bengali for the first time. 'How amiable are thy tabernacles, O Lord of hosts!' Krishna said he was full of praise. Felix and I accompanied him to his home. We talked with unusual feeling to the women *[and to Krishna's relatives there from Chandernagore and Calcutta]*. About nine o'clock Krishna came joyfully to the Mission to tell us that they again wished for baptism. Blessed day!

> *Christ set them in the ecstasy*
> *Of His great jubilee;*
> *He gave them dancing heart and shining face,*
> *And lips filled full of grace*
> *And pleasure, as the rivers and sea.*

Carey says he was charged with 'having desecrated the *Ganga*', but he knew that his own soul's gladness only echoed Heaven's. That Felix led (for the first time) that evening Serampore's family worship added another deep happiness.

Krishna (unless it was Fakira) was the first convert. 'He was only one, but a continent was coming behind him.' As Marshman put it, 'The conversion and transformation of one Hindu was like a decisive experiment in natural philosophy, of universal application. The divine grace which changed one Indian's heart, could obviously change a hundred thousand.' Krishna was the first-fruits of Bengal and of North India.

He openly accompanied the preachers; no loathing of his countrymen, nor rage of his *guru*, shaking his soul. His Brahmin landlord evicted him; another robbed him of land he had partly paid for.

Jaymani was baptised in a fortnight, the first Bengali woman to brave this confession. Asked how many rupees it brought her, she replied, 'I have obtained great riches indeed, and in Jesus a treasure beyond the world's wealth.' Every evening sick Brunsdon went to read with them. 'Before he could stammer out the New Testament words, they caught the meaning.' 'They never felt the cold when learning of Jesus.' Jaymani called her heart 'a book, wherein was written everything she had heard of the Saviour'. She so encouraged her sister Rasamayi that by the end of February she was also bold enough for baptism, with Annada, a *chamar's* (skin worker's) widow. Considering the traditional reserve and reticence of India's women, it was amazing that these three were so soon prepared to follow Krishna's lead, with all its social cost. Of these women Marshman wrote: 'We count these more precious than the most beautiful gems. They are also pillars by the wayside to remind us of our Master's faithfulness.' Carey would have baptised his son William with Jaymani, assured of his sincerity, and not afraid to baptise a boy of twelve, but a colleague counselled postponement until deeper experience was his.

Serampore was never wiser than in its early and deliberate decision to give no recognition to caste in the Bengal churches which they laboured to establish. They knew that in Southern India chaplains and missionaries had permitted its retention within the compass of the Church, as if it were as innocuous as their own Western recognition of a person's status, and also in fear, lest defiance of this Indian practice should doom their work to failure. But the Serampore missionaries believed that caste was the bulwark of Hinduism, and diametrically opposed to the spirit of the Gospel, so they resolved to refuse it the least sanction from the outset. They would not bow the knee. They knew that by this drastic course their progress would be slower, but at least it would be sure.

Increasingly the South Indian concession yielded grievous and even scandalous results – separate communion cups (for the low-born and the high), and even separate churches for the low-castes and the high-castes. There was no 'love and humility and union' – the very genius of Christianity. 'Caste proved a noxious weed by the side of which the Christian graces could not grow.' Serampore escaped these evils by the clear-cut principle on which they acted. Brahmins (the priestly caste) and Sudras (the lowest of the four castes) were treated as equals and brothers. At the Lord's Supper this equality was absolute. The castes were also daily encouraged to a cordial friendship with one another. As we shall see, they also intermarried.

Blest almost as Krishna's baptism day was Thursday, 5 March, 1801, when they placed on the communion table the bound Bengali New Testament. It was *the first people's book* ever printed in Bengali, the fruit of seven and a half years of Carey's toil. He was now close on forty. The last page was printed on 7 February. Through the nine months of its printing Ward had not known an hour's sickness. He writes in his *Journal*:

5 March – This evening we had thanksgiving for the finishing of the New Testament. Carey spoke in English and Bengali, and the rest of us prayed. A comfortable meeting!

For India, this was an historic evening! Marshman tells us that

Carey's text was: 'Let the word of Christ dwell in you richly.' Marshman had composed a hymn for the occasion:

> *Hail, precious Book divine!*
> *Illumined by thy rays,*
> *We rise from death and sin,*
> *And tune a Saviour's praise:*
> *The shades of error, dark as night,*
> *Vanish before thy radiant light!*
>
> *Now shall the Hindus learn*
> *The glories of our King:*
> *Nor to blind gurus turn,*
> *Nor idol praises sing;*
> *Diffusing heavenly light around,*
> *This Book their Shastras shall confound.*
>
> *Deign, gracious Saviour, deign,*
> *To smile upon Thy Word;*
> *Let millions now obtain*
> *Salvation from the Lord:*
> *Nor let its growing conquests stay,*
> *Till earth exult to own Thy sway.*

That Krishna, Jaymani, Rasamayi, and Annada were with them, with the Word of Christ already richly dwelling in their hearts, and Krishna sharing in the leadership of prayer, crowned their rejoicing.

Along with a hundred copies of the book despatched to Ryland for home distribution, Carey sent a case of Indian butterflies which he and Ward had caught and set.

Andrew Fuller took care to send one of these New Testaments to Earl Spencer, of Carey's own county, to enrich his incomparable 'library of Bibles'. The Earl congratulated Edmund Carey on the achievement of his son, and sent £50 to Serampore towards the publication of the Old Testament. He also instructed that a copy of the New Testament should be presented to the King, as at his own request. Soon after, a 'Richard Bowyer, Esq', a skilled engraver of London, and a warm friend of the Mission, was received at Windsor to present the gift, expressing the hope that 'the King might live to see New Testament principles prevail throughout his Eastern dominions.' A lord-in-waiting whispered an uncomfortable fear that the communication should have come, if at all,

Joshua Marshman and William Ward, courtesy of Regent's Park College, Oxford

through the East India Company Directors, but the King replied that this was a thing beyond the Company's jurisdiction, and to Richard Bowyer he said, 'I am greatly pleased that any of my subjects should be employed in this manner!' A copy was also sent to the King of Denmark.

This first Bengali New Testament has been described as 'the first stroke of the axe levelled at the banyan-tree of India's superstitions'.

PART OF THE SOCIETY'S LETTER TO KRISHNA, JAYMANI, ETC

LEICESTER
19 August, 1801

Dearly loved in the Lord,

The joy of our hearts was great, when the news of your conversion reached us. In you we see the first-fruits of Hindustan, the travail of our Redeemer's soul, and a rich return for our imperfect labours, to which the love of Christ constrained us. Now, we beseech you, stand fast in the Lord.

To unite with the Church below is to be akin to that which is above. Satan divides men from God and one another. The Gospel makes us one. You were once darkness, but are now light in the Lord. Walk as children of light. Put off all that is evil; put on Christ's new man. Abhor every kind of idolatry. Lay your account with persecutions. This was the Master's lot, and must be yours. Blessèd is the man that endureth temptation. Let your chaste and holy conversation, your uprightness and gentleness, your firm adherence to the Truth continue to refresh us. Pray and strive for the salvation of your fellow countrymen. Recommend to them the Gospel by your long-suffering and love.

A. FULLER

THE SERAMPORE MISSION AND DR VANDERKEMP OF THE LONDON MISSIONARY SOCIETY

In 1799 Dr J. T. Vanderkemp, a Dutchman medically trained in Leyden and Edinburgh, reached Capetown as the missionary pioneer to South Africa of the London Missionary Society. When the Serampore missionaries learned of him there in 1801, they wrote at once the following (abridged) letter:

SERAMPORE, BENGAL
14 February, 1801

Very dear fellow-helper Vanderkemp,

. . . You and your colleagues are called to a most arduous but important work. You may meet with many discouragements, and may have to face many trials: you may labour long with no sign of success; many apparent first-fruits may be blasted, or for long may seem so. Yet be not weary; you shall reap in due time, if you faint not. He is faithful Who has promised, and will stand by His servants to the end of the world.

Seven years have passed since we, who have been here the longest, came first to this country to publish the Gospel. Throughout, the faithfulness of God has been our stay and our encouragement – our *only* encouragement till this last year, save for His mercy in our family and the conversion of some Europeans, to whom we had access. But now God has begun to add Indians themselves to His Church. We baptised two some little time ago, and have very lively hopes of three more. Which gives fresh vigour to our spirits – though, had we not been blessed with even this success, we should have waited *still* upon God, assured that all things are under the rule of an infinite wisdom.

Experience has taught us that God's ways are best, and that our little plans are often frustrated in great mercy. As, for instance, in the matter of our settling *here*. Far to the north of this we *were* settled, and to that place every heart was bound, when our colleagues arrived in this country. Not till we could choose no longer, and even with the utmost reluctance, did we bring ourselves to relinquish what we had begun in Mudnabati: we only painfully complied with dire necessity. But now we see that the divine hand was in it, and we are convinced that this is the very place where we ought and are best advantaged to be. Therefore, dear friend, be sure that, even when you are most disturbed, disappointed and discouraged – whilst God leads, you can never go astray. Be strong in Him and in the power of His might. Make mention of His righteousness – even of His only.

We shall greatly esteem a letter from you or from any of your colleagues – telling us where is the seat of your labour, what your success, your difficulties and your prospects. We long to know you intimately, that we may the more sympathise with you affectionately, and rejoice with you in a more lively strain, and pray for you more heartily. We wish you to do the same with us. Let us by such mutual communications cement a union between Asia and Africa.

Very affectionately yours in the bonds of the Gospel,

W. CAREY

JOSHUA MARSHMAN

W. WARD

D. BRUNSDON

FELIX CAREY

SERAMPORE IN 1800

Then the town was well ordered and beautiful, the neat Danes taking pride in their Bengal outpost. Whatever threatened public health or contravened public order, even on private estates, was summarily dealt with. An inspector went on a fortnightly round, and (after due warning) righted the wrongs without more ado, sending the account to each offender. The population was much less than today's; yet was it no sleepy hollow – witness the surviving fine buildings on the river front. An official map of the 1760s credits it with having a large bazaar. The place was alive with shipping of the world. Then the novel sound of machinery could be heard from Ward's long paper-mill and printing works, folk coming from far to see the magic *steam-engine*. We may bemoan the short-sightedness which sold to the Jute Company such acres of Mission property. The only buildings associated with the Mission which survive from Carey's time are Marshman's and Carey's houses, the Mission Church (which was the original Mission House), the college, the Danish Church, the Governor's house and gateway, the Jail gate, 'Aldeen', and Henry Martyn's hideously restored and plastered pagoda.

S. PEARCE CAREY, 1920.

16. The Fort William Professor

No longer were young men, fresh from Eton or Harrow, to be flung loose upon the surface of Indian life, to acquire, as best they could, without any formal training or scholastic discipline, the knowledge that was to fit them to become judges and ambassadors and ministers of finance. Earnestly and assiduously had Lord Wellesley addressed himself to the great work of improving the administrative machinery of the Anglo-Indian Government. And foremost amongst his projects was the establishment of a college for young Indian administrators, under efficient direction and control.

SIR JOHN W. KAYE, *Life of Lord Metcalfe.*

If the Court of Directors should abolish this institution, it is my fixed and unalterable resolution to propose to Parliament, immediately after my return to England, a law for its restitution. For I *know* it to be absolutely requisite for the good government of these possessions. So convinced am I of its necessity, that I am determined to devote the remainder of my political life (if needs be) to establishing it, as the greatest benefit which can be imparted to India's public service, and as the best security for the welfare of our Indian subjects.

LORD WELLESLEY to Lord Dartmouth, 5 August, 1802.

No sooner did Lord Wellesley find himself freed from 'the uncongenial bonds of war' in the south than he devoted himself to various measures of internal administration with an ardour seldom equalled. The Company's civil servants, although they produced a few men of first-rate ability, had sunk into lowest depths of ignorance and vice. The Service had its origin in a mercantile staff, well-versed in the mysteries of the counting-house; and its training, since the factory had grown into an empire, had not been sufficient for the more important duties now devolving upon it. The system, which Burke had

[202]

reprobated fifteen years before, was still unchanged, and lads of fifteen to eighteen were being sent out to India, before their education could be finished, with no opportunity nor inducement on their arrival to complete it. At the close of three or four years' residence, the young civilians, endowed with an affluent income and unchecked authority, had not only lost the fruits of their English studies, and gained no useful knowledge of Asiatic literature or business, but were abandoned to pursue their own inclination without guidance or control.

DR SUSIL KUMAR DE (University of Calcutta),
History of Bengali Literature from 1800–1825.

Carey was the centre of the learned Bengalis whom his zeal attracted around him. The impetus which he gave to Bengali learning is to be measured, not merely by his productions and his educational labours, but by the influence he exerted and the example he set.

DR SUSIL KUMAR DE

I must acknowledge that whatever has been done towards the revival of the Bengali language and its improvement must be attributed to Dr Carey and his colleagues.

RAM KOMAL SEN, Secretary to the Asiatic Society, 1830.

Carey was the pioneer of the revived interest in the vernaculars.

SIR RABINDRANATH TAGORE, 1921.

Turning suddenly to the north, at the end of Garden Reach, the 'City of Palaces', with its lofty, detached mansions and the masts of its innumerable shipping, appeared before us on the left branch of the Ganges. A range of magnificent buildings extended eastward from the river.

THOMAS TWINING, English merchant, arriving at Calcutta in 1792, astonished by the scale and splendour of British colonial buildings.

16. The Fort William Professor
Calcutta, 8 April, 1801 – 31 May, 1830

MODEST AS CAREY WAS, he was pleasantly excited on the morning which Marshman thus describes:

Wednesday, 8 April, 1801 – This morning Carey came to me in great haste, almost before I was awake. He had received a note from our very good friend Rev David Brown concerning a matter of great moment, to which an immediate answer must be given. 'He wishes to propose him as Professor of Bengali in the new college. Would he give his consent?' Going over to C.'s room, I found Ward summoned in the same earnest manner. We laid our heads together with the gravity of a conclave of cardinals. After discussing the subject pretty liberally, we agreed that, as it came unsought, and might in easily-imagined circumstances be of essential service to the Mission, we would consent, leaving it to God to fulfil or frustrate, as was best – there being yet much uncertainty in the business.

This new college – the Fort William College – was the first administrative reform of Lord (Marquis) Wellesley. In 1800, in the third year of his governor-generalship, he was freed for a while from military anxieties by Britain's conquest of Mysore. The victory was itself a further illustration of how the Indian 'responsibilities' of Britain were stretching. The East India Company had become an empire. It was clear to the Marquis that the civil servants on whom its increasing administration would rest, would need a far better Indian training than had sufficed when the interests of the Company were chiefly commercial. If they were to govern India, they ought to know its peoples' thought and history, as well as their languages, literature and laws. He therefore resolved to establish a Government college in Calcutta to provide this instruction for arriving British civil servants. Such would pursue courses of two to three years.

His initial overtures concerning this scheme evoked little response from the majority of the Company's London Board of Directors. They reckoned him a sentimental idealist, and his college a waste of money and of years. But they could not divert him from his path. He postponed the erection of any special building for his Fort William College, and contented himself with renting one in Calcutta's central square, and with arranging for the students to be lodged in the same square.

He made David Brown and Claudius Buchanan, the two chaplains of the city, the Provost and Vice-Provost of the college, and drew into its staff the most gifted European linguists of the land – like Gilchrist, the brilliant Hindi and Urdu scholar, and Judge Colebrooke – the former to be the college Principal, and the latter the head of the Sanskrit department (though seldom lecturing); with Sir George Barlow as the Professor of Law. The post of Bengali Professor had its own special importance, seeing that Bengali was the native tongue not only of the capital, but of the largest number of the stations which civil servants would fill.

Lord Wellesley, of course, knew nothing of Carey until he was nominated for this professorship by Chaplain Brown. But when his qualifications were cited (his just-printed Bengali New Testament, and his project to translate the whole Bible) this was a record which no other nominee could match. And when it was added that he could *speak* Bengali as readily as he could write it, the Marquis was satisfied, and the appointment was fixed. On Sunday, 12 April, the Vice-Provost and Danish Governor Bie brought eagerly to the Mission the good news.

When Carey enquired whether the Marquis had been informed that he was a Nonconformist, he was assured that the provosts had faithfully reported all the facts. To override the difficulty of a

A *View of Writers' Buildings* (Calcutta) by J. B. Fraser, 1819, where Fort William College students lived. Courtesy of The Oriental & India Office Library.

Nonconformist being a professor in a Government college, it was suggested that he should be named *tutor*. And so it came to pass that Carey, who had been unable to secure from the East India Company any licence to enter Bengal, and who had been forced to lie low for six years, and to camouflage his Christian purpose under a business pursuit, and then, with his new colleagues, to accept the protection of the Danish Government by reason of the continuing hostility of the British authorities to missionaries, was now called to a position of high trust in the educational service of the British Government!

Furthermore, the work which established his linguistic fitness for this service had been pursued in fulfilment of the very function which the British authorities opposed. And what had brought him, against his design and desire, within range of Calcutta, where he became noticed and proposed for this post, but the hostility of the British Government to his work!

He himself was burdened with a sense of his inability to fulfil such an engagement adequately, but the provosts insisted they were better judges of his ability than himself. 'For my own part,' he told Principal Ryland, 'I am almost sunk under the prospect, having never known college discipline. My ignorance of the way of conducting collegiate exercises is a great weight on my mind. Give me your counsel and your prayers.'

The other Serampore missionaries could only feel more secure, now that their senior was in the Government's conspicuous service. 'Being thus appointed,' Carey wrote to Sutcliff, 'our English friends may now be at ease respecting our safety.' Except for this safeguard, how anxious they might have been on the morning after Carey's first return from his college duty, when Felix roused them very early in the highest excitement, saying that the British flag was flying over the Danish Government buildings. They discovered that while Serampore slept, a British detachment from Barrackpore had taken possession of the town, and had hoisted the ensign 'without firing a shot or beating a drum'. Then the missionaries were summoned before the British Commissioner, and were assured of their freedom to pursue their callings as before.

> Now [*says Marshman*] we could unravel the providence in respect to Carey. We could recall our uneasiness eight months back, when such questions as these were being asked: 'What press is that at Serampore?

Ought it not to be forbidden?' The tokens of divine care over us are almost as visible as over Israel in the wilderness.

In the event, with the restoration of European peace the next year, Serampore was given back to the Danes.

When Carey persuaded his colleagues at the founding of their Serampore base to disallow all labour for personal gain and to pool all earnings, one wonders what his own hopes were of acquiring funds for the Mission. When the Marshmans were soon making large contributions from the profits of their schools, he must have almost envied them their joy. But now it fell to him, most unexpectedly, to be a chief contributor, out of his monthly salary of Rs 500, which was soon to be doubled. The day after his appointment he sent £20 home to his father, 'who must be suffering much in this wartime dearth'; £10 to his invalid sister Mary, and £20 towards his nephew Peter's apprenticeship. For the rest, he lived exactly as before, reckoning his salary as the Mission's, except that a modest allowance was made him for 'decent apparel'.

He could have no qualms about giving two days a week, and soon three days, to this so-called secular service, for, although he would not be permitted to be an evangelist in his class-room, he would have many opportunities to witness to the Government's future administrators.

The students were in their later teens, and from Britain's aristocracy. Charles Metcalfe and Butterworth Bayley, in Carey's first classes, were fresh from Eton. Of his first 45 men, 21 rose to be judges, with 9 of the Court of Appeal. Metcalfe and Bayley became Provisional Governors-General, Plowden became Secretary to the Board of Trade, Morton rose to be Deputy Accountant-General, Barwell was ultimately Comptroller of the Treasury, Fraser and others became Commissioners of the Revenue, Pakenham attained Secretary to the Governor-General, and Siddons Postmaster-General. His first care was to choose pundits – a chief at Rs 200 a month, a second at Rs 100, and six others at Rs 40. For his chief he appointed Mrityunjay, one of India's best Sanskrit scholars. As one of his lesser pundits he re-engaged Ram Ram Basu (who was living close to Serampore), thus opening a new career to him in spite of the past, and to avail himself of his undoubted gifts.

For his classes on two and soon three days a week, he needed to go up to Calcutta each Tuesday, returning by Friday evening, crossing each time the unbridged Hooghly. These regular goings and comings appeared to profit his health.

A chief trouble was the lack of vernacular textbooks and tools. Halhed's *Grammar* (1778) was almost out of print. Forster's *Vocabulary* was only English-Bengali. No Bengali literary prose work was at hand, though he had seen certain MSS. in Nadia. He goaded his pundits to produce textbooks, himself in his first year leading the way with a Bengali *Grammar* and *Colloquies.* The *Grammar* was, of course, based on Halhed's, but has been applauded as an original contribution to the study of the language. Professor H. H. Wilson of Oxford described the *Colloquies* as 'a lively picture of the manners and notions of the people of Bengal'.

In this same first year his pundits published excellent Bengali translations from the Sanskrit, while Ram Ram Basu produced a graphic history of Raja Pratapaditya, the hero of the Sundarbans. These were the beginnings of modern Bengali literature.

Before Carey's first term ended, he was appointed to teach Sanskrit as well as Bengali. The examination week in February 1802 gave him no anxiety for his men had made 'good Bengali progress'. At the annual disputations in the throne room of Lord Wellesley's newly-built Government House in 1803, they came through with great honour, debating in Bengali before the Provisional Governor and the educated people of Calcutta that – 'Asiatics were capable of as high a civilisation as any nation of the West' (for which Carey had coached them). On Thursday, 20 September, 1804, in the presence of Lord Wellesley and his brother (the future Duke of Wellington), along with the Supreme Court judges, the Supreme Council, an envoy from Baghdad, and the city's intelligentsia, Carey was required to address the assembly in Sanskrit, the first such public act by a European. 'Carey,' Dr Smith says, 'was the only European scholar with the exception of Colebrooke who could speak Sanskrit as fluently as the Brahmins.' In the course of his speech he said:

> The institution of this college . . . will help to break down the barrier of our ignorance of India's languages, which has long opposed the influence of our principles and laws, and has despoiled our administration of its energy and effect. 'Sanskrit learning,' say the Brahmins, 'is an extensive forest abounding in varied and beautiful foliage, in flowers and delicate fruits.' But it has hitherto been surrounded by a thick and

thorny fence. Scholars like Sir William Jones and Charles Wilkins have here and there broken the fence. This college, by the wisdom of Lord Wellesley, will make a highway through the wood.

Marathi was soon added to Carey's tutorial responsibilities, and in 1805 the Marquis congratulated him and his pundit Vidyanath on the progress of their first five students in this tongue.

He had been Bengali tutor only nine months, when Lord Wellesley (at the instigation of George Udny, now a member of the Supreme Council) instituted an inquiry into the religious murders of the Hindus, especially the atrocities at Ginga Saugor, where the sea and the Hooghly branch of the Ganges meet. Childless wives were taught to vow to the sacred river that if she would grant them children, they would give one back in solemn sacrifice. In due time many would return mournfully to execute their vow. The doomed infants were pushed down the mud banks, either to drown or be devoured by crocodiles and sharks. Carey wrote to Fuller early in 1803:

> As teacher in Bengali, I have received an order from the Vice-President to make every possible inquiry into the number, nature and reasons of these murders, and to make a full report to Government. You may be sure I shall do it with great readiness.

He gathered in a month full up-to-date information, resulting, along with the reports of others, in the Government's immediate banning of the horrors, with the exception of widow-burning. To the bliss of the Mission, when they went preaching during Saugor's religious festival in 1804, not a babe was sacrificed to the river. The innocents had found ransom at last.

Distressed at the excepting of widow-burning, Carey immediately sent careful investigators to every village within thirty miles of Calcutta to learn how many widows had sacrificed themselves in the previous twelve months, and their ages (for they were sometimes mere girls) and the children they had left doubly-orphaned behind them. *Four hundred and thirty-eight* was the damning total in this specific area alone: the toll of a single year's superstition, cruelty, and contempt of life. The victims were India's pearls. Serampore implored the Government's prohibition. With George Udny on the Supreme Council (an ardent abolitionist) they hoped to prevail. But Lord Wellesley's reign was ending, and with a swarm of critics in London and Calcutta he feared to risk so contentious a reform, though he did not fail to leave on record (on his retirement in 1805) his own approval of a ban. The Mission never ceased to lodge its protests, nor to publish the detailed death-rolls. But not for another quarter of a century were the Hindu widows redeemed.

Carey strove with all his heart to win his students to Christ. Before the end of his first term he had a few men gathering round him in his rooms for spiritual talk, men like Lang, and like the brilliant Byam Martin, whose conversion and transformation greatly perplexed the pleasure-loving wife of the Chief Justice. 'I never converse with him,' said Carey, 'without the liveliest pleasure.' Gifted and rich William Cuninghame, converted earlier under Carey's witness at Dinajpur, was now stationed near Calcutta, and frequently joined these young men in Carey's rooms, helping to establish and advance their Christian faith. He also brought along a young man from his office named King.

Late in 1802 Cuninghame sailed home, under Carey's persuasion, to take legal steps to free the slaves on his newly-inherited West Indian estates.

In his second Fort William year Carey was incensed to hear that the Jamaican House of Assembly had prohibited both the education of the negroes and their holding of religious assemblies. He immediately wrote to John Williams of New York (in November 1803):

We must wrestle in prayer for their deliverance. Certainly God's hand will fall heavily on those Isles *[ie: the British]* whose trade is maintained by robbery and cruelty. When He maketh inquisition for blood, He will not forget the sighing of the poor and needy. Yet may their oppressors be rather converted than destroyed!

In a letter to Prof Rogers, Carey said:

I was much shocked at seeing in some American newspaper advts. headed:

TO BE SOLD
A NEGRO MAN

I hope no Christian keeps a slave; if this should be the practice (for cus-tom often blinds the eyes of even good men) in the southern parts of the United States, it will not be difficult to answer the inquiry in a cer-tain Association letter you sent me, why the churches there are in so languishing a state; but I hope that every one who names the name of Christ departs from the iniquity of holding their fellow creatures in slavery, and that it is the practice of those only who are *enemies* of God.

The minutes and correspondence of the Fort William College Council trace its vivid history through the time of Carey's long service. We observe the fight of Lord Wellesley with the London Directors over their decision to strangle it almost as soon as it was born. We follow also the students and their progress, the insubordinate and indifferent, and the loyal and keen; the problem of the slackers and their expulsion; their debts; their expensive entertainments, which they compelled one another to maintain; their shooting crows with pistols and catapulting of passers-by; and the keenness of the military men from the Fort who were admitted to classes from 1812.

Carey grows very real in these records. With his subjects and classes increasing, he asks and gets (from 1806) equal pay with the Hindustani professor, Rs 1,000 a month, plus the full title of 'Professor'. He mourns that 'though the far greater part of the junior Civil Service are men of good abilities, they are of such indolent habits, or so inclined to pleasure, as to need perpetual incentives to study or to self-restraint.' Yet he refuses 'to treat them as boys in a grammar school'. He saves one from expulsion by a generous word. He remonstrates with another for boxing his pundit's ears. He delights in yet another for having translated four books of the *Aeneid* into Bengali, but more for 'his greater achievement of subduing himself, and breaking the chains of indolent habit'. 'Schalch,' he writes, 'is one of our brightest ornaments, few having left the college with a better knowledge of Bengali.' Other students defeat him: 'Duntze has so completely absented himself from lectures as to put it out of my power to admonish him, without requiring his special attendance for this purpose.' 'Barton has been distinguished by a marked aversion to study, a neglect of preparation, and an endeavour to escape before the lectures are concluded.'

Henry Smith, suspected of cheating in his written Bengali examination, protested his innocence and was given a second chance. 'I chose,' says Carey, 'one of the easiest exercises in the appointed book. He sat over it till 12.00, and then requested me for another less difficult. This I chose, but in about half an hour, he wished another. *I then gave him the choice of the whole book,* and after some time he fixed on one to attempt. But I am constrained to say that, except for the title and one or two loose ideas of the story, his translation bears scarcely any resemblance to the original. His English into Bengali is worse.'

He says he did all he could to make his classes agreeable. When Bengali newspapers began to be published, he often utilised these, for he strove for liveliness. For the English into Bengali the juniors brought prepared work, while of the seniors he demanded translation on the spot. It was usually, he says, some story from the *Arabian Nights,* or a passage from Montesquieu's *Spirit of Laws* – 'chosen for its short and well-defined sentences, its appeal to their understanding, and because most of them were looking towards the judicial branch of the Service.' He was also authorised by Lord Wellesley to use as textbooks the translations he had made and published of *Psalms* and *Isaiah.*

It is interesting to see Carey – in the college records – defending the tongue he so ardently loved:

> Bengali is the language of the extensive province, which holds the seat of the British Government, and which is the centre of the commerce of the East. It is the language constantly spoken by its inhabitants in their domestic intercourse and business, the great majority of whom can converse in no other. It must, therefore, be a painful thing that only a few servants of the Government should be found able to read or speak it.
>
> Its structure is such that it abundantly uses words requiring much care for their right formation, and which yet yield it its peculiar perspicuity and elegance. Its multitude of inflexions and its syntax present difficulties, which few, who have not laid the foundation in their college years, will later care to encounter, however much they may be conscious of their lack of the knowledge.

By 1818 he alone of the professors had been at the college since its foundation. By 1825 he was senior to the next longest serving professor by 12 years, and the rest by at least 20. He served for 30 years, and was the only one of its professors to be pensioned.

The college professors were also the Government's literary advisers in the languages they taught. Thus nothing was published by the Government through 30 years in Bengali, Marathi, or Sanskrit without Carey's endorsement. The keys of this triple kingdom were his!

Carey sought to be not just adviser and censor, but literary inspirer. 'His college rooms,' says Dr Susil Kumar De, 'became the centre of literary activity. The best intellects and scholars of the country met in friendly intercourse at Fort William, and Carey drew around him a band of enthusiastic writers bent on removing the poverty of their vernaculars.'

Sixteen works his own pundits published, being mostly Bengali translations from the Sanskrit or the Persian. But three of the sixteen were original, and the beginnings of modern Bengali literature.*

Carey did not disdain to be what Johnson with so much feeling called 'the drudge and slave of science'. He produced six grammars (being often the first ground-breaker), of Bengali, Sanskrit (1,000 pages), Marathi, Punjabi, Telugu, and Kanarese, not to mention a Bhutia grammar, worked up jointly with Marshman from the notes of missionary Schroeter. Three dictionaries he compiled – Bengali, Marathi, and Sanskrit – as well as a Bhutia vocabulary. The Bengali dictionary, with its eighty thousand words in three volumes, resulted from the toil of thirty years, and was for long *the* standard work. Professor H. H. Wilson of Oxford said: 'Local terms are here rendered with the correctness which Carey's knowledge of the people's manners and his long domestication amongst them enabled him to attain; and his scientific acquirements and familiarity with natural history qualified him to employ, and not infrequently to devise, characteristic terms for the animal and vegetable products of the East.'

In closest alliance with the college was the Asiatic Society, of Sir William Jones' founding. Carey was admitted to its membership in 1806, and met there Calcutta's most open-minded intellectuals. For the first ten years he missed only eight of its fifty-six meetings, and served on its 'Committee of Papers' from the beginning until within a year of his death. It was before this society and the College Council that in 1805 he laid his project of publishing (with the help of his Serampore colleagues) a series of Indian classics, with the original text, English translation, and notes, to make the Western world partakers of India's

---

*These were: Ram Ram Basu's *Raja Pratapaditya*, the story of Jessore's daring challenger of Akbar, whose subdual cost the emperor the serious output of his military strength; Rajib Lochan's *Maharaja Krishna Chandra Charitra* (from whom he himself claimed descent), who took Clive's part in Plassey, and then in Nadia became an ardent royal patron of learning and music; and Mrityunjay's *Chronicles of India's Kings*. These three gave distinction to Carey's pundit circle.

literary riches. Both bodies strongly approved his scheme, and under-took its financing. The Asiatic Society's president (the Chief Justice) communicated its prospectus to the learned societies of Europe, whose interest in the long-sealed literature of India had been recently aroused. Carey and Marshman began with the *Ramayana* – the epic which mirrors India's soul – and hoped to offer this Eastern 'Iliad' to the English-reading world in nine or ten volumes. But when by 1810 they had issued only three volumes, pressure of other work thrust aside this purely literary labour; and then a catastrophe, of which a later chapter tells, forbade its resumption.

To Andrew Fuller in far insular Britain, and exclusively absorbed in the religious interests of the Mission, the *Ramayana* was 'that piece of lumber'! He was impatient and unsympathetic to the project. But Carey's grief over its polytheistic aspects could not blind him to its human interest, its cultural information, and its literary power.

During these same years Ward, keen and open-minded as his colleagues, published in four considerable volumes *A View of the History, Literature, and Religion of the Hindus,* with translations from their principal writings. This was a standard authority for over half a century, exhibiting a familiarity with Indian society which was 'unsurpassed' by any other work in its time.

17. The Astounding Advance

As the age of Carey recedes, his work will be seen in a truer perspective, and the heroic proportions of the man will fill the new generations with wonder.

DR JAMES H. RITSON

1801 – In the month of August, Gokul, one of the earliest enquirers, was received into the church by baptism. Such accessions brought under consideration the question of giving Christian names to the converts on their baptism. The missionaries were decidedly adverse to the practice. They could not perceive any positive connection between the rite of baptism and the alteration of a name. They found, moreover, that in the apostolic age it was not deemed necessary to repudiate names of heathen origin, such as Sylvanus, Olympias, Hermes, Nereus and Fortunatus, and they decided therefore, that the converts should be baptised with their original surnames. It was not till a later period that the anomaly of Matthew Chukerbutty or Timothy Tarachand was introduced into the missionary system, which only served to import a foreign and repulsive character to Christianity in the eyes of the people of India.

JOHN CLARK MARSHMAN

This Protestantism was characterised by an abounding vitality and a daring unequalled in Christian history. Through it, for the first time, plans were seriously elaborated for bringing the Christian message to all men and to make the life of all mankind conform to Christian ideals. In the first century some Christians had believed it to be their obligation to 'preach the Gospel to every creature'. Never before, however, had the followers of any faith formulated comprehensive plans covering the entire surface of the earth to make these purposes effective.

PROFESSOR KENNETH SCOTT LATOURETTE,
A History of the Expansion of Christianity, speaking of the period of
missionary enterprise commenced by Carey's Society.

17. The Astounding Advance
1801–1803

THE STORY OF Carey's Fort William professorship has unavoidably carried us through nearly thirty years of his growing authority and influence. We must keep this story in mind, as it runs concurrently with everything else, but we must now take ourselves back to his second year at Serampore, when the Mission was seeing the very first of its spiritual fruit.

Krishna Pal paid heavily for his Christian faith, especially in the distress of Golok, his eldest child, who, though now only thirteen, had been contracted by her parents in their pre-Christian days to be married to a certain Mohan. When she learned about Christ, she revolted from this arranged marriage with one who was an ardent idolater. 'Why should this poison be given me?' she cried. 'Cannot my father save me?' But he was legally helpless.

One April morning in 1801, Mohan with others seized her while she was fetching water. Tying a cloth over her mouth, they hustled her by minor paths and fields the fourteen miles to Calcutta. They savagely beat Krishna Pal, who pursued. In Calcutta Golok told the police, 'I am not willing to go with this man. I have heard of the grace of Christ, and have chosen to follow Him.' The next day she repeated this to a magistrate, who would have preferred to break her yoke, but could only pledge her protection. Left in the hands of the idolaters, she refused herself to her husband, vowing that 'live or die, she would be Christ's'. Nor could he break her will. Presently, Carey exhorted her to endure the indissoluble marriage, and by patience win Mohan to the faith. He even dared to enter Mohan's home to bring about some understanding, but an angry mob arrived and he only narrowly escaped.

Krishna's meekness throughout was remarkable, given his naturally fiery temper. Christ's grace subdued him, and was his constant theme. Europeans and Armenians reviled him just as much as Hindus. Two critical Europeans he silenced with talk of Christ's matchlessness. 'If you knew Christ's love as well as His name,' he said to an angry Portuguese man, 'you could restrain your passion.' Close to his home he built a preaching-shed, holding about forty, where he talked of Christ with his neighbours. He gathered lads about him to be taught with his own children. He composed to Bengali tunes hymns soon sung everywhere, the spirit of the most-famed one breathing in them all:

> O thou, my soul, forget no more
> The Friend Who all thy misery bore.

Speaking Hindustani as well as Bengali, Krishna Pal craved to be sent even to Allahabad and Benares with the message of the Cross, saying 'he would go to the end of the world for the Gospel.' 'We think,' said Carey, 'of encouraging his gifts to the utmost, that he may preach to his countrymen, as he is growing singularly free from Hindu prejudice and error.'

> I followed the Hindu worship [he would oftenest say]. I bathed in the Ganges. I worshipped dumb idols. I prostrated myself times without number, at my *guru's* feet. I gave my gifts to the priests. I visited holy places. I kept repeating the name of my guardian deity. But it brought me little good, little relief from my sin. Then I heard of Jesus Christ, that He became flesh and dwelt among us, and was as one that served, and even for our ransom gave His life. What love, I thought, is this? And here I made my rest. Now, say if such love was ever shown by our gods. Did Durga or Kali or Krishna die for sinners? And think. Whilst *gurus* put their feet upon their prostrate *chelas*, Christ washed His disciples' feet. Was ever such lowlihood?

Jaymani (Krishna's wife's sister) and Annada (a widow) became like-minded with him, wooing for Christ their women neighbours, and in Chandernagore the three sisters of Krishna. Jaymani said, 'The Gospel has long been planted in Europe; now a sapling is transplanted in Bengal, and is beginning to yield fruit. I want to taste it abundantly, that I may tell all its sweetness to others.' To Rasamayi (Krishna's wife) 'one line of the Gospels was more than all the legends of the Mahabharata.' Gokul, who, after breaking his caste alongside Krishna, had recoiled from baptism, now braved its ordeal. And his wife, Kamal, who had sworn to die sooner than eat with a Christian, was conquered by the love shown in the Mission and at Krishna's, and so by the love of Christ, she was added to the Church in spite of a bitter social boycott – their landlord stripping the thatch from their roof (which he had been paid to repair), leaving them only a hovel in which to shelter from the monsoon rains. 'Better than Christ's lot,' they answered, 'with not where to lay His head.'

The Mission devoted its best strength to this home group of Krishna's through 1801, Carey returning every Friday to teach them. Every free Sunday hour was made theirs, and the Bengali preachings were in Krishna's hut. The whole home became Christian – father, mother, aunt, the nearest friends and the children – Anandamayi surprising them with her quick reading of the New Testament, and Keshori able to say, 'I am a little child, but my soul is not little.' Colonel Bie invited them to Government House and was surprised at their reading and their knowledge of hymns. The greatest pleasure the Mission could offer their new recruit John Chamberlain on his arrival, was an evening's singing in this transformed Indian home, most of the hymns having been written by Krishna. Soon the Governor put Krishna in charge of the woodwork of the Danish Church he was building.

Mohan (Golok's husband) repaired his blemished caste by eating cow dung as penance, and by giving gifts of money and a feast to the Brahmins. But he treated Golok so harshly that one night she fled home. At Krishna's, she grew apace spiritually, and was later granted her great desire for baptism.

Krishna's home became the base of all advance, progress which was very wonderful after the long wait for blessing. Krishna's teaching of boys along with his own children became the nucleus of the free school. Most of the inquirers in the next two years were encouraged in their spiritual progress through this household, for it bridged the distance between the Mission and themselves. To Krishna and his family circle they could open their minds when they were shy of the British missionaries. The guests were numerous. They would smoke, talk, and eat with them far into the night, the Mission making them an allowance toward these simple hospitalities.

When Krishna and Gokul broke their caste, many marvelled, but most shrugged it off. 'What great thing is it that a joiner or distiller breaks caste? Have any Brahmins or Kyasts *[the writer caste]* believed?' But on New Year's Sunday, 1802, Carey baptised a Kyast named Pitambar Singh. He was just over 60, had travelled far for peace of soul, had outgrown idolatry and forsaken his own *gurus*. Coming across a Serampore pamphlet (distributed by Wood and Krishna in the Sundarbans), he found information about preachers from far with 'news of instant salvation for penitent sinners'. 'This is what I have been seeking,' he exclaimed. 'This must be the way.' Noting the origin of the tract, he journeyed the thirty miles to Serampore. Soon, persuaded by the Mission's graciousness, he fetched his belongings and returned. Krishna found him a man after his own heart. At Christmas he broke his caste, and ate with the missionaries and with Krishna. Bengal had never before seen a Kyast and a carpenter dwell as equals together. The day he put on Christ, Carey wrote, 'I trust a spark is struck, which will never be extinguished. The fire is kindled for which Christ expressed a strong desire.' Pitambar became to them a tower of strength and a trophy of integrity and steadfastness. He possessed great reasoning powers and would brilliantly answer challenges from pundits.

That month Syam Das, also of Kyast rank (till degraded by marriage to a Portuguese woman), gave his whole heart to the Saviour. He witnessed to a Moslem named Peeru, also married to a Portuguese woman. In the summer of 1802, Peeru was their first Moslem to be baptised. Then Kamalakanta, a Kulin Brahmin (a Brahmin of the purest and most honoured blood), 'drank in the Gospel', and though not yet venturing to baptism, broke caste, ate often at the Mission and 'loved to get other Brahmins under Carey's knock-down blows'. He also brought his son for Christian training, became a teacher in the Mission's free school, and gave Carey his *paita* (the sacred thread of the high castes). When Hindus saw this Kulin Brahmin and Krishna Pal walking together, they cried, 'What will this joiner do? Will he destroy the caste of us all? Is this highest-caste Brahmin to be as a low caste?'

Early in 1803 another Brahmin, young Krishna Prasad, a native of Nadia, came from Debhatta on a quest for truth, heard of Christ and believed. He was the first of these highest-borns, these Brahmins, to be baptised. At the Lord's Supper he received the cup from the lips of Krishna Pal as a way of renouncing his pride. Before his baptism he had on his own initiative discarded and trampled on his *paita*. Boldly he confessed Christ amongst his cultured Calcutta companions, even when they smashed his hookah (his pipe), and pelted him with dung. 'Insults,' he said, 'are sweet to me for Christ.'

In that April he was married to Krishna's Anandamayi – a Brahmin to a carpenter's child! Under a tree near his house Krishna gathered the company. Carey conducted the service, and the couple signed the covenant – the first time a Hindu woman had done this. The missionaries all signed as witnesses, and were happier men that day than proud fathers attesting a flattering alliance. The following day all except Carey partook of the wedding supper.

The day before the wedding another Kyast, Ram Ratan, a young man, had braved the baptismal confession, together with Carey's William, whose faithful walk was the Mission's joy. Krishna Prasad and Ram Ratan dared to preach Christ openly in the streets, though the mob sometimes mauled and beat them. Carey wrote, 'God is laying the foundation of His temple in India.' And Ward: 'God is famishing the gods of the country, and making His own name glorious.'

> What hath God wrought? *[Carey wrote to John Williams in the summer of 1802.]* Eighteen months ago we should have been in raptures to have seen one Hindu eat with us; now it is sometimes difficult to find room for all who come. Nine Hindus have been baptised, of whom seven walk so as to be an honour to the Gospel. We expect to baptise a Mussulman and another Hindu, before Captain Hague leaves us.

But there was the pain of trials and reverses also. Indian Christians were derided. Traders refused to serve them, landlords refused to accept them. Syam Das was murdered within nine months of his baptism. Fakira was more than probably put away. Ram Dahn was decoyed home on the pretext of his mother being snake-bitten, and never permitted to return. Pitambar Mitra, a Kyast, was drugged by his own father and fell into melancholy that nothing could relieve. Kasi

Nath was flogged by his neighbours, till in fear he recanted. Halidhar, on the verge of baptism, was dragged off and hidden.

Yet almost more heart-breaking were the stumblings of Krishna and of his whole home circle. They pierced the Mission through with many sorrows. Its very devotion to them made them heady. Krishna had to be rebuked for undue fierceness with Brahmins, harshness towards Gokul and Krishna Prasad, injustice to Pitambar Singh, rudeness to Marshman, and grave misordering of his home. Rasamayi and Jaymani also had to be rebuked for indiscretion, tale-bearing and strife. Even Golok needed reprimand for untruthfulness and immodesty, and Anandamayi, for a letter that wrought grievous harm. Gokul, too, warranted reproof for sustained bitterness towards Krishna Pal, an assault on Pitambar Singh (in the Bengali school), long abstention from worship, and 'hard words about Christ', after Carey's remonstrance.

> How discouraged we sometimes are *[says Ward]* by their accusations, quarrels and apparent untruths! Truly a missionary's hardest work is not travel in a hot climate!

They understood Christ's sighs over the Twelve, and Paul's heartaches over Corinth. Ward wrote (after a temper tantrum of Krishna Pal's) – 'Carey got no sleep again last night.' As pastor, his burden was heaviest.

> Compared with Europeans *[Carey would say]* they are a larger sort of children. We are obliged to encourage, strengthen, counteract, disapprove, advise, teach, and yet all so as to retain their warm affection. We have much to exercise our patience from the uncultivated state of their minds; but, also, much to rejoice us in respect to their conduct and their acquisition of evangelical knowledge. Even when viewed at their worst, we can truly call them the excellent of Bengal.

Most of the faltering young believers soon gave evidence of a contrite heart and a renewed spirit. Annada, for example, in token of regret, swept of her own will Krishna Pal's verandah – a lowest-caste service – even though there was smallpox in the house. Rasamayi and Jaymani wept night and day over their realised transgressions. Gokul declared he would die if not restored to communion. 'We can bear others to mock us, throw dung at us – but not to have you vexed with us,' they would say. By Christmas 1803 all (save one) were back in the fellowship, humbled and not hardened, and much the tenderer on account of their trespasses: Carey's Felix and William also, after sadly deserved reproofs.

Evidence of new-born character was also seen in the two-month illness and death of Gokul. Refusing all native charms and incantations to *debtahs*, he stayed himself on Christ. Even Hindus said, 'May our end be as Gokul's!' Nor were they less impressed by his widow's tender calm.

His burial in the Mission's newly-bought burial acre was a further revelation to the hundreds of witnesses. Krishna Pal, greatly forgiving, had made at his own cost the coffin. After singing, the body was carried on the shoulders of Marshman and Krishna Pal, Felix and William, Peeru (their first Moslem convert), and a Christian Brahmin – an amazing abandonment of caste. Hitherto, the only Indian bearers of Christian coffins had been *doms* – degraded outcastes. 'The crowd,' says Marshman, 'was much struck by the reverent love Christians show, even in death, to one another.'

Ward proposed that the missionaries should dig the graves of both Europeans and missionaries connected with the Mission, in order to teach Indian converts to practise self-denying duties, and that they should do for one another the most lowly and caste-forbidden things.

From early in 1802 Carey devoted his three weekly Calcutta evenings to gatherings for prayer and preaching, especially to the so-called 'Portuguese', the half-caste descendants of the early Portuguese adventurers, who were now 'disowned by their fathers' race, and outcasts from their mothers' kindred, more ignorant than the heathen and universally despised'. It was, for Carey, a Sunday morning of special joy when Bhairab Chandra, a Kulin Brahmin, did not hesitate to be baptised alongside John, a Moslem who had sunk into the hands of the despised 'Portuguese'. Before the end of 1803 Carey also baptised Padmanabha, a Brahmin from Assam, and Saduk Shah, a Moslem of 38, who became a faithful preacher through half a century.

Carey still had to be doctor at the weekends, as before at Mudnabati. Widow Grant describes 'the maimed, halt, and blind suing his mercy – some to have their wounds dressed, some with the ends of their fingers and toes eaten off by leprosy. He gives them medicine for their bodies, and the best of medicine for their souls.' The missionaries were already discussing with the Government Chaplain the establishment of a first hospital for Indians in Calcutta.

To train their gifted converts for work as evangelists, the leaders took them on extensive itinerations. Carey took Pitambar Singh to Sukh Sagar, and Krishna Pal to Jessore. Ward took Krishna Pal to Debhatta, and later, Krishna Prasad and Ram Ratan as far as Dinajpur and Mudnabati. At Debhatta (where Carey had been earlier) the eagerness for pamphlets passed all bounds. They could not meet a tenth of the demand. At Mudnabati the people talked much of 'Carey's flower-trees and book-making and good doctrine'. Siva Nath, one of his former scholars there, was advanced enough to read to the village the New Testament which Ward left in his hands. Almost wherever the preachers travelled they were prospered by the Mission's spreading fame.

Four Europeans died in these three years within the Mission circle: David Brunsdon, John Thomas, Charles Short and Samuel Powell. 'Every death,' as Ward said, 'made the rest cling the closer to one another.' Brunsdon would have made a good linguist and preacher, but was unable to survive the climate of Bengal. He died at 23. Thomas never fully recovered from the over-excitement of Krishna Pal's conversion. When he died of malaria in October 1801, Carey likened him to Simon Peter for his strength of impulse, and extolled him as the first Englishman to so care for the souls of Bengalis as to learn to preach the Gospel in their language, to translate for them books of the Bible, and to be their voluntary, honorary physician. Nor should it ever be forgotten that he led Carey to India, opened the way for him to gain his early paid employment, and was the principal instrument in the conversion of Fernandez, Fakira, and Krishna Pal.

Charles Short, the Good Samaritan of Debhatta, after sailing to England with his wife for his health, was compelled to return to Bengal, but had not the strength to recover. To the end – March 1802 – he kept in close touch with Carey, but there is no word that he ever espoused the faith. He was buried in Calcutta.

Samuel Powell, who had grown fervently mission-minded, died unexpectedly in Dinajpur in the malarial September of 1802, and was buried alongside John Fountain and John Thomas. Before their deaths all four had been permitted to see the auspicious beginnings of the Mission's advance.

FROM KRISHNA PAL'S LETTER TO THE HOME CHURCHES

SERAMPORE
12 October, 1802

To the Brethren of the Church of our Saviour Jesus Christ, our souls' beloved, my affectionately embracing representation. The love of God, the Gospel of Jesus Christ, was made known by brother Thomas. In that day our minds were filled with joy. Then judging, we understood that we were dwelling in darkness. Through the door of manifestation we came to know that sin confessing, sin forsaking, Christ's righteousness embracing, salvation would be obtained. By light springing up in the heart we knew that sinners, becoming repentant, through the sufferings of Christ, obtain salvation. In this rejoicing, and in Christ's love believing, I obtained mercy. Now it is in my mind continually to dwell in the love of Christ: this is the desire of my soul. Do you pour down your love upon us, that, as the *chatak*, we may be satisfied – the bird that opens its bill, when it rains, and catches the drops from the clouds. I will tell to the world that Christ hath saved me. I will proclaim His love with rejoicing. Christ, the world to save, gave His own soul! Such love was never heard; for enemies Christ gave His own soul! Such compassion, where shall we get? For the sake of saving sinners He forsook the happiness of Heaven. I will constantly stay near Him. I will dwell in the town of joy.

KRISHNA

KRISHNA PAL'S BEST KNOWN HYMN

1. Never again forget. Make this the essence *[core]*.
   Jesus, the *[true]* Brahma. For salvation His is the name.

2. Forsake, leave far behind all other works:
   Keep Christ's love-wealth in your heart.

3. Truth, grace and forgiveness all boundless:
   Jesus by His own blood delivers the sinners.

4. I say it again and again: He is the *[true]* Saint and Friend.
   It is the name of Jesus that takes me across.

   Chorus –
   That One Who gave up His own life,
   Sinners to redeem,
   O my soul, do not forget Him.

The familiar (though very free) version of the hymn is, of course, Joshua Marshman's:

1. O thou, my soul, forget no more
    The Friend Who all thy misery bore,
    Let every idol be forgot,
    But, O my soul, forget Him not!

2. Jesus for thee a body takes,
    Thy guilt assumes, thy fetters breaks,
    Discharging all thy dreadful debt;
    And canst thou e'er such love forget?

3. Renounce thy works and ways with grief,
    And fly to this most sure relief;
    Nor Him forget Who left His throne,
    And for thy life gave up His own.

4. Infinite Truth and mercy shine
    In Him, and He Himself is thine;
    And canst thou, then, with sin beset,
    Such charms, such matchless charms forget?

5. Ah no! – till life itself depart,
    His name shall cheer and warm my heart;
    And, lisping this, from earth I'll rise
    And join the chorus of the skies.

6. Ah no! – when all things else expire,
    And perish in the general fire,
    This name all others shall survive,
    And through eternity shall live.

18. The Increasing Purpose

The frowning providence was big with mercy. Had the seat of the Mission not been removed to Serampore, the professorship in the college, the English schools and the printing-press as means of large pecuniary help would not have been obtained. What threatened the extinction of the Mission was the very source of its prosperity: for this removal led to the appointment of my beloved colleague to the professorship in the college of Fort William, and this put him in possession, so far as it was necessary to his plans, of all the learning of India.

WARD to an Edinburgh friend, 10 May, 1820.

Never have men addressed themselves to the holy work of evangelisation in a purer spirit nor with more earnestness of purpose; and yet at the same time with sounder good practical sense and steadier perseverance in the adaptation of all legitimate means to the great end they set before them. They expected no miracles to be wrought on their behalf. They knew that much toil was necessary for even scanty success, and they never spared themselves. They gave up everything to the one object of their lives. Most thrifty in their own expenditure, casting everything into a common stock, they were glad, by any fitting labour, to realise this world's wealth, that they might devote it to the costly requirements of printing the Scriptures in the native tongues. They believed that only by sowing these broadcast, could the conversion of India on any great scale be accomplished.

SIR JOHN W. KAYE

Last Lord's Day a Sunday School was opened, superintended by Felix and William and John Fernandez. It will chiefly be confined to teaching catechisms in Bengali and English.

WARD'S *Journal*, July 1803, recording the first
Sunday School in India.

[228]

18. The Increasing Purpose
1803 – August 1806

I T WAS ONE of the happiest times of Carey's life when he woke to the missionary possibilities of his position in the college of Fort William. He was brought into close touch there with not only Bengal's most learned Europeans, but with many of India's ablest scholars of the various languages. Fifty of these received college appointments, a dozen serving under him. Of the many others who from time to time came seeking employment, Mrityunjay discovered the worthiest and introduced them to him.

Then it was borne in on Carey that through this array of multi-lingual Indian scholars he might develop and multiply his own powers massively, and translate the Word of God into all the chief languages of the land.

This was all the more plausible because Lord Wellesley, under the influence of Vice-Provost Buchanan, had even included in the Fort William College project the idea of a Bible translation department – an astonishing ideal, given the British Government's hostility to missions.

Carey's earliest ambition had been to give the Scriptures in increasingly accurate versions to Bengal. Soon he added the hope of producing a Hindi version. As far back as the winter of 1795, he declared that 'he would always be poor till the Bible was published in Bengali and in Ḥindustani,' by which he meant Hindi. As late as 1802 he wrote to Ryland hoping to accomplish both Testaments in both languages before his death. In other words, this had clearly been the extent of his dreams.

But now he heard the word – 'Thou shalt see greater things than these.' His Nottingham sermon came again to him. 'Enlarge thy tent. Stretch forth thy curtains. Lengthen thy cords. Expect greater things from God. Attempt greater things for God. Dare a bolder programme. Dwell in an ampler world. Launch out into the deep. God is able to do for and through you exceeding abundantly above all your past asking or thinking. Ask and you shall receive, that your joy may be full. Hitherto you have asked a mere nothing in My name. *Much* fruit the Husbandman designs from your branches. Aim to give God's Word to *India,* not simply to Bengal and to the nearer Hindustan.'

The idea rang through him until the vision was almost blinding. He who had traded with one talent, and was hoping at the best for two, seemed suddenly entrusted with ten.

Marshman soon felt and saw with Carey, and believed in his belief. He was swiftly of one will with him, and was resolved to share to the full his multiplying tasks. Ward, however, was at first cautious and critical. He said:

> I fear lest your strength may evaporate in schemes of translations into tongues you can never hope to master, and for peoples we can never hope to reach; whilst the good within our grasp and at our doors we may leave unaccomplished. In such a case we should leave the Mission at our deaths so unestablished in Bengal that it might come to nothing. On the other hand, if we root and ground it in Bengal, all these translation schemes of yours will in due time be undertaken by others, and be achieved more reliably; and their products will be distributed more directly. I warn you that Jesuit missionaries have made grammars, dictionaries and translations in abundance, which are now rotting in the libraries of Rome.

Such were the wounds and admonitions of this faithful friend. But soon he also realised the uniqueness of the presence of the many multilingual pundits in Calcutta, and the possibilities of their co-operation with Carey and with the whole Serampore team. He agreed with his colleagues that it was a providence which it would be sinful to neglect. Writing to an Edinburgh friend, he said:

> Learned men from every part have crowded to Calcutta, seeking employment in the new college; and the senior Sanskrit pundit in the college, who attends Carey constantly in the discharge of his college duties, informs him from time to time of the arrival of some learned Indian, now from Benares, then from Kashmir, and then from the Punjab. These are, of course, introduced to Carey, who sees all India thus coming to pour its treasures at his feet. Nor can he fail to recognise the hand, which thus brings him help from afar.

Once again, where three were gathered and agreed in that name, He was burningly in the midst.

Of course they knew it meant for each of them a fuller cup and deeper baptism of service and of sacrifice, especially for Carey who would need to become a thorough master of these many languages. To simply delegate the translation work to scholarly pundits without his own superintendence and revision would be out of the question. The task was supremely spiritual, demanding the direction of a trained and fervent Christian mind. He would need to supply the finer shades of meaning. The task, however, was not impossible, considering Carey's familiarity with Sanskrit, and its very magnitude was strangely inspiring.

Marshman, too, undertook to speed forward his own Sanskrit, and Ward set himself to get the various types prepared, which for most of the languages had never yet been made. He also would need a close familiarity with the languages to fit him to superintend the printing of the versions.

They blessed God for their earnings – the college salary, the profits from the boarding-schools, and the proceeds of the press – rejoicing that they were able to pay towards the engagement of pundits, and the printing of the Bible translations. Carey said that in the translation work it was impossible for them to expect too much from God and to attempt too much for Him.

They began this widened translation work with Hindi. Carey was at that time 'only a poor hand at it', as Ward said, although he had been able as early as 1796 'to converse in it and preach intelligibly'. Now he made Hindi his especial study, and, with Vidyanath's help he made by the end of 1803 the first draft of the Epistles – Marshman and Ward preparing themselves to render the Gospels.

At the same time he set himself to Marathi and Oriya – both Sanskritic languages. Orissa was India's most revered though idolatrous province, and Carey longed with great desire to put the Word of God into its hands. Marathi was Vidyanath's mother tongue, and he taught it to Carey both for college class work and for translation.

Having tested his potential pace of translation over many months Carey wrote to Fuller at the end of 1803:

> If we are given *another fifteen years,* we hope to translate and print the Bible in *all the chief languages of Hindustan.* We have fixed our eyes on this goal. The zeal of the Lord of hosts shall perform this.

At this moment, in England, the formation took place of the Bible Society, whose first communication with India crossed with the following letter of Carey to Fuller in 1804. He says:

> We are engaged in translating the Scriptures into Bengali, Hindustani *[ie: Hindi]*, Persian, Marathi and Oriya, and we intend to add more. Perhaps so many advantages for rendering the Bible into the Eastern tongues will never again meet in any one situation, viz:
>   1. The possibility of securing native scholars from all these countries;
>   2. A large printing establishment and letter foundry, capable of any expansion;
>   3. The best library of critical writings to be found in India;
>   4. An acquired habit of translation, and a disposition to do it.
> I am more in my element *[Carey added]* translating the Word of God than in any other employment.

They only asked of the home base £1,000 a year, to supplement their own resources.

Even they who knew Andrew Fuller best could little dream how this bold programme of widened biblical translation would kindle his imagination and intensify his passion and his power. He soon travelled 1,300 miles and raised £1,300 for this purpose.

Before the Serampore missionaries learned of Fuller's success, they were overjoyed when, at the end of 1804, they learned of the new-born Bible Society's appeal to Chaplains Brown and Buchanan to join with their Mission in promoting and securing Bible translation!

While undertaking this new translation work, Carey had also to revise that which he had done earlier. From his now closer familiarity with Bengali, and his association with Bengali scholars who were more frank and bold than his earlier helpers, he learned that his Bengali New Testament was much too 'English' in style and idiom, in both the use and order of its words. Indeed, after his second Mudnabati pundit's death at this time, he had reason to suspect that this man had often deliberately misled him in order to frustrate his work. From midsummer, 1803, he set himself to the total revision of his Bengali New Testament, leaving hardly a sentence unaltered, and (to Marshman's surprise) throwing whole pages aside. Yet that version cannot have been altogether bad, for Krishna Das, one of their ablest preachers, long preferred its wording to the later more accurate edition. Still, the revision marked an unmistakable advance.

Soon Carey decided that the surest path to his multilingual goal lay in translating the Scriptures straight into Sanskrit, the ancient and sacred language of Hindus, and parent of so many tongues, as Latin is of many European languages. To do this faithfully would be half-way to translating them into its Indian and Asian daughter tongues. All his pundits knew Sanskrit. If he could put a Sanskrit Bible into their hands, they could from this make first-draft translations into their own languages. By this approach he would catch many birds in one net. Moreover, this, as nothing else, would secure for the Bible an entrance into India's cultured circles, and people of recognised rank. He wrote:

> Sanskrit was the vehicle by which the learned shared their literary information; the depository of their records, and of all the science they possessed. It had, too, a sacred character, as the tongue in which were treasured the stories of their theology, the rites of their religion, the exploits of their gods. To translate the Scriptures thereinto would be to deposit them in the country's archives, and to secure for them a degree of reverence in the Indian people's eyes.

Carey felt he could produce such a version with the help of Mrityunjay, one of the greatest Sanskritists of the East – whom he often astonished. 'What kind of body has Carey Sahib?' Mrityunjay once asked Ward. 'I cannot understand him. He never seems hungry nor tired, and never leaves a thing till it's finished.'

Soon Ward, who had at first been cautious and critical, became a *leading* enthusiast. In his diary on 6 June, 1806, he writes:

I have urged Carey and Marshman to press forward the preparation of their Sanskrit New Testament, as a faithful translation into Sanskrit will render all the translations into the other Eastern tongues easy and certain. For all the Eastern pundits know the Sanskrit, and, making this the original, every true pundit will make therefrom a good translation into his own vernacular tongue. I have told them that, by translating the Scriptures into Sanskrit, they at once translate them into a host of the languages of Asia.

Events ultimately corroborated Carey's judgement. Once the Sanskrit citadel was taken and Scripture enthroned therein (after four years the New Testament, and a further ten the Old), the conquest of other languages was swift. And the Sanskrit version did give Truth the hoped for access to India's academic circles. One pundit, for example, on being presented with Carey's Sanskrit New Testament said, 'Had you offered me your sacred book in any modern tongue or vernacular I should have spurned it, as I should milk from a vessel of dog skin. But this I receive with delight.'

How Carey's pundits fared in their translations of his Sanskrit version into their vernaculars kept revealing to him its weak spots. Whenever more than one of them was obviously puzzled, Carey would suspect his Sanskrit rendering and promptly set himself to amend it. He was able to say in May 1810, that 'these passages were few'. 'The difficulty lay often,' he says, 'in the obscurity of the original Greek or Hebrew text.' Nevertheless, he greatly profited from this constant practical testing of his work.

Carey's diary shows how packed his days had to be for him to accomplish his objectives:

Thursday, 12 June, 1806, Calcutta:

5.45 – 7.00	Dressed. Read a chapter of Hebrew Bible. Devotions.
7.00 –10.00	Family worship in Bengali and with servants. Read Persian with *mûnshi [language teacher]*. Revised Scripture proof in Hindustani. Breakfast. Translated portion of the *Ramayana* from Sanskrit into English, with help of Sanskrit pundit.
10.00 – 1.30	Government college classes.
1.30 – 2.00	Dinner.
2.00 – 6.00	Revised proof of a *Jeremiah* chapter in Bengali. Translated most of *Matthew 8* into Sanskrit with Mrityunjay's help.

6.00 – 7.00	Tea. Read Telugu with a pundit. A son of the Rev Timothy Thomas of London called.
7.00 – 9.00	Prepared and preached an English sermon. About 40 present including Judge Harington, who afterwards responded to my plea and gave £63 10s towards our Calcutta Chapel building fund.
9.00 –11.00	Translated *Ezekiel 11* into Bengali. Have cast aside my first edition translation. Letter to Ryland. Read a Greek Testament chapter. Commended self to God.

I have never more time in a day than this.

We should note that he was studying two such opposite tongues as Telugu and Persian, the latter of most difficult script. Towards its acquirement he had been greatly stimulated and aided by a precious gift from Judge Colebrooke – the manuscripts of his own recent Persian translation of the Gospels and of *Genesis*. No wonder he wrote thus to his sisters:

> I shall never more see either of you on earth, and, considering the work before me here, and the loud calls on my powers, had I a thousand bodies strong as this, I dare not entertain a thought of seeing England. I do not know, indeed, how I could bear an English winter.

The Calcutta Chapel referred to in this diary entry was to be built in Lall Bazar, where sailors of a dozen races jostled. Some said that this was rightly pronounced *Loll* Bazar, because so many lolled about in its drink dens and brothels. On both sides of their site there were brothels. It was also known as Flag Street, each cheap liquor shop sporting its own flag. Nothing could have been more missionary-minded than to set the chapel there.

They began with a bamboo and mat preaching place, into whose friendly openness both Hindus and Mohammedans flocked. 'Multitudes used to hang upon our lips,' Ward said, 'and stand in the thick-wedged crowd for hours together in the heat.'

Though the multilingual translation and publication of the Scriptures was Serampore's main objective, they aimed at even more. Taking Paul as their pattern they sought to establish strategic bases for the Gospel in the far-flung cities of 'Rome's empire', and so to possess India for Christ. The south they left in the care of Danish and Dutch missionaries, together with the London Missionary Society. To the untouched remainder they gave their thought, mapping out mission

View of the Lall Bazaar (Calcutta), by J. B. Fraser, 1919, courtesy of The Oriental & India Office Library, London

stations some two hundred miles apart, to be operated jointly by a missionary and an Indian pastor or evangelist, so long as English reinforcements should arrive and their Indian colleagues be ready. Such reinforcements from home they confidently looked for in response to their recent successes and their earnest appeals. America also might send help, seeing that several of her Baptist churches were in close touch with Serampore.

They had sound hope of raising a succession of Indian pastors, for scarcely a month now passed without baptisms, often of men possessing considerable gifts. Krishna Prasad, for example, was preaching in Calcutta with power, to the dismay of Brahmins who had known him as a devoted idolater. Phatik Chandra, though expelled from his village with his eyes, ears, nose and mouth stuffed with mud, and cursed, proved a fearless evangelist. Krishna Pal and grand old Pitambar Singh had already been ordained as preachers.

Ordination seemed too soon in Krishna's case, for within six months the promotion made him heady again, and he and all his household grew rebellious and difficult. For three months he was sullen, and his womenfolk for six. 'The Mission is in deep waters,' wrote Ward. 'These things,' cried Marshman, 'rend the soul.' Those who had been their pride and joy now seemed like Jude's trees – without fruit, twice dead, plucked up by the roots. But at length they all returned in lowly contrition, and with one exception (Bhairab), went on to lasting faithfulness.

Even Mohan, Krishna's wicked son-in-law and Golok's legal husband, saw at length the glorious light of the Gospel and humbled himself, repenting of his stubborn idolatry, and seeking baptism. He went on to learn carpentry from Krishna and continued faithful, but for a few speedily-repented-of lapses, until his death.

One midnight Krishna was thought to be dying. The Mission was aroused, and Ward and others ran to his relief, thinking, 'Satan will be happy, if now we lose Krishna.' But the gladness was theirs, for he lived and did great exploits. After all, they had no fear of lacking such Indian evangelists for their programme of strategic advance.

As for the cost of their extension plan, they hoped to be able to bear each station's initial outlay themselves, and after that Carey depended on the policy of partial employment in a profession or trade, by the regional missionaries, as the means of supporting their work. He therefore begged the home base to send them only such people as, alongside clear spiritual fitness, 'could make paper or glass, print cloth or dye chintz, teach drawing or music, be apothecaries or surgeons, etc.'

The attitude that was in the Serampore missionaries is seen in their covenant, dating from these days, which was read three times a year in each station:

1. To set an infinite value on men's souls.
2. To acquaint ourselves with the snares which hold the minds of the people.
3. To abstain from whatever deepens India's prejudice against the Gospel.
4. To watch for every chance of doing the people good.
5. To preach 'Christ crucified' as the grand means of conversions.
6. To esteem and treat Indians always as our equals.
7. To guard and build up 'the hosts that may be gathered'.
8. To cultivate their spiritual gifts, ever pressing upon them their missionary obligation – since Indians only can win India for Christ.
9. To labour unceasingly in biblical translation.
10. To be instant in the nurture of personal religion.
11. To give ourselves without reserve to the cause, 'not counting even the clothes we wear our own'.

Let us often look at Brainerd [they say] in the woods of America, pouring out his very soul before God for the people. Prayer, secret, fervent, expectant, lies at the root of all personal godliness. A competent knowledge of the languages current where a missionary lives, a mild and winning temper, and a heart given up to God – these are the attainments, which, more than all other gifts, will fit us to become God's instruments in the great work of human redemption.

Prior to this time, in line with most of their home churches, and in keeping with Fuller's insistence, they had kept the bounds of their Lord's Table communion 'strict', though they found this an embarrassment when honoured non-Baptist sea captains and Congregational and Anglican comrades had to be 'fenced' from their Table.

Now, under Ward's especial entreaty, they resolved to admit *all* who were truly dedicated Christian believers to the Lord's Supper.

We could not doubt [wrote Ward] that Watts, Edwards, Brainerd, Doddridge, and Whitefield, although not Baptists, had been welcomed to His Table by our Lord. On what grounds could we exclude such? Rather than engage in a furious controversy about baptism to the gratification of Satan, whilst the people perish, we rejoice to shake off this apparent moroseness that has made us unlovely to our fellow Christians.

I am more than ever anxious to know no man after his sect, as an Independent, Episcopalian, Presbyterian, Methodist or Baptist. Everyone who wears the image of Christ, and brings beauty and fertility into the spiritual desert around him, is my 'brother and sister and mother'. Let us conscientiously profess our own convictions; but let us love the man of our own sect but little, who possesses little of the image of Christ; whilst we love him exceedingly, in whom we see much of Christ, though some of his opinions are contrary to our own. So shall we know we are passed from death unto life, and sectarian quarrels will cease.

Abnormal and distressing experiences, however, drove them, a few years later, to bend back from this course.

At this point in their labours the missionaries found their longing for expansion widened to an undreamed-of degree. The Government Chaplain, Vice-Provost Buchanan, long a friend of the Mission, and also long concerned for China, now offered them, from funds he controlled, £600, if they would send two scouts overland to China to test the possibility of planting a mission there, and to make the acquaintance of the peoples *en route*. They eagerly accepted the challenge, and Felix was the first volunteer. But before he could leave, a stranger's arrival recast the whole scheme, and in the person of Johannes Lassar China reached Serampore instead of Serampore seeking China.

Johannes Lassar was the son of rich Armenians of Macao, opposite Hong Kong. Proving apt at the Chinese language he had been sent in his teens to Canton for thorough training in both Mandarin and Cantonese. After seven years of this discipline he became a Portuguese commercial correspondent with official Peking until at twenty-four he went tea-trading to Calcutta, a venture which failed and left him with nothing. Learning of Chaplain Buchanan's interest in China he made his acquaintance, and when he revealed that he was able to speak, read, and write with equal freedom Armenian, Portuguese, and Chinese, he was warmly welcomed and offered an excellent salary to remain and to render the Armenian Bible into Chinese. He sprang to the task. Chaplain Buchanan soon transferred him to work with the missionaries at

Serampore, where he was hailed with great delight. Still vaster things than their recently conceived hopes seemed to be emerging.

The presence of Lassar, as China's 'representative' in their very compound at Serampore seemed an opportunity too golden to be missed. If one or two of their sons could thoroughly acquire through him the Chinese language, they might grow so familiar with its literature and speech by the time he had translated the Scriptures as to be fitted to enter China as Christ's prepared pioneers. Equipped with the Chinese Bible, they might spend their lives there in Christ's name. This was the hope which now allured them.

We might have expected Felix to be Carey's selected son for this undertaking, since he had so instantly volunteered. But judging Jabez (bilingual from infancy, and not yet in his teens) likely to absorb this hard language more surely, Carey laid the burden upon him, and Marshman also designated John, his gifted first-born. Then Marshman himself made a typical sacrifice in humility and commitment. Adding to his work-load he joined the Chinese class himself, unashamed to be a pupil with his own lad and with Jabez, partly in sheer avarice for knowledge, but chiefly in the hope that he might have so learned to collaborate with Lassar as to make some contribution to the translation's worthiness and truth. Nor was this just a passing enthusiasm, but the new passion of his life. He grew in time to be an accepted European authority on Chinese language and literature, and became an editor of *Confucius*. He published his own Chinese grammar in 1814, and in 1815 superintended Serampore's printing of Robert Morrison's grammar, nor did he rest until the whole Bible was complete and issued in Chinese (the product of fourteen years of labour). His lad Benjamin would sit with him and with his brother in the little class, and Marshman writes: 'You may laugh at a child of six becoming a Chinese pupil, but in memory he keeps pace with me, and in pronunciation goes beyond me. Lassar insists that he will make a Chinese scholar. He teaches his sister the characters in play.' As long as Chaplain Buchanan remained in India, he encouraged the boys with gold medals and Indian gold coins according to their achievements.

Commenting on the manner in which the Mission approached their projected expansion, Marshman wrote:

> We imitate an experienced general, who, unable to take an important position by storm, retires a short distance, erects a fort, where he

disciplines his forces, takes measures for new levies, and holds all in readiness for assault at the first fair chance.

Encouraging local developments intensified their longing to give to the East the soul-quickening Scriptures. Ward had in 1801 chanced to leave Carey's Bengali New Testament in Ram Krishnapur (in what is now Howrah). A certain Krishna Das read it, and kept rereading it to his neighbours, till the village was transformed. After three years they sent three men to seek and thank its publishers. These were Jagannath Das, who had long since smashed his idols, Sebak Ram, former ring-leader of lewd songs, and fisherman Gobardhan. Serampore was transported with joy, and before the three at length went home they were baptised. Next month Krishna Das came himself, with his wife and the wives of two others seeking baptism. On their baptism morn-ing Carey also led through the waters Krishna Pal's Anandamayi, and Chandramoni – a girl snatched from a procuress – and also three printers from Ward's press. (The latter had been converted from fierce hostility to the Gospel.) Through this service two of their Brahmin believers (Krishna Prasad and Ram Mohan) renounced their *paitas*. 'How much better,' writes Ward, 'is love and illumination than force! Had we compelled them to discard these, they would have been attached to them for life.'

It cost Krishna Das himself much courage to remain faithful in Ram Krishnapur. The Hindus gnashed upon him with their teeth, and did him every violence and wrong, even jailing him for a debt he had already paid. He preached very tenderly to his fellow prisoners the Word of Life.

There was much talk in Serampore at the end of 1805 of sending to England with John Fernandez (the son of Ignatius) Ram Mohan, who had become a skilled preacher. Carey consistently opposed it as unwise, but Ward was very keen. For years at home Ward had been in the newspaper world, and had still something in him of the journalist's instinct and outlook. He writes to Fuller:

There will never have been a sight like this in England since the world began – a converted Brahmin! The missions on the south coasts have been established, I suppose, for a century, and they have many thous-ands of converts, but they have not been able to baptise a single Brahmin! The sight of Ram Mohan may stop the mouths of infidels and of cold Calvinists. It will electrify whole congregations. Let John

Fernandez and Ram Mohan sing a Bengali hymn after a sermon on behalf of the Mission, and in every place you will be laden with gifts and contributions! Take them with you on a missionary tour through Scotland! Don't make a show of them, but don't be afraid of showing them.

But through the colour-prejudice of the ship's captain the arrangements broke down in Calcutta. So the experiment was never tried.

During this same season of blessing Jessore, too, showed how Christ could use the least literate once His power was in their hearts. Early in 1803 a Jessore peasant named Sita Ram heard of the Mission at Serampore, tramped seventy miles to get there, and was welcomed, instructed, converted and baptised. On his return he spoke so continuously of the Gospel that in two years, though he could neither read nor write, he led into the faith, and either brought or sent to Serampore for baptism, a whole group of people, including a Moslem, a Hindu of the writers' caste, this Hindu's nephew, a Hindu widow, a field-labourer, his own sister, and others. The Mission itself had the joy of leading into Christ's peace an old priests' slave named Raghu Nath, who six times had swung on the flesh-hooks. And early in 1806 they baptised the first two Indian disciples from Carey's seed-plot in the north. The missionaries wrote to England:

> We only want men and money to fill this country with the knowledge of Christ. We are neither working at uncertainty, nor afraid for the result. We have tried our weapons, and have proved their power. The Cross is mightier than the caste. We shall be more than conquerors.

Missionaries from other societies often received from them their first guidance and training. They sometimes remained for weeks. Carey, for example, initiated Dr John Taylor into Marathi and Sanskrit, in exchange for which the physician gave many hours of medical training to Felix. Of all such welcomed associates none won their hearts like Henry Martyn (appointed to a military chaplaincy in India), who owed his missionary aims to Charles Simeon's frequent talk of Carey's Indian labours. On arriving in Calcutta he quickly met his hero, and soon was dwelling near Serampore at Aldeen, in a dismantled Hindu shrine which Chaplain Brown had had transformed to serve as his junior's lodging and study. It was picturesque then, beneath its peepul-tree. Martyn gloried in filling the deserted shrine with Christian intercession. 'The echoes of my prayers,' he said, 'resound from its vaulted roof. May I learn so to pray that they may resound from very Heaven!'

After tea at Serampore on his first Friday (with, to his surprise, 150 at the tables), Henry Martyn joined their usual weekly conference, the theme being 'the relation of Christ's death to the salvation of sinners'. The Brahmin converts he met there seemed 'a miracle as convincing as the resurrection of Christ'. Two days later Carey heard with delight his first Calcutta sermon – 'very honest, evangelical and bold' – and wrote: 'As the shadow of bigotry never falls upon us here, we take sweet counsel and go together to God's house as friends.'

Marshman and Martyn became close companions, and would walk by the Hooghly for hours, arm in arm. The latter wrote to Simeon, 'Three such men as Carey, Marshman, and Ward, so suited to one another and their work, are not to be found, I think, in the whole world.'

Henry Martyn was very struck by the grandeur of Carey's proposal of decennial world mission conferences at the Cape, which Carey had already urged on Fuller, proposing the first for 1810. 'We should understand one another better in two hours than by two years of letters.' But Fuller had replied:

> I admire Carey's proposal, though I cannot say I approve. It shows an enlarged mind, and I have heard say that great men dream differently from others! This is one of Carey's pleasing dreams! But, seriously, I see no important object to be attained by such a meeting, which might not quite as well be reached without. And in the gathering of all denominations there would be no unity, without which we had better stay at home.

In August of 1806, Serampore sent home their most challenging message yet, revealing to the British churches their own wider aims and their plan of campaign, and pleading for a proportionate increase of money and of men.

They pointed out that their base in Bengal was providentially central for all Asia, Orissa, Kurnata and Mahratta lying to the south and south-west, Hindustan, Nepal, Bhutan, and Tibet to the north-west and north, Assam, Burma, China, and the Malay Isles to the north-east and east. China was only 600 miles from Serampore. Could they reach a certain river only 60 miles from Assam, they could be conveyed into Yonan. Had they been deaf (they said) to the cries of men's souls, they could hardly be unconcerned about this vast Chinese Empire with its three hundred millions. But God had opened to them the door of its speech in a way as unexpected as it promised to be effective. Six months of patient and diligent improvement of the language had convinced them that neither its speaking nor writing were beyond their attainment. They hoped to publish the Scriptures in Chinese – indeed it was daily proceeding apace.

As far as Indian languages were concerned, the missionaries were able to report that the New Testament was already translated into Oriya, and the New Testament with a large part of the Old into Marathi. The Gospels were printed in Hindi, and the *Psalms* and *Isaiah* were in the press. They had good hope also of the work of Bhutia, Nepalese, and Assamese pundit-scholars. A Burmese Gospel would probably be ready as soon as their earliest recruit from England could arrive. Six lads were in their school who could speak Malay with the utmost fluency, bringing their mastery of this language within the sphere of the possible. They meant to speed translations into all these tongues with their whole strength. It surely could not be that God meant His translated Word to be food for worms, instead of seed to be disseminated. True, some of these lands were as yet sealed. But

Lall Bazar Chapel, Bow Bazar, Calcutta, as it was opened in 1807

courageous and wise efforts might throw them open. It was not God's way to remove obstructions till His hour of challenge arrived. The Red Sea was not divided a month before Israel needed to cross. They proposed to make Serampore not just the translation centre, but the language school for Asia, from where their trainees should go forth into the many lands already acquainted with their speech, furnished with their printed Scriptures, trained in proven missionary methods, and linked together in an inspiring missionary fellowship. There was nothing, they said, wild or fanciful in all this, nor would they be building on other's foundations. They asked for *forty new missionaries* to enter these vast lands; nor could they believe the demand preposterous from *four hundred churches.*

> We are debtors *[they pleaded]* both to the Greeks and the barbarians. Woe is ours, if we preach not the Gospel. To him that knoweth to do good and doeth it not, to him it is sin. We must work the works of Him that sent us. Whatsoever our hands find to do, must be done with our might. Not to have the heart to improve the prize of a God-given opportunity is to deserve the epithet of fool.

19. The Foiled Opposition

I find myself here in a sphere so vast that I cry out with unfeigned astonishment, 'Who is sufficient for these things?' I am somewhat dispirited at finding myself at a stand; not knowing what course to take to acquire the language of the people – for the fine language of my Mussulman *mûnshi [Indian clerk]* is as unintelligible as English to the country people, and I have very limited opportunities of being much with them. I cannot be absent a night from this station without permission from the commander-in-chief. However, these are small difficulties. Our great obstacle is the dominion which Satan has obtained over the hearts of men. Yet through the support and power of God, I think I am willing to continue throwing in the net at the Lord's command through all the long night of life, though the end may be that I have caught nothing.

Wishing you all success in the common cause and much divine consolation in your own soul, I conclude by saying that I am,

Your affectionate though unworthy fellow labourer in the Gospel,

HENRY MARTYN

Letter to Rev J. Chamberlain, Katwa, from Dinajpur,
6 December, 1806.

The brethren in Serampore are men to be wondered at: I speak of Carey, Marshman and Ward; or, if you will, Peter, James and John. The former is most remarkable for his humility; he is a very superior man, and appears to know nothing about it. The great man and the little child unite in him, and, as far as I can see, he has attained to the happy art of ruling and overruling in connection with the others mentioned, without his asserting his authority, or others feeling their subjection; and all is done without the least appearance of design on his part.

E. PRITCHETT, Missionary to Burma, to a London friend,
12 August, 1811.

I have long made the language of *Psalm 51* my own. 'Have mercy upon me, O God: according unto the multitude of thy tender mercies blot out my transgressions.' Should you outlive me, and have any influence to prevent it, I earnestly request that no epithets of praise may ever accompany my name, such as 'the faithful servant of God', etc. All such expressions would convey a falsehood. To me belong shame and confusion of face. I can only say, 'Hangs my helpless soul on Thee'.

WILLIAM CAREY to John Ryland, 30 January, 1823.

Krishna labours at Calcutta with great success. He is a steady, zealous, well-informed, and, I may add, eloquent minister of the Gospel. He preaches on an average twelve or fourteen times every week in Calcutta or its environs.

CAREY, September 1811.

Krishna Pal's work schedule while posted to Calcutta:

Lord's Day – at eight o'clock I preach at the Chapel and again at four in the afternoon.

Monday – at four in the afternoon I preach in the jail and at seven at Mr Pogose Petruse's.

Tuesday – I preach at nine o'clock in the morning at Mr Gilbert's, in the afternoon at Mr Humphrey's, and at six in the evening at the Chapel.

Wednesday – at nine in the morning I preach at Mr Charles Pigot's, at four in the afternoon at the Chapel, and at six in the evening at Mr Thompson's.

Thursday – in the morning I preach at Mr Leonard's (the charity school) and at seven in the evening we have a prayer-meeting at the Chapel.

Friday – at four o'clock in the afternoon I preach at Mr Jefferson's and at seven in the evening at Mr Thomas Kramer's.

Periodical Accounts, Vol IV, 1811.

19. The Foiled Opposition
26 August, 1806–1812

INTO THE MIDST of the Mission's redoubled efforts for expansion fell an unexpected and devastating bombshell. The might of the Government was turned absolutely against them. The ear of the Acting Governor-General, Sir George Barlow, was caught by both the European and Indian foes of Christian missions, who unjustly but plausibly attributed the recent mutiny in Vellore, which had involved the British garrison in such tragedy, and then the sepoys in dire retribution, to Indian resentment at missionary activities.

The arrival from Britain of two fresh missionaries for Serampore precipitated action. Captain Wickes was refused his clearance, and James Chater and William Robinson were given unchallengeable orders to return. Carey was summoned on 26 August, 1806, before the Supreme Court, and, in the Governor's name was instructed to see that – 'the Mission preached no more to the native people, nor distributed pamphlets, nor sent out native preachers.' 'The Government,' they said, 'did not interfere with the prejudices of the people, and neither should Mr Carey nor his colleagues.'

Refraining from any promise or undertaking Carey withdrew, but with a very disturbed spirit. His projects seemed broken like eggshells.

All the anxieties of the last thirteen years returned to haunt him. Was this the alarm-bell of war between the British Government and Christ's little Serampore flock? As senior shepherd, *he* must confront its chief onset. He trembled to think what wisdom and courage he would need.

His news reached his colleagues that midnight. They roused Henry Martyn, and together laid their distress before God. Martyn consoled them with the assurance that influential mediation on the morrow would re-establish their freedom, especially as Mr Udny was now second in rank in the Council.

But the Government authorities were resolved and determined, although they were forced to admit that no complaint had ever been lodged against the missionaries. They would allow Serampore to print and publish the Scriptures, and to preach within their own precincts or in any private home, but not again in the open, and certainly not in Lall Bazar without express leave from the London Court of Directors. Their Indian converts might preach, should they wish, but they must no longer be sent out by the Mission. 'At one stroke,' said Marshman, 'we are become dead as respects spreading the Gospel.' And Carey wrote to England:

> We are all of us prisoners at Serampore, and you have sent us two new brethren to keep us company. We are in much the same situation as the apostles when commanded not to teach nor preach any more in the name. The opening doors for usefulness, which a few days ago engaged our attention and animated our exertions, are closed by this cruel message. The shutting of Lall Bazar is a very cutting thing.

Except for Denmark's protection they would have been 'swallowed up quick'. 'Our enemies,' they said, 'want to shut us out, but God had shut us in.' Danish Governor Krefting reminded Sir George that the Mission was under his sovereign's specific patronage. But all their contemplated wider British-Indian campaign was brought to a sudden halt.

Carey refrained from counselling defiance of the hostile Government.

> To act in open defiance of the Governor-General [*he said*] might occasion a positive *law* against evangelising the native peoples, and at once break up the Mission, which has been settled at so great expense. On the other hand, if we yield a little to the present storm, it may blow over,

The Government House in Calcutta by Frederick Fiebig, c1845, courtesy of The Oriental & India Office Library, London

and we may not only enjoy our present privileges but obtain the liberty we have so long wished for.

It dawned on Carey in mid-September that being barred from *Indian* advance 'might be their fit opportunity to make trial of *Burma*'. They had turned their thoughts there before, but 'the impassable forests, which separated it from Bengal had seemed to put it beyond their reach.' Now, perhaps, was God's hour for making an attempt to enter Burma. As Marshman said, 'their way north, south, and west suffering obstruction, like Paul's to Bithynia, was, perhaps, the divine signal for their moving east.' Indeed, they realised that a campaign into Burma could eventually lead them into China. They set apart an extra Friday evening hour for prayer.

Meanwhile, two newly arrived official British chaplains, Daniel Corrie and Joseph Parson, brought them joy, 'their hearts beating in unison with Serampore's own', men who, as Smith says, 'made the words *chaplain* and *missionary* synonymous'. They and Henry Martyn were soon appointed to districts, which the Serampore Baptists had hoped to serve. The Mission was in a measure reconciled to the restrictions laid on them by the Government, while such Gospel-preaching chaplains could function. Before the chaplains left, they warmed one another's hearts in Martyn's 'temple'. 'The divine presence,' writes Corrie, 'filled us with joy. But, oh, my dullness in comparison with these burning ones!' The Mission was able to furnish Martyn with their newly-issued Hindi Gospels, thankful that, though they were shut out of the north-west provinces, this fervent chaplain would scatter the good seed.

They were also thankful for their courageous Indian converts, who persevered in their preaching, even though they were no longer commissioned by Serampore. Krishna Pal and Jagannath Das ventured into Burdwan with, as Ward put it, 'the spirit of martyrs'. The brethren could endure to be silenced so long as men like these openly preached. Indeed their speech was often more compelling than their own – as Ward felt when listening to a gifted young evangelist in Hindi. 'Oh, I saw that the Gospel was as sweet in this as in any other tongue! At his aptness and tenderness I could scarcely hold back tears.'

The Mission was saddest over the closed preaching place in Lall Bazar, to which so many had been flocking. But Aratoon Petruse, an Armenian whose wife had been converted to Christ through the

Mission, enlarged his own Chitpore Road house (in a densely popu-
lated area) for their preaching, and Robert Griffe lent his school for the
same purpose.

Through more than two months the Government refused Captain
Wickes his clearance, till at length Chaplain Brown's intercession prevailed and the Mission gathered late that 4 November in the hall and
sang Watts' version of *Psalm 40* –

> *The wonders, Lord, Thy love has wrought,*
> *Exceed our praise, surmount our thought:*
> *Should I attempt the long detail,*
> *My speech would faint, my numbers fail.*

Nevertheless, the injunction against new missionaries Chater and
Robinson remained in force. The Mission therefore decided to send
Chater to Burma, outside the area of British administration, while
Robinson would, for the time being, 'lie low'.

The Serampore Mission became amazingly multilingual in these
months of repression. On the very day of Chater's sailing for Rangoon,
a well-travelled Burmese man, familiar with Hindi, offered them his
services, and he was engaged to translate their Hindi Gospels into Burmese. Chinese craftsmen also lodged there to teach Bengalis to cut
wood-blocks for the Chinese Gospels. Even a Hebron-born Jew stayed
with them, equally fluent in Arabic, Hebrew, and Syriac. 'They showed
him peculiar courtesy, to incline him to the Gospel.' Carey could tell
Ryland that:

> There were written, spoken, or read amongst them Lat., Gk., Heb., Ara-
> bic, Syr., Sansk., Pers., Beng., Hindi, Oriya, Gujarati, Telugu, Marathi,
> Armenian, Portug., Chinese, and Burmese.

He himself, the most diverse linguist of all, had well earned the doc-
torate which Brown University, Providence, USA, conferred upon him
in 1807.

To counter the prohibition of public preaching in Lall Bazar, the
Mission began to build there its long-planned Union Chapel. Again
the Government threatened a ban, but surrendered to the petition of
more than a hundred city men, who, at Marshman's urging, took their
stand in its defence. 'Our hearts leapt for joy,' cried Ward. 'His mercy
endureth for ever.' 'The archers shot at them to grieve them,' said
Fuller, 'but their own bow abode in strength.'

While the officials in Calcutta were suspicious and unfriendly, Bombay's new (and first) Recorder, Sir James Mackintosh, a friend of Robert Hall, took a quite opposite course, even inviting Carey to plant a mission there. Carey recommended Dr Taylor of Surat, who was soon breakfasting daily with Sir James, and teaching him Sanskrit. In no time he sent home for a press, Persian type, and more colleagues. Sir James became the rallying centre of the 'Western progressives'.

So cheering was Chater's report of his Rangoon survey (when he appeared unexpectedly among his colleagues one May evening of 1807), that they prepared all that summer for a larger Burma undertaking. They even considered transferring the entire Mission there. But before Chater could return with his chosen companion, a second bombshell struck Serampore.

The European and Indian foes of the Mission seized on the arrival of a new Governor-General to exploit his inexperience and excite his anxieties. They described the Mission to Lord Minto, within seven weeks of his landing, as a most dangerous source of racial disharmony. The public peace would be threatened, they claimed, particularly among Moslems, until its publications were totally suppressed. By way of proof they produced a Persian pamphlet printed at Serampore in which Mohammed was described as an impostor and a tyrant. To let such seed be scattered was simply asking, they said, for trouble.

Carey was summoned to the Chief Secretary's office. He had never heard of the obnoxious tract. On inquiry he found that Ward had translated into Bengali extracts of Sale's dissertation on Mohammed, but a Moslem convert who had been commissioned to translate this into Persian had himself inserted the offensive terms. Unfortunately this had escaped Ward's notice during its passage through the press.

Serampore withdrew the tract, sent Ward's original manuscript to the Governor-General, and confessed the regrettable mishap to both the Danish and British Governments. Yet on Friday, 11 September, 1807, Carey received a fresh injunction from the British authorities, demanding the immediate transfer of the Mission press to Calcutta, and the termination of all attempts to convert the Bengalis, and also of all services, even those in the house of Aratoon Petruse.

Serampore used to look forward to Friday evenings and Carey's return with the week's news of the city. This night he was much later than usual. At his shock news they were deeply dejected, more than they had ever been. They feared that Carey might even lose his college professorships. It was a sinister inauguration of a Governor-General's reign.

'We are a few poor sheep, despised of every one,' wrote Mrs Marshman. They agreed to meet for prayer at earliest dawn. The long night's thoughts brought little comfort to Carey. In the morning prayer session 'he wept,' says Ward, 'like a child,' knowing, as Marshman put it, that 'the press, if removed to Calcutta, would not be safe a single day. So long as it remained in Serampore, many redoubts [*defensive outworks by way of political complications*] had to be surmounted before it could be touched, giving time for investigation. But in Calcutta it would only be for some *mûnshi* to fancy something offensive in a publication, and get the ear of a Government officer, and the press might be seized, and its printers deported.'

They urged Carey to send a delaying answer to the Government, and to request an interview with Danish Governor Krefting, with a view to securing an audience with Lord Minto. But the next day's news was even worse.

All preaching was forbidden in Calcutta, except by the East India Company's own chaplains. Rumour ran through the district, to their critics' glee, that the Government intended to expel the missionaries from the country. Even the men of the Fort William garrison joined in the hue and cry with the catch-phrase, 'Ten pounds for catching the Methodists!'

'Had some rajah or *nabob [prince or official]* forbidden our preaching, we should not have wondered,' wrote Hannah Marshman, 'but that those who should be our nursing-fathers should do this is most strange!'

'Yet in a few days,' wrote Ward, 'will be the Durga Puja, and all Calcutta will be in motion. Business will be stopped at the public offices. Idol processions will parade the streets, and crowds of Europeans will go to the homes of rich Indians to watch the idolatrous dances!' Carey mourned that at such a time 'the Gospel was bidden to sneak into a corner like a thief.'

> Many [*said Carey*] would rejoice to see us expelled. We have no security but in God. The experience of Abram, who was alone when called, supports me. I have for many months had my mind drawn to *Isaiah 40. 27-28*: 'He fainteth not, neither is weary, etc.'

I have no doubt but our troubles will tend to the furtherance of the Gospel; but to what extent they may be carried, it is impossible to say. We mean to inform Lord Minto that *we are prepared to suffer in this cause, rather than abandon our work*; but we hope to do all in the most respectful manner possible. Such a letter was never written by a Christian government before. Roman Catholics have persecuted other Christians as heretics; but since the days of heathen Rome, no Christian government, however corrupt, has, so far as I know, prohibited attempts to spread Christianity amongst the heathen. We are all in mourning. I do not know that anything ever so affected me. My mind is full of tumultuous cogitations. I trust Jehovah will appear for us.

And wondrously He did appear. Carey was granted an interview with Governor Krefting, and then Marshman and he (by the intercession of Dr Leyden, a linguist) were given an audience with Lord Minto.

Dr Leyden shrewdly advised them to present to his Lordship what of the *Ramayana* they had translated and printed. Considering the gravity of the whole crisis for Serampore, and their inevitable apprehension, it is interesting to note from Ward's diary that they still retained a sense of humour.

Carey and Marshman having settled their plans, and Marshman having borrowed a coat of Mr James Rolt, a Calcutta architect-friend of the Mission, they set off to wait on Lord Minto. A friend of Dr Leyden had undertaken to introduce them. It was lucky for them that an attendant required them to leave their hats in a passage, or Carey would most likely have stuck his under his left armpit, and Marshman would have squeezed his into the size of a black pocket handkerchief – for they were carrying the *Ramayana* and other Serampore volumes. Making, no doubt, therefore, very awkward bows, they entered into the presence of India's Governor-General, and offered to him the books, and the first sheet of Marshman's Chinese New Testament.

They then told him that they wished to present to him a private memorial. His Lordship blushed, and said he would be happy to receive it. They then *[Lord Minto having bidden them be seated, as we learn from a letter of Carey's]* entered into a long conversation with him, and he asked a number of questions, and declared that he entertained no hostility towards them or their work; that he thought the conversion of the Indian people in a peaceable way desirable, though he felt the danger of provoking the Mohammedans; and that he had heard of their work from Lord Spencer. He said that it was expected that missionaries should be more enthusiastic than others, and should also be able to bear sometimes the frown of those in power. In such conversation twenty minutes passed. He added that they might depend upon his reading their memorial, and, although it could not be brought into the business of Government, he promised that he would show it to his colleagues.

In the memorial which they left with him they told of the hundred Indians – both Moslem and Hindu – whom they had already baptised, who had come to them from near and far *seeking* Christian instruction. They mentioned that among them twelve had been Brahmins, sixteen of the writer caste, and that at their public baptism there had never been any suggestion of disquiet. They proved to him that the enforced removal of their press to Calcutta, what with high city rents and wages, would load the Mission with an impossible expense. They declared that in the last resort they would elect to suffer rather than betray their trust. All this deeply impressed him. Danish Governor Krefting, too, challenged the British Government's right to order the transfer of the Mission press to Calcutta (indeed, with great courage, he forbade its removal). Lord Minto discerned that he had been ill-advised. Within a month he and his Government climbed down and a large part of their orders were revoked. Carey could write to Andrew Fuller on 14 October, 1806:

> I rejoice to inform you that the storm is gone over. The Governor of Serampore has received a letter from our Government revoking their Order concerning our press, and only requiring to be apprised of what we print. A similar letter has been sent to me. We had little expectation of this formal revocation, though we hoped it might not be enforced. The crests of our challengers have much fallen. Our dispersal of pamphlets in the Company's dominions is now recognised in these letters of revocation, and, as we wish to avoid everything inflammatory, I have no doubt we shall be permitted to print nearly all we desire. I believe the obstacles which yet remain will gradually be removed. There are, however, many in this country who would rejoice to see Christianity wholly expelled, and particularly any embarrassment thrown in our way. But our confidence is in God. I preached this (Tuesday) evening from *Isaiah 59.1-3*, 'Is My Hand shortened, etc?'

At their next Sunday's thanksgiving they were 'like them that dreamed', their mouths filled with laughter, at their captivity so turned. To crown their gladness, Carey's son William (now twenty-one) preached to the Mission family for the first time, and with fluency of Bengali which surprised them all.

By the next month they heard that their Malda friend William Grant had left them Rs 30,000 for their translation work, and they heard in his great legacy their Lord's 'I am with you!'

Of all the mountain lands behind Bengal, Bhutan was most deeply engraved on Carey's heart. He could never forget his early visits to its border country, and yearned to possess it for Christ. The Company's territories being still closed to them, it seemed an ideal time to enter Bhutan. With Robinson's Bengali exceptionally good, Serampore judged him specially equipped for the mastery of the tongue, and urged him to go. The Bhutias, however, were found at war, and the way of the Mission was blocked.

Though yielding in the matter of the press, the Government still forbade the Mission's preaching in Calcutta, even at Aratoon Petruse's, or at any provincial station. They were free to go to Chittagong to grow coffee or plant teak, but not to preach Christ. The authorities were deaf to every patient and respectful plea. Lord Minto was personally friendly, inviting Marshman and Carey to his table at Barrackpore but conceding them no freedom toward 'the making of Indian Christians'.

> You mistake us, Your Lordship *[Carey said to the Governor-General].* We have no faith in makings. You can make hypocrites by pressure: but not Christians. We only solicit the right to present the Truth to each man's intelligence and conscience, as our Master enjoined.

But Lord Minto was afraid to permit them. Therefore, Carey pressed Fuller to besiege Parliament with a million signatures for the sanction of missions, an objective made all the more pressing as by the spring of 1808 they were stripped again for a time of Denmark's protection, through Britain's resumption of control of Serampore.

Early in 1808, Carey met the most revered scholar and saint of the then living Hindus. He does not name him, and all efforts to identify him have failed. Carey was overjoyed to elicit from him an unqualified condemnation of *sati*. When, at this time, Carey learned that one of his own Serampore pundits had lit the pyre for the burning of his sister-in-law, he drove him from his presence as a murderer.

Lall Bazar Chapel was opened on the first Sunday (and day) of 1809.

All the Serampore missionaries, except Mrs Marshman and Mrs Robinson, went to the eventful services, which were conducted jointly by Carey and Nathaniel Forsyth of Calcutta, of the London Missionary Society (and the only missionary in Bengal not belonging to Serampore).

A garden was planted on either side of the wide paved way from the gates to the sanctuary, a pleasant welcome off the hot and dusty street, and a suggestion of the greater blessing within the church. The land and building had cost Rs 30,000. A third of the money had been raised from private friends, a third from business houses in the city, and it was hoped that the last third would be given by the Company's civil servants. Marshman had been tireless in canvassing the city merchants for this fund – raising £1,100 in ten days. In order to be as near to Lall Bazar as possible for fullest availability, Carey rented rooms in 34, Bow Bazar close by.

> There [says Dr Smith] for nearly a generation he, who was training the governing class in Bengali, Sanskrit and Marathi, and was translating the *Ramayana*, returned, when the sun went down, to preach to the poorest in India in their own tongues the good news of the kingdom, with a loving tenderness and a patient humility only learned in the school of Christ.

For, although for thirty years he was a Government professor, and mingled daily with his fellow European officials, he never allowed himself to catch their prevailing haughty manner. The love of Christ made him the lover of India's poorest and most outcast.

Tradition says that once, on entering the pulpit, he found a pair of old shoes hanging from its desk – a scorner's reminder of his early employment as a *chamar* (a worker in skinning, one of the most despised of India's low castes). He simply said, 'the God Who can do for and through a poor shoe-maker the much He has done for and through me, can bless and use any. The very humblest may trust Him.'

One Sunday a British ship's officer named Ebenezer Kemp drifted into the chapel – just one of the thoughtless ones with whom the street abounded. God spoke to him through Carey. That night he turned from sin and embraced Christ, privately vowing that should he ever be a ship's master, he would bring out a colleague for Carey free of charge. By 1814 he was captain of the *Moira,* and gave free passage the next year to Yates. Fuller says, 'We wished to pay him for the voyage, but he pleasantly replied that he would consider Mr Yates as his chaplain.'

On his return he took plants back for Carey to Ryland, and the next year gave free freight of business wares to Carey's merchant nephew, Jesse Hobson, and earned the name in the whole Mission circle in India and in England of 'the missionaries' friend'. His cousin, he was surprised to find, had some years before been baptised in Northamptonshire (his own county) with Carey's niece Phoebe: so small is the world! He himself became a member of Lall Bazar till his death in Calcutta at 51, and his son was also baptised there. A few months before he died, his ship was wrecked at Krishnapatam, his crew and himself only just escaping.

Carapeit Aratoon, a schoolmaster, son of an Armenian merchant in Calcutta, once dropped into a service conducted by Ward, and was afterwards invited into Carey's house. Knowing no other church than the Armenian, he was shocked to learn that the Mission did not believe in transubstantiation, prayers to the Virgin, holy ointments, and crosses. 'You cannot be faithful Christians,' he said. Answered Carey, 'Friend, do one thing: bring all you would say from God's Word.' 'I will,' he replied. 'At least I will convince you from Scripture that you should pray to the Virgin Mother.' However, he was dismayed to find himself quite unable to do so. He consulted his church clergy for help, but in vain. At his next attendance at the Mission service, he tried to slip away unobserved, but Carey intercepted him. 'Well, friend, have you found it?' Carapeit stood helpless, only to be led into a truer understanding of the New Testament and the Gospel. When he was at length baptised, his angry Armenian vicar dismissed him from his teaching post, bidding the boys even spit in his face. Yet he stood firm and began preaching, and continued faithfully for the rest of his life.

Adam Gordon, the Governor of Calcutta's prison, was converted together with his wife at Lall Bazar, and became fervent for the Gospel. He opened the prison week by week to the missionaries, services there being held in English and Bengali.

Major-General Hardwicke, a close natural history friend of Carey's, admitted them for a while into the Fort William garrison, where they held services at the house of a poor Hindustani woman converted through Krishna Pal's preaching. Up to 100 gathered to hear. Sergeant

William Cumberland, superintendent at Cossipore (near the city) of the gun-carriage works of the East India Company, had possessed a violent and uncontrollable temper until, through the Mission, Christ cleansed him and calmed him. Then he became the wonder of his 500 army workmen. Whenever he did relapse into passion (with even the humblest) he would beseech his forgiveness and bring him a peace-offering. It was not surprising that, when he opened his house to the missionaries on Saturday evenings, they often found it full, and there were many conversions. The first baptism at Lall Bazar was of John Axell, a soldier. John Peter, an Armenian's bearer, was often drunk until converted in the Mission. He developed such preaching power (in Bengali) as to be called their 'Robert Hall'. They ordained him and sent him with the Oriya New Testament into Orissa, as its pioneer evangelist, together with Krishna Das.

Carey wrote to Fuller:

> I do not know that I am of much use myself, but I see a work which fills my soul with thankfulness. Not having time to visit the people, I appropriate every Thursday evening to receiving inquirers. Seldom fewer than twenty come, whose confession of their sins and of their former ignorance and of their grateful trust in the Saviour, told often with tears which almost choke their utterance, presents a scene no English pastor could imagine.

And yet he felt constrained to write in 1810 to Ryland in honest and distressed self-accusal:

> Marshman is all keenness for God's work. Often have I seen him, when we have been walking together, eye a group of persons, like a hawk, and go up to try on them the Gospel's utmost strength. I have known him engage with such for hours, more eager for the contest when he left off than when he began. It has filled me with shame. In point of zeal he is a Luther, I an Erasmus. Ward, too, has such a faculty of addressing things to the heart, and his thoughts run so naturally in this channel, that he fixes the minds of all who hear him; whilst I, after repeated efforts, can scarcely get out a few dry sentences, and, if rebuffed at the beginning, sit like a silly mute, and scarcely say anything at all. Yet I do desire to give myself, such as I am, to the cause of God, and to be wholly employed in His service. None stands more in need than I of the prayers of God's people.

The truth is that, whilst he revelled in spiritual talk with the earnest, he was painfully shy of religious approach to the indifferent and to strangers. Marshman was much more at ease in unfamiliar company, and more able in close argument. But God knew his soul's ardour.

The storm which the Mission had to weather in India after August 1806, broke repeatedly over its supporters in Britain during the three following years, in gales of much violence. Thomas Twining (once of the Calcutta Customs), Major Scott Waring (Warren Hastings' chief champion), and the notorious Colonel Steward (who, renouncing Christianity, became an exuberant Hindu) filled the air with wild assertions and alarms.

'If religious innovation be still suffered in India, the fifty millions of our Empire there will drive thence the British with as much ease as the wind scatters the desert sand.'

'If India is worth preserving, we should try to regain its confidence by the recall of every missionary.'

'They are invading the dearest rights, and wounding the tenderest feelings, of the native peoples.'

'They are as illiterate, ignorant, and enthusiastic as Hinduism's wildest fanatics.'

'Their preaching is puritanical rant of the worst kind.'

'No Hindu of any respectability will ever yield to their remonstrances.'

'Their converts are renegades from the faith in which they have been nurtured; most despicable characters, who have espoused a new religion, because excommunicated from the old.'

'The distribution of the Scriptures in Marathi is not unlikely to produce another Mahratta War.'

We might have thought that the British influential class would have discounted such intemperate words, but 'Vellore' was on their nerves. Even Sydney Smith, founder of the *Edinburgh Review*, the lion and idol of London, to whose preaching in Berkeley Square and lecturing in the Royal Institution the fashionable thronged, joined the opponents of missionary work and twice used his trenchant pen to protest against any toleration for 'the nest of consecrated cobblers', seeing that they themselves were so intolerant, insulting the religions of others.

If a tinker is a devout man, he infallibly sets forth for the East. Let any man read the accounts of the Anabaptist Mission. Can he do so without

deeming such men pernicious and extravagant, and concluding that
they benefit us much more by their absence than the Hindus by their
advice? If no other instruments remain but such visionary enthusiasts,
some doubt may be honestly raised whether it is not better to drop the
scheme entirely. For these instruments are calculated to bring ridicule
and disgrace upon the Gospel.

Missions in India stood in grave danger. Directors of the East India
Company were ready to vote for the immediate recall of the missionaries. However, friends stood in the breach, statesmen like Viscount
Melville, Charles Grant, the Marquis Wellesley, and Sir James Mackintosh (the three last familiar with Carey). These communicated with the
Directors to protect the slandered missionaries. Lord Teignmouth
(former Governor-General), the secretary of the Bible Society, and
preachers Robert Hall and Andrew Fuller, put forth tremendous
efforts to defend the Mission, especially Fuller, who was never so
mighty. The antagonistic onslaught was finally routed when Southey,
whom no one could suspect of extravagance, published a powerful
defence. What answer could there be to Southey's facts?

Carey and his son have been in Bengal fourteen years, the others only
nine. They have all had a difficult language to acquire, before they could
speak to the people; to preach and argue therein required a thorough
and familiar knowledge. The wonder is not that they have done so little,
but so much. The anti-missionaries cull from their journals and letters
all that is ridiculous, sectarian, and trifling; call them fools, madmen,
tinkers, Calvinists, and schismatics; and keep out of sight their love of
man and zeal for God, their self-devotement, their indefatigable industry and unequalled learning. These 'low-born and low-bred mechanics'
have translated the whole Bible into Bengali, and by this time have
printed it.

They are printing the New Testament in Sanskrit, Oriya, Marathi,
Hindi, and Gujarati; and are translating it into Persic, Telugu, Kanarese,
Chinese, and the tongues of the Sikhs and of the Burmans; and in four
of these languages they are going on with the whole Bible. Extraordinary
as this is, it will appear more so when it is remembered that of these
men one was originally a shoe-maker, another a printer, and the third
the master of a charity school. Only fourteen years have elapsed since
Thomas and Carey set foot in India, and in that time these missionaries
have acquired this gift of tongues; in fourteen years these 'low-born,
low-bred mechanics' have done more towards spreading the knowledge

of the Scriptures among the heathen than has been accomplished, or even attempted, by all the world's princes and potentates, and all its universities and establishments into the bargain.

20. The Home Circle

His was the even tenor of family devotion and loyalty to friends unbroken either by passion or coldness, and ever lit up by an unwavering geniality. The colleagues who were associated with him for the third of a century worshipped him, in the old English sense of the word. The younger missionaries who came to the fore on the death of Fuller, Sutcliff and Ryland, in all their mistaken and self-seeking conflicts with Carey's colleagues, always attempted to separate Carey from those they denounced.

In nothing, perhaps, was Carey's true Christian character so much seen as in his relations with his first wife, whose illness – with all its hostile, suspicious delusions – so clouded the last twelve years of her life. Never did complaint escape his lips regarding either her, or John Thomas, whose eccentric impulses and oft-darkened spirit also gave way to mania. The brotherhood arrangement, Ward's influence over the boys, and Hannah Marshman's domestic management, relieved Carey of much that his wife's illness had thrown upon him at Mudnabati.

DR GEORGE SMITH

The 'wildered brain,
The pain,
The phantom shapes that haunted,
The half-born thoughts that daunted –
    All became plain.

The fever-fit all vanished with the night,
When God's kind light
Pierced through the veiled delusions,
The errors and confusions;
And pointed to the tablet where
Her name was graven all the time:
    Yes, all the time!

S. PEARCE CAREY, after T. E. BROWN.

20. The Home Circle
1806–1812

G REAT CHANGES passed over Carey's home life in the period of the foiled opposition. Dorothy, his wife, died. Her mental distress had greatly worsened throughout her last five years. Her state of delirium complicated by deep misery and violence, was such that the Danish authorities begged and even told Carey to send her to an asylum. (Twice she had made an attempt on his life.) However, his Leicester friend, Dr Thomas Arnold, had so filled him with horror about the average institution of the day that he insisted on keeping her under his own compassionate care. 'He was,' says Dr George Smith, 'her tender nurse.' At length, in the first week of December 1807 she emerged from her long tunnel of morbid fears into Heaven's light and peace – 'the rest that remaineth for the people of God'. He was deeply touched during her last fortnight by the devotion of her Serampore 'sisters'. In a very literal sense, hers was a life 'offered upon the service and sacrifice of the faith'. Her name is no doubt written in Heaven, in the Lamb's Book of Life, in the Lord's Roll of Honour.

As soon as her sister Catharine (Charles Short's widow, now home in England) received the news she wrote to Carey from Clipston (North-amptonshire):

My dear brother,

I have received your letter respecting the death of my poor sister. I loved her much, but I can say, 'The Lord gave; the Lord hath taken away.' The river she has crossed you and I, dear brother, must pass, before we can serve God as we would. Till then may His grace be sufficient. Oh that I may be kept doing the Lord's will, till He come. It is a great consolation to me that our Father is a God nigh at hand, and not afar off . . . I hope my brother will never cease to be my brother, though the ties of nature are broken. I feel a stronger tie than these . . . I long to know if there is any soul coming to the feet of the Saviour from Debhatta . . . My dear brother, pray for me and be to me as a father, for I am an orphan, and I need your help. My love to all the dear children, and to all the friends. Pray write to me, if but two lines. I shall love to hear from you all. *[Catharine lived at Clipston for a further twenty years, and died there at the age of sixty-five.]*

Then Carey had to learn to do without Felix. Ever since he had missed the overland survey of China he had 'longed to be out somewhere', and in the summer of 1807 Chater begged to have him as his colleague when he returned to Burma. His father could not really spare him from proof-reading and other work at the press, but his tested character, his ardour and initiative, his linguistic attainments, and his considerable medical training in the Presidency Hospital, Calcutta, established his unique readiness, and at twenty-one he was ordained. 'What a day!' wrote Hannah Marshman. 'What must Dr Carey have felt! May I see another such with a son of mine!' On the eve of his going, 'Take heed to *thyself* and to thy doctrine' was his father's public charge, supplemented by these written injunctions:

Let the Burmese language occupy your most precious time, and your most anxious solicitude. Do not be content with its superficial acquiring. Make it yours, root and branch. Listen with prying curiosity to the forms of speech, the construction and accent of the people. All your imitative powers will be wanted, and, unless you frequently *use* what you acquire, it will profit you little. As soon as you feel your feet, compose a grammar, and some simple Christian instruction. Begin your translations with the *Gospel of Mark*. Be very careful that your construction and idiom are Burman, not English.

Observe a rigid economy. Missionary funds are the most sacred on earth. Cultivate brotherly love. Think of our friends Creighton and Grant, who lived for near twenty years in Goamalti without one painful difference. You cannot be so much as shy with each other without hurt to the Mission. Union, like every other blessing, must be prized and sought.

Preach the never-failing Word of the Cross. Be instant in season and out. Do not despise the patient instruction of one Burman. Let us hear from you regularly. Make memoranda of all you see. Be meek and gentle amongst the people. Cultivate the utmost cordiality with them as your equals. Never let European pride and superiority appear at the Mission House, Rangoon. The day when our Saviour says to you and to us 'Well done!' will make amends for all we feel at parting.

To Chater, Carey said:

If you should happen to be called into the presence of the king, avoid all reserves, put on a cheerful and winning confidence, offer your services to him in a way becoming your character, and testify your loyalty as a true Christian. If you should be introduced to Roman Catholic priests, show towards them every degree of frankness, and in a prudent manner seek their confidence, and do them good offices.

Felix felt almost as much sorrow at leaving Ward as leaving his own father. He loved him as himself, as well he might. From Diamond Point he sent him the shell of a huge turtle he caught there – either to adorn his study, or make a bath for his babe.

His first letters were most optimistic. The Burmese viceroy was interested in their mission, especially in the introduction of vaccine. The whole city was friendly. The fact that the houses were miserably built, the streets filthy with vermin, the rents wickedly oppressive, the taxes absurdly high, and the punishments barbarous, only proved the country's urgent need of the Gospel together with Christianity's impulse toward social advance. Soon, however, portents of war darkened the sky, and the missionaries were forced to return.

At the next cool season Felix went back, and was swiftly followed by the news of his wife's death in Calcutta during childbirth. Yet he courageously remained at his post. He pleased his father by the discovery that Pali, the learned language of Burma, was another cognate of Sanskrit, bringing him fresh incentive for his Sanskrit Bible. He pleased him even more by his intercession for a Burmese criminal whom he found being crucified. He ran and pleaded for his reprieve with the inexorable viceroy for hours, and prevailed just in time to save the dying man from final collapse. Then he had him carried to the Mission

House, and for a fortnight nursed him back to strength. His acts brought renown to the Gospel in the region, and exhibited the concern of a Christian missionary for the doomed and the lost. His father was deeply proud of him, and wrote every detail to friends.

In the summer of 1808, Carey remarried. Years after, he told William that 'if he had searched the whole world, he could not have found a truer helpmate' than in this Danish lady, Charlotte Rumohr, the youngest daughter of Count Rumohr of Rundoff (near Schleswig), and of the Countess of Alfeldt. They were just of the same age. Yet their marriage seemed preposterously ill-advised, for Charlotte was an invalid. One tragic night when she was a girl her father's mansion was destroyed by fire. Charlotte gave the alarm and saved the household, but she herself sustained a degree of shock and injury which left her a lifelong invalid, unable to walk up or down stairs, and compelled to rest her back daily. Severely affected by the cold, she at first lived in Italy and the South of France, but even here she was often unable to stand or speak. Advised by doctors to try India, she arrived in Serampore the same year as the Mission, and was 'settled' there by Governor Bie, who was related to her. In the heat of India she regained her speech, and enough strength to stand and walk a little. She was, however, still a very fragile invalid, 'both diminutive and somewhat deformed', as Ward wrote.

The Governor requested Carey to teach her English, which he did. He also taught her the Gospel, leading to a clear work of salvation in her life. It was in this new love for Christ that she took Krishna Pal by the hand after his baptism, and blessed him from her heart. The next June – despite her spinal weakness, she was baptised, the first European woman in India to bear this witness. From that time she was the Mission's generous friend, and her entire life was thrown into its work and worship. She even learned Bengali so that she might encourage the Indian converts.

For all this she was hopelessly fragile. For days on end the phlegm on her lungs produced such pain as to make death seem preferable to life. Not marriage but death seemed more likely to claim her. She no more dreamed than did Elizabeth Barrett, the invalid poetess, years later, that 'love's silver voice was to ring through her, and teach her the whole of life in a new rhythm.'

Carey's colleagues and their wives were distressed at the

engagement, even sending him a round robin of protest. 'How did my whole body tremble,' wrote Hannah Marshman in her diary, 'when I was called upon to sign the letter!' The next Sunday she adds, 'My husband preached, but I could not listen. I felt in such an agitation about Dr Carey.' But in a few days comes this unsurprising entry: 'All things settled with Dr C. The opposition to his marriage withdrawn.' The suddenness of the engagement was possibly the problem. But had he not for ten years been lonelier than a celibate? If her alarming frailty was a handicap, Carey had the answer in his own gentle and caring soul, and also in his faith, and length of days lay within the gift of his love. They were married in May 1808 in her own recently-built house, which she at once gave to the Mission, its rent to support Indian evangelists. Most of her dowry she added to Carey's income in sending help to his English relatives, and to buy a small business for his brother Thomas. 'I could not be easy,' he wrote, 'to possess property, and know that my brother was in need.'

Though she was often pitifully ill – compelled at times to keep her couch for months on end – they lived in love's perfect understanding for thirteen years. Her refinement and her intimate knowledge of Danish, German, Italian, and French, and her delight in the study of Scripture in all these versions, made her his invaluable companion in biblical translation work. Like Mrs Browning, she had 'a soul of fire in a shell of pearl'.

Thomas, Carey's brother, to whom he and his wife sent aid, had been retired from the army on a small pension after receiving severe wounds in Holland, and like many another ex-serviceman found it impossible to get employment, though of higher than average education. When at length he became a night-watchman at the West India Docks, on scant pay and in much danger, he dared not tell his sisters. His letters, in neat handwriting, reveal an affectionate, devout, but very apprehensive spirit. His brother was his comfort and his pride. 'Your liberality to us all affects me not a little ... Every scrap of paper you have used and every word you have written me, I keep as sacred treasure.'

The year of Carey's wedding was also that of the ordination of his son William, and the father could thank God for a second ordained and missionary son. Deterred by the Government from opening a mission station in provincial Bengal, he went to Ignatius Fernandez, the

Christian merchant of Dinajpur and Sadamahal to help him in his business and his mission work. Carey was blest to have him serving in the district of his own early labours, and he wrote to cheer him:

> You are in a post, my son *[he wrote]*, very dear to my remembrance, because my first Indian years were spent in its neighbourhood. I, therefore, greatly rejoice in your exertions. The conversion of one soul is worth the labour of a life. 'Unto us is this *favour* given that we should preach among the Gentiles the unsearchable riches of Christ.' Hold on, therefore; be steady in your work, and leave the result with God. I have been contemplating a mission to the Afghans of Kabul.

Presently, with five Indian converts to help him, William transferred to Mudnabati itself and saw the home of his boyhood, now derelict, together with the indigo factory and all its plant. However, the village folk flocked to hear him, and his father wrote:

> Be encouraged, my dear son. Devote yourself wholly to your work. For this is the cause God has had in His mind from eternity, and for which Christ shed His blood, and for which the Spirit and the Word were given. So its triumph is certain.

And again:

> Be steadfast, dear William. Walk worthy of your high calling. Be a pattern to others, who may engage in similar undertakings. Much depends on us who go first to Christ's work in this country.

Sadamahal, where William dwelt, was a very lonely spot, with not another European for miles round. The buffaloes (or 'buffelows', as he always spelt them) were wild and dangerous (he was gored once in arm and thigh). The *dacoits* (armed robbers) were even worse. But when he begged for somewhere safer, Carey was roused to stern reply. The iron in his own blood he expected to see in his sons.

> There is much guilt in your fears, dear William. Mary and you will be a thousand times safer committing yourselves to God in the path of duty than neglecting duty to take care of yourselves.

He reminds him of what perils and loneliness soldiers and their wives must brave, in a calling inglorious compared with theirs. He himself dwelt, he says, in just such perils through five and a half years in Mudnabati, 'as lonesome a place as could be thought of', and 'with many of his own *ryots [peasants]* in league with the *dacoits*. 'Mount your horse,' he urges, 'and be out on God's work.'

Determination, however, was to be accompanied by great humility. On one occasion William took a particular action in the work of the mission which offended his senior, Mr Fernandez. Carey's advice to him was thus: 'I would rather see you stoop as low as you can to effect a reconciliation than avoid it through pride. You will never regret having humbled yourself to the dust that peace may be restored.'

By the end of 1811, however, William was needed in Katwa. He was very apprehensive about following a missionary so vigorous and able as John Chamberlain. 'Five like me in body and zeal,' he wrote, 'could not do what he did alone.' 'Disputing does not suit me at all, whereas Chamberlain could run them down with perfect ease.' 'To govern a church is no small thing. I could with joy itinerate and evangelise all my life, but I am not formed to rule a church.' He often begged for a sphere of less responsibility. 'I doubt whether this is the right side of the ship for me to cast my net.'

Yet despite all this self-distrust and much ill-health, through more than twenty years he served there, making glad the heart of his father with his sustained evangelism, his trained band of native preachers, his many schools (his wife's and his own), his vocational weaving school, his large coffee plantation, and his many attempts with cloth and silk, sugar and indigo, to meet the costs of his station. (Carey had sent six boatloads of coffee plants from Calcutta.)

'I think William,' Carey often wrote to Jabez, 'one of the most useful missionaries we have, and I believe all the brethren have a growing confidence in him.' His Bengali was native. A colleague tells of 'the pleasure approaching to ecstasy with which Bengalis heard a minister speaking their language with such fluency and force.'

Carey kept all his sons' letters – even their brief notes. An extraordinary number of them survived – almost all of them most filial and affectionate. Only once does William write as one aggrieved: 'I must beg that you will not write so sharply again, for I am not made of stuff hard enough to bear it, and particularly when it is unjust.' But he was a chief joy of his father, who would often say, 'Religion flourishes at Katwa more than at any other station in the Mission.'

Towards the close of 1808, who should arrive in Serampore but Carey's nephew Peter. Learning of a regiment bound for Bengal, he had impulsively enlisted for ten years just for the joy of seeing his hero-uncle and his cousins. He was a fine lad, winning rapid advancement for his intelligence and keenness. In three years he was promoted to sergeant, and attached to his adjutant's office. We hear of his buying and borrowing books of educational value such as vernacular grammars, a life of Akbar, etc. He had courage also.

> I was given a nice-looking horse, but a very bad one to ride in the ranks, always fighting and kicking, and he got me a kick from another horse in the ankle. I rode all the morning, and when I came in, I was obliged to be carried into my tent, and have my boot cut off, and to go to the hospital. I was obliged to ride with one boot for a good while, and now I would not exchange my horse for the best in the troop. I was obliged to have some hard battles with him, before I was master.

Tragically, by July 1814 this letter was sent from Cawnpore:

> I am very poorly owing to an accident I met with on the 7th. The Regiment [H.M. the 24th Light Dragoons] was out at exercise, and my horse reared up, and fell backwards on me, and broke my left leg all to pieces. There have been several bones taken out of it. It should have been taken off ere this, but it has a violent inflammation. I shall be sure to lose my leg, and, perhaps, my life.

Two days later it was his life. And this was the first news Carey had to give Eustace, Peter's only brother, upon his arrival in Calcutta.

In the heat of 1809 Carey fell desperately ill. He had toiled inordinately at the second edition of his Bengali Bible. On 26 June the revision was complete, and his colleagues talked with him at dinner of all he had seen achieved, and asked his further purposes and plans. He said he had translation work mapped out for *twenty years*. That very evening he was seized with strong fever, and in a fortnight they despaired of his life, and watched every hour for his passing. William, Jabez and Jonathan all served as unwearying nurses, and Ward was convinced that they and the Mission were 'soon to be orphans'. His revised Bengali Bible seemed to be the end of his career. Yet he felt himself to be possessed of tremendous strength.

> In my delirium [he wrote afterwards] I was busily employed, as I perfectly remember, in carrying a communication from God to all the princes and governments in the world, requiring them instantly to abolish every political establishment of religion, and to sell the parish and

other churches to the first body of Christians who would purchase them. Also, to declare war infamous, and military officers the destroyers of the race. I was attended by angels in all my excursions, and was universally successful. A few princes in Germany were refractory, but my attendants struck them dead! I also pronounced the doom of Rome to the Pope.

In the midst of the blaze of this hallucination, a doctor, urgently sent for from Barrackpore, entered the room in military dress, to the patient's great agitation. Carey shouted, 'How dare you come to me in that red coat? Don't you know that God Almighty has decreed that all war shall be abolished?'

The doctor withdrew, and returned in a black coat of Marshman's, but he was recognised and rejected at once. Upon Carey's recovery, he would never accept that his fever had been simply brainstorm. 'There were truths in my delirium whose force I wish to feel, and for whose triumph to strive, to the end of my life.'

Though his anti-military views were so vehement, he was thrown much amongst soldiers, and learned deeply to love them. Among his military friends were Captain Moxon, Levi Hobson (Carey's own nephew), who was Moxon's ensign, not to mention his many military students in Fort William College, and young Henry Havelock (in the days of his adjutancy of the Chinsurah garrison, and of his marriage to Miss Hannah Marshman) and Major-General Hardwicke of Fort William (who possessed a passion for natural history like his own).

After the anxiety of Carey's delirium was over, Ward wrote to Fuller:

When I looked at the printing office containing usually fifty workmen, then almost stript and silent, I could not help anticipating a time when not for three days but for ever this whole machine would be still. Carey has just been raised from the dead, and the machine goes on a little longer. But we cannot expect these resurrections oft repeated. The men who live sixteen years in India are not so numerous as to justify us in presuming that he will be spared much longer. Every year of the continuance of us elders you may count a miracle. No one else in India will do for Serampore, except, perhaps, Dr Taylor. When any one of us goes, the machine will crawl on a little longer, but as a cripple. What would you think if the safety of the whole Baptist interest in England depended on yourself, Ryland, and Sutcliff? Would you not tremble for the Ark?

When we thought we had lost Carey, we were ready to ask, 'Who will finish his Marathi and Bengali dictionaries? Who will complete his Sanskrit and Oriya Old Testaments? Who will carry on the Hindi, Marathi and all the other translations?'

Ward urged Fuller to send them men of undoubted quality and spirit. And Carey also wrote to Ryland:

Hindustan needs ten thousand ministers of the Gospel; and China as many. England has done much, but not a hundredth part of what she is bound to do. Ought not every church to turn its chief attention to the raising up of such missionaries and the nurture of their spiritual gifts, with the express design of sending them abroad? Difficulties would soon disappear, if the trial were once made.

Carey was very happy in November 1811, when Phoebe, the sweet daughter of his sister Ann, reached Serampore, not just on a visit, but to share his home. Reporting her safe arrival to her mother, he had other good tidings to tell:

My wife's health has experienced a great change for the better. For thirty years she could not bear the motion of a carriage, nor even of a palanquin; but she is now able to ride down to Calcutta and back every week without the least inconvenience, and I believe it is of great use to her to do so.

Then he expresses the fear that the Chaters will feel obliged to abandon the mission to Burma because of the very troubled and threatening conditions of the country, and because of Mrs Chater's poor health. 'But Felix,' he says, 'has just united his interests with those of Burma by marrying a wife born there, whose mother and sister dwell there, the sister being married to a Dutch merchant in Rangoon.' And he adds:

I would rather hear of Felix losing his life in the cause of the Gospel than see him quit his station.

The remarriage of Felix in March 1811 followed a widowerhood of nearly three years. His bride was a Miss Blackwall, aged twenty-two. She had been born in Bassein on the Burmese coast, to a British ship's captain. Her familiarity with the Burmese language and customs promised to be invaluable to Felix – all the more as he had been unable to secure any reliable pundit. The bride's brother, a lad of thirteen, was sent to Serampore, to Marshman's boarding-school, and proved 'steady and diligent'.

Carey completes his letter to his sister with this cheer:

> I expect to baptise six next Lord's Day, which will make the number in Calcutta for this year more than sixty. Very considerable additions have also been made elsewhere. Krishna Pal and Sebak Ram preach in more than thirty places in Calcutta and its environs every week. Young men, too, of promising gifts frequently preach in the open and are useful. They have found the pearl of great price and they commend it to others.

Lawson arrived from England as a layman helper of the Mission just as Carey was convalescing from his illness, and in an early letter wrote home:

> I had formed an idea of Serampore before my arrival; but, notwith-standing my very high expectations, I was perfectly astounded. Dr Carey, lately recovering from a dangerous illness, said, when I went to see him, 'God has spared my life. I hope it is that I may serve Him better. I have been but a loiterer – but a half-hearted servant.' This from such lips filled me with shame and confusion.

Carey's illness made the home leaders anxious to secure his portrait, and they commissioned Ward to arrange it. He engaged Robert Home, Calcutta's chief artist, who had already painted Lord Wellesley, and his great soldier-brother, for Government House, and Sir William Jones for the Asiatic Society which he had founded. (Indeed, Robert Home was himself a prominent member of this society, where he had often met Carey.)

> In compliance with your wish, though not my own [Carey writes to Ryland in his fifty-first year], I have sat for my portrait. Ward has greatly desired that I should be drawn as engaged in the work of translating the Scriptures. So the artist, Mr Home, has introduced the pundit, whom I employ as my amanuensis, as sitting by me. His likeness is a very good one. [His name Carey does not give, only his title, 'Nyayalankara' – one who has gained distinction in reasoning, literally 'an ornament of logic'.] He has also introduced a number of books such as I use in translation, and, in short, has made it as much as possible like my table. He has copied parts of Acts 2.11 from my Sanskrit New Testament into the manuscript before me – 'We do hear them speak in our tongues the wonderful works of God.'

The following (sole-surviving) letter from Carey's father and step-mother merits presentation in this home circle chapter. The handwriting is firm, but the reiterated phrases tell the tale of his seventy-four years. 'Mother' was not, of course, Carey's own.

PAULERSPURY
3 January, 1811

Dear Son and Daughter,

We received your letter dated 3 May, 1810, on 28 November following, and are glad to hear that after your illness you are so bravely recovered again. We hope the Lord will preserve and bless you both together for many years to come. We have been comfortably provided for by the blessing of the Almighty and by both your kindnesses, for which we return our grateful thanks. For my own part I have been blessed with extraordinary good health for the whole year. Your mother is tolerably well in health, only very lame and helpless. We are glad to hear of your success in the Mission, and that the translation of the Scriptures into the Oriental languages goes so rapidly on.

We are glad to hear that Felix is likely to do well in the Burma empire. Give our kind loves to him. We must include in one letter our loves to them all. They are all young. We should be glad to be favoured with a letter from each of them at any opportunity. We are glad to hear of William's escape from the danger you mentioned [the wild buffalo]. Our kind loves to him and his wife. We are glad to hear of the proficiency Jabez and Jonathan make in the languages. We are glad that Peter [Carey's nephew] is well, and that he is steady and careful. Poor boy, he must be among great temptations in the soldier-line. Eustace makes great progress in his studies at Mr Sutcliff's. He often preaches at one place or another in the neighbourhood. Mr John Hands, son of Mr Charles Hands of Roade, who is lately arrived at Madras as a missionary, we read in the *Evangelical Magazine,* was at Rangoon with Felix and Mr Chater. You don't mention his being at Serampore.

We conclude with our kind loves to you both,

Your affectionate father and mother,

EDMUND AND FRANCES CAREY

Could there have been a more interesting situation in the Bengal of those days than Serampore? The three elders in their prime, overjoyed by their widening effectiveness under the felt impulse and guidance of God; each reckoning the others greater than himself; each engaging his particular skill; each responsible in his own domain; and each able to produce an income for the furtherance of their missionary aims. Their wives were all a source of great strength and blessing: Carey's with better health than she had known since girlhood, shedding abroad such calm by her own peace; Marshman's, though carrying the burden of the boarding-schools, always unflappable and motherly; and Ward's, the widow of John Fountain, the 'Martha' of the community, the mistress of supplies, but with a fine balance of 'Mary' as well.

Then there were the families: Carey's two older sons being devotedly mission-minded, and the two younger, as it proved, 'not far from the kingdom'. The Marshmans had conspicuously clever and interested sons, and tender-hearted daughters, and the Wards' little children romped around.

In addition, there were more than seventy boarders, to add life and laughter to the settlement.

And the many guests: relatives from England, fiancées (and then wives) of Felix and William; soldier-friends; parents of the boarders (never a month without some of these) and visiting chaplains from Calcutta and afar; newly-arrived missionaries of other societies in all the zeal of their youth; and sea captains from Britain and America. (Among the latter was once a tall grandson of Jonathan Edwards, who took Carey aback and amused him by his blunt reply to his congratulations on his distinguished ancestry – 'Yes, sir, but every tub must stand on its own bottom.') Considering these sharers in the household and these visitors, the daily food supply might well have needed to be as ample as Mrs Marshman tells:

> Always we need four very large dishes of boiled rice piled high, four dishes of curry, three or four joints of meat (or sometimes eight or nine large fish), seven or eight dishes of vegetables from our own garden, and three tureens of soup. A chest of tea at Rs 80 (about £10) lasts three months and a fortnight. We use nine quarts of milk daily.

Then beyond those taking food together were the Indian spiritual-seekers, the Indian converts and preachers, all with thrilling personal stories; the pundits, Indian, Armenian, Persian, Arabian, and others; the craftsmen (at least sixty in Ward's service); the cooks; the servants; Carey's gardeners, etc. What animation and colour it all meant! This all-aliveness of Serampore must have kept renewing the elders' vitality and strength! They needed it to nerve them for the distresses which were fast approaching.

The following communication sent from the only son of Carey born in India, to a young lady of his youthful admiration, reflects an environment of humour and ingenuity.

> Madam,
> After a long consideration
> Of the great reputation
> You have in the nation,
> I have an inclination
> To become your relation.
> To give demonstration
> Of this my estimation,
> I am making preparation
> To remove my habitation
> To a nearer situation,
> To pay you adoration.
> If this declaration
> Should meet your approbation,
> 'Twill confer an obligation
> From generation to generation.
>   JONATHAN CAREY,
> A man of observation.

And this was her reply:

> Sir,
> I received your oration,
> With much deliberation
> Of the seeming infatuation
> That seized your imagination,
> When you made your declaration,
> And expressed your admiration
> On so slender a foundation.
> But, after an examination
> And some little contemplation,
> I deem it done for recreation,
> Or with some ostentation,
> To display your education
> By an odd renumeration

Of words of like pronunciation
Though of different signification;
Which, without disputation,
May deserve commendation.
So I shall give much meditation
To your quaint communication.

21. The Fire

We are only scholars. It rests with the Great Teacher to decide which lesson shall come next – a hard one or an easy one.

WARD to Dr Nathaniel Wallich.

As you enter, you see your cousin, in a small room, dressed in a white jacket, reading or writing, and looking over the office, which is more than 170 feet long. There you find Indians translating the Scriptures into the different tongues, or correcting proof-sheets. You observe, laid out in cases, types in Arabic, Persian, Nagari, Telugu, Punjabi, Bengali, Marathi, Chinese, Oriya, Burmese, Kanarese, Greek, Hebrew and English. Hindus, Mussulmans [Moslems] and Christian Indians are busy – composing, correcting, distributing. Next are four men throwing off the Scripture sheets in the different languages; others folding the sheets and delivering them to the large store-room; and six Mussulmans do the binding. Beyond the office are the varied type-casters, besides a group of men making ink; and in a spacious open walled-round place, our paper-mill, for we manufacture our own paper.

WARD to a cousin, three months before the fire.

21. The Fire
Wednesday, 11 March, 1812

CAREY WAS STARTLED at the woe in Marshman's face when he burst into his home in Calcutta so unexpectedly that Thursday morning of 12 March, 1812. What fresh sorrow could have befallen the Mission? They had recently been smitten with breach upon breach. There had been five burials at Serampore since Christmas, yet without an epidemic: 'Sister Mardon' on Christmas Day, leaving three children; a woman servant of Mrs Marshman's, of eleven years' faithfulness; Herbert, a boarder of Marshman's, who was almost as dear as a son; Ward's darling Mary, aged six years; and, only a week back, an infant of Marshman's own, named 'William Ward Marshman', for love of the colleague. Of what more distressing bereavement was Carey to hear?

When he learned that the Mission printing works were a shell of burnt and naked walls, with only a few business documents rescued, he was dumb with silence. His heart froze within him. Marshman hasted to assure him that the bulk of the translation manuscripts were safe, because they had been kept in a warehouse. But portions of most of them had perished, and in grammars and dictionaries it was feared that Carey's losses would be very heavy – as they proved. As Marshman told his story, Carey was overwhelmed by the blow of God's hand. 'About six last evening,' Marshman said, 'the workfolk having left, I was musing at home on the loss of my little one, when I heard Ward shout to me from his office where he tarried with the day's accounts. Running and looking in, I saw at the south end of the long building a twenty-feet sheet of flame from a stage stacked with paper. We both rushed thither, till the smoke thrust us back. A workman pressed further, but fell senseless, and had to be dragged out.

'All the window shutters but one were bolted from within. We would fain have torn them open, to save things; but an expert forbade us, and, indeed, shut the open one, to stifle the flames. We organised carriers, and Ward mounted and pierced the roof over the area of trouble, and for four hours we poured in water to the great abatement of the fire. But injudicious friends, counting it safe at last, forced a shutter, and I saw flame leap to the centre of the building.

'In half an hour, all was ablaze, and salvage was the only thing possible; though precious little of that. We could rescue the five presses, for they were in the room adjoining, which as yet had not caught fire. They were only transferred there two or three weeks since. Had they been still in the main room, they could not have survived. Then we broke the windows of Ward's office, and pulled out the *almirah [cupboard]* and his desk; but except our title deeds and the translation fund ledgers, they held nothing of account.

'Our concern was now for the near buildings: the Mission House, the boys' dormitories, and the girls'. So we cleared all that was combustible from between them and the printing works, besides all their furniture and the bedding. A friend took the children and the girls. The office roof fell in about midnight, and our greatest fear was then; for a body of flame, two hundred feet by forty, rose into the sky, and we dreaded the conflagration spreading – with the wind blowing sometimes pretty hard. But it mercifully fell, and the flame kept straight as a candle. We could only watch it in solemn silence, and, I think I can say, solemn serenity, interrupted by the crash of beams. By two o'clock of the morning it had spent itself, and we went to lie down. At daylight I took boat to you. I could not bear that you should hear the terrible news from any stranger.

'But the building and all its contents have gone. Nothing could survive such a furnace. The loss in English paper is immense. We never had so much in stock before. A thousand reams arrived only a week since for the Sinhalese and Tamil Testaments, which the Calcutta Bible Auxiliary had commissioned us to print. Ward had it stacked in the office to save it from being thieved. Then the just-cast Tamil type and the new Chinese metal-type have gone, and are pitiful losses! But, thank God, no life was lost, though many were in danger, particularly Ward.

'How the fire originated? We know nothing. Perhaps from a work-man's hookah *[pipe]*; arson possibly, by an Indian enemy, enraged at the Scriptures getting printed in all his country's tongues.' (Later, they assured themselves that it was an accident.)

This was Marshman's heart-rending story, retold here almost entirely in the words of his immediate letters.

But a blow stings the brave to resistance. Carey went to his classes at Fort William, and to get exemption for the next day. Professor Cole-brooke braced him with words that he oft afterwards repeated: 'However vexing it may be, a road the second time travelled is usually taken with more confidence and ease than at the first.' He resolved that his grammars, dictionaries, and translations should gain by the disaster. Marshman scoured Calcutta to learn what printing materials were purchasable, never dreaming of stopping the work. They were able to just catch a mail to send to Ryland an instant S.O.S. That letter described the calamity as 'another leaf of the ways of providence, calling for the exercise of faith in Him Whose Word, firm as the pillars of Heaven, has decreed that all things shall work together for good to them that love God. Be strong, therefore, in the Lord. He will never forsake the work of His own hands.'

Carey added the bare facts to a letter written overnight to his nephew, who was contemplating a missionary life. The whole letter has interest, written as it was in the security of his Bow Bazar home, while his colleagues were hustling the children and the Mission's belongings from the increasing roar of the fire.

My dear Eustace,

Whether you come to India or not, be assured that the work of publishing the Gospel is the most important you could have chosen. Engage in it with humble dependence on God, and with a single eye to His glory, and He assuredly will bless you. Every one to whom God has given abilities for such work is bound to devote himself to it: he has no option. Nor has a church, whether it will send such into the ministry. If the church neglect to do so, the guilt is theirs. The number now required to spread the Gospel through the world is unspeakably great. If fifty thousand ministers, besides those already employed, were now to go forth, they would be so thinly scattered as scarcely to be perceived. The harvest is indeed great, the labourers very few.

Then comes the undreamed-of addendum:

I began this last night; I close it hastily this morning, having received intelligence of a dreadful loss, which befell the Mission last night. Our printing office was totally destroyed by fire, and all its property, amounting to at least Rs 60,000 or 70,000. Nothing was saved but the presses. This is a heavy blow, as it will stop our printing the Scriptures for a long time. Twelve months' hard labour will not reinstate us; not to mention loss of property, MSS., etc, which we shall scarcely ever sur-mount. I wish to 'be still, and know that the Lord is God,' and to bow to His will in everything. He will no doubt bring good out of this evil, and make it promote His interests; but, at present, the providence is exceed-ing dark. No lives were lost. We cannot tell what was the cause of the fire.

Your affectionate uncle,

W. CAREY

With the turn of the tide Marshman and Carey were rowed to Ser-ampore, drawing close to each other in the fellowship of suffering and faith. Marshman talked of a scripture that had strengthened him dur-ing the recent weeks of the Mission's bereavements, and especially in his own: 'Every branch that beareth fruit He purgeth it, that it may bring forth more fruit.' 'Last night,' he said, 'when all hope of saving the building had to be abandoned, this fell again upon my spirit with peculiar sweetness and power, as the clue to all. It stilled me into tran-quil submission, enabling me to look up and *welcome* God's will, assured that the end was not destruction, but chastening towards peaceable fruit.' And Carey told how he had been steadied by the word he had passed on to Eustace, 'Be still, and know that I am God.' They both drew solace from the fact that with the boarding-schools and Carey's professorship unaffected, no main source of Mission income was depleted.

The desolation in the Mission compound was horrifying, and the fire still smouldered. Yet Ward they found not just submissive, but jubilant, because he had spent the day removing the debris where his steel punches lay buried, and to his delight he had found them *uninjured* – four thousand punches of the types of fourteen Indian tongues – the product of more than ten years of labour. He later said that this changed the face of everything, coming to him as God's plain 'Take heart! Carry on! Go forward!' For with these punches undamaged, and with multitudes of matrices *[type-moulds]* also recovered, and with hundredweights of salvageable lead, they could at once begin recasting type. Then, with the presses rescued and their paper-mill safe, they might hope to be reprinting in a month.

There was no need to await rebuilding; no need to rebuild at all. Only the previous Saturday (they had all thought of this) Palmer & Co. had vacated the Mission's warehouse, to their grief at the time, because of the heavy rent-loss, but now God's place was prepared for them, a convincing token of His care. Being larger than the burnt-down building it even allowed for the growth of their work. So they counted their blessings and extolled the mercy of their God.

Next morning they gathered their fifty or sixty anxious Indian colleagues and surprised them with their optimism and vigour. They directed the pundits to immediately begin the re-rendering of the Scriptures in the damaged versions, and arranged for the type-casters to work in relays day and night. The compositors, printers, and binders were paid full wages and enjoined to be back from their homes refreshed and ready for strenuous labour in not more than a month.

The three spent the morning in careful calculation of their losses. First, they identified destroyed manuscripts which no money could replace. Here Carey was the chief sufferer. Lost were nearly all his Indian Scripture versions; all his Kanarese New Testament; two whole, large Old Testament books in Sanskrit; many pages of his *Bengali Dictionary*; all his *Telugu Grammar*, and much of his Punjabi; a year's work of Marshman and himself on the *Ramayana*; and every vestige of his well-advanced *Dictionary of Sanskrit and its Indian Cognates* (the *magnum opus* of his linguistic life – an overwhelming disaster).

Concerning this Carey had written to Ryland only three months before the fire:

> I have long been collecting materials for a universal dictionary of the Oriental languages derived from Sanskrit, of which that language is to be the groundwork; and to give the corresponding Greek and Hebrew

words. I wish much to do this for the sake of assisting biblical students to correct the translations of the Bible in the Oriental languages, after we are dead. Perhaps, another person may not in the space of a century have advantages for a work of this kind that I now have. I, therefore, think it would be criminal for me to neglect the little I am able to do while I live and enjoy these privileges.

Also destroyed were 1,400 reams of English paper, and much more of their own; 4,400 lbs of English type, and many founts of English-cast Hebrew, Greek, Persian, Arabic and Tamil; not less than 104 founts of Nagari, Telugu, Bengali, Burmese, Marathi, Punjabi, Oriya, Tamil, Chinese and Kashmiri (all these having been created and cast by them). In addition the fire took all the building, books, printing materials and tools. Allowing for all probable salvage and the recovery of their safe, they judged their material loss at between £9,000 and £10,000.

Chaplain Thomason came in the afternoon to console them.

The scene [he wrote] was indeed affecting – the long printing office reduced to a mere shell, the yard covered with burnt paper. Carey walked with me over the smoking ruins. The tears stood in his eyes. 'In one night,' he said, 'the labours of years are consumed. How unsearchable are the divine ways! I had lately brought some things to the utmost perfection I could, and contemplated the Mission with, per-haps, too much self-congratulation. *The Lord has laid me low, that I may look more simply to Him.*' I saw the ground strewn with half-consumed paper, on which the Words of Life would soon have been printed. The metal under our feet amidst the ruins was melted into misshapen lumps – the sad remains of types consecrated to the service of the sanc-tuary. A few hours ago all was full of promise – now all is rubbish and smoke.

Yet that evening they reviewed their blessings and abundantly uttered the memory of God's goodness. In twelve years their one Ben-gal church of eleven members had become eleven churches, with an average of thrice eleven in each. They had twenty native evangelists. Calcutta's membership had doubled in the previous year to 110, and its missionary spirit was most active. Owen Leonard, a converted sol-dier, promised to develop into a most moving Bengali preacher. 'The leaven,' they said, 'was spreading: the little one was becoming a thou-sand.' 350 children were being educated in their free Portuguese schools. Jessore was greatly prospering. Next to Serampore it was the most promising of the stations. Chamberlain was in Agra, John Peter was in Orissa, the Chaters were on their way to Ceylon to plant there its first Protestant mission, Robinson was preparing for Java, Felix was steadfast in Burma, and Carey's youngest son, Jonathan, was newly baptised, and rarely prayed without voicing his desire for missionary service. The fire could not touch these considerable encouragements.

There was only one possible text for Carey on the Sunday – 'Be still, and know that I am God.' His divisions were as simple as at Nottingham:

1. God's right to dispose of us as He pleases.
2. Man's duty to acquiesce in His will.

He led them into a most heartening remembrance of God's principles and purpose, promises and providence.

Help flowed to them the next week in letters, money, printing materials, and furniture. Rs 7,000 were swiftly subscribed by such as Chaplain Thomason, George Udny, John Ellerton, Prison Governor Adam Gordon, a Javanese prince in Marshman's school, Carey's Fort William students, past and present (Rs 1,200), and even Scott Waring, a son of the major who had attacked and misrepresented them in England. A Calcutta journal extolled them in full rhetoric:

> Zeal and perseverance distinguish the missionaries. Their ardour derives a new impulse from misfortunes. They embody the advice of the Mantuan bard, 'Ne cede malis; sed contra audentior ito.' We confidently trust that their printing establishment at Serampore, lately destroyed by fire, will, like the phoenix of antiquity, rise from its ashes winged with new strength, and destined, in a lofty and long-enduring flight, widely to diffuse the benefits of knowledge throughout the East.

Carey wrote home:

> Much ground must be laboured over again, and I have suffered most. But we are not discouraged. We are chastened and not killed; cast down, but not destroyed; perplexed, but not in despair.

By the end of July they could *print* again in Bengali, Sanskrit, Hindi, Punjabi, Marathi, Oriya and Tamil. The Sinhalese fount was almost ready, and the Persian well advanced. By the year-end they were as rich in Oriental type as ever, and had even sent a Tamil fount to Tranquebar 'the best ever handled there'. By the next April they were printing in more languages than before the fire, and the pundits' better renderings saved Carey hours of revisionary toil. He told Ryland that 'he seemed to have just overcome the chief obstacles, which had blocked up the threshold of the door.'

The news of the fire did not reach Ryland till 9 September, nor Fuller till the 18th. But how Fuller rallied the helpers as soon as he felt this rope tug from the depths of the mine! Britain was at the time in a tense struggle with Napoleon, America was sinking her frigates, and food prices were dreadful. Yet the churches rushed to make a large response, not just the English but the Scottish also. From the Society's twentieth anniversary at Kettering, Fuller wrote:

> When your late disastrous intelligence reached us, a strong sensation was felt throughout the kingdom, not only in our own denomination but amongst Christians of every name, each vying with the rest to repair your loss. Norwich had just raised £200 for the Society, but added £500 more. I spent the 20th at Cambridge, and about £165 were collected. The Bible Society has voted you 2,000 reams of paper, and the L.M.S. a hundred guineas.

A few days after, he could report £170 from Northampton, £160 from his own Kettering; Edinburgh already £800; Greenock, with collections in every place of worship, £170; Leeds, £300; Bristol, nearly £400; Birmingham, £320; Leicester, between £200 and £300; etc, etc.

> If the loss [he writes] be made up in two-and-fifty days, and the hearts of Christ's enemies be dismayed, the work being so clearly of God, I should not be surprised. Cf. Nehemiah 6.15.

Britain did repair the losses in two months. Dr F. A. Cox tells of Fuller entering the Society's committee and exclaiming 'with sparkling eyes': 'Brothers, the money is all raised, and so constantly are contributions still pouring in that we must in honesty publish an intimation that the need is removed.' Among the gifts of special interest were £15 from Thomas Scott, Carey's early spiritual counsellor; £10 from Wilberforce; £5 from ex-Governor-General Lord Teignmouth; £20 from Mrs Beeby Wallis; £10 from Thomas Potts; £22 from Clipston; £7 from little Hackleton; £76 from Friar Lane, Nottingham, where the deathless sermon was preached; and £156 from Olney. Almost every church of the denomination (in village and town) in Essex, Hampshire, and Norfolk helped. Jesse Hobson, Carey's nephew, wrote: 'You will rejoice with me when I tell you that poor Moulton has raised upwards of £50 towards your loss by the dreadful fire. I fear your loss of MSS. is great, and perhaps irreparable. Mr Sutcliff asked me if I could form any idea, but, as I had no account, I could not tell him.'

An event thus dramatic seemed needed to reveal the work to British Christendom, which learned with *astonishment* that the Mission *could* lose, and in one building, from £9,000 to £10,000, and still more that the translations involved so many languages. Till then they had heard without hearing. This catastrophe unstopped their ears. In the blaze of this fire they at last saw the grandeur of the enterprise. The facts were broadcast, and thus the destruction proved to be a beacon, multiplying the Mission's zealous friends. So loud a fame it brought them as to reverse the nature of their risks, as Fuller faithfully warned them. In the first week of 1813 he wrote:

This fire has given your undertaking a celebrity which nothing else, it seems, could; a celebrity which makes me tremble. The public is now giving us their praises. Eight hundred guineas have been offered for Dr Carey's likeness! If we inhale this incense, will not God withhold His blessing, and then where are we? Ought we not to tremble? Surely, all need more grace to go through good report than through evil. I have less jealousy of you than of ourselves; but we are all in danger.

The promptitude with which you have been enabled to repair the loss of types, and to renew your printing of the Scriptures, is as extraordinary, says Dr Stewart of Edinburgh, as if we had repaired your pecuniary loss in *one week*. The specimens of Tamil, Nagari, Oriya, and Punjabi that you sent me, printed from the recast types, I clipped in pieces, as Saul hewed his oxen, and sent in letters through England, Scotland, and Ireland, calling them 'feathers of the phoenix'.

I said I trembled lest we should be injured by men's applause, and should incur God's displeasure. But now another thing strikes me. When the people ascribed 'ten thousands to David', it wrought envy in Saul, and proved a source of long and sore affliction. If some new trials were to follow, I should not be surprised; but, if we be kept humble and near to God, we have nothing to fear.

Wise Fuller was right, but even he failed to conceive how swift and severe the 'new trials' were to prove.

22. The Routed Foe

An invitation having reached us from Dr Carey, as soon as we moored, to spend the night in his Calcutta home, I got into a palanquin, whilst Mr Judson walked. It was with considerable fear I rode, the streets being so full. I soon lost sight of Mr Judson, and did not know where they might carry me. They stopped, however, before a large building, which I found to be Dr Carey's house. We were directed up a pair of stairs, through one or two large rooms into his study. He rose, and gave us a cordial welcome. His house is curiously constructed, like all European homes here. No fireplaces nor chimneys; the roofs flat; the rooms twenty feet high, and proportionately large. Large windows without glass open from one room to another, that the air may freely circulate.

In the evening we attended a service in the English Episcopal Church. We spent the night at Dr Carey's. Very near is the Mission charity school, with 200 boys, and nearly as many girls – chiefly children picked up from the streets, of no caste. We could see them kneel in prayer together, and hear them sing. It was most affecting.

In the afternoon we left for Serampore. We were met by Dr Marshman and Mr Ward, who, with their wives, received us very cordially. The three families live in separate houses, but eat together in a large hall. The buildings stand close to the river. The bell rings at 5 for the boys to rise for school; at 8 for breakfast, and immediately after breakfast for prayers in the large and elegant chapel: a hymn, Bible chapter and prayer. On Sunday, English worship 11 to 1; Bengali in the afternoon, and English again in the evening. Monday evening, a conference for the native Christians; Tuesday evening, an hour spent in examining difficult Scriptures; Thursday and Saturday evening, conferences.

The garden is as superior to any in America, as America's best is to a common farmer's. It consists of several acres, under the highest cultivation. Fruit, flowers and vegetables grow in abundance. The pineapple grows on a low bush, the plantain on a tall stock, and the cocoa-nut on a high tree.

The day after we came here there was Jagannath worship. The crowd was immense. The idol, painted with large black eyes and a large red mouth, was taken from his temple, and water poured on him to bathe him. The more

[290]

solemn act of worship will be in a fortnight. After bathing their god, they bathe themselves. They know not what they do.

O Mary, Americans know nothing of poverty compared with the multitudes of India.

MRS ADONIRAM (ANNE HASSELTINE) JUDSON to her sister, mid June 1812.

We were affectionately received by the good Dr Carey at his Calcutta house, and treated with the greatest hospitality. Imagine a small bald-headed man of 60 (nay, 51): such is he whose name will be remembered to the latest generation. He is now advanced to a state of honour, with 6,000 dollars a year. We accepted his invitation to visit the Mission family at Serampore, and took boat the next evening, and reached the happy dwelling of these friends of Immanuel. Here peace and plenty reign, and we almost forgot that we are in a land of pagan darkness. Mrs Carey is ill. Only Dr Carey's youngest son, Jonathan, now lives here, and has lately begun preaching at 16. Felix is in Rangoon, William at Katwa, and Jabez studies law in Calcutta. Mrs Ward has the care of providing for the whole Mission family, and is a motherly woman, very active and kind. Mrs Marshman has a lovely school of English young ladies. Miss Phoebe Hobson, Dr Carey's niece, is a very pretty girl. Captain Moxon from the Mahratta country is also here (and devoted to Phoebe, who made it her study to promote the comfort of them all). Mr and Mrs Carapeit Aratoon, Armenians, are on a visit. These, with the families of Drs Carey and Marshman and Mr and Mrs Ward, and all the pupils, make the Mission company very large. A hundred or more sit down together in the dining hall.

Serampore is a charming place. We frequently walk out to admire its beauty. The Mission garden is larger and much more elegant than any I ever saw in America. The view across the river is delightful. I love these dear missionaries very much. You would love them too, could you see them. I never experienced so many kindnesses.

HARRIET NEWELL to her mother and her sister, July 1812.

On the 6th instant [of September] was baptised at Calcutta by Bro. Ward, the Rev Adoniram Judson. Dr Judson was sent out as a missionary by the American Board of Commissioners of Foreign Missions formed from Congregational churches in the States of New England, and a few days before his baptism sent us the following note:

'To the Rev Messrs Carey, Marshman and Ward,
Sirs,

As you have been ignorant of my late exercises of mind on the subject of baptism this communication may occasion you some surprise. It is now about four months since I took the subject of baptism into serious and prayerful consideration. My enquiries commenced during my voyage from America, and, after much painful trial, which I will not now detail, have issued in the entire conviction, that the immersion of professing believers is the only Christian baptism.

In these exercises of mind I have not been alone: Mrs Judson has been engaged in a similar examination and has come to the same conclusion. Feeling, therefore, that we are in an unbaptised state, we wish to profess our faith in Christ by being baptised in obedience to His commands.

A. Judson'

Members' Circular Letter of Lall Bazar Chapel,
September 1812.

22. The Routed Foe
1812 – 1813

NO REINFORCEMENTS from the home base were sent to Serampore through six long years, by reason of the Government's unrevoked injunction against missionary evangelism in the Company's territory. But when, at the end of 1811, Lord Minto himself eased Chamberlain's going to Agra, Carey concluded that the Government's restrictions were relaxed, and its veto moribund, and he so advised Fuller. But he was soon disillusioned. Fierce anti-mission forces once more gained the ascendancy within the British Indian administration, and the wolves again chased Christ's few shepherds. They planned to deal the Mission the severest possible blow before the East India Company charter was reviewed in Parliament in 1813.

John Thompson of the London Missionary Society, who was designated for Madras, was the first victim. He was instantly ordered to return to England, the disappointment possibly aggravating the fever from which he died. Then America's first Asian missionaries were similarly excluded – the Judsons, the Newells, the Notts, Gordon Hall and Luther Rice. Regardless of the fact that the Government was assured that they were only calling at Serampore, and did not intend to settle in Bengal, they were barred from every British Indian presidency and dependency, and from every Eastern possession of Britain's allies. The preposterous ban was absolute. When they were at length obliged to go to Mauritius, Lord Minto's recent conquest (though still under French law), they were mercilessly saddled with heavy expense. Those who could not get passages quickly enough to satisfy the impatient authorities were ordered to go to England, almost as prisoners, by the Company's next fleet – a fate which they only just escaped. Even a year later, when the Judsons headed east again from Mauritius, they only eluded arrest in Madras by immediate embarkation for Rangoon. Official eyes were sleepless.

It may be thought that the fact that they were Americans was the reason for their harsh treatment, especially in those days of strained relations between the States and Britain, and doubtless, this counted. But the administration was just as hostile to British missionaries such as Dr Johns and John Lawson, who arrived with the Americans. Indeed, they were even hostile to Robinson, in spite of his six years' residence. They banned them all, and demanded their withdrawal. They did not ban them because they thought them likely to commit any indiscretion or misdemeanour, but solely because they had no formal licences from the East India Company (a lack shared with hosts of others at whose presence the Government winked). Their misdeed was that they were missionaries. This was the crime which could not be condoned. The deportation order reached Serampore on the anniversary of the fire, and was felt as a more severe disaster.

Lawson, a trained artist and engraver, was eventually allowed to stay to work on the perfecting of the Chinese types, in which the Government had an interest. But the Johns were expelled at the cost of the Mission. They were bundled home on the *Castlereagh* with no chance of escaping. As a chemist and surgeon, Johns could have nobly served India on the humanitarian side of the work, but, being a missionary, he was anathema to the administration. Even Robinson, who had gone to Java on the strength of an earlier permit, was ruthlessly pursued and ordered home to England, but he was protected and retained by Lieutenant-Governor Stamford Raffles, an ardent friend of the Mission, and as keen a naturalist as Carey. But the British Indian administration was out to break every possible British mission. They would have deported even the Serampore leaders if they could have done so, and all the more when they heard of the open identification of three of the American missionary party with the Baptist tenets of Serampore.

On their separate sea journeys to India the Judsons and Luther Rice had made further study of the New Testament, in order to equip themselves to plant Asian churches on scriptural foundations. As they studied they were strongly drawn towards baptistic conclusions, against all the bias of the paedo-baptism of their upbringing, and to their own consternation! Not wanting to disappoint and vex their denominational supporters, they strongly resisted these conclusions. At Serampore, despite the missionaries' refusal to discuss this question with them, conviction at length grew absolute, and before the end of 1812 they adopted Baptist views and were baptised at the Lall Bazar Chapel, Calcutta. When this got abroad, as it soon did, it darkened the official frown on the Mission.

The administration's bitter hostility distressed Carey more for Britain's sake than for his own, stung though he was by its ungraciousness after his twenty years' devotion. He wrote:

> I mourn, on my country's account, that preaching the Gospel should be regarded in the same light as committing a felony. In every way I have tried to acquit the Government and the London Directors of intention to persecute; but I am driven to conclude that, whilst Lord Minto himself is friendly and of liberal enlightenment, the presidency secretaries are largely infidel and inimical, and that they so shape the information and advice they lay before the authorities as almost to necessitate adverse decisions.

The Mission, however, bore itself with wise restraint. In their circular letters of this period, reporting the work monthly to their stations and to the home base, no hint was dropped of the rough weather they were experiencing. They kept the door of their lips. They let their moderation be known unto all men, in the faith that their Lord was ever at hand to guard both them and His kingdom. 'Jehovah reigneth' was their perpetual refrain.

What pained Carey more than the violence of the Government was the contention it brought within Serampore. Johns would not believe that sufficient pressure had been brought to bear on the authorities for his retention, though they did all they could to secure this, motivated by their desire to have in their ranks one of his valued profession. Furthermore, he had raised in America £1,200 for the work. But he could not rid his mind of the idea that more effort had been taken to secure the retention of Lawson than of himself. He particularly blamed Marshman, who had conducted the negotiations. Carey laboured as never before for reconciliation, but to no effect. Johns' bitterness remained, and when back in England he sowed seeds of suspicion over Marshman, the harvest of which was tragic. The distress of it made Carey 'alarmingly ill', so that he even 'looked for death'.

That Carey could see the virtues of Johns as well as his defects is clear from his words to Ryland:

> He was a very irritable man, but he certainly devoted himself to his work. I confess that I thought more highly of him when he went away than when he arrived. He was not suited for missionary life, but he had many excellent qualities.

Carey's solace in the midst of the Government's opposition lay in what he had already seen of the Gospel's power. He wrote to Ryland in the April of 1813:

> It is too late to eradicate the Gospel from Bengal. The number of those born in the country who are now preaching the Word is very considerable.

They had by this time baptised more than five hundred people. Five Kulin Brahmins had recently confessed their faith, saved through the unaided study of the Scriptures. These reported that 100 other truth-seekers in their district were on the brink of an identical profession of Christ. The Mission was currently translating the Scriptures into eighteen languages, and printing them in fifteen. Not even their eight presses could meet the increasing demand for their various New Testaments. Beyond India, the Judsons were settling into their Burmese service, and Felix could say, 'They are just cut out for this mission. I thought so, as soon as I first met them. In six months Mr Judson has a splendid grasp of the language, and is the very colleague I wanted.' Then, in Batavia, the Mission's most eastern outpost, Robinson had already a baptised church of twenty meeting in the home of a former member of Lall Bazar. They had great rejoicing over a cultivated Bengali convert named Tara Chand Datta of Bansbaria (20 miles from Serampore) who later authored a Bengali hymnbook, with tunes of his own, and who made his home a centre for evangelism and spent almost all his wealth in the service of Christ.

But Carey's sweetest comfort was the conversion of Jabez, for which he had long cried to God, and also enlisted the prayers of Fuller and Ryland. The lad was filial, but not Christian. Though he diligently learned Chinese for the Mission, still he lacked personal devotion to Christ, and also any missionary interest. In December 1810 he had written to Carey:

Very dear Father,

As you have once or twice suggested to me that you would be glad if I would let you know in what line of life I would wish myself permanently fixed, I now take the liberty of laying open my mind to you, for I have frequently of late been thinking of it. If you would endeavour to get me into the Civil Service, I should be glad, both on account of my being near yourself for the first two or three years, and on account of my not mixing with any mean company. You once mentioned to me yourself that you wished me to get into some honourable employment. I can think of none more honourable in secular life than the Company. I hope, my dear father, that you will not take this amiss, for, if it does not meet your approbation, I shall drop all thoughts of it.

Unable to arrange this, Carey did the next best similar thing, and articled him to a firm of Calcutta solicitors.

Ryland, preaching on the Society's twentieth anniversary to a gathering of the Mission's friends in London on 'The zeal of the Lord of hosts shall perform this,' spoke of Carey's joy in Felix and William: 'but he has a third son,' he said, 'giving him pain; because, though dutiful, he is unconverted.' Pausing, he asked their instant prayers for Jabez, and a deep quiet fell on all, and they knew God was near and was hearing. Indeed, before they had called, God had answered. The very next Indian mail brought them the news that in the summer of 1812, Jabez had come to Christ as Saviour and as Lord.

This happy event heralded an astonishing turn of events. The very administration which had been so churlish, suddenly sought the Mission's help.

Byam Martin, whom we remember as one of Carey's early and brilliant students and college converts, had just become first 'Resident' of the Moluccas, which had been taken from the Dutch. Upon entering into his task, he grew convinced that what his islands most needed was missionary-hearted educationalists. In a comprehensive (and courageous) dispatch to the Calcutta authorities in the summer of 1813, he urged them to secure him such from Serampore, and wrote the following by the same mail to Carey:

> My dear Sir,
>
> What shall I say for having so long neglected to write to you? I can only acknowledge my fault and resolve to make amends. I have written to the Calcutta Bible Society Auxiliary earnestly entreating them for an edition of the Malay Bible in the Roman character for the 20,000 native Christians of these islands. What a field is here opened for your labours at Serampore! Be assured, my dear Sir, that, so long as I remain here, my authority and influence shall be exerted to support those who think it worth their while to turn their attention thither. I earnestly beg of you to concert means *for sending a missionary to Amboyna.* The advantages would be incalculable. As the head of the administration here, I should consider it a sacred duty to give all the assistance in my power. Pray, therefore, lose no time in setting about this. I am sure I need say no more to interest the feelings of one so humane and good as yourself. I am writing in a great hurry, and can say no more at present than to assure you that I shall ever be, with the utmost gratitude and attachment,
>
> Your sincere and faithful friend,
>
> W. B. MARTIN

Within a week of this letter's arrival, Jabez volunteered. His conduct for a year and a half had left no doubt in the mind of his father about his Christian spirit. Yet Carey set before him the attractive professional prospects he would be surrendering (the Supreme Court's second judge was already interested in him), and contrasted these with the privations he would be accepting. By January the British administration invited the Mission's assistance, with the promise of free passage to whoever would go, and Jabez, though not yet twenty, was approved and appointed.

On the 12th he wrote to his father:

> Before I embark, I wish to follow the example of Christ, my Lord and Saviour, in baptism, to Whose service I have devoted myself. Pray for me, my dear father, that I may be enabled to give myself to God without reserve and with a heart of sincerity.

Marriage, ordination, and farewell were then crowded into three days. Felix, by a happy coincidence, was there to collect lymph for Burma's Crown prince; William was also there, home from Katwa. So, at the joint ordination and valediction, the two brothers with the father laid their hands on the new missionary and invoked God's blessing. All went direct to the docks, and Jabez sailed away in the *Streatham* for Christ's service, going further east than any had yet gone from Serampore, and by the request and in the pay of the British Indian Government which had recently done its best to expel the Mission from the East! It was indeed more than conquering. It was a routing of the foe! In the midst of his tears Carey was inexpressibly happy.

> Oh praise the Lord with me *[he wrote in his next letter to England]* and let us exalt His name together. God has been very, very gracious to me. I trust all my sons love Him. Three out of the four are engaged in the active work of the Gospel, and two in new countries.

He told William that 'he would rather have Jabez a missionary than Chief Justice of Bengal.' He made time (though very unwell) to write the following letter (here slightly compressed) towards his son's embarkation:

My dear Jabez,

You are engaging in a most important undertaking, in which you will have not only my prayers for your success, but those of all who love our Lord Jesus, and who know of your engagement. A few hints from a father who loves you tenderly will, I am sure, not be wasted.

Trust always in Christ. Be pure of heart. Live a life of prayer and of devotedness to God. Be gentle and unassuming, yet firm and manly.

You are now married. Be not content to bear yourself toward your wife with propriety, but let love be the spring of all your conduct. Esteem her highly that she may highly esteem you. The first impression of love arising from form or beauty will soon wear off, but the trust arising from character will endure and increase. I hope that, as soon as you are settled in your cabin, you will begin and end each day together in prayer and praise to God.

Behave affably to all, cringingly and unsteadily to none. Feel that you are a man, and always act with that dignified sincerity, which will command men's respect. Seek not the society of worldly men, but, when called to be with them, act and converse with propriety and dignity. To this end labour to gain a good acquaintance with history and geography, with men and things. A gentleman is the next best character after a Christian, and the latter includes the former. Money never makes a gentleman, much less a fine appearance; but an enlarged understanding joined to engaging manners.

Consult Mr Martin on every occasion of importance. As soon as you are settled, get a Malay, who can speak a little English, and make a tour of your islands, visiting every school. Keep a journal of each, and encourage all you see worthy. Compare their periodic progress. Consider yourself more than a director of schools – even their Christian instructor, and devote yourself to their good. God has committed to you the spiritual interests of these islands; a vast charge, but one which He can enable you to fulfil. When you meet with a few who truly fear God, form them into Gospel churches. As soon as you see any fitted to preach, call them to the ministry, and settle them over these.

Shun all indolence and love of ease, and never try to act the part of the great and gay in this world. Labour incessantly to become a perfect master of the Malay. With this in view, associate with the native people, walk with them, ask the name of everything you see, visit them when they are sick.

Every night arrange your new words in alphabetical order, and use them as soon as you can.

Do not unnecessarily expose your life, but incessantly endeavour to give to the aboriginal Alfoors the Word of the Gospel.

Learn correctly the number, size and geography of your islands; the number and character of their inhabitants, their manners and customs, etc, and regularly communicate with me.

After elaborate natural history instructions he adds:

But your great work, my dear Jabez, is that of a Christian minister. May you be kept amid all temptations, supported under every trial, and made victorious in every conflict; and may our hearts be mutually gladdened by accounts from each other of the triumphs of God's grace. He has conferred on you a great *favour* in committing to you this ministry. Take heed to fulfil it. We shall often meet at the throne of grace. Write to me by every opportunity, and Eliza to mother. Now, my dear son, I commit you both to God and to the Word of His grace, which is able to make you perfect in the knowledge of His will. Let that Word dwell in your hearts. Should I never see you on earth, I trust we shall meet with joy before His throne.

Your very, very affectionate father

Jabez wrote on his voyage in reply:

We have never failed, dear father, since we left you, to bow our knees together at our family altar morning and evening, according to your advice and the dictates of our consciences, and have spent very pleasant hours thus. We have often read your kind and dear counsel, and wept over it, too. Pray that I may to the end of my days be enabled to walk in your footsteps.

And soon he wrote from Amboyna:

I can scarcely express the joy I felt at the receipt of your kind and affectionate first letter here. May my conduct deserve a father so good.

Ward writes to England in the last week of 1813:

We are here carried forward, the prospects still widening. *Ten* presses are going, and nearly *two hundred* are employed about the printing office. The foundation is surely not being laid to this extent and depth for nothing. But our hands are too few, our days too short, our strength too small for the expanding work. Serampore, Jessore, Katwa, Dinajpur, Patna, Digah, Allahabad, Agra, Sirdhana, Nagpur, Surat, Orissa, Calcutta, Ceylon, Burma, Java have messengers of salvation. Now we have been *called by the Governor-General himself to send help to Amboyna.*

Fuller's first letter to Jabez at Amboyna overflowed from his fatherly wisdom:

LONDON
18 August, 1814

My dear Jabez,

We are informed of what God has wrought for you and in you, and hope soon to hear of what He has wrought through you. Our hearts have participated in the joy of your dear father over you . . . Shall I say, you have honoured God by preferring His service to your own? I might rather say that God has honoured you, and I trust will make you a blessing amongst the islands. May you see better days than we have, though we have seen what gladdens our hearts. May you outdo us in devotion. Cleave to God, and there is no difficulty He will not help you to surmount. You lived just long enough without God in the world to know what you would have been, had you been left thus. Your being so early turned to God is a token of the much He designs for you. I hope my children will love and correspond with you, as I have loved your father. A word to you, dear Mrs Carey. We rejoiced that you were willing to have your husband give up his flattering prospects in Calcutta, and to go with him to Amboyna. Blessed be thou of the Lord. I pray that you may continue thus till death.

I am, my dear young people,
Your faithful, though unknown, friend,

ANDREW FULLER

Resident-Governor Martin gave Jabez and his wife a great welcome, but regretted that they were alone. He wrote to Carey:

> I experienced the greatest pleasure from the arrival of your son. He commenced very shortly after to apply himself most diligently to the Malay language; and I have no doubt that, in the course of a short term, he will have sufficiently qualified himself to initiate his system of instruction in the schools. But I am a good deal disappointed that no other missionary came with him. It appears that you have very little intelligence in Bengal respecting the opportunities here for the diffusion of Christianity. Let me entreat you, my dear Sir, to exert your influence to send us *more* labourers into this field, which gives promise of a most abundant harvest.

Carey grieved to have no other reapers available, but the blame was not Serampore's. The guilt lay at the door of Byam Martin's own superiors and colleagues who had so restricted and thinned the Mission's ranks. But to have a governor of that same administration soliciting Christian help for his province, like the Macedonian at Troas, was a wonder and a triumph.

Jabez quickly approved himself in his many-isled new 'kingdom', and Governor Martin kept reporting to Carey his fine service. He was never content with just an educational directorate, but pressed people to Christ – young Anglo-Indian J. W. Ricketts first, from Governor Martin's staff, who was ultimately chosen to lay before both Houses of Parliament the famous Petition of 1830 which secured the abolition of the colour-bar from India's civil and military services. Such respect and confidence did Jabez inspire in the Malays by his development of the schools, his preaching, and his Scripture translation work on the one hand, and by his civic service as State almoner and member of the College of Justice, that, in the very troubled days which followed the restoration of the islands to the Dutch, he was able to be the chief arbiter and peacemaker. Carey could be very proud of him. His intimate knowledge of Chinese, too, opened avenues of service. When he eventually left the Moluccas because the Dutch Governor would allow no preaching nor baptising except in the name of their State church, he could say, 'It gave me the greatest satisfaction to see so many wet eyes, as I parted from the people.'

Through his years there Carey had written to him, by every ship he heard of, letters that reveal his fatherly love. I cull a few sentences:

I want to assure you how much you lie upon my heart. I follow you with my prayers.

As a parent who tenderly loves you, I feel all your anxieties keenly.

Tell me all your difficulties. I am your father.

Everything relating to you is of great importance to me.

I generally become anxious when the time of the month arrives, when I may expect your letter – anxious about your health and family and work.

When I am long in hearing from you, my heart sinks, and I begin to be full of fears.

I have stated times of intercession with God for my children.

Never step an inch out of the path of righteousness and Truth, to curry favour or avoid disgrace.

Examine the Word of God for every step you take. Rightly understood, it will never lead you astray.

Seek to gain a constant and intimate acquaintance with evangelical Truth.

All that is not built on the foundation of Christ crucified will fail.

Make mention of His righteousness, even of His only.

The character of a minister of the Gospel should be the highest on earth.

If true godliness prosper in your own soul, duty will be easy. If personal religion is low, your work will be a burden. Personal religion is the life-blood of all your usefulness and happiness.

The more unreservedly you devote yourself to God, the more will you know His peace.

I do not write thus because I have any suspicion of you, but because I am jealous over you with a godly jealousy.

To persevere in doing good in the midst of discouragement will give you more happiness and win you more respect than a crown could.

If duty leads us to any place, however unhealthy, we may safely trust God to take care of us.

If God gives us work to do, fits us for it, and strengthens us in it, that is enough.

Watch against the temptation just to gossip with the Europeans. Show them every respect, but always remember that *your* chief duty lies among the Malays.

Communicate to these the knowledge of divine things you possess, and you will find your stock soon increase.

You must not expect them to pay much attention to what you say, unless you win their love. The more attention you pay them, the more will they pay you. Let nothing short of a radical change of heart satisfy you in your converts.

You are the sole director of your own affairs, nor would I interfere with them, but as an affectionate father I give you my advice, which is dictated also by my care for Christ's kingdom.

Your honour is as dear to me as my own.

During 1813, when the East India Company's charter was reconsidered by Parliament at its ten-yearly review, and while the British administration in India was reluctantly moving away from its fierce hostility to Christian missions into an acknowledged indebtedness, the friends of missions at home won a notable victory. Nine hundred petitions urged the Houses for the sanction of missionary activity. Fuller described it as 'not a shower but a set rain'. His own activity was phenomenal, until Britain's Christian conscience waked and thundered, and politicians took alarm. Three days in the Commons were devoted to this particular debate, though many more to the whole charter.

On 22 June Wilberforce was the Christian advocate in a speech of extraordinary fulness and power, which contained these words:

These 'Anabaptist' missionaries, as among other low epithets they have been contemptuously called, are entitled to our highest respect and admiration. One of them, Dr Carey, was originally in one of the lowest social stations; but, under all its disadvantages, he had the genius as well as the benevolence to devise a plan, which has since been pursued, of forming a society for communicating the blessings of our Christian light to the native peoples of India.

His first care was to qualify himself to act a distinguished part in this truly noble enterprise. He resolutely bent himself to the study of the learned languages. After reaching considerable proficiency in these, he applied himself to several of the Oriental tongues, more especially to that which, I understand, is regarded as the parent of them all, the Sanskrit, in which his proficiency is acknowledged to be greater than even that of Sir William Jones, or any other European. Of several of these languages he has already published a grammar; of one or two of them a dictionary, and he has in contemplation a still greater literary enterprise. The very plan of these would excite the highest admiration and respect in every unprejudiced literary mind.

All this time, Sir, he is labouring as a missionary with a warmth of zeal only equalled by that with which he prosecutes his literary labours.

Merit like this could not escape the distinguishing eye of Lord Wellesley, who appointed him Professor of Sanskrit and Bengali in the college at Calcutta. Another of these 'Anabaptist' missionaries, Dr Marshman, has established a seminary for the cultivation of Chinese, a language which he has studied with a success scarcely inferior to that of Dr Carey in the Sanskrit. On more than one occasion at the annual examinations of the college in Calcutta, the highest eulogiums have been pronounced both on Dr Carey and Dr Marshman by the Governor-General, and the happiest consequences predicted from their literary toils.

It is a merit of a vulgar sort, but, to those who are blind to their moral and even their literary excellences, it may afford an estimate of value better suited to their principles and habits of calculation, that these men, and Mr Ward, another of the missionaries, acquiring from £1,000 to £1,500 a year each by the varied exercise of their talents, throw the whole into the Mission's common stock, which they thus support with their pecuniary contributions only less effectively than by their researches and labours of a higher order. Such, Sir, are the exertions, such the merits, such the successes of these great and good men; for so I shall not hesitate to term them.

The Commons could not withhold its applause either from the men or the cause so defended. Amongst the ten later speakers, however, a Mr Prendergast alleged:

The conduct of Dr Carey, which was excellent during Lord Wellesley's government, totally changed from the day of his departure. Recently, he so abused the religion of the Hindus from a tub, that he would have been killed, had it not been for the intervention of the police.

Despite this allegation (which Carey later called 'a gross falsehood') and the five other anti-mission speeches, Wilberforce won by 89 to 36. The rout of the Mission's challengers was complete. On 1 July, when the debate was resumed, the attendance on both sides was much thinner – Indian questions generally drawing small Houses. But Charles Marsh (ex-barrister of Madras), member for East Retford, gave a speech as extensive as Wilberforce's of the 22nd, in which he emptied on the Mission the vials of his scorn.

Will these people [he said] crawling from the holes and caverns of their original destinations, these apostates from the loom and anvil, these renegades from the lowest handicraft employments, be a match for the

Adoniram Judson

cool and sedate controversialists they will have to encounter, should the Brahmins condescend to enter into the arena against the maimed and crippled gladiators that presume to grapple with their faith? What can be apprehended but the disgrace and discomfiture of whole hosts of tub-preachers in the conflict? And will this advance us one inch nearer our goal?

Wilberforce immediately followed him:

Far different was the impression produced by these men on the mind of a Marquis Wellesley; far different his language. Even a philosophic mind, if free from prejudice, could not but recognise in them an extraordinary union of various, and in some sort contradictory, qualities – zeal combined with meekness, love with sobriety, courage and energy with prudence and perseverance, great animation and diligence as students with no less assiduity and efficiency as missionaries. I can only admire their eminence of merit, which I myself despair to reproduce.

The progressives won again – this time by 22.

In the Upper House Lord Wellesley himself stood in the Mission's defence. The three leaders had lived under his very eyes from Barrackpore.

> I must say *[he confessed]* that, whilst I was in India, I never knew of any danger arising from the missionaries' proceedings. The greatest number of them were in the Danish settlement of Serampore. Some of them were very learned men, particularly Dr Carey, whom I employed in the College of Fort William. I always considered the missionaries who were in India in my time a quiet, ordered, discreet and learned body. I employed them in the education of youth, and the translation of the Scriptures into the Eastern languages. I thought it my duty to have the Scriptures translated into the tongues of the East, to give India the advantage of access to the sacred fountain of divine Truth. I felt that a Christian Governor could not do less: I knew that a British Governor could not do more.

The victorious resolution ran thus:

> That it is the duty of this country to promote the interest and happiness of the inhabitants of the British Dominion in India, and that such means ought to be adopted as may lead to the introduction among them of useful knowledge, and of religious and moral improvement. That in the furtherance of the above objects sufficient facilities should be afforded by law to persons desirous of going to and remaining in India for the purpose of accomplishing these beneficent designs.

Wilberforce always declared that 'this cause of the recognition of our Christian obligation to British India was the greatest he had lived for, not even excepting the emancipation of the slaves.' He thus records his feelings after his great first victory. 'It was late when I got up. I thank God I was enabled to speak for two hours and with great acceptance, and we carried it by 89 to 36. I heard afterwards that many good men had been praying for us all night.'

Years later the Marquis of Hastings told Carey and Marshman that 'the revision of the charter and the freedom of entry therein given to Christian missionaries was the fruit under God of their own prudence and wisdom and zeal.'

23. The Threatened Woe

The conflict of the first quarter of the century in the history of the Society's Indian Mission yielded a series of victories; the controversy of the second quarter, though both sides were zealous for God, squandered a part of the strength of the strongest, and saddened the hearts of the three noblest workers of the century. It was doubtless to Ward and Marshman, as Carey said it was to him, 'a greater trial than all his many sorrows'. To forget the Serampore controversy altogether is to close the book on one of the most profitable warnings in modern church history.

SAMUEL VINCENT

The old economy of missions, under which Dr Carey and his associates embarked, had passed away. Missions had attained the maturity and organisation of a national enterprise. Missionaries no longer went to India with the understanding that they must depend for the means of subsistence mainly on their own exertions, which would be eked out by slight or occasional aid from England. The societies were endowed with ample resources, and were enabled to give adequate salaries to their missionaries, and this brought in its train a new principle of subordination, to which the Serampore missionaries were strangers.

JOHN CLARK MARSHMAN

23. The Threatened Woe
1814 – October 1817

THE REVISAL of the Company's charter with its now sanctioned ingress of missionaries brought to Serampore a good sequence of accessions. Carey's own nephew Eustace was the first, of whom Robert Hall said that 'they had engaged no one concerning whom they had formed a more raised expectation.' Then Yates, once shoe-maker, like Carey, and from Leicester's Harvey Lane. Then engineer Randall, a convert of Saffery's, to run the paper-mill; and school-expert Penney; and printer Pearce, son of Samuel, after years at the Clarendon Press.

Carey himself was more occupied than ever. Earl Moira and Bishop Middleton were amazed at Serampore's translation room, with pundits from nearly every Indian language area, as well as from China and Afghanistan, and with Carey supervising twenty-two Scripture versions.

The winters of 1814 and 1815 brought Carey home news of devastating deaths. First, Sutcliff, a most valued friend and correspondent, the Society's shrewd counsellor, and scholarly tutor of its aspiring missionaries. Then, to the extreme grief of the Serampore missionaries, Fuller himself, the Mission's *Colossus,* as Ward termed him – 'the

shadow of a great rock'. He had never recovered the strength he had
exhausted in his fight with Parliament. He had purchased the revised
charter with his life. Indeed, through all the twenty-three years from
that Nottingham morning, he had been of one mind and soul with
Carey, and 'in labour and travail and much patience, in journeyings
and watchings and fastings, in necessities, in hunger and cold', he had
spent himself for the Mission. His doctor said 'he was as completely
worn out by intense application as any one he ever knew in the last
stage of consumption.' 'Staying by the stuff', he had been as valiant as
any who went forth to the battle – the Mission's Minister of Muni-
tions. In loyalty to his vow to 'stand by Carey until death', he had
refrained from passing his work as secretary of the Mission to any
other, even when he knew he had long been overtaxing his strength.
No cause could have had a nobler captain, nor could Carey have found
in all the world a more steadfast home colleague. He had been able to
build on him 'an absolute trust'. 'I loved him,' Carey wrote to Ryland.
'There was scarcely any other man in England to whom I could so
completely lay open my heart.' Saffery rightly condoled with him as
'the chief mourner', for his death increased the weight of his every subsequent load.

Staughton wrote from America, 'The cedars have fallen; yet, I doubt
not, God has in England an undergrowth, which, ere long, will tower
to His praise.' Carey had lifelong occasion to bewail the fall of the
cedars.

Things were already running far from smoothly in the Mission. The
newcomers had either brought with them (through the influence of
Johns) some critical attitudes, or were quickly thus infected. The
criticism was not directed at Ward or Carey, but Dr Marshman.
Though their missionary record amply demonstrates their high aims,
the newcomers soon became aggravated by the yoke which the Serampore elders had deliberately chosen, and which had become their
second nature. Arrangements, which suited the Mission's early stages,
were no longer appropriate. Serampore was full of discord and distress.
Carey had never known such friction and grew dangerously ill. Three
of Calcutta's chief physicians attended him – one, the son of his warm
Leicester friend, Vicar Robinson. 'He was brought to the brink of the
grave.'

There were also other causes of disquiet. Even before Fuller's death, intimations had reached the Serampore elder missionaries from the home base of the proposed run-down of the island mission stations of Java and Ceylon. These intimations now increased. At this threatened deflection from his whole policy Carey wrote:

> I entreat, I implore you in England not to think of the petty shop-keeping plan of lessening the number of stations so as to bring them within the bounds of your present income, but to bend all your attention and exertion on increasing your finances so as to meet the work's pressing opportunities and demands. If our objects are large, the public will contribute to their support. If you contract them, their liberality will contract itself in proportion.

An axiom which Ward endorsed:

> I think with Carey that you must not go into the plan of giving up stations because they are costly, unless they are at the same time unnecessary or hopeless. Rather make England, Scotland, Ireland and America ring with the cry of your need.

The three soon received another stinging blow. Some Doeg whispered at home that they were 'making private fortunes', which a few began to believe. In reality, they had never swerved a hair's-breadth from their original self-denying rule. After meeting the settlement's simplest necessities, and those of their nearest English relatives, they had never ceased to lavish on the Mission the rest of their large earnings, making them beyond comparison its princeliest contributors. Of their super-sensitive honour let this from Hannah Marshman's diary, almost amusingly, suffice:

> 12 October, 1814 – We lately purchased a palanquin-carriage for the use of our school. But what a burden it was on my mind, more particularly since we heard of Felix's severe trials! Nor could I bear to see either of our brethren become coach-drivers: it does not become a minister of the Gospel. I feared, too, lest my own children should be elated with pride, and think themselves better in the carriage than out of it. I also thought it unsafe for them. But my chiefest dread was lest it might prove a curse to us, and bring God's anger upon us – being a deviation from the simplicity of our manners for the last fifteen years. But today the carriage has gone, and I desire to thank and love God, Who has mercifully delivered us from this burden. I rejoice therein more than if I had found great riches.

Carey writes to a home leader on 22 April, 1817:

> I confess I am a little indignant at some of the hints in one of your
> letters about our interested conduct. Beloved Fuller, with one scowl of
> his brow, would have dissipated a thousand such insinuations! I have
> devoted my all to the cause, and so have my colleagues. When Felix
> loaned from the Mission sums of money, which (through his misfor-
> tunes) he could not repay, I became responsible, and, with the little
> private property I possessed through my wife, paid the whole. Nor do I
> complain. We are trustees for the public and for God. Had my col-
> leagues wished, they could not have remitted the debt; nor could I have
> allowed it. I am now in my old age destitute of a rupee. I have become a
> fool in glorying; but you compelled me.

And later:

> Were I to die today, I should not leave property enough for the pur-
> chase of a coffin, and my wife would be entirely unprovided for. We are
> coarsely clad, and certainly not overfed, and, I believe, he who possesses
> the most among us has not so much as he contributes to the public
> stock in four months. I had Rs 6,000, but now I have none.

Some dared to hint that they were feathering nests for their *sons* in
the property at Serampore, though Ryland insisted that they were taking steps of the precisely opposite kind, namely, to make such family
succession impossible, unless the clearest proof of fitness was forthcoming, and any sons were properly elected to office. 'They are
wanting,' Ryland told the committee, 'not to seize what was ours to
make it theirs: it is theirs, and they want to make it ours. Not to secure
it *to* their children, but *from* them.' For his own part Carey wrote:

> I have striven my utmost to place my children in situations in which
> they would be independent of the Mission. William *is* dependent
> thereon; but, I believe, is by far the most efficient European labourer in
> Bengali now amongst us, and I am sure he has had a smaller allowance
> than that of any other European worker. Jabez left good earthly pros-
> pects for God's work. He has hitherto supported himself, and has repaid
> the 1,000 dollars, which the Mission advanced for his outfit; in which I
> glory.

In regard to this last he had written to his son:

> Your resolution to pay the 1,000 dollars most fully meets my appro-
> bation, and I am sure you will never be the poorer for it. And it will gain

you the confidence of all, and will be blessed of God: though, had you not done it, the brethren would not have thought you obliged to.

Still other communications from the home base indicated trouble ahead. Even Fuller, in his last two years, had sensed a new tone and attitude in the Society's councils, and had written to Serampore forebodingly of some who were impatient for a more authoritative executive. He had, he said, rebuked them in the following way:

> We never considered ourselves as legislators for our brethren, but just as their co-workers. If ever the committee begins to legislate for India, I should expect them to issue a declaration of independence, and I should not be sorry if they did. We never pretended to govern them, for two reasons – they were better able to govern themselves, and their distance is too great for them to await our directions. Our business has been to furnish them, as far as we were able, with means, and to send them a few recruits.

However, the old guard was passing from the scene. Fuller, Sutcliff, and Ryland had virtually *been* the committee, and their personal intimacy with the three, especially with Carey, made control (though not frank counsel) inappropriate. But now with Fuller and Sutcliff gone, the committee increased to thirty-five, and a finance committee chosen, the relationship became business-like and official. This finance committee can scarcely be blamed for wanting to know the precise terms of the trusts of the Indian properties. Yet it was wholly unfortunate that this was its earliest and most emphasised question, and that it immediately advised the appointment of *eight* British trustees to serve with the Serampore *three*.

However unintended, it lent confirmation to Ryland's written forebodings: 'I dread men's getting the reins in proportion to their eagerness to seize them.' 'I have unbounded fears for the future.' 'I tremble for the Ark of God, when it shall fall into the hands of mere counting-house men.' 'The confidence of young men in their competence makes me distrust them the more.'

When the official notification of the proposed election of trustees reached Serampore at the end of August 1817, it aroused the gravest concern, which was heightened by the arrival of Pearce under novel conditions. This highly trained son of 'the seraphic' Samuel Pearce was sure of a warm welcome, but it was an innovation that he (with his

wife) should be commissioned to reside in the *Serampore family* as
Ward's colleague in the press. No one had previously been pre-
assigned from home to Serampore's joint corporate fellowship, but
only adopted thereinto after mutual acquaintance, and by its members'
unanimous vote. This change touched the Serampore family at a very
sensitive spot. It looked like an expression of the new home regime's
aggressiveness, and an indication of much that would be fatal to Serampore's freedom and peace. The repeated forebodings of Fuller and
Ryland, the friction in the brotherhood, Ward's ill-health, and Marshman's woundedness under the juniors' distrust, and Carey's anxieties
over Felix and over Jonathan (who had brought him much sorrow),
combined to produce heightened sensitivity to offence. Carey poured
out his distress to Ryland in a long, sad letter. 'I have scarcely ever
written,' he confessed, 'under such depression of mind.'

> We are yours to live and die with you; but as your brothers, not your
> servants. I beseech you, therefore, not to attempt to exercise a power
> over us, to which we shall never submit. Bear with me a little, even if I
> speak foolishly: for my heart is exceedingly wounded at the Society's
> proposal of the eight British trustees, and at several concomitant symp-
> toms.

Then he reminds the Society that, even including the gifts to repair
the losses of the fire, Britain had only sent them some £33,000 from the
first, ie: enough to have covered the cost of their European staff, if they
had all been salaried throughout. The money for all else – for the
native preachers, the schools, the lands and buildings in Serampore,
Calcutta, Katwa, Patna, Rangoon, etc – they themselves had supplied,
including Serampore's type-foundry, printing works, paper-mill, with
all their equipment and stock.

> We borrowed the money, and paid it with interest, and became trustees
> thereof on the Society's behalf. Now we are required to associate with
> ourselves a large majority of persons in England as trustees. We have no
> objection to a single one proposed. We have always most highly
> esteemed them; but we will never consent to put power over these
> premises and over ourselves into their hands, at a distance of a quarter
> of the globe's circumference. The premises belong to the Society. We
> have made the Society a present of them. But, if the Society insists on
> the measure proposed, we will, much as we are attached to the place,
> evacuate it, and purchase other premises – which, whilst given to God,

shall not be given to the Society, and there we will carry on our work, subject to no control but His most holy Word. In this we are of one mind, and here we shall make our stand.

We have always thought ourselves masters of the funds produced by our own toil. We devote the whole to the cause of God, and wish to do so to our dying day. But the funds we produce, though devoted to the same object, have never been so merged into the Society's funds as to put them under others' control. We are your brothers, not your hired servants. We have always accounted it our glory to be related to the Society, and with them pursue the same grand purpose, and we shall rejoice therein, so long as you permit us; but we will come under the power of none. I do hope that the ideas of domination, which Fuller never thought of, but which the Society has imbibed since his death, will be given up, as we shall never 'give place by way of subjection, no, not for an hour'.

Concerning Pearce, he adds:

I think persons intended to dwell together for life should be placed within the sphere of each other's attraction, so that, after they know one another, they may voluntarily come together. In that case their union may be expected to abide. But the love of those *thrown* together will, I fear, in most cases increase in proportion to the squares of their distance.

Three weeks later he announced the deliberate and joint remonstrance they were sending to each member of the home committee, together with a new deed of trust, 'from which they would never swerve a hair's-breadth'. He also thankfully records the growing cordiality between the Pearces and themselves.

The 'remonstrance' was drafted by Marshman, but accepted and signed by the three. Marshman's son declares it 'one of the least happy of his father's productions, and prolix to an excess'. But it was written 'out of much distress and misery of heart with many tears', like Paul's to Corinth. Indeed, save in its length, it recalls that Pauline letter, that 'vibrated,' as Moffatt says, 'with anxiety and anger.' There is the same stung sense of grievance, the same irony, the same enforced self-boastings, and the same pressure of incalculable peril. It ended thus:

Nothing has ever caused us sorrow like this. Nothing ever so strongly threatened the destruction of the Mission. Your letter found us preparing a review of our work, but we had no spirit to go forward. We saw that, if your contention was right, we had delivered ourselves over to be bound to we scarcely knew who. The spirit of the oldest amongst us began to break. It had borne up against everything from enemies; but this from brethren it seemed unable to sustain. For a moment the cause looked hopeless, overwhelmed thus by its friends, who hitherto had been the centre of our affections only next to our Master Himself.

But the God of mercy and righteousness has enabled us to roll our burdens on Him, and to discern the course by which alone the Mission can be saved. We mourn that such a letter as this should have been requisite, and we have written with feelings of anguish never before experienced.

We entreat you for love's sake to lay aside this spirit for ever. The attempt repeated may destroy that love which has so long existed between us; whilst the solid rock does not more firmly resist the wave than shall we every attempt at interference with our funds, our union, and the premises originated by us for the Mission at Serampore.

Carey told Jabez that he was very near losing his life at the beginning of 1817:

I was returning from Dum Dum, when the belly band of the harness broke, and the shafts were drawn out of the saddle-slings and fell on the ground, in which condition the horse, which was spirited, continued to drag the buggy. I could not stop him, and I was afraid he would run off, which would have been very dangerous. I therefore jumped out and in so doing sprained my foot very badly, and fell down and cut my face, and I am still *[ten days later]* very lame.

Carey's anxieties through this entire period were intensified by the overwhelming sorrows, and then the stumblings, of Felix. After three years' widowerhood, he had married a Eurasian lady in Rangoon, his father willing to have him link himself thus closer with Burma. There he kept growing in the favour of the King, who charged him to establish a mission station, with a press, in his capital at Ava. When early in 1814 he returned to Rangoon with lymph for the Prince, and Burmese language copies of the *Gospel of Matthew* for the people, his father's hopes ran high. On the last day of that August, with wife and two little ones, and a printing-press (the willing gift of Serampore), he embarked at Rangoon for the capital. But within three hours of sailing, the ship overturned in a squall, and they all were flung into the Irrawaddy. Felix held up his wife and babe, till he sank, exhausted. When he came to the surface again, they had vanished. He thought he saw his little boy at a distance, but, strive as he would, could not reach him. He himself struggled to the river bank, where, still in much danger, he was rescued by *lascars* (sailors). Once again he had lost his wife, and half of his children had perished.

> My affliction *[he wrote to his father]* has indeed been great – I had almost said, more than I can bear. I have lost all I was worth in the world. Let it go. But the loss of my dear wife and dear infants goes very near my heart. What can I say? With Job I will be silent.

On the Sunday after this dreadful news came, Carey preached; but Mrs Marshman wrote in her diary, 'He appeared very low; his trials have been surely very heavy.'

Carey wrote to Jabez:

> We are overwhelmed with distress at these most heavy tidings, but we are dumb with silence, because God has done it. I mourn for Felix in silence.

And William wrote to his father:

> Your last melancholy letter cast us into a state of mind that I cannot describe. My poor brother! And in his distress he had not a friend to comfort him. So sudden a death, and almost a family at once! We shall expect you next week. Do spend some time with us.

The press and the Burmese copies of *Matthew's Gospel*, together with Felix's Burmese dictionary manuscripts, were all lost in the disaster.

His monetary loss the King quickly repaired, but his mental and spiritual health he recovered only slowly. For four years he was eccentric. Yet outwardly he seemed at first to advance. Towards the year's end he announced to Serampore his impending return to Calcutta as Burma's ambassador to the British Government, his commission being to ease the two peoples' strained relations, an errand in which Carey rejoiced. But he was pained to have him therewith resign from the staff of the Mission. 'I start,' he says, 'from the idea with a kind of horror, as if I realised it to be a great crime;' and to Fuller: '*Felix is shrivelled* from a missionary into an ambassador.'

However, soon after Felix had entered Calcutta in the glory of his rank – gold sword, scarlet-silk umbrella, and fifty Burmese

attendants – and after the Government had placed a city mansion at his
and his retinue's disposal, his credentials were found defective. He did
indeed bring letters from the King of Ava and the Viceroy of Pegu, and
commissions to execute, but apparently not a responsibility of ambas-
sadorial uniqueness. After having read the whole correspondence
between him and the British Secretary of State, I am unable to determine if the fault was with the royal secretary at Ava, or whether Felix
had misunderstood and exaggerated the nature of his mission. This,
however, is certain, that his strange, injudicious letters can only be
attributed to the drowning tragedy.

To Carey the whole affair must have been an unspeakable humiliation. 'It is very distressing,' he says, 'to be forced to apologise for those
you love.' All the more so, as Felix felt obliged, throughout the seven
months of his stay, to keep up the social circumstance of his claimed
position, and so incur debts which his father had to impoverish himself to extricate him from. He began to give way, too, to an excess of
wine. All the waves and billows rolled over Carey. 'Felix's drifting from
God,' he wrote to Jabez, 'has nearly broken my heart.'

Jabez answered from afar:

> O my dear father, were I able I would immediately be with you, and do
> the little I could to comfort and serve you, who have so long taken care
> of me. But, as my leaving the post I am stationed at, for any other
> reason than that of being obliged, will have a great effect in lowering
> your opinion of me, I submit. Never did I know as now the pain of
> separation.

William wrote to his father:

> My heart is ready to break when I think of all the anxiety you have lately
> had to go through. I do hope that like Job you will have sevenfold of
> your former comforts.

When Felix returned to Rangoon and heard of the King's mood-
iness, he feared his displeasure and fled. For three years he roamed
over the frontier borders between Burma and Assam – exploring,
botanising, learning vernaculars, serving the Raja of Cachar, gathering
and transmitting to Calcutta political information of the much-
agitated tribes and peoples, and once even captaining a little force
against hopelessly-outnumbering Burmese raiders. Throughout the
three years he kept in touch with his father, whose letters, he said,

'cheered my soul'. At length, at the end of 1818, he was met near Chittagong by Ward, his tender-hearted spiritual father, and was persuaded to return to Serampore, to the solace of them all. With his dear prodigal home again, Carey could be happy.

24. The Master-Builders

They proceeded on the assumption that the evangelisation of India was to be accomplished by Indians. Convinced that a purely theological training was objectionable, inasmuch as it tended to produce professionalism and contracted views, they planned to let in light from every quarter. They hoped thus to secure men who should be able to deal with religious questions under a full comprehension of Indian ways of thinking and feeling. It seemed to them that what was required was not to translate European books into Eastern tongues, or to clothe European ideas in an Eastern dress, but to raise up men loyal in heart to Jesus Christ, who would build the truths of revelation into an edifice answering to the genius of the East.

DR JAMES CULROSS

Neither the ungenerous suspicion nor the charge of unfaithfulness, with which their character was assailed in England, was allowed to slacken the prosecution of their plans. It was while their reputation was under an eclipse in England, and the benevolent hesitated to subscribe, that these men were engaged in erecting a noble college for the promotion of knowledge and religion, at their own cost, the expense of which eventually grew to the sum of £15,000.

DR GEORGE SMITH

24. The Master-Builders
1818–1819, & The Charter, 22 February, 1827

SERAMPORE WAS particularly nervous of home officiousness and control at the beginning of 1827 because it was just launching a project, the wisdom and urgency of which far-away Britain was not competent to assess. It was an enterprise which had occupied their thoughts since the beginning of 1816, although Carey had dreamed of it years earlier. They proposed to build at Serampore a college of Eastern, Western and biblical learning.

As early as 1794, Carey had written to the home committee, saying that he and John Thomas had contemplated opening advanced classes in each of their existing stations, for six Hindu and six Moslem boys. Pundits would be employed to teach them Sanskrit, Bengali and Persian, while they themselves would instruct them in the Bible and in Western science. The youths would be provided with food, clothing and lodging during their seven-year course. At the time they failed to secure suitable boys, but clearly the project was the germ of the later programme and achievement.

Then again, in February 1802, as soon as the first group of converts had brightened their whole outlook, Serampore drew up a plan, as J. C. Marshman tells us, 'for educating the children of native converts, and youths who might renounce their caste. It was intended to give them instruction in divinity, history, geography and astronomy, and in the English and Bengali languages.' In the prospectus of this institution Serampore says that 'to provide for the education of these native youths in those principles which enlarge the mind, and which lead to the worship of the true God and to a worthy life, cannot fail to be essentially advantageous to society, and may be the means in a few years of sending out men who shall be peculiarly instrumental in turning their fellow-countrymen from dumb idols to serve the living and true God.' A considerable amount was done in this direction in their several free Bengali schools.

In 1817 Carey wrote to Ryland:

> The work of duly preparing as large a body as possible of Christian Indians for the duties of pastors and itinerants is of immense importance. The pecuniary resources and the requisite number of missionaries for the Christian instruction of Hindustan's millions can never be supplied from England, and India will never be turned from her idolatry to serve the true and living God, unless the grace of God rests abundantly on converted Indians to qualify them for mission work, and unless, by those who care for India, these be trained for and sent into the work. In my judgement it is on native evangelists that the weight of the great work must ultimately rest.

To meet the need, Serampore College was conceived, and its scope and purposes went beyond the thinking of even the most progressive Anglo-Indian educationalists, and far beyond that of untravelled British Baptists, so many of whom were shy of college training for even *their own* ministers. Had Serampore been required to seek and await the home Society's approval, the three leading missionaries would have been in their graves first! They knew they must be free to act upon their own experience and insight.

Carey had been in India a quarter of a century, Marshman and Ward eighteen years. Had they ever expected its rapid conversion, which Carey confessed was his own first expectation, they now felt (in spite of their six hundred baptisms and their thousands of adherents) that the spiritual transformation of India's millions would of necessity be slow.

The Serampore missionaries' manifestos, prospectuses and letters of this period all show that they were closely restudying the history of the

Reformation, and that they were deeply impressed by the *length* of the struggle. They realised that its victory had cost centuries of witness and effort. They saw that if Rome's perverted form of Christianity yielded only to *long-sustained* pressure, even in the advanced West, India's ancient religions would never be overtaken, nor Islam's progress be retarded, without long-term measures. To the American Baptists Carey had written:

> We are ready to think that our labours may operate on the people more slowly than we once expected, but in the end more effectually; as knowledge, once fermenting, will leaven the whole lump. This may not be so encouraging, and may require more faith and patience; but it appears to have been the process of things in the Reformation, during the reigns of Henry, Edward, Elizabeth, James and Charles. Should the work of evangelising India prove thus slow and silently progressive, still the grand result will be our recompense. We are certain to take the fortress, if we can but persuade ourselves to sit down long enough before it. We shall reap, if we faint not.
>
> But when it *shall* be said, the infamous swinging-post is no longer erected; the widow burns no more on the funeral pyre; the obscene dances and songs are seen and heard no more; the gods are thrown to the bats, and Jesus is known as the God of the whole land; the Hindu goes no more to the Ganges to be washed from his uncleanness, but to the fountain opened for sin; and the crowds say, 'Let us go up to the house of the Lord, and He shall teach us of His ways;' the anxious Hindus no more consume their property, their strength, and their lives in vain pilgrimages, but come at once to Him, Who can save to the uttermost; the sick and the dying are no more dragged to the Ganges, but look to the Lamb of God, and commit their souls into His faithful hands; the children are no more sacrificed to idols, but are become 'the seed of the Lord'; the public morals are improved; benevolent societies are formed; civilisation and salvation walk arm in arm together; the earth yields her increase; and innumerable souls from this vast country swell the chorus of the redeemed – shall we then think that we have laboured in vain?

The missionaries felt that a broad education should be extended throughout India, an education covering India's philosophy, literature, religion and science, and also the Christian Scriptures and Western science.

But this enlightened education would need to be sown and grown in

Serampore College

Indians themselves, not just brought to them by accomplished strangers from without. It would never do to have Western Christian scholars make India their home, acquire there a critical knowledge of India's philosophy, religion, literature and science, and then bear their witness. India's own sons would have to become the scholars, just as England had grown her own Wycliffe and Tyndale.

India's sons from every class, also, would have to be educated, not just from the high castes. Too long had Indian education been the prerogative and monopoly of Brahmins. Now, the missionaries felt, the *people's* gifted sons must share the inheritance. The Mission had laboured in this spirit from the beginning. Free schools for low castes and for outcastes had always been a chief feature of their work in Mudnabati, Goamalti, Serampore, Calcutta and Katwa. Within twenty miles of Serampore they had founded a network of free vernacular schools, pioneering popular education in Bengal before the Government had done anything. By 1818, according to Dr George Smith, they had 10,000 boys on their rolls and in their care. But all this was only elementary education, whereas now they were planning to furnish a vastly higher education.

The Marquis Wellesley had been the first to supply a higher Indian education for the British Civil Service, but Serampore was the first to provide a higher education for Indians themselves: at least, for India's rank and file. The Government had recently established in Calcutta an Arabic college for well-to-do young Moslems. Rich Hindus, too, had just founded there an English and Western science college for their sons. The Serampore Mission first brought a higher education within the grasp of India's poor.

The translation of God's Word had already been greatly advanced, so that the whole Bible was now published in North India's five chief tongues, and the New Testament in most others. They might be said to have given India God's Word. Now they must educate the community to reap its full profit.

The cardinal question was whether the education they set themselves to provide should be chiefly Western or Eastern; and whether its vehicle of communication should be English or Indian. Young India itself would have voted for the Western and the English, for this was just the curriculum that affluent Hindu youths were getting in their new Calcutta college, which led them to coveted appointments to

Government clerkships. But Serampore was not considering the popular course, which would provide quick profit. It rather looked to the far-off interests of India and the Gospel. They did not seek to make India after their own British image or likeness. As Ward said, 'The college we are building rests on the same principle we have acted on for years, to make India evangelise herself and the surrounding peoples. We carefully avoid whatever might Anglicise our students and converts.'

The training would be conducted in Indian languages, English being taught only to those who were conspicuously able. India's sacred writings and classics would be laid open to students in the original Sanskrit, which would be a basic subject. This was revolutionary, for Sanskrit literature had been denied to the multitudes as too sacred for common use. The people were not permitted to learn Sanskrit. More than Rome sealed the Scriptures (by means of Latin) from the multitudes in the Middle Ages, the Brahmins had sealed from India's masses the literary sources of their own philosophy. Serampore intended to make an outright challenge upon this exclusive monopoly of learning. The Indian people would no longer be all their lifetime subject to mental disfranchisement and bondage. Nothing was covered that should not be revealed. Being themselves lowly-born Englishmen, they offered to the lowly-born of Hindustan (provided they were prepared to pay the price of hard work) India's most esteemed education and the accepted canon of her true culture – the Sanskrit learning. They would lay open to them the Vedas, Upanishads and Puranas side by side with the Christian Scriptures in their own vernaculars, enabling them to prove all things, and to hold fast whatsoever they judged to be good. They were naturally concerned to provide this higher education *especially* for the gifted sons of their native converts, so as to lift the reproach of illiteracy from their Christian community.

They made the college, as they said, 'free as the air, not thinking it right that any should be deprived of its benefits for having had the misfortune to be born and brought up within any particular circle; nor that the gates of knowledge should be barred against those who differed in opinion from themselves.' One difference, of course, remained. While the sons of their Indian Christians could dwell together in the Mission, the Hindu and Moslem students, on account of their own social custom and caste, arranged to board out – 'since nothing was to be asked of any which was repugnant to his conscientious feeling, nothing to which he attached the idea of moral wrong.'

Their supreme, but by no means their sole, concern was to grow India's would-be native preachers and teachers, 'on whom the weight of the great Christian work would ultimately rest'. But they were mindful also of the schoolmasters, writers, journalists, lawyers, etc, which the changing India would need. So they built on a scale large enough for two hundred students, though they reckoned that only a tenth of these were likely to be preachers of the Word.

For many reasons they judged it to be vital for their theological men to mingle and train alongside those who were destined for secular vocations. For 'Carey and his colleagues had always felt,' as John Marshman says, 'that a strictly theological seminary for missionary students, whether native or East Indian, was calculated to produce contracted views, and to give too much of a professional bias to the character.' So they called them into this diverse and invigorating comradeship.

Things were not to be made easy for the 'theologicals'. The utmost was demanded of those who aimed at the service which the Mission reckoned the highest.

'What could early Christianity have wrought in the Greek world,' they asked, 'without a Paul, a Luke, an Apollos? Or what could the Reformation leaders have effected, had they been ignorant of Latin, Hebrew and Greek?' 'In the same manner let no man be able to despise you,' was their incessant exhortation. 'Out-Sanskrit the pundits, and then add such knowledge of the Scriptures and of Western science that, stronger than your antagonists, you may foil them with their own trusted weapons, and capture their spoil.'

Furthermore, it is clear that in all this breadth of purpose they were thinking of more than their own denomination. They were not just bent on growing *Baptist* preachers and teachers.

In a country so destitute *[they said]* of all which elevates the mind, and so dependent on us for both political freedom and moral improvement, it is surely our duty to forget the distinctions which divide society in England, and to make common cause for the promotion of its welfare. It will be time enough a hundred years hence, when the country is filled with knowledge, and Truth has triumphed over error, to think of sects and parties. *Every public institution, aiming at India's betterment, ought to be constructed on so broad a basis as to invite the aid of all denominations.*

Looking far into the future, the Serampore Mission hoped that their most advanced divinity men would become India's own future biblical translators; for India, they said, 'would no more rest in non-native versions of the Scriptures than England would in an English version by a German.'

They dared to believe that even some Brahmins would let their sons enter a college confessedly Christian, and their faith was vindicated, eleven such joining in the first sessions, and from households of rank. Serampore was unafraid to have their children of Indian Christians share with these all the intimacies of college life, for they aimed to produce not sheltered invalids but mature men. By the healthy freedom and enlightenment of the college they hoped that many would become Christian. Even those who remained non-Christian would be 'freighted with blessing', 'their minds enlarged by general knowledge, acquainted with Scripture, freed from their former prejudice against Europeans and Christians, filled with pleasant recollections of their Christian instructors and companions, and, therefore, prepared for a candid examination of divine Truth in the future, and not easily rallied to the side of superstition.'

The very buildings reflected the college programme's height and breadth, especially the central one, long declared to be 'the noblest of its kind in India', with its halls, its double brass-pillared staircase (one of the most handsome Birmingham could then produce), its apse, later riven by earthquake, and its noble Greek portico.

Its projected observatory was for some reason never built. The cost of the eight acres of land and of the buildings eventually grew to the sum of £15,000, a sum the missionaries supplied from their own earnings, justifying their freedom from their home committee's approval or control. For the salaries of the professors and tutors (European and Indian), the support of the poorer students, the educational accessories and the maintenance of the high school, they looked to the generosity of Indian, British and American friends, but they gave their own services unsalaried until the staff should arrive. Nor was their trust misplaced. The Marquis of Hastings, their willing first patron, gave Rs 1,000, concerning which (with many other encouragements) Carey wrote to Jabez, 'The kindness of Lord Hastings is very great, and has bound my heart strongly to him.' The King of Denmark conveyed to them royal grounds and premises, the deeds enclosing a gold medal for each of the three, after they had respectfully declined the Danish Order of the Dannebrog as out of keeping with their Mission's character and work.

Many civil servants contributed. Charles Grant (late Chairman of the Court of Directors) bequeathed them Rs 2,000. Bryant Connor, a recent pupil of Marshman's, left them Rs 6,000, after Marshman had nobly declined this as a personal gift. An Edinburgh friend gave £500 towards the laboratory. The Government offered to meet the cost of a medical professorship. Captain Gowan raised a Delhi fund for the continuous maintenance of two students from that district, and himself added Rs 500 for the support of a third. Ward's powerful advocacy in Britain and in America secured £5,000 further.

Most of the American and British Baptist money, however, was strictly earmarked for the theological department, the donors being uninterested in the wider scope of the design. Even a zealous supporter like Staughton refused to aid the teaching of science. 'Can young men,' asked Carey, 'be prepared for the American Christian ministry without science?' Indeed, many strongly dissented from the scheme for student enrolment. They would have excluded all who were not definitely Christian, and would have admitted these only for biblical training. All this was further proof to the Serampore missionaries of how vital it was for them to retain their freedom from home intervention and control.

The all-Indian scope of the college was expressed in its first pupils and students, among whom were several Brahmins, a few Moslems, a Punjabi, a Mahratta, two Khasis, three Garos (sent by Scott, Commissioner of Cooch Behar, one of Carey's early students), two Arakanese, and many Bengalis.

To the advanced theological students, Greek, Latin, and Hebrew would be available, tasks fairly simple after long Sanskrit discipline! From the best would come, they hoped, India's own Christian theologians, and biblical translators.

Carey renewed his youth as the buildings rose, and especially as he arranged the new library and museum, and at last welcomed the students. At the weekends he took his full share in the collegiate work. He was blest, too, to have Felix again beside him, now tender and faithful, translating into Bengali for the college abridged *Histories of British India and of England*, along with articles on anatomy and jurisprudence for his planned Bengali *Cyclopaedia*, also a chemistry primer of Mack's, and best of all, Bunyan's *Pilgrim's Progress*.

So full were Carey's days throughout these great developments, and so invasive of the night, that the Marquis of Hastings (at Barrackpore for the weekends), himself a late-hour worker, would often, on retirement, note the lamp still burning in Carey's study.

The college opened some of its classes early in 1819, but its main building was not even roofed till July 1821, as Carey tells Jabez. They had been kept so long waiting for the great stairway from Birmingham. This protracted delay, after classes had begun, explains the absence of an inaugural ceremony, so unlike the usual habit of Serampore, which loved to mark its red-letter days and to keep its anniversaries.

Carey was 60 when the college building was complete. We may be sure that no home committee would have approved such a venture at an age so advanced, had the decision rested with them.

At the first public examination of the students, 30 learned Brahmins were present from the many provinces of India.

Years later, in 1827, Dr Marshman, when in Europe on furlough, obtained by personal interview with Denmark's King Frederick VI a charter for their Serampore College. It was as complete as that of the Kiel and Copenhagen Universities, with identical authority to grant degrees in all faculties, making it the first such college in India with power to confer divinity degrees. (This right was allowed to lie neglected and unused through later years until 1909.)

In all this devotion to India's sons, her daughters were not forgotten. Marshman's niece, and his and Ward's daughters, established most successful free schools in Serampore for Indian girls at a time when hardly anyone in India cared at all about the education of women.

In the same zeal for India's education they were encouraged in 1818 to publish a monthly vernacular magazine, the *Dig Darshan*, or 'Showing the Direction', and also a Bengali weekly newspaper, the *Samachar Darpan*, or 'News Mirror', to be a kind of school for the people to bring the world's history and current events into the general knowledge of Bengal. The monthly was Bengal's first, and the weekly its second, having been preceded by the short-lived *Bengal Gazette*.

Carey trembled lest these, especially the weekly, should become political, and involve them in disputes with the Government. But, under the prudent editing of Marshman and of John, his eldest son, and under the encouragement of Lord Hastings, his anxieties soon receded.

To these two educational ventures the Marshmans added a third, though this time for Europeans, the *Friend of India,* a monthly in which they strove to turn the hearts of Anglo-Indians and Europeans towards India's peoples and problems in sympathetic understanding. In both the *Samachar* and the *Friend of India* they kept recounting the constant widow-burnings, doing much by this emphasis to create the public opinion, both Indian and European, which in due course led to the abolition of widow-burning. India's lepers, too, found in these journals, which campaigned unceasingly for them, their friends and defenders. Their plight is shown in the following letter from William in Katwa in September 1812:

Last week I saw the burning of a poor leprous man. I got there too late, as he was lifeless before I arrived. I find that it is a very common practice here. The poor man was well enough to go about himself. They had dug a pit about ten cubits deep, in which they made a fire. After all was prepared the poor man rolled himself into it: but, when he felt the fire, he prayed to get out, but his sister and another relation thrust him down again, and he was burned to death! What horrible murder!

That the outrage was not exceptional, this note of J. G. Potter witnesses:

At Agra I was accustomed to visit the leper asylum with Pundit Hari Ram, a Brahmin convert. One day I saw this good man with tears in his eyes, as he spoke to the lepers thus: 'Brothers, you owe much to the Lord Jesus. Here you are housed and fed, clothed and cared for by those who are His followers. How different was your condition under Brahmin rule! At my village of Bisarna, whose priest I was, a leper was once brought to me, and the villagers asked me what they should do with him. I replied: "Dig his grave and bury him." Under my instructions the grave was dug, and the leper forced into it, where he was buried alive.'

Serampore's college and its journals were to drive out this darkness. The fourth issue of *Friend of India* is filled with rejoicing over Kali Sankar Ghosal's offer of land and money for the founding of a leper asylum. Dr George Smith says, 'Carey never rested till a leper hospital was established in Calcutta, near the centre of the Church Missionary Society's work.' And after Carey's death, Marshman commented: 'Scarcely an undertaking for the benefit of India has been engaged in, of which he was not either a prime mover or a zealous performer.'

Abbreviated Data Translated From The 'Samachar Darpan'

---

30 January, 1819 – Either from the woe of the pain or in concern for her children, a widow in Benares leapt from the pyre. Her relatives thrust her back, but a *chowkidar [a watchman or lower rank policeman]* pitied and saved her.

6 February, 1819 – A month before his appointed wedding day a man died at Chandernagore. His bride-elect immolated herself with him.

7 March, 1819 – On the third day after a Brahmin's death, his young wife burned with him – the delay being occasioned by her youth, since Government forbids the burning of those with child, or not 15. *Sati* is more common in S. Bengal than in the United Provinces: but most, in Rajputana. Recently, a Rajput raja died, and his thirty-three wives burned with him.

19 June, 1819 – Permission not being obtainable for the burning of the widow of Ram Chandra in her own district, the body was brought to Serampore, and she immolated herself there.

July 1819 – One of a man's two wives at Ballabhpur burned with him. The other, forbidden by her pregnancy, beat herself in her grief, and vowed to burn after her babe's birth. But by then, in her mother's home, she relented – to the vexation of her relatives, who feared a loss of caste.

10 August, 1819 – A widow, who was not held down by bamboos, because she swooned before the pyre was lit, was waked by the fire, and escaped. Sepoys seized her and thrust her back. Again she fled, and again was thrust into the flames. A third time she escaped, and was saved by Europeans. She has since been outcasted. Europeans have raised a local fund for her support.

25 January, 1820 – The wife of a Rishra betel-leaf seller has just burned with her husband. Also, the two wives of a man in Ballabhpur.

25 March, 1820 – The Madras Collector, with the help of peons and sepoys, prevented the burning of a Brahmin's widow, to the wrath of the relatives. He has promised her maintenance. Some Englishmen pleaded in vain last Sunday against the *sati* of a widow at Calcutta's Chitpore Ghât.

12 August, 1820 – A week ago the two wives of a Brahmin burned with him at Peliti's Ghât, Calcutta.

23 September, 1820 – Last Sunday Ram Sundar Basu died. That very afternoon his wife was burned with him.

30 September, 1820 – Ganga Kanta Chattopadhyaya of Krishnagar died a fortnight since – at the age of 40. His widow sacrificed herself with him, leaving a daughter of 5 and a son of 1 .

17 October, 1820 – The relatives of a Mahratta Brahmin declared that his widow was 15, so that she might burn, and his wealth be theirs. But her pundit insisted that she was only 11.

7 September, 1821 – Tarini Charan Banerji died at Sulka at 1 o'clock. By 5 o'clock his beautiful wife of 17, the only daughter of a high-caste, was sacrificed with him.

14 April, 1823 – The widow of Ram Kumar Sen, a Serampore doctor, burned with her husband: he 45 and she 37. Her only child, a daughter, was not allowed to see her, to dissuade her.

5 November, 1823 – The four widows of a Konnagar man burned with him, the youngest being 26.

September 1824 [Friend of India] – The wife of a Telugu Brahmin insisted on being immolated with her husband, saying that she had been a *sati* in three former births, and must be four times more, and then would attain eternal felicity.

25. The Schism

The greatest trial of a missionary is often another missionary.

FORBES JACKSON

Mr Rowe was for some time at 'Bristol'. He prayed, the night before they set off, that they might all sink to the bottom of the sea sooner than ever live to hurt the precious cause of Christ; and his wife told Mr and Mrs Skinner, at whose house they lodged for a month before they went, that her husband could not have prayed more according to her own heart's wish had he asked her what he should say. I charged them over and over again to make this the great object of their ambition, viz. to see who could be the least and the most willing to be servant of all. Herein is true greatness!

J. C. RYLAND in a letter to Chamberlain,
9 May, 1804.

I disapprove as much of the conduct of our Calcutta brethren as it is possible for me to disapprove of any human action. The evil they have done is, I fear, irreparable . . . I trust you will excuse my warmth of feeling upon this subject when you consider that by this rupture that cause is weakened and disgraced in the establishment and promotion of which I have spent the best part of my life. A church is attempted to be torn in pieces, for which neither I nor my brethren ever thought we could do enough. Now we are traduced, and the church rent by the very men who came to be our helpers.

I think their plans anti-missionary, and forced on them by their circumstances. I certainly think it a monstrous waste of money and strength for four missionary brethren, beside Pearce and Penney, to be *crowded* together in Calcutta, when there are besides them four paedo-baptist brethren and four evangelical clergymen, besides four native brethren, and where we also preach. My plan for spreading the Gospel has been, for several years, to fix

European brethren at a distance of 100–150 miles from each other, with native brethren stationed within that circle as preachers, schoolmasters, etc, and that he *[each European]* should as a brother, not a lord, visit and superintend them.

I would not wish you to entertain the idea that we and our brethren in Calcutta are resolved upon interminable hatred. On the contrary, I think that things are gone as far as you would expect them to go, and I now expect that the fire of contention will gradually go out.

CAREY, from a very long letter to Rev John Dyer,
antagonistic secretary of the home Society, 15 July, 1819.

25. The Schism
April 1818 – July 1820

WE MUST BEND BACK a little on our course. Serampore had yearned so long for the revised charter of the East India Company, with its proper sanction of missions, and for the open arrival of permitted recruits, that the four gifted colleagues who arrived between 1814 and 1817 were most joyfully welcomed. Yet by April 1818 these four, together with Lawson, had broken away from the seniors to form a missionary auxiliary of their own. It should not have happened, and it is a painful story. The senior men merited better treatment. Their record and age should have saved them from such a challenge from their juniors. None of the four newcomers was more than 26. Two had had less than three years in India, and two only one year.

The circumstances had offered promise of a happy outcome. Eustace was Carey's nephew, son of his much-loved, oft-helped only brother, a pupil of Sutcliff's, and a student of 'Bristol'. Yates had been, like Carey, a shoe-maker, and again, like Carey, he was an intensely diligent student of languages. Furthermore he hailed from Harvey Lane, and possessed an infectious sense of humour with a ringing laugh. Penney was strongly recommended to Carey, having trained numerous schoolteachers, and been an instrument of spiritual blessing to many. Pearce was the like-minded son of a much-loved and supportive preacher. Lawson shared Carey's botanical enthusiasm and was also a skilled musician. Surely here was the material of good colleagues.

All the juniors were sound in the faith and possessed undoubted dedication. The will to toil was theirs, together with a most useful diversity of trained talent. Eustace, orator and preacher; Yates, scholar; Lawson, artist; Penney, schoolteacher; Pearce, from the Clarendon Press (the three last being designated for supporting roles). They had the very gifts the Mission needed – Eustace for the Lall Bazar pulpit and pastorate, Yates to be Carey's understudy and successor in translation, Penney to superintend the Bow Bazar free school, and Pearce to be Ward's colleague in the press, especially now that Ward's health appeared to be breaking.

At first all went well. Eustace could write, 'My admiration for my uncle increases every day. He has not a half-hour in a month in which he relaxes from hardest labour.' Carey could tell his sisters that Eustace was 'universally beloved, and had much personal religion, and preaching ability far above the common stamp'. Yates wrote to his home folk, 'More and more of my time will be spent with Dr C., and I am glad: he is so great a scholar, and so kind a man. It is my chief earthly satisfaction to please him. He has treated me with the greatest affection, and told me he will do everything in his power to promote my happiness.' Carey could say he could see 'none so likely as Yates to succeed him in translation work', and that he was drawn to him by his 'personal piety, quiet spirit, and habits of diligence'. Then Penney was 'clear as a running stream'. At the end of a day's hard work he would come into the midst of his fellows, his wit flashing. Of Pearce, Carey could write that he and his wife had gained the affection of everyone.

What changed things who can tell? Much of the blame must rest, I fear, with Johns, whose unjust talk at home – of which they heard echoes – prejudiced the newcomers against Marshman before they left home for India. Added to this, Penney and Pearce left England under 'post-Fuller' conditions, and persuaded of the new home committee's aim to control the Mission from England. They had been prepared to encourage direct government from home – a sure source of friction.

Perhaps, too, the elders were at less than their best. Marshman was

embarrassed and unhappy, knowing himself misjudged. He and Ward
and their wives were in poor health. Indeed, all the seniors were paying
the price for their long unfurloughed labour in the heat of Bengal. The
threatened woe, too, depressed them. They *may* not have been (though
of this there is no proof) sympathetic enough with the dreams and
ideas of the newcomers, whose youth made them one.

Nevertheless, it was quite out of order for the juniors to withdraw
from Lall Bazar, where their help was so needed, and to found a new
church in Entally. Equally it was wrong for them to open or to serve in
schools in Calcutta on lines similar to the Marshmans', and also to
plant a press there. To reproduce, and so near, the very activities of the
seniors was 'indelicate', as Ward said, and heralded the Mission to the
world as a rifted and discordant thing. Finer feeling would have
restrained them from any semblance of competition, and would have
disposed them to pitch their tents well afield, where loud voices were
calling them.

In Chittagong, for instance, a leader was urgently needed to fill the
place of the assassinated De Bruyn, and to shepherd his many Arakanese converts, whom he had so loved. Carey would willingly have gone
there himself. Sir Stamford Raffles, Singapore's first Lieutenant-
Governor, spent a whole day in Serampore, partly to see Carey's
garden (for he was a keen fellow botanist) but chiefly to plead for a
press and mission helpers for Sumatra. David Scott, early student of
Carey's, and now Judge of Rungpur, begged in a twelve-page letter for
a mission settlement amongst his Assamese and Garos. The Marquis of
Hastings himself, after correspondence with Marshman from his military camps in Rajputana, pressed him and Carey and two of their sons
at his Barrackpore dining-table to inaugurate and organise schools in
this newly-conquered province. 'He could not yet,' he said, 'make it
the business of Government, though he would subscribe Rs 8,000 as a
beginning, and Resident Sir David Ochterlony would be both enjoined
and eager to help them.' Carey called this 'one of the greatest openings
in the divine providence since the beginning of the Mission.'

To the three senior missionaries, who had toiled so long under the
Government's displeasure and harassment, to have the highest official
authorities flinging open these gates and urging their entrance seemed
almost miraculous. And for the young men to choose Calcutta, already
comparatively well supplied with Christian agencies, in preference to

these virgin outfields, seemed incredible and criminal. It distressed them almost as much, Carey said, as the division in their ranks. As it was, Ward's nephew went with the press to Sumatra, and Carey's Jabez to Rajputana. By the end of 1818, Jabez set out upon the four months' river voyage for Ajmere with his father's newly-completed Hindi Bible in his hands, to labour there with noble faithfulness for fifteen years. But the recent recruits from England offered themselves for none of these outposts. 'I am greatly afflicted,' Carey wrote.

His patience and desire for peace is attested by the fact that, whereas the trouble had been brewing from the summer of 1815, he sent no syllable of it home, *till the schism was complete,* and the juniors had formed and made public their 'Calcutta Missionary Union'. Carey wrote of it then, in vexation of spirit, as 'a Counter-Baptist Mission, to be more pure than the former, and to answer higher purposes!' The entire episode had been 'supremely unlovely, but we are resolved to bear everything rather than contend, and I have told them so.' They invited him to join their Union – having with him no quarrel – but he would not consider separating himself from Marshman, with whom they would not work.

> I have lived *[he wrote]* with Dr Marshman for eighteen years, and have seen him in all relationships, and I do not think I am blind to his faults. I have seen all his so-called 'tortuosities' and every other defect with which he is charged. But I cannot caricature him, as I am sure our brethren do. That would be like publishing a print of a man with a long nose, and elongating it to the extent of several yards. Marshman's excellencies are such that his defects are almost concealed by them, and I believe him to be one of the firmest friends the Mission ever had, and I hope it may never stand in need of one like him.

At this very time the Marshmans' schools were contributing to the Mission not less than Rs 2,000 a month.

A little later Carey wrote to Ryland:

> I do not recollect in my whole life anything which has given me so much distress as this schism. Many sleepless nights have I spent examining what we had done to give it occasion, but can discover nothing on which I can fix. The Mission, however, is rent in twain, and exhibits the scandalous appearance of a body divided against itself. We could easily vindicate ourselves, but the vindication would be our and their disgrace. We have, therefore, resolved to say nothing, but to leave the

matter in God's hands. I trust that my pouring out these my distresses into the bosom of an old and much-beloved friend will not be accounted a deviation from this resolution.

And later:

I have repeatedly said to the brethren that the only way of correcting a misunderstanding is to come to a right understanding. I have with all the earnestness I could command, and my feelings made me truly in earnest, requested that we might labour to put an end to this evil. I have repeatedly said that I would on my bended knees ask pardon of any one I had offended; that, if it was proved that I had either said or done what was wrong, I should count it an honour to acknowledge it, and would do it without hesitation. But ... I must do all in connection with my brethren, who, from many years' close union in the same work I esteem. I can scarcely see what more I can do to put an end to this dishonourable division. I have said that I do not wish to mortify them by proving them to be in the wrong, but I wish we may understand one another and be heartily reconciled. I have known my colleagues in all situations, and have seen all their faults and foibles. Yet, were I to make another choice with all the knowledge which eighteen years of experience can furnish, I would again choose them as my associates in the Gospel.

To his unspeakable comfort he could tell Ryland on 30 March, 1819:

I hope the spirit which so long prevailed with our brethren in Calcutta begins to subside. Eustace *[who had been the bitterest]* has lately been twice to see me, and Pearce once. I am determined to do all I can for peace. I think of the schism, as I always did, as a very wrong and most unnecessary thing; but there is no doubt much on both sides to be forgiven. Only of pride cometh contention. There has been much pride, and still, I fear, much exists on both sides. I think, however, that nothing has been said or done, which ought not to be immediately forgiven on both sides, and that there has been no misunderstanding which Christians ought not to use their utmost endeavour to remove.

And again:

I have lately thought that all the little grudges and collisions of parties, which, in their beginning, are often the cause of so much distress, resemble the springs from which rivers take their rise. Many seem so near each other as almost to reduce the country through which they flow to a morass, and their apparent interferences with each other's courses seem rather hurtful than otherwise. Yet, after a time, they either fall into each other, so as to form a river large enough to enrich a whole district, or, as not infrequently, diverge so widely as to fertilize regions lying far apart. I trust this will be the final result of our painful differences in the Mission.

And on 15 August, 1820, he delighted to write thus to Jabez:

I am sure it will give you pleasure to learn that our long-continued dispute with the younger brethren in Calcutta is now settled. We met together for this purpose some three weeks ago, and, after each side giving up some trifling ideas and expressions, came to a reconciliation, which I pray God may be lasting. Nothing I ever met with in my life – and I have met with many distressing things – ever preyed so much upon my spirits as this difference.

26. The Woe

The Society has long ceased to approve of the Dyer period *[secretaryship of Rev John Dyer]*. Its opinion has become that of J. C. Marshman. The worst result of the Dyer mistake was not merely that it outraged justice in the case of the men of Serampore, but that it arrested for nearly half a century the progress of a healthy, because indigenous, church in India.

To us the long dispute is now chiefly of value in so far as it brings into Christ-like relief the personality of Carey.

DR GEORGE SMITH (in 1885).

Had it been possible to create a dozen establishments like that of Serampore, each raising and managing its own funds, and connected with the Society as the centre of unity in a common cause, it ought to have been a subject of congratulations and not of regret.

JOHN CLARK MARSHMAN

26. The Woe
1817–1830

THE WORST of the schism was its influence on the home base. It presented to the home committee the Indian Mission broken into opposing camps, for banning or blessing. To this new and enlarged committee the seniors were personally almost unknown, while with the juniors they were intimate. Sharing as these juniors did the committee's viewpoint, and representing their policy, they were naturally esteemed the loyalists, and the seniors the rebellious and obstinate ones. Sympathy with the enterprises of the seniors waned, while to those of the juniors it grew. Help for the elders was made to depend upon embarrassing conditions; for the younger men it flowed unconditionally.

The home committee could not grasp in their minds the difference between the self-supporting seniors and the salaried juniors. Control, which the latter desired, the former could by no means accept, for to them liberty had become the breath of life.

When I came out on this Mission [Carey wrote] I certainly did not think myself the servant of the Society, but a brother. *A work was to be done at the bottom of a well,* as it has been expressed. Some person had to descend to the bottom, whilst others held the rope. I agreed to descend, if my brothers would hold the rope; but I surely did not become thus their servant.

This claim to equal comradeship and freedom they had made absolutely valid by their long self-maintenance and their own liberal gifts to the Mission. Carey received no more than £600 from the Mission's home committee for personal support in all his 40 years in India. Through his business years in North Bengal and his government service in Calcutta, he earned over £46,000, all of which, apart from grants to needy relatives, he devoted to the Mission. In addition, the income-earning operations of the Serampore Mission raised £40,000 to £50,000 by the year 1818, and a further £24,000 in the next nine years. Altogether, at least £105,000 was raised and donated by the efforts of the missionaries. Independent public donations added around £80,000, to help them buy and equip their many buildings. Of all these properties the ultimate proprietorship was vested in the Society. They only demanded to be trusted, as in Fuller's day, in their use of the properties, to be left free to choose their own colleagues, and (with certain reservations) to appoint their successors.

Not even the Serampore succession question presented any difficulty, for neither Carey nor Ward claimed such distinction for any of their own, but the three were unanimous in their recognition of the conspicuous fitness of John Clark Marshman.

One marvels that demands which were so reasonable cost a decade of disharmony with the home committee, disharmony which home trips by four of the Serampore missionaries failed to resolve. Ward was home in England from 1818–22, Mrs Marshman from 1820–21, J. C. Marshman from 1822–23, and Dr Marshman himself from 1826–29. Certainly, Serampore (and at its own expense) took pains to state and interpret its case. Alas! Eustace, just when the waters had calmed, when compelled to return home in 1825 for health reasons, released the storm winds again through irreconcilable animus against Marshman. At length, on 17 March, 1827, in Marshman's presence, and despite his every effort, the breach came.

The committee claimed that everything they had done over the years to sustain and develop the interest of British churches in the Mission justified their demands for much greater control. They could not grasp the realities of Serampore, nor could Marshman accept their arguments and terms. They strove, however, to part as Christian men, resolved to serve the cause from differing standpoints. They pledged to each other goodwill.

Yet, presently, in the denomination's magazine, there broke on the Serampore missionaries hail-storms of accusation, for which the leaders in the committee were by no means free of blame. And this became the signal for a three years' woe of conflict. The almost continuous challenging of Serampore's honour caused Carey deep distress, deepening loneliness and premature ageing.

I ought to be believed.

I hope Marshman will be a thousand times more calm and temperate than I am.

It is like the king of Moab, not content with killing the king of Edom, but burning his bones.

I have lived too long.

I had formerly friends, whose hearts beat in unison with my own; but, except for Mr Burls and Ryland, no person belonging to the committee has, since Fuller's death, written me a single letter of friendship, and I suppose I am unknown to almost every one. I do not complain, though I acknowledge that I have occasionally felt it.

I cannot write freely to the Society's secretary, because his letters resemble those of a Secretary of State.

Dr Marshman is no more perfect than any other partaker of the grace of God. But I wish I had half his piety, energy of mind, and zeal. I believe the charges brought against him are unfounded. I have not forsaken him, nor shall I. There is no man in India more respected than he. I love him. Where is his family aggrandisement? He is as poor as I am, and I can scarcely lay by a sum monthly to relieve three or four indigent relations in Europe. We might have had large possessions, but we have given all to the Mission.

When Jabez let himself be drawn for a season into the camp of Marshman's slanderers, his father indignantly reproved him:

You express a very indecent pleasure at the opposition which Dr Marshman has received. What you call a 'set down', I call a falsehood.

Remember I was a party to all his public acts and writings, and from that responsibility I never intend to withdraw. I despise all the creeping, mean assertions of those who say they do not include me in their censures, nor do I work for their praise. 'Thine own friend and thy father's friend forsake not.'

It added wormwood to their cup that for a period – by the representations of Eustace – even Robert Hall's trust in them was shaken, as well as that of Carey's own sisters, and that *Ryland* hardened towards Marshman. When this 'last and most unkindest' thing happened, Carey, in defence of his colleague, wrote the sharpest letter of his life. He lashed even the honoured leader who had baptised him.

> My dear Ryland,
> Your letter to Bro. Marshman was absolutely insulting, and I will confidently say unmerited. You are bound as a Christian man to acknowledge the evil of what you have said; and, if you have mentioned such things to others, you are bound as an act of simple justice to contradict what you have said.
> I am,
> Your very affectionate but deeply wounded brother,
> W. CAREY

All the sweeter was John Foster's staunch championship, and the allegiance of Dr Chalmers. But Carey felt unspeakably the controversy's disgrace for Christians of the same denomination. To Christopher Anderson he wrote:

> The present contentions are not those of different sects touching the particular doctrines and disciplines of each. Upon the contrary, there was scarcely ever a time when greater harmony and a better spirit prevailed amongst Christians of different denominations. But the present disputes are between brethren of the same Christian name. Satan has indeed gained an advantage over us. Our Lord prayed that His disciples might all be one, so that the world might believe that the Father had sent Him. Whence it appears that Christian union is necessary to the success of the Gospel in the world. Blessed will be he who is the instrument of removing this great obstacle, and of introducing harmony and love amongst the followers of our Lord. Let prayer after reiterated prayer, and fasting, public and private, be persevered in, that God's Spirit, which is certainly withdrawn, may return and bless us with peace and with prosperity.

To his sisters he made answer, 'I detest the misrepresentations so long and so unjustly maintained. I hope you will never say another word to me of this.'

He declared that 'if he had to live through such calumnious years again, he would scrupulously abstain from offering any reply to any censures which might be passed upon him, and would inform his opponents that they had his full permission to say whatever it would afford them pleasure to believe or propagate concerning him, provided that they did not encroach on his invaluable time.'

The only public parts he took in the controversy were to secure, in 1829, the verbatim publication of his letters to England, to counter the unjust and mischievous use which had been made of excerpts torn from their context; and then, as late as 1830, to express in a few temperate pages his final 'Thoughts on the Discussions' which end thus:

And now, what is our trespass and our sin, that ye have so hotly pursued us? Whereas ye have searched all our stuff, what have ye found of all your household stuff? These thirty-seven years have I been with you – Dr Marshman thirty. Your ewes and your she-goats have not cast their young, nor the rams of your flock have we eaten. In the day the drought consumed us, and the frost by night, and our sleep departed from our eyes. Now, therefore, let us make a covenant with each other.

To his faithful friend Steadman, who was pressing him to visit England, he wrote in this same 1830:

I wish from my heart that success may attend all the efforts of the Society, but I cannot approve of many things they do, and I should be obliged to say more than I am disposed to. So I fear my going to England would neither be useful nor comfortable. Crimination and recrimination are disagreeable to me. I dread the stirring up of that unholy spirit which spread itself through the churches, when Dr Marshman was in England. Serampore does not deserve the blame which has been so industriously cast upon it, and I trust that in the end our righteousness may appear as the light. I rejoice that Christ is Lord over all things to the Church, which is His body.

That same 1830 they brought the quarrel to a close for their part by transferring the Serampore properties to eleven home trustees, simply stipulating that they should occupy them rent-free for the brief remainders of their lives, and then Professors Mack and Swan for a further three years, though paying rent. 'Blessed be God!' they cried, 'that we have lived to see this day! Now shall our grey heads go down to the grave in peace!'

'Never,' said one of their sons, 'did men rejoice more in the acquisition of property than did these elders in divesting themselves of all interest in the Mission premises.'

27. The Comforted Mourners

Serampore is a handsome place, kept beautifully clean, and looking more like a European town than Calcutta, or any of its neighbouring cantonments. The guard, which turned out to see me, consisted of a dozen sepoys in the red Danish uniform: they were extraordinarily clean and soldier-like looking men, and the appearance of the place flourishing.

BISHOP HEBER'S *Indian Journeys*, 1824–25.

We have been at Serampore more than a week, and have received much kindness from every member of the Mission family. Dr Carey is a vigorous old man, very like the portraits in England, only that he looks rather older. He had a fall several months ago, which occasioned him a very serious illness, and which has left him lame; but still every step he takes, and every sentence he utters, denote such vigour and activity as are truly surprising in a man who has been so many years in India. Europeans resident here are generally listless to a degree, of which you can form no idea. The first Sunday we spent here, Mr Leslie preached in the morning, and Dr C. in the evening. The good Doctor exceedingly animated and methodical; it was the best sermon I have heard since I left England. Yesterday morning Dr Marshman preached, and in the evening Dr C. administered the Lord's Supper to Bengalis and English together, and addressed us in both languages. There are several native girls' schools here, under Miss Marshman and Miss Ward. I went to see one this morning, and was much delighted.

MRS LESLIE to her mother, June 1824.

Dr Carey, who has been very ill, is quite recovered, and bids fair to live many years. Both he and Dr Marshman are active to a degree you would think impossible in this country. Dr C. is a very equable and cheerful old man, in countenance very like the engraving of him with his pundit. In body, however, he is now much inferior, being rather less in size, and not so robust. Nor does he wear such a fine dress as is given him in the plate. His general costume is white stockings, nankeen breeches, a white waistcoat, a round white jacket and an old black hat hardly worth a shilling.

He is of very easy access and great familiarity. His attachments are strong, and extend not merely to persons but to places. About a year ago, so much of the house he had lived in ever since he had been at Serampore fell down, that he had to leave it – at which he wept bitterly. There is a manliness in an old man's tears – something far removed from the crying of a child.

Serampore is one of the most beautiful places I have seen in India. Built quite on the bank of the river, the air is pleasant and healthy, and the scene is enlivened by the plying up and down of numerous boats. Much harmony and Christian spirit prevail among the Mission family; and their kindness to all who visit them is most abundant. They received us with warm and open hearts.

The breach made by the death of Mr Ward is deeply felt, and is not likely to be filled up. Our good friend Mack is tenfold more a missionary than a professor.

ANDREW LESLIE to R. R. Sherring, 7 June, 1824.

We found Dr Carey in his study; and we were both much pleased with his primitive, and, we may say, apostolical appearance. He is short; his hair white; his countenance benevolent. Two Hindus were sitting by, engaged in painting some small objects in natural history, of which the Doctor has a choice collection, both in specimens and pictures. His garden is enriched with rarities.

DANIEL TYERMAN and GEORGE BENNETT,
London Missionary Society deputation, May 1826.

At Barrackpore, about fifteen miles from Calcutta, the Governor-General has a country residence, delightfully situated in a park of uncommon beauty. The opposite bank is adorned with a thick robe of drooping bamboos, overtopped by stately palms and feathery cocoa-nuts; with lawns of gardens laid out round dwellings; and, immediately in front of the Governor-General's house, the beautifully clean and quiet-looking town of Serampore. This is a Danish settlement, and the chief seat of that Baptist Mission, over which the venerable and devoted Dr Carey presides. How great and how blessed have been the labours of himself and his able colleagues will appear, when I state that upwards of a hundred schools are under its fostering care, and that in its ever-busy presses either the entire Scriptures or separate Gospels are being printed

in sixteen of India's languages and dialects. *[A considerable understatement.]*
The Marquis of Hastings, whose eye rests every morning on the buildings and
garden of Carey's establishment, must derive great inward peace from the
consciousness of having always encouraged it.

Sketches in India by an Officer to Fireside Travellers at Home,
4th edition, 1826.

One of my earliest introductions was to the venerable Dr Carey in 1826. In
person he was somewhat under middle size: his dress neat, but antiquated.
The aspect of his countenance was mild and benevolent. There was, however,
nothing in his general appearance to indicate to a stranger anything extraordinary about him. It was only in *conversation* that the vast stores of his mind
became apparent . . . I could not therefore but gaze upon him with admiration and love.

G. E. PEARCE, *Reminiscences.*

I had recently to prepare for the Government a fount of the Ahom type, from
the foundation up. The time and care it called for in designing the face, cutting
the punches, preparing the matrices and casting the type, made me appreciate
afresh the whole-souled and remarkable work of Ward.

C. H. HARVEY, Baptist Mission Press, Calcutta, 1920.

27. The Comforted Mourners
1821 – 1830

THE DISAPPOINTMENTS arising out of these years of controversy were intensified for the elders by a succession of grievous deaths. First, Carey lost his Charlotte after thirteen years of marriage. The frail little Danish lady died in May 1821. She had been unable to walk for three years, and for months before the end Carey had daily carried her in his arms down to her Bath chair, to give her the fragrance and pleasure of his garden. Her very soul was as a garden. J. C. Marshman speaks of her 'blended patrician polish and Christian simplicity', and of the 'peace' she shed abroad. Her letters to Carey from Monghyr, to whose dry air she had gone for health, tell the warmth of her love.

> My dearest Love,
>
> I felt very much in parting with thee, and feel much in being so far from thee. I am sure thou wilt be happy and thankful on account of my voice, which daily gets better, and thy pleasure adds greatly to mine. I hope you will not think I am writing too often: I rather trust you will be glad to hear of me. Though my journey was very pleasant, and the improvement of my health, the freshness of the air and the variety of objects enliven my spirits, yet I cannot help longing for you. Pray, my

love, take care of your health, that I may have the joy to find you well.

I thank thee most affectionately, my dearest Love, for thy kind letter. Though this journey is very useful to me, I cannot help feeling much to be so distant from you, but I am much with you in my thoughts. I bless God for the protection He has given to His cause in time of need. May He still guide and prosper it, and give us all hearts growing in love and zeal! I felt very much parting with thee. I see plainly it would not do to go far from thee: my heart cleaves to thee. I need not say (for I hope you know my heart is not insensible) how much I felt your kindness in not minding any expense for my recovery. You will rejoice to hear me talk in the old way, and not in that whispering manner.

I find so much pleasure in writing to you, my love, that I cannot help doing it. I was nearly disconcerted by Mrs — laughing at my writing so often; but I feel so much pleasure in receiving your letters that I hope you may do the same. I thank thee for thy kind letter. I need not say that the serious part of it, too, was welcome to me, deprived as I am of all religious intercourse. I shall greatly rejoice in seeing thee again. I need not say how much thou art in my thoughts day and night.

For years Charlotte had been Serampore's constant and tender correspondent with Carey's large family circle, and she was dearly loved by all of them. 'I hope,' wrote William to his father, 'we shall never forget her great affection, and very motherly care to us. They were very great indeed, and have often drawn tears from me.' And Jabez wrote in similar vein from Ajmere:

My ever dear and affectionate father,

I have just heard with astonishment and grief from Felix of the death of my dear mother. Nothing was so unexpected. I hope, my dear father, that God has supported you. I little thought when I left Bengal that I should never see her again, and never hear any more of that motherly counsel from her own lips, which she was wont to give me when near her, and which could only have been dictated by the love she bore me. It was only about eight or nine days ago that I thought of writing to her, knowing how happy she would be to hear of the providential escape I had from being bitten by a black cobra, which got into a box in which I kept a few fowls for fear of rats, which are very troublesome here. The fowls began to make a noise in the night, which I imagined was occasioned by the rats teasing them. The first time I went and gave a few thumps on the box and quieted them a little, but, hearing the noise again very shortly after, I went and opened the box, and put my hand in to feel whether there was anything else besides the fowls, when the snake raised his crest and made at me, and touched my hand with his mouth, but providentially did not bite me. I immediately called for a light, and killed the cobra, but not before he had killed four of the fowls. Had he bitten me, I do not know what I should have done for assistance in the night, and might have been long before this a dead man.

I am grieved that I was not near to minister in her sickness, nor to receive her last blessing. When I was leaving Serampore about three years ago for this place, she very prophetically took leave of us, and blessed us, saying that she never expected to see us again. I little thought it would be a reality. My dear father, may you have strength to come out of this furnace like gold doubly purified. May you yet live for many days for the furtherance of the Gospel and the good of us all!

In the middle of June, Carey wrote to him:

A month ago I was not able to write on a subject so very afflictive to my mind. Your dear mother was one that truly feared God. Her soul was continually engaged in meditation or in prayer or in the reading of God's Word. Next to that she lived for me. She never did a thing during the thirteen years we lived together without consulting me, even though she was sure of my consent. She watched every change in my countenance with the utmost solicitude, and often was full of anxiety if she perceived the least sign of weariness, illness, grief, or distress. Often has she come to me and requested me to forgive her anything, in which she had unknowingly offended me. She certainly had no occasion for such a request, but her heart was exceedingly tender upon that point. My loss is irreparable.

And a little later:

I am exceedingly lonely. I hope you will never fail to pray for me.

Very human was her godliness. The blind and the lame, to whom her own frailty drew her, were 'her pensioners'. She bequeathed them to Carey as 'a very sacred legacy'.

Then, in March 1822, the Marshmans lost their eldest, and married, daughter Susan, during pregnancy. She was twenty-five, and left two little children. To the grief-stricken husband (an official in the Bengal Civil Service) Marshman wrote daily for nearly two years, indeed, till his son-in-law's death. The letters are full of tender comfort, revealing the heart of a man so misrepresented by his slanderers.

Then in the August of 1822, when aged only fifty-six, Krishna Pal was snatched from them by cholera. In Jessore (where he was mobbed and beaten), in Calcutta (through five years), in Katwa, Birbhum and Berhampore, in Dinajpur and Malda (through seven years), and in Dacca, he had watered the seed sown by the pioneers and others. At the foot of the Khasi Hills he was for eight months himself a pioneer. For the baptism of his first seven converts – sepoys, two Khasis, and an Assamese – the resident magistrate welcomed them to his house, and set a silver bowl before him, expecting the baptism indoors. But Krishna Pal said he knew nothing of such a mode, and led them to the river, where eight native princes and six hundred Khasis assembled. The magistrate watched the ordinance with reverent surprise, had cannon fired to mark the importance of the occasion, took Krishna back to his bungalow, and wrote a full record to Carey. Owen Leonard used to say that 'to see him engaged in his pastoral work you would suppose him a warm young convert, with at the same time the experience of a father.'

John Mack was in time to hear Krishna preach in Calcutta, and was struck by 'his considerable grace of manner and address – something to gratify common sensibility and taste, how much more a Christian and a missionary!'

As he lay dying at Serampore, Krishna was asked if he still loved Christ. 'Yes,' he replied, 'but not as much as He loves me.'

Then, towards the end of this sad year, Felix died following six months of stubborn fevers. The voyage to China, which the doctor had counselled, might possibly have saved him, but could not be arranged. 'A prisoner of hope', he contritely called himself after his wanderings and return, but he became again his father's invaluable colleague, especially during Ward's long furlough. Carey could confidently lean on his scholarship, acknowledged as he was to be the best Bengali linguist amongst India's Europeans. Though Felix never entirely recovered his earlier energy and fervour, he did win back his colleagues' trust in his steadfastness of service. He died with his father's name upon his lips. It was very hard for his father to carry him to burial at only thirty-seven, and immediately to return to a multiplied burden.

But, on Friday, 7 March, 1823, came a further staggering bereavement. *Ward died of cholera*. Eight years younger than Carey, and fresh from his four years' busy furlough, he had seemed full of vigour.

Already he was drawing to Christ students of the college (built in his absence), just as he had drawn each son of Carey's long before. He perfectly understood the Indian mind, and none could match him as the converts' counsellor. Dr Wallich (head of Calcutta's Botanic Institution) regarded him as 'by far the best preacher in Serampore'. Marshman called his death 'a tremendous stroke', and Carey wrote to England:

> We are all plunged into the greatest distress. *Ward died yesterday* about 5.00 in the afternoon. He preached to us very impressively on Wednesday evening. He breakfasted with us on Thursday, was in the printing office till 1.00; then came into dinner, and complained of drowsiness. About 3.00 I was called, and found him very ill. The doctors attended him, and through the night hopes were entertained. I found him apparently asleep about 5.00 in the morning, when I went to Calcutta. I returned about half an hour before his death that same day. He had not been able to speak for some hours. He is happy, but oh, what a breach! Who can fill it? We hope in God. We need your prayers.

When Carey preached the memorial sermon in Calcutta the next Sunday Lall Bazar Chapel was, he recorded, 'crowded with such an assembly as he had never before seen in India, for few men were so beloved as Ward.'

The two surviving elders could scarcely go on functioning with the third torn from them. William wrote from Katwa:

> Very dear father,
>
> I was out for two days at a fair, and on my return received your melancholy and affecting letter. My heart bleeds for you all. I have not got over the death of my most affectionate brother Felix. This has awakened all my feelings again. Mr Ward was very dear to me. How often has he upheld me, when my feet wellnigh slipped! He was my spiritual father. How is his place to be supplied? Had John Marshman been in India, he would no doubt have taken it. Now I do not see how it can be.

Then, before very long, came news of the passing of Ryland, the last of Carey's home covenanters. Carey wrote:

> It appears as if everything dear to me in England has now been removed. Wherever I look, I see a blank. Were I to revisit that dear country, I should have an entirely new set of friendships to form.

Only a few months after Ward's going, it looked as if Marshman was to be called to a final, overwhelming grief as the sole survivor of the three. For, returning at midnight on 8 October, 1823, from Calcutta preaching duties, both Carey and a doctor friend slipped on the Serampore landing jetty steps in the dark, Carey being so injured that he had to be carried into the house in utter helplessness. His thigh was not dislocated, as was first thought, but it took 110 leeches through two days to reduce the inflammation. A strong fever ensued, an abscess on the liver was diagnosed, so that they despaired for his life. But the skill of several voluntary doctors, including the Governor-General's, pulled him through. He could not, however, lift his foot from the ground until the end of the year, nor limp across the room for a further two months. Nevertheless, he resumed his Fort William classes from New Year's Day, and his Serampore lectures from February. Bearers lifted him out of his palanquin and carried him to his class-room. He sat whenever he lectured or preached.

He was fortunate to have remarried not long before his fall and illness, and to have found in Grace Hughes, forty-five, a most gentle and affectionate partner. Like himself, she had been already twice married. Her second husband had been dead ten years. Carey told Jabez that 'her constant and unremitting care and excellent nursing took off much of the weight of his illness.' To his joy she was presently baptised, and her daughter by her first marriage became an enthusiastic helper in the Mission's native girls' schools. 'We live in great happiness,' said Carey.

In the early days of his recovery, when he was still confined to his bed, another catastrophe had overtaken them. Indeed, disaster chased disaster. Phenomenal overflowings of the Damoodah had flooded the southern triangle between this river and the Hooghly, drowning scores of people and hundreds of cattle. The floods at length reached Serampore. They destroyed around six hundred homesteads, made fissures in the walls of Carey's house, forcing his hurried removal, made a mud tank of his garden, and greatly damaged the Marshmans' school buildings. The losses and poverty inflicted on the town, and on their converts, was appalling, while their own losses wiped out their ability to give relief. Moreover, Andrew Fuller was no longer alive to send them emergency aid from home. On the contrary, slander was drying up the usual channels of supply. They were pitifully unaided.

Nevertheless, they slackened none of their labours. Carey added to his tasks the Bengali translatorship to Government, thankful, for the Mission's sake, for the extra monthly Rs 300. The office was no easy task. Its work was eighteen months in arrears and included the translation of involved legal documents, a single sentence sometimes filling a page of printed foolscap.

At the same time Carey joined in establishing a mission to Calcutta's seamen, buying a small boat for the purpose – with Lord Hastings as patron and Carey as preacher at the dedication of the boat. They even increased their mission stations, and established three Christian villages – at Jannagar close to Serampore; at Barripore, south of Calcutta; and the third (with as many as fifty families) as far east as Arakan. The Lord gave them some great encouragements. Buckingham, a soldier's son, was transformed into a most effective missionary preacher. He travelled by horseback to all the villages around Jessore, living frugally, refusing a salary, and being accepted warmly in every place.

They had remarkable baptisms – Pundit Siva Ram in Benares; the first Telugu and Delhi Brahmins; in Java, the first Chinese; and at Serampore a Mag Brahmin and a notable *fakir* (Hindu begging 'monk') of Kalighat. The *fakir* arrived covered with amulets and charms and wore a necklace of snake bones. Even after his conversion wealthy Indians – who could not grasp what had happened – prostrated themselves at his feet. They could also take comfort from the fact that nearly 700 Hindus had given up all their worldly connections and prospects for Christ since the year 1800, and that eight Indian students were currently being trained in their college for missionary service. Carey also set himself to the restoration of his ruined garden, sending home by the first mail for bulbs and seeds.

At this time the first General Baptist missionaries arrived, and accepted Carey's counsel to labour in the region of Orissa. William Bampton was eager to become wholly Indian in diet, clothing and housing. Carey, while admiring his dedication, felt compelled to add many cautions. 'The Master won't thank you for committing suicide. It is yourself, and not these externals, that will make the abiding impression.'

Carey had wonderful fellowship with Ignatius Fernandez when the old merchant-missionary at 74 came down to Serampore to die. He was too weak to be carried from his pinnace into Carey's house, but his spirit was radiant. He was leaving in the north a church membership of

eighty. Carey and he could gauge, as no others could, the advance of
Christ's kingdom in India.

This was the comfort Carey communicated to an assembly of missionary societies in Lower Circular Road, Calcutta, in 1825, as he spoke
from the text – 'In due season we shall reap, if we faint not.' 'Faith
grows, as the distances widen, which you are able to compare. I, who
have seen the work from the beginning, know what an abundance of
wheat has been already garnered.'

Carey had many a grandchild about him in these years, the children
of each of his four sons.

Carey was shocked and alarmed in May 1829, upon Marshman's
return from his three years' absence, to find him 'looking fifteen years
older', the troubles at home had so told on him. Nor could Carey wonder when he learned the story of all the ingratitude, injustice and
indignity his great colleague had suffered within his own denominational borders, where he should have been welcomed with
full-hearted confidence and affection. The two had never felt so dazed,
lonely, and wronged. They did indeed tread the winepress together.
Then they strove to bury it all out of sight and out of reference, and
Carey found every leisure moment that he could to hear the positive
aspects of Marshman's fascinating British, Irish and Continental journeys, and of the fellowships which had given these their joy.
Marshman had met Carey's staunch friend Dr Steadman, and also
Christopher Anderson, the Hopes of Liverpool, and the son of the
Leeds surgeon who had aided all their translation work. For months
Marshman had been the lovingly-detained guest in Bristol of their
stoutest champion, John Foster. He had been honoured, too, by inti-
mate talks with many of the renowned – with Robert Hall, Hannah
More, Gutzlaff, the Haldanes, Chalmers, Wilberforce, Daniel
O'Connell, Sir Walter Scott and young William Gladstone; and with
Denmark's King Frederick himself, who had been proud to give them
their college charter. He had, indeed, despite the troubles, 'come again
rejoicing, bringing sheaves with him'.

It must have been one of Carey's most galling experiences to find, in
the September 1829 issue of the *Asiatic Journal,* a savage and extensive
onslaught on his Marathi Bible by an anonymous critic – a version
which (with its two New Testament editions) had cost him toil
through more than eighteen years. The assailant protested that it

'swarmed with every fault of taste', and severely criticised the Bible Society for subsidising 'the work of such a bigot, whose translations were exactly fit for worms'. Carey writhed, but refrained from self-defence, saying, 'Those who are not prepared to follow their Lord through evil report, cannot follow Him at all.'

At length an unsolicited champion made answer for him, in what Carey described to Jabez as 'a most triumphant reply'. William Green-field, the editor of *Bagster's Syriac New Testament*, took up the case point by point, and established the version's praiseworthy, skilled care. Its single drawback, Greenfield maintained, was its local dialect, which was the native speech of pundit Vidyanath, who had been the Marathi pundit chosen by Fort William College, and praised for his attainments.

One very great comfort that the Mission received in these years of disruption, bereavement and calamity was the abolition of *sati* (widow-burning), just when the slander at home was at its fiercest.

Lord Cavendish Bentinck assumed the government of India in July 1828, and immediately set himself to face every aspect of this long-vexed question. After many consultations with representatives of every side, he formed his own judgement and determined to legislate. On Friday, 4 December, 1829 – a date for enduring remembrance – he carried, in the teeth of Brahmin protestation, a Regulation in Council declaring the practice both illegal and criminal. Mrityunjay had long before proven that 'according to the great Shastras, a life of abstinence and chastity was the Hindu *law* for a widow, whilst burning with her husband was only an alternative, which could never have law's force.'

Sir Charles Metcalfe and Butterworth Bayley, two of Carey's earliest Fort William students and prizemen, and now leading members of the Council (presidents respectively of the Boards of Revenue and Trade), who had already forbidden the practice in the various districts they had governed, were eager for the reform.

At such a time it was bliss for Carey to be the Government's Bengali translator. The edict arrived early on Sunday, 6 December, when he was preparing for the pulpit. Arranging with another to preach he, with his pundit, gave the day to their translating. He would not lose an hour with women's lives at stake. In the Bengal Presidency alone some six thousand had been sacrificed in the previous ten years. The transla-tion required meticulous care, every sentence and phrase needing to be weighed with the most careful deliberation. But by the evening it was done, and this age-long abomination was doomed. It had existed in India, as Marshman pointed out, since the days of Alexander the Great. This was truly for Carey a 'Sabbath task after Isaiah's own heart'. It was fitting that he who had lodged the first protests with the Government twenty-five years before, and had striven more than any other man for its abolition, should be used to announce the end of *sati*. Often this scripture from *Proverbs 24* had burned in his heart:

> If thou forbear to deliver them that are drawn unto death, and those that are ready to be slain; if thou sayest, Behold, we knew it not; doth not he that pondereth the heart consider it? and he that keepeth thy soul, doth not he know it? and shall not he render to every man according to his works?

Of course, the reform was met by a Brahminic uproar as an unwarrantable interference with the people's religion; and as a breach of faith with India. Appeal was even carried to the King. But Lord Bentinck would not waver, and his humane decision was upheld by the Privy Council.

Several occasional attempts were made in the following years to pursue the condemned practice. The son of a rich Rajput pleaded with the British Resident to allow his mother to burn with her dead husband's body, it being a point of conscience with herself and her family, and the British Government being famed for its regard for the people's conscientious convictions. 'Of course, your mother may do as her conscience enjoins her,' replied the Resident, 'and you, as her first-born son, may light the *sati* fire. Only then you must permit me to follow my conscience and my Government's, and hang you for murder.'

28. The Calcutta Crashes

The last days of William Carey were his best. His sun went down in all the splendour of a glowing faith and a burning self-sacrifice. Not in the poverty of Hackleton and Moulton, not in the hardships of Calcutta and the Sundarbans, not in the fevers of the Dinajpur swamps, not in the apprehensions twice excited by official intolerance, not in the most bitter sorrow of all – the sixteen years' persecution by English brethren after Fuller's death – had the father of modern missions been so tried as in the years 1830–1833. Blow succeeded blow, but only that the fine gold of his trust, his humility, and his love might be seen to be the purer.

DR GEORGE SMITH

The brightest page of the Serampore controversy story is that which tells how John Mack and John Marshman cheered the closing years of the two older men by their noble service of Serampore and its missions; and to them belongs a large share of the honour of the peace in which that long controversy closed.

SAMUEL VINCENT

28. The Calcutta Crashes
1830 – 1833

CALCUTTA CAN PASS with startling suddenness out of sunshine into storm, but it had never known a gloom more unexpected than when, in January 1830, the princely mercantile house of Palmer & Co., the bankers of so many, reckoned safe as the East India Company itself, failed. The debts were from three to five million pounds sterling. Hundreds of European and Indian families were hit, including many whose children were in Serampore's boarding-schools, and who were now cast upon their charity.

In June that same year the Indian administration – compelled to retrench after the costly Burmese War – reduced Fort William College from a teaching institution to a purely examining body, terminating all lectures, and discharging the professors. In recognition of his unique length of service, Carey was treated considerately, and was given the only professorial pension, equal to half his salary. Even so, his monthly income shrank instantly by Rs 500. Later in the same year, due to further retrenchment, Carey's post of Bengali translator to the Government was suspended, involving him in a further monthly loss of Rs 300.

Robinson tells how the elders were 'dissolved in tears' as they gave themselves to prayer, and how Marshman, in particular, 'could not find words for his feelings'. 'It was, indeed, affecting to see these fathers of the Mission entreating God not to forsake them in their grey hairs.' Carey wrote to the Rev Christopher Anderson, now the British secretary of the Mission –

> I confess that the prospect of this great reduction of my salary lay very heavily on my mind at first, particularly as it would *put it out of my power to support our missionary stations. [He had been giving Rs 600 to these monthly.]* I am, however, convinced of God's infinite wisdom, and have implored Him to bend my mind to His will. We cannot give up our stations, nor do I see how we can maintain them. *[They had added eleven workers the previous year.]* But God can raise us up. It is His wont to make us realise our complete dependence on Him.

And chivalrous Marshman wrote:

> Carey can contribute little to the stations out of his pension, after he has supported his sister Mary, his late wife's eldest sister in France (for her sake as dear to him as his own) and an orphan, whom he has sent home to be educated in England, the expense of whose board, education and clothing lies wholly upon him; not to mention the expense of his own family, now five persons – and of his garden and palanquin, which contribute so essentially to his health, and which he shall never discontinue, while I live, if I can prevent it . . . You ask, perhaps, how we expect to carry forward our thirteen stations and the college. I answer, 'Through divine aid.' Whether this shall be from Britain or from India, I humbly leave to Him.

In July, John Mack wrote to Lauchlan Mackintosh of Allahabad: 'Carey is left without a *pice [farthing]* to give to the stations, which are dearer to him than his life.' Of the Khasi station he had borne the whole cost from the beginning. They appealed to the home churches:

> Only a few years have passed since the Protestant world was wakened to missions. Since then, the annual revenues collected for this purpose have grown to the once unthought-of sum of £400,000. Is it unreasonable to ask that some fraction of this should be entrusted to him, who was among the first to move in this enterprise, and to his colleagues? . . . We know God can provide. We as firmly believe that He will, as if we saw it accomplished.

This appeal did not reach England till December, but Christopher Anderson and Samuel Hope (the Mission's home treasurer, and a leading Liverpool banker) immediately gave it the utmost publicity – 'that the declining years of the seniors might be cheered, the hands of their youngest colleagues be strengthened, the native missionaries feel a new impulse in the cause, and this crisis, like that of the fire, turn out to the furtherance of the Gospel.' They forwarded in faith at once, by the *Aurora*, £1,000, which reached Serampore, with heartening letters, just as the elders were at the end of all their material resources, and the allowances of many of their station missionaries were two months in arrears. On 17 May, Carey wrote to Anderson:

> Four days ago we received your exceedingly welcome letters. I was just recovering from nearly a month's attack of fever. These letters did much to revive me. To God is all praise due for thus graciously removing the embarrassments, under which we must soon have sunk. All our stations lie very near our hearts; our brothers there are men of God; and the stations are maintained at the least possible cost: we, therefore, could not feel willing to relinquish any one of them.

The same day he wrote to Steadman:

> Your very welcome letter, dated 27 December, arrived with several others a few days ago, and all contributed to raise our drooping spirits, and, I trust, to call forth gratitude to God. We had been a long time without letters, and the last we had received were rather of a gloomy cast. Our difficulties were also great and discouraging. All we could do was to hope and pray. But letters from you and Mr Gibbs of London, and from our kind friends Hope and Anderson, with the remittances contained in them, removed our burdens, and we have now only to devote ourselves and our all more entirely to God's service. All our stations are very dear to us, and the relinquishing of any one of them would be most distressing. All who occupy them are tried and faithful men, and even those who have gone forth to the work within the last year give us as much pleasure as the older.
>
> Among other things in your letters both to Marshman and myself you express a wish that I would pay a visit to England. To this, my dear friend, there are many serious objections, the chief of which is the necessity of my getting a new edition of the Bengali Bible through the press, which is now being printed. Another twelve months will scarcely suffice to bring it to a close. I also wish to get another edition of the Sanskrit Bible, which has been begun, completed. I could leave India then, so far as regards my work, but not before, unless God should call me away by death.

With respect to myself, were I in England, all my friends would be greatly disappointed. I am now within three months of 70. My recollection is so shattered that I am almost afraid to assert anything. I could not travel day and night, as Ward and as Marshman did. Besides, England presents to me a great blank: nearly all my old acquaintances are dead, and I should have a new set of religious connections to form. You, my dear Steadman, were known in all the churches before I left England, and, I believe, sent the first half-guinea to the Mission. At least, either you sent the first half-guinea, or Elkanah Winchester the first guinea, for I received them nearly at the same time, and, so far as I can recollect, before the Missionary Society was formed. I, however, never saw you, though I am sure I should feel myself at home with you immediately on sight, but how few others could I similarly embrace. I thank you, my dear friend, for that kind and steady co-operation with Serampore, which you have so long maintained.

Three, and five, days later he acknowledged to treasurer Hope the receipt of Rs 11,400 and Rs 11,700:

How shall we sufficiently praise God, Who, in our great extremity, stirred up His people thus willingly to offer their substance for His cause! My heart is toward them all, but most I desire to re-consecrate myself to that God, Who has wrought for us wonders.

To Jabez he wrote:

I am always prone to be fearful and unbelieving as it respects supplies, and yet God has appeared beyond my most sanguine expectations.

John Mack blessed Anderson for the burst of good news, and for help from Edinburgh, Glasgow, Liverpool, London and York. John Marshman wrote:

I cannot look back on the feelings which filled our hearts this time twelvemonth without the strongest emotions of gratitude. Then our stations seemed deprived of all support; our means had reached the fatal point of exhaustion. A hundred times, as I trod the weary way from my office to my home after a fatiguing day, with no prospect for the morrow less dreary and sickening, I thought we must give up the struggle to maintain the stations. We seemed to be driven to retire. Yet the promises of God would dart across my mind, and invigorate both soul and body, and revive every power and faculty, till I thought it was impossible we should fail. Now how different the prospect – how lively and cheering – funds which relieve us from anxiety – friends who sympathise with us, and *who give us their whole trust!*

The 'hurricane' of 1830–31, however, was succeeded by other Euroclydons, which struck Calcutta and the Serampore Mission between 12 December, 1832 and 5 January, 1833, when the banking companies Alexander & Co., and Mackintosh & Co., each failed with huge losses and 'the city of palaces' became a place of panic. Following the second crash, John Marshman wrote:

> Dr Carey has lost his last farthing in Alexander's. Now Mrs Grace Carey's competency, £3,000, has all gone in Mackintosh's. They both feel the loss most poignantly. Every farthing of money my father had is also gone; after three-and-thirty years' labour, of the tenth reserved for old age nothing remains but the house in which he lives, and two small houses in Barrackpore. All Fernandez' legacy for Dinajpur has gone, about £1,600; Jessore's schools' fund, £720; the Delhi school fund, £800; all, all is gone.

Yet he adds:

> What, then, is to be done? Shall the conversion of India be arrested by the failure of two houses of agency? No. 'Speak unto the children of Israel, that they go forward.' We must go forward, trusting to that all-wise God, without Whose foreknowledge these things have not arisen. We must rekindle the flame of love and the ardour of faith, and labour incessantly. How we are to carry on the stations, I know not. As a missionary committee we have nothing; as individuals, nothing. Yet we dare not faint.
>
> The whole nation of the Arakanese, the whole nation of the Assamese, the whole tribe of the Khasis, the whole Bengali districts of Chittagong, Dacca, Barisal, Jessore and Dinajpur have not a soul from whose lips they can hear the Word of Life, save our own workers. We dare not recall them.

John Mack writes:

> Distress is now universal. Mackintosh & Co. were our bankers. We can obtain no more money now to pay the salaries of our brethren, till fresh supplies arrive from England. What we shall do, I know not. I know God can provide: how He will we cannot tell. It would be shameful to distrust Him, Who has before so singularly helped us; nor will we distrust your zeal and affection.

Young John Leechman, newly arrived from Glasgow, wrote home:

We have been under the greatest apprehensions, lest we should be compelled to give up some of our stations. Were that day to arrive, we should soon have to lay Dr Carey in his grave.

Carey told Steadman that the relinquishment of any of the Mission's stations would be 'like tearing limbs from his body'.

Their friend Judge Garrett of Bakarganj (a former student of Carey's), who, with his wife, had submitted to Christian baptism in a pool there, despite the derision of their fellow Europeans, secured them a bank loan. The Mission asked all their branch station colleagues whether they would be willing to forgo any portion of their allowances, and cut their own Serampore expenditure to the bone.

Yet before their urgent January letters reached England, Colvin & Co., another great Calcutta banking house, collapsed, bringing a further tidal wave of troubles. The largest trees of the forest were falling.

We cannot see [says Marshman] how the work is to be carried on without funds, but He, Who is the same yesterday, today and for ever, knows what He purposes. On Him we must wait, whilst doing all within our own ability. The failure of these houses has left many of our boarders destitute.

Like the Serampore elders, Mackintosh of the Allahabad mission station had lost his all in these houses. Mack comforts him:

I am grieved at your loss. But do not let it too greatly depress you. God will never forsake you, nor those dear to you. He would have us live by faith. By these painful disciplines He teaches us both how it is to be done, and how sweet it is to do it. We are heirs to riches which will never fail. Only let us be faithful.

Before they called, God was sending them answer. Three 'five hundreds' were on their way to them in successive dispatches – which, had they come sooner, would have been lost in the failed banking houses. In the hard waiting time Carey's themes and texts were bracing – 'The might of Gideon's three hundred in God's hands;' 'Lord, increase our faith;' 'This is the victory that overcometh, even our faith.' On the fortieth anniversary of his leaving Leicester he brought them strong encouragement.

Rather than abandon their posts, their station colleagues were,

almost to a man, willing to take sharply reduced allowances, and agreeing to maintain themselves by secular labour while they pursued their
mission work. Serampore could be proud of them. Carey wrote to
Christopher Anderson in May 1833:

> The replies from our station brethren breathe the spirit of the Gos-
> pel . . . I fear that but a small part of our losses will be recoverable. Yet I
> am firmly convinced that all these distressing circumstances are under
> His control, Who is Lord of Heaven and earth. Therefore would I 'be
> still, and know that He is God.' Pray that more completely I may take
> hold of His strength, and go about my work fully expecting the accom-
> plishment of His promises.

That very May, after an exceptionally hot season (when, as Carey
said, 'the earth was iron, the heavens brass, and the rain powder and
dust'), South Bengal was stricken by the most terrific gale it had known
for a generation. 'Nearly every vessel in the river was injured or
destroyed. The shore was strewn with carcasses and wrecks. The misery
from starvation and from lack of drinking water was indescribable, the
number of lives lost immense.' Serampore felt its full violence. Carey's
mahoganies and other great trees in his garden crashed across his conservatories, and destroyed the treasures of twenty years. It seemed to be
Nature's counterpart to the recent commercial devastations.

Then, that July, the Bible Society, under the insistence of non-
Baptist Calcutta subscribers, felt compelled to withhold any further
grants to Bible translations (like those from Serampore) which *translated* instead of transliterating the word 'baptizo'. The money loss to
Serampore was grievous, especially on top of the other recent disasters.
Yet Carey and Marshman judged that they could do no other than
maintain the course they had so long followed, and which was followed by contemporary translations in German, Danish and Dutch.

As soon as secretary Christopher Anderson and treasurer Samuel
Hope learned of the Mission's destitution, they spread the news
throughout Britain. Despite the short time since their previous appeal,
they raised this second cry with an even greater certainty of faith:

> We must not permit them to be hindered in their labour. Not one of
> their stations must be crippled; not one of their infant churches be
> neglected. By God's help they *shall* be nourished. Nor will we turn a
> deaf ear to the cry of other districts. We entertain no shadow of doubt

but that this mission loss will be made up, and, notwithstanding all the pressure of the times, perhaps as speedily as on former occasions. At all events, that it is not in the power of any Calcutta house of agency to stay the progress of His cause, Whose is the silver and gold, the friends of our common Christianity will soon demonstrate, to the abundant comfort of our colleagues in India.

To a trumpet call so confident the home churches could do no other than respond, and, when the self-denying acts of the station missionaries were eventually published, people's hearts were stirred, and gifts poured in, and were constantly forwarded, until 'thankfulness and praise rang from one end of the Mission to the other.' John Mack could write joyously to Mackintosh on 18 September, 1833:

We are now able to restore all your former salaries. God has supplied all our wants. Today we have received from England a fourth remittance of £500, and there is every prospect of more. We need fear no longer lack of means for our work. Our most distinguishing necessity is His Spirit to make all our toil effectual for the conversion of men. Unite with us, dear friend, in imploring this blessing.

And later:

We have received most encouraging letters from friends Anderson, Hope, Gibbs, and Barclay. By them all we are assured of continued support and of their fervent affection. One lady has given £1,000, half for the college, and half for the Khasis. When we see the hearts of God's people thus at His command, and that He so inclines them to help us, why should we ever doubt Him any more – even if, to keep us dependent upon His grace, we should again be made to pass through straits? We have not yet learned a proper importunity in respect to our spiritual necessities. His mercy in hearing us for the lesser things should goad us to pray for His Spirit.

29. The Satisfied Years

Bless the Lord, O my soul, and forget not
    all his benefits:
Who forgiveth all thine iniquities;
Who healeth all thy diseases;
Who redeemeth thy life from destruction;
Who crowneth thee with lovingkindness
    and tender mercies;
Who satisfieth thy mouth with good things;
So that thy youth is renewed like the eagle's.

KING DAVID, Psalm 103.

[The first meeting of Carey and Alexander Duff, missionary of the Church of Scotland to India, and founder of the college that became the University of Calcutta.]

Landing at the college *ghât* one sweltering July day of 1830, the still ruddy Highlander strode up to the flight of steps that leads to the finest modern building in Asia. Turning to the left, he sought the study of Carey in the house 'built for angels', said one, so simple is it, where the greatest of missionary scholars was still working for India. There he beheld what seemed to be a little yellow old man in a white jacket, who tottered up to the visitor, of whom he had already often heard, and with outstretched hands solemnly blessed him. A contemporary, soon after, wrote thus of the childlike saint:

'Thou'rt in our hearts – with tresses thin and grey,
    And eye that knew the Book of Life so well,
And brow serene, as thou wert wont to stray
    Amidst thy flowers, like Adam ere he fell.'

The result of the conference was a double blessing, for Carey could speak with the influence at once of a scholar, who had created the best college at that time in the country, and of a vernacularist, who had preached to the people for nearly half a century. The young Scotsman left his presence with the approval of the one authority whose opinion was best worth having.

DR GEORGE SMITH'S *Alexander Duff.*

I was a private pupil of John Mack's at Serampore for about three years, and attended the college classes. John Mack lived at the south end of the college house, Dr Carey at the north end. I remember old Dr C. very well. He was very fond of me. I dined with him once a week, and had a standing invitation to tea at any time. The portrait of him with his pundit is just like them both, as I have often seen them sitting at work. The college windows overlooked Dr C.'s study, and that is just how they used to sit. I saw the meeting between C. and Duff. The latter came up the steps and they embraced each other. I heard C.'s lectures on botany. He would go first into the garden and pluck some leaves and flowers, and bring them to the class-room. He spoke quietly, but without hesitation, and very interestingly. His notes were on a slip of paper about three inches wide. Some fifteen of us would listen and take notes. Outsiders, also, were often present. He would tell us many anecdotes of his Mudnabati years. He struck us as being of a very retiring disposition – devoted to study. At prayers, Dr Carey would read a chapter, emphasising important parts with a sharp drop of the forefinger of the right hand – its whole length – on to the book or the table.

His wife was devoted to him and looked after his every want. Every morning he took his walk in the garden (near the big tank), his hands clasped behind him, and engaged in audible prayer. This was a habit only interrupted at times, as he bent to examine a flower: then he resumed his onward tread. He was very short. He wore white in the summer and black in the winter. In fact, this change of attire was to us the sign that the season had changed. He always wore gaiters and stockings.

J. H. REILLY, retired Chief of Detectives,
recalling (in 1892) his attendance at Serampore College.

I am now in the Hooghly going to Serampore. I shall be very thankful to get my prejudices against this station removed. May God prepare my heart not to expect too much from man, but to be very thankful for all that I see that is according to His will. The banks of the Hooghly near Serampore are very beautiful, the houses very handsome, the verdant lawns shaded by magnificent trees.

I have just seen Dr Carey, who is sinking into the grave, after more than forty years' Indian service, leaving the world, as to temporal things, as poor as when he entered it.

Never, I think, were men more overwhelmingly belied than these: not, perhaps, that they have done all things well, but they are certainly as far above those who censure them as the blue vault of heaven is above the clouds.

ANTHONY GROVES (Church Missionary Society), 1834.

At this time I paid my last visit. He was seated near his desk in the study, dressed in his usual neat attire. His eyes were closed, and his hands clasped together. On his desk was the proof-sheet of the last chapter of the Bengali New Testament, which he had revised a few days before. His appearance, as he sat there, with his few white locks and his placid, colourless face, filled me with a kind of awe; for he seemed as one listening to his Master's summons, and as ready to go. I sat there for about half an hour, without a word, for I feared to break that silence, and to call back to earth the spirit that seemed almost in Heaven. At last, however, I spoke, and well do I remember the very words that passed between us. I said, 'Dear friend, you seem to be standing on the very border of the eternal; do not think it wrong, then, that I ask your thoughts and feelings.' The question roused him, and, opening his eyes, he earnestly answered, 'I know in Whom I have believed, and I am persuaded that He is able to keep that which I have committed unto Him against that day. But when I think that I am about to appear in God's holy presence, and I remember all my sins, I tremble.' He could say no more. The tears trickled down his cheeks, and he relapsed into the silence from which I had aroused him.

GEORGE GOGERLY, *The Pioneers.*

On one of the last occasions on which Duff saw him – if not the very last – he spent some time talking, chiefly about Carey's missionary life, till at length the dying man whispered 'Pray.' Duff knelt and prayed and said goodbye. As he passed from the room, he thought he heard a feeble voice pronouncing his name, and, turning, he found himself recalled. He stepped back accordingly, and this is what he heard, spoken with a gracious solemnity: 'Mr Duff, you have been speaking about Dr Carey, Dr Carey; when I am gone, say nothing about Dr Carey – speak about Dr Carey's Saviour.' Duff went away rebuked and awed, with a lesson in his heart that he never forgot.

DR JAMES CULROSS

29. The Satisfied Years
1830 – 9 June, 1834

CAREY HAD BEEN STARTLED and distressed to see how Marshman had aged on his return from furlough in 1829. If Marshman had been equally shocked to see how much Carey also had aged during that time, it would not have been surprising, considering the griefs and pressures of those years. Yet this was his contrary impression:

> Though soon to enter on his seventieth year, he is as cheerful and happy as the day is long. He rides out four or five miles every morning, reaching home by sunrise; goes on with his work of translation day by day; gives two divinity lectures and a natural history one every week in the college, and takes his turn at preaching both in Bengali and English. I met with few friends in England near their seventieth year so lively, so free from the infirmities of age, so interesting in the pulpit, so completely conversable as he.

Moreover, although in the next three years he was to be greatly shaken by fevers, and twice by what appeared to be paralytic strokes, he would rally surprisingly. John Marshman, in February 1832, would say –

> Were Dr C. not beyond 70, I should say he was quite well. His

improved health has brought back his fine flow of spirits, making him again, what Lady Hastings emphatically called him, 'the cheerful old man'.

In that September Carey described himself to Jabez:

I am exceedingly emaciated. This does not appear particularly in my face, but is so great in all other parts that my clothes hang about me like bags.

But he found it easy to be cheerful, for, as he himself said, he had 'scarcely a wish ungratified'.

The last sheet of his final revision of his Bengali Bible (the passion of his closing years) had been sent to the press in June 1832. Carey wrote:

God has graciously preserved me to bring the last edition of the Bengali Scriptures through the press. The last sheet was ordered to be printed last week. I have done all in my power to make it correct.

At John Mack's ordination to the Serampore co-pastorate with Marshman and himself, Carey took its first copy (a single volume now) into the pulpit, and, having used it, made the swan-song of Simeon his own. Like the Venerable Bede, he felt that his life-work was finished.

Not quite, however, for an urgent task claimed him – the drawing up with the Marshmans, father and son, of the 'unalterable statutes of the college' as required by its charter, and on the character of which its future would depend. The document is confessedly one of Serampore's noblest – the elders' fitting legacy. Its chief elements speak for themselves.

All degrees, considering India's economic poverty, were to be free of charge to their winners. No oaths were to be administered to any. Marriage (early in India) was to bar no position in the college, from that of master, to that of the humblest servant. Members of the council might be chosen from any in India, Europe or America, of the due 'piety, learning and talent'. No caste, colour, country nor creed was to disqualify any from attending the classes. The college councillors and professors were to be true believers in Christ's divinity and atonement, and to vacate their office if they changed their views, any such change being proved from their writings or lectures, and its evidence published to the Christian world.

How completely the seniors could rest in those who were succeeding them – especially in the three Johns – Mack, Marshman, and Leechman. John Mack made an ideal leader – from Edinburgh University, Bristol College and Guy's, with his classical and medical attainments, his sound sense, his influence over the young, his power of utterance, and his love of Indian Christians. 'I do not envy,' he said, 'the favourite minister of the best and largest congregation in Great Britain, when I am preaching in Jannagar.'

John Clark Marshman was acknowledged by all to be outstandingly able and devoted. John Leechman – who had attended Glasgow University – was of vigorous intellect and apostolic soul. Into hands so capable the elders could entrust the future without fear, and all the more, as there was no discord between them and these junior men. Furthermore, the three were now joined by William Robinson, returned back from faithful work in Java and Sumatra. He had become pastor of Lall Bazar. In the time of schism and disruption he had taken his own independent line, and at length published in Britain a defence of the seniors. Now he fully identified with Serampore, and became one of Carey's most valued assistants.

Then, beyond their own Baptist borders, Alexander Duff, of the Church of Scotland Mission, was furthering the cause. His vision and methods differed from Carey's – but 'we love him,' wrote Marshman, 'as though he were one of ourselves.'

In a first letter home John Leechman writes, 'I arrived at this lively place on 24 November, 1832, and bless God daily for bringing me hither.' A lively place it certainly was, with the high school and the college students now added to the Marshmans' schools. When Carey led the weekly service designed specially for these, he would set the time, in spite of his seventy years, and stamp energetically with his foot at the start of the singing.

The theological men of the college were the elders' pride and joy. Among them was Samuel Mackintosh, the son of their much-loved colleague in Allahabad, 'a budding tutor, with his fine capacity for clear thinking and research'. There was Carey Barclay, son of a manse, showing exceptional promise. Panchu Gopal, a grandson of Krishna Pal, was another whose progress warmed them. All these, and others, were fervent missionaries already, who went out as opportunity came to preach the Gospel.

John Marshman tells how, in his last days, Carey would plead for volunteers in the outfields, more than once repreaching his Nottingham challenge: 'Stretch forth the curtains of thine habitations; lengthen thy cords; strengthen thy stakes.' Students of fine spirit responded, most of them ready to maintain themselves, as Carey wished, while they served the Gospel of Christ. Smylie, in Dinajpur, won the grateful confidence of people for miles round as much by his mechanical expertise and services as by his message. John Smith and W. H. Jones conducted the first modern schools in Barisal and in Rungpur, of which two Christian judges – friends of Carey's – had borne the cost. Greenway was esteemed as highly in Cawnpore as a man of business as an ambassador of Christ. Rae exchanged the Assam superintendency of public works for a missionary's calling, and soon, as Mack said, 'stretched his limbs there, Serampore's senior student having nine Garos and three Khasi princes under Christian instruction.'

Rowe and Alexander Lish, to Carey's special joy, settled in Chirrapoonji in the midst of the Khasis (and near to Commissioner David Scott). These hill people were particularly dear to Carey, who had translated the New Testament for them and strained his own reserves for years to plant a mission station among them.

At the ordinations of most of these, he, their white-haired elder, gave the charge, bidding them – 'Be sober, be vigilant;' 'turn men from darkness to light;' 'occupy till Christ come,' and 'make full proof of your ministry,' or, as he rendered it, 'put your ministry to the test in every way and by every means, seeing and showing what it can do.' By the year of his death they had strategic mission centres in more remote places than ever, eighteen in all, stretching from Delhi to Akyab, manned by fifty workers, of whom half were wholly Indian, and a quarter were Indo-European. A nineteenth station was formed by young Henry Havelock, who was by this time a son-in-law of the Marshmans.

One afternoon, over teacups, in the Society's fortieth year, Carey talked to Marshman of 'his earliest thoughts about missions, and of how God had sustained these within him, even when Fuller had been unable to embrace them, and senior Ryland had denounced them as unscriptural. They spoke of how different India would have been, had these thoughts and yearnings been stifled.'

They contrasted the Indian administration they had both first known (suspicious of missions, refusing them countenance, and forbidding them outright), with the India they now knew. The Governor-General and his lady were now their warm personal friends. So were governors such as Sir Stamford Raffles of Sumatra, and residents like Byam Martin of Indore, and supreme councillors like Butterworth Bayley and Sir Charles Metcalfe, and commissioners like David Scott of Assam, and judges like Garrett of Barisal. These were not only friendly towards their purpose, but sought their aid.

It gladdened the missionaries particularly to have lived to see the colour-bar removed from India's civil and military services; and, on the other hand, Europeans granted permanent leases at easy rentals in the Sundarbans. They immediately secured many hundreds of acres there, and, by the energy of young Conrad Rabeholm, their Barripore colleague, had them cleared and tanks dug, with the Rs 10,000 of the legacies of Grant and Bryant. Then they sublet the plots to peasants on reasonable terms, especially to the Christians of a dozen villages there, freeing them from oppressive landlords, and at the same time providing an endowment fund for the college.

But the Mission's future could not depend solely on Indian resources. Survival would also depend on the spirit of the home base, and on the quality of its leadership. On this account, they could now feel greater hopefulness. Christopher Anderson and Samuel Hope, Serampore's home secretary and treasurer, had proved themselves sympathetic leaders. Fuller himself had, years before his death, marked out this Christopher Anderson as the most suitable next leader. If his nomination had not been overthrown at Fuller's passing, the Mission would have been saved immeasurable hurt. The schism would have been improbable, the disruption impossible. He had all Fuller's strength of mind, heart and will, and rejected the policy of keeping down the field expenses at the risk of starving the work and depressing the workers. Like Fuller he preferred to keep up the commitment of the churches, and to urge them to the heroic. His letters to the missionaries were never formal; never those of a Secretary of State, but the drawing of men's hearts to his own by an individual sympathy. Take the following, for instance:

My beloved Mackintosh,

How often I have gazed, on my large map of India, at Allahabad, and thought of you, I cannot tell. But in view of the close and endearing bond by which you and I are now united, I know that I have frequently purposed in my heart to sit down and write to you; indeed, to you all. For the truth is that, familiar as I now am with most of the Eastern countries, so far as the best maps and books can make me, I find it easy to rove in imagination from Delhi to Arakan, going to every station in succession, and not only associating with them each your well-known names, but entering in some small measure into your various trials or disappointments, sorrows and joys.

The loss of your dear daughter was felt by me with all the tenderness of a brother's sympathy. This you will fully believe, when I tell you that such things have befallen me, and to no common extent. A beloved wife and *five* beloved children I have laid in the grave, and amongst these a son, who, though young, yearned to become a missionary; and since then, I have been left alone. But it is well, I can *now* say, and all as it ought to be. They are safe every one, with your own child. My relief is in *work*, in plunging into efforts on behalf of that cause which can never die; and such, I trust, my dear friend, will continue to be your relief. Mercies you have still. You have a son whose voice and example will be of use and value, I trust, long after we have joined the song of Moses and the Lamb.

The accompanying appeal is another effort to rouse our churches. You have as much need to pray for us as we for you. At a leisure moment if you were to send me a few lines, it might serve the common cause. Do try and I will write to you. Remember me very affectionately to Sertul Das. Tell him there is none like the Master, no service like His.

CHRISTOPHER ANDERSON

Isolated missionaries felt their work power trebled under a home supporter like this, and the churches' bounteous response to this Greatheart's appeal kept reaching Serampore in Carey's last months and weeks. 'His colleagues valued the liberal gifts on no account more than for their effect upon him.' John Mack would read to him, as he was able to bear them, the affectionate letters. He would rally from even his extreme prostrations, and would stir himself to rejoice that the stations were once more free of debt. He would beg to be taken to his desk long after this was possible, that he might acknowledge gifts. Thankfulness to God and to the loyal home friends were his last emotions and delights. As John Leechman put it, 'the last chord that vibrated in his heart was gratitude to God and to His people.'

Another mercy, through his last months, uplifted his soul. Dr Wallich read him a letter which he had received from London in September 1833, reporting that the Cabinet meant to free trade with India, and to emancipate the West Indian slaves. 'This latter news,' says John Marshman, 'has rejoiced us all, but especially Carey. For many years, in his every prayer, he has been pleading for the destruction of slavery. In no public question has he taken a deeper interest. When the particulars of the measure were named to him, with tears in his eyes he thanked God, though in some points it fell short of his benevolent wishes. He proposed that for one month we should give special thanksgiving to God in all our meetings – a proposition with which we cheerfully complied.' And while the subject was hot in the public mind, they issued to all their stations this questionnaire:

> We are anxious to call public attention to the subject of *slavery in India*, and shall greatly value any information you can send us from your part of the country. By whom are the slaves chiefly held, by Hindus or Mohammedans? By what means are they obtained, and for what purposes – domestic, agricultural, or for prostitution? Trustworthy answers to such questions will be a work of mercy.

Another event excited them in 1833 – *steamboats* bringing news from London to Calcutta, via Egypt, in sixty-four days! 'We here,' they wrote, 'know all that has been going on at home up to the beginning of February: yet it is only 24 April!'

Carey was blest in his last months and weeks with the presence of his three surviving sons, William and Jabez (from Katwa and Rajputana), still faithful missionaries, and Jonathan, a Supreme Court attorney, but also Indian financier of the Serampore Mission. (Jonathan, sadly, was already widowed after brief wedded happiness with the daughter of Samuel Pearce.)

Jabez had a good story for his father. On his way down from Ajmere, his boat was capsized by the tidal-wave effect which afflicted the Hooghly, and almost within sight of Serampore. No lives had been lost, but when they reached the eastern bank, and the boat had been righted, he declined to trust himself again to his boatmen from the north, inexperienced as they were in the Hooghly, so he sought local rowers to take him across to Serampore. These demanded an exorbitant fare, and he refused, and moved away. However, when they discovered that the sahib was a son of Carey, they asked to be allowed to row him free of charge.

Well might Carey say that he had 'scarcely a wish ungratified'. His Bengali Bible was now, once more, revised and reissued (the third time for the Old Testament, and the eighth for the New). The college statutes were sound and fixed. He had juniors of the finest mind and spirit to fill the elders' places. The Mission's schools and college fulfilled their best expectations. Their stations were more numerous and far-flung than ever before, and were demonstrating on a large scale Carey's organising principle, that Indian preachers were best in India. *Sati* was no more. The Indian administration was now sympathetic, appreciative and co-operative. An endowment had been inaugurated for the college. Their supporters in the home churches were generous. The West Indian slaves were to be emancipated. West and East were being brought into more rapid interrelation. His own sons were with him, two with honourable missionary records, and the third the Mission's treasurer! Surely, his years were satisfied with good.

Two days after Carey's passing, Marshman said:

> The peculiarly hot weather and rainy season of 1833 reduced him to such extreme weakness that in September last he had a stroke of apoplexy, and for some time his death was daily expected. But he revived a little. During the last cold season he could again take a morning and evening ride in his palanquin, and spend much of the day in an easy chair with a book or in cheerful converse. But, as the hot weather advanced, he sank daily into still greater debility, till he could take no nourishment, and lay helpless and speechless on his couch.

Carey was too physically exhausted for spiritual ecstasy in the Last Valley. In June 1832, at the burial of Mrs Ward, he had spoken 'with much feeling and elevation of the holy happiness of the redeemed', as one who almost anticipated his own blessedness. But in his own final weeks just two years later there were 'neither raptures nor fears', but that which accorded more with his life's steadfast evenness, a tranquil trust in his crucified and glorified Saviour. John Mack could say that 'respecting the great change before him, not a shadow of anxiety had crossed his mind since the beginning of his illness.' By the labour of over 30 New Testament translations into Indian languages he had woven its triumphant affirmations into the very texture of his soul. He rested his sin-stained soul – as on the several earlier occasions when he thought he had come to his crossing – on his atoning Redeemer, and testified with thankfulness that there he, as ever, found his peace.

The vigour that had characterised him through his forty-one Indian years rallied so often that it was rash to say the end was near.

On Sunday, 8 June, 1834, Joshua Marshman, his companion in tribulation and in the kingdom and patience of Jesus Christ, felt an unusual burden of spirit as he visited him before setting off to Calcutta for the duties of the Lord's Day. Kneeling by his side, he felt certain he did so for the last time, and prayed from a full heart blessing God for the goodness of Carey's Indian years. When he concluded, Carey's wife of twelve years – the gentle Grace – asked, 'Do you know, dear, who is praying with you?' 'Yes, I do,' whispered Carey, and pressed the hand of his loyal and dear colleague. So they parted, to be divided (in Marshman's case) for a little season of three and a half years, for before he returned the following day, Carey was home with the Lord. 'The eternal gates,' says Culross, 'were opened for him at sunrise on 9 June, 1834.' His dependence and trust had proved secure:

> *A wretched, poor and helpless worm,*
> *On Thy kind arms I fall.*

Never wretched, poor, nor helpless, however, in the safety of those arms!

He instructed that these 'two lines and nothing more' from his beloved Isaac Watts, should be added, when his name and dates were inscribed on his previous wife Charlotte's monument in the Serampore graveyard.

'And now,' wrote Leechman to Serampore's friends in England, 'what shall we do? God has taken up our Elijah to Heaven, He has taken our master from our head today. But we must not be discouraged. The God of missions lives for ever. His cause must go on. The gates of death, the removal of the most eminent, will not impede its progress, nor prevent its success. Come: we have something else to do than mourn and be dispirited. With our departed leader all is well. He has finished his course gloriously. But the work now descends on us. Oh, for a double portion of the divine Spirit!'

30. The Translation Achievement

At an early period each new pundit's first attempts were brought to the test, when, after he had advanced some way, his MS. was put to the press, and the first sheet was examined by an initiated native assistant sitting by the side of this original native translator. The first and second proofs were thus corrected, which brought the sheet as near as these could to the original Sanskrit. The third proof was then carried to Dr Carey by the translator himself, and they went over this together, and over as many more proofs of the same sheet as the Doctor thought necessary, sometimes more and sometimes fewer, and after this the sheet was ordered to the press.

WARD to an Edinburgh friend, 10 May, 1820.

The principal work to be done in future as to India is that of printing from time to time *improved editions* of the Scriptures, the labours of the late Dr Carey and his colleagues having left comparatively little to be further attempted in the way of new translations . . . The only translations of the Old Testament which he left unfinished were the Pashto and the Kashmiri . . . His delight in the work of translation and his ardent desire to give the Scriptures to the Indian peoples were infused into the minds of his fellow missionaries, and, before he was called to leave the scene of his labours, he saw a succession of helpers in the work, who would carry it forward.

Eleventh Memoir of Translations, 1838.

[384]

30. The Translation Achievement

WHEN CAREY REACHED BENGAL, the only printed Christian Scriptures in India's vernaculars were the whole Bible in Tamil (the work of Ziegenbalg, Schultze, and Fabricius), the New Testament and the *Psalms* in Hindi (by Schultze), and the New Testament and the Pentateuch in Sinhalese (by Philipsz). The Hindi translations of Schultze scarcely counted, so little had they been approved, or fulfilled their purpose. Practically, only the Tamils and the Sinhalese had God's Word in their own tongues. Thus only two lamps were burning; and these in India's southernmost corner and its adjacent isle. The vast remainder lay in darkness. But before Carey's course was finished, he had festooned the darkness with inextinguishable lamps throughout its length and breadth.

We found him writing to Fuller at the end of 1803:

> If we are given *another fifteen years,* we hope to translate and print the Scriptures into all the chief languages of Hindustan. We have fixed our eyes on this goal. The zeal of the Lord of hosts shall perform this.

He was thinking, he elsewhere tells us, of

> Bengali, Hindi and Punjabi in the north, of

Oriya, Marathi and Gujarati in the midlands, and of
Telugu and Kanarese in the south.

The Scriptures were, he hoped, to be translated and printed, or at least the New Testament, in these eight languages within this term. It is startling to note how much, by the end of 1819, he had accomplished. He had rendered –

> The whole Bible *[in more than one edition]* both into Bengali and into Hindi – the latter with the aid of his two colleagues – plus the whole New Testament and half the Old into Punjabi;
> The whole Bible into Oriya and Marathi, and almost all the New Testament into Gujarati;
> The whole New Testament into Telugu and Kanarese *[though the latter had perished in the fire]* plus the Pentateuch into Telugu.

He had surely gone far towards realising his programme. In truth, he had much more than outdistanced his anticipated progress, having carried through many great accomplishments beyond his original design. He had translated the *whole Bible into Sanskrit* and seen it through the press – an undreamed-of achievement. He had produced the whole New Testament in Pashto (Afghan), and in Assamese, and the Gospels in Kashmiri. He had completed the whole New Testament again in Konkani (for the Brahminised multitudes south of Bombay), and in Lahnda (Multani) for cities as old as the time of Alexander the Great. Moreover, to Balochistan he had given three Gospels, and *Matthew* to a people south of Rajputan. His inclusion in his translation programme of the Afghans and Balochis on the west and of the Assamese on the east, had immensely stretched his range, and his Bible in Sanskrit had provided God's Word for Hindu scholars throughout India, and had eased the work of translation into every cognate Sanskrit tongue.

Carey's earliest procedure was to publish a Bible in five volumes, *Volume I* being the New Testament. He supplied all five volumes in the case of six Indian languages, in the following order: (1) Bengali, (2) Oriya, (3) Hindi, (4) Sanskrit, (5) Marathi, and (6) Assamese.

In this sequence there was great intelligence. Bengali was the speech not just of Carey's own province but of India's densest area of population. Oriya was the vernacular of Carey's best pundit, and of Jagannath's chief temple and realm. (Its script was very distinct from

Bengali, but its structure was very alike.) Hindi swept the widest northern and central field, and was the Hindus' speech in cities of world fame. Sanskrit, while not a language currently spoken, was the language of literature and learning. Marathi was the tongue of the province most recently added to British rule. Assamese completed a chain of languages through North India from Burma to Bombay.

The Oriya version was in the first instance executed by Mrityunjay from Carey's second Bengali edition, and was then corrected by Carey, verse by verse, with continuous reconsulting of the Greek and the Hebrew. The spadework for the Marathi version was the work of Vidyanath.

Carey's Hindi New Testament of 1811 was so welcome in the upper provinces that a large second edition was demanded within a few months of the first, and this was also quickly exhausted. That it was well understood by its readers is shown by J. T. Thompson, a later translator. He tells of visiting in 1816 a cultured old man of Patna, whom he found familiar with Christian teaching, though he had never before met a Christian. Not until his third interview, however, did he disclose the source of his knowledge, which was Carey's Hindi New Testament, which had come into his possession after thirty years of dissatisfaction with the Hindu religion, and had seemed to him a gift from Heaven. From that time he had broken with all idolatry, and through four years had taught doctrines of the treasured Book to up to seventy disciples.

Of course, there were many inelegancies of expression, and a degree of harshness of construction in Carey's versions, but Professor H. H. Wilson of Oxford attributed these chiefly to his strict adherence to the exact text of the original, which with him was a point of honour. But in the past, fidelity was always the aim of the truly scholarly translator. 'I call God to record,' said Tyndale, 'against the day when we shall appear before the judgement seat of Christ, to give reckoning of our doings, that I never altered one syllable of God's Word against my conscience.'

At the end of 1803, Carey had hoped for fifteen years in which to render God's Word in all the chief tongues of Hindustan. God gave him twice fifteen. He spent this unlooked-for second term translating the whole Old Testament into Assamese, plus ten-elevenths of it into Punjabi and four-ninths of it into Pashto and Kashmiri; but chiefly he spent his time in *translating the New Testament into a multitude of minor Indian tongues.* The names of these languages were at that time scarcely known to the linguists of Europe. Carey says that he had once supposed them to be varieties of Hindi, but found that they were all distinct languages – derived from Sanskrit, yet so differently terminated and inflected as to make them unintelligible to the inhabitants of the surrounding regions.

Several were the vernaculars of only a few hundreds of thousands. Yet they had been distinct languages from times immemorial, and some had substantial literary traditions. Awadhi, for example, was the standard epic tongue in all the Hindi districts, for the *Ramayana* of Tulsi Das had been composed in this language during the days of Shakespeare, and the *Mahabharata* had also been recast in the same mould. How right that the *true* Christian 'Epic of Redemption' should enter that realm of language.

Braj Bhasha was the purest of the Hindi dialects, with the highest percentage of Sanskrit. Kanouji had been spoken from the eleventh century, and was for generations the vernacular of the most powerful Indo-Aryans before the rise of the Moguls. Malvi also had been the tongue of many an Indian king.

But even if a 'lesser' tongue had no such regal or literary glory, Carey was keen to make it a new vesture for God's Word. He has been reproached for wasting valuable strength on these subordinate dialects. But he who would cheerfully have laid down his life for Tahiti was not likely to grudge the toil, which would give to a few hundreds of thousands more people the Word of God in their own speech. And in this he was also responding to Dr William Hey, a Leeds surgeon. In Serampore's *Sixth Translation Memoir* it was affirmed that 'such were their facilities that £500 should cover the cost of producing a thousand copies of the New Testament in any further Indian vernacular into which they might be able to render it.' This so stirred the mind of Dr Hey that he set to work to raise such sums of £500, later uniting his fund with the efforts of the new British and Foreign Bible Society. The sum of £1,500 was soon forwarded to Serampore to facilitate the printing of Carey's Konkani, Pashto and Telugu New Testaments, at which he had laboured for six, eight and fourteen years respectively.

Carey often remembered, and made mention of, the experience of Britain, which had needed the Scriptures not just in the tongue of the predominant partner, but also in Welsh, Gaelic, Irish, Cornish and Manx. Indeed, until the Bible was available in these fireside dialects, it remained aloof, barren and unloved. These were the considerations which persuaded Carey to his extraordinary output in the lesser tongues. Perhaps, too, it was something of the scholar's and lexicographer's feeling such as animated Dr Johnson, when he said, 'I am very unwilling that a single language should be extinguished.'

Unexpected circumstances would often thrust Carey into schemes outside his plans. He never planned to undertake the Pashto (Afghan) New Testament. But when the brilliant orientalist Dr John Leyden (Professor of Hindi at Fort William College) left Calcutta he offered Carey the services of a capable Afghan scholar, together with a pundit, to work on the New Testament. For the next seven years they worked together to complete the New Testament. When Dr Taylor in Bombay passed into the full-time service of the Government, having rendered *Matthew* into Gujarati, Carey felt that he must complete the whole New Testament. And when Chamberlain's early death left his Braj Bhasha New Testament unfinished, Carey was constrained to supply the untranslated books.

So far were he and his colleagues from vaunting how many versions they could count to their credit that they postponed until 1811 the publication of their translated Hindi Gospels, leaving the field to Judge Colebrooke's version for five years. And later, in 1820, when a third edition of Carey's Hindi New Testament was demanded, he chose to publish Chamberlain's instead, so that 'by the comparison of independent renderings an idiomatic and standard version might be ultimately formed.' In the same spirit he discontinued his Kanarese Old Testament upon learning about the projected work of John Hands of the London Missionary Society, and he relegated further Telugu translating, after completing the New Testament and the Pentateuch, to the Madras Auxiliary of the Bible Society. In due course Carey withdrew, except for Gujarati, from the whole western field of translation, as soon as Dr Wilson and his colleagues had settled in that sphere. Then he resigned even this Gujarati work to the London Missionary Society in 1820, after completing the New Testament.

For each first translation he was compelled to await the appearance of a suitable pundit in the coveted vernacular, preferably a man who was at the same time familiar with Sanskrit, together with one or two other vernaculars in which the Scriptures had already been translated. Then from one of these versions this pundit would build the new one, with many fellow pundits close at hand for consultation. His understanding of the text might often be mistaken, but his style could be trusted to be tolerably 'native'. By the time the pundit had completed a Gospel, Carey had acquired from him the peculiarities of this fresh language or dialect, and was able to appreciate his manuscript and before long he advanced enough for the task of correction.

For such an adequate pundit he sometimes sought for years. When, in December 1813, he at last secured one for Khasi, he said he believed he was the only one in that nation who could read and write. Twice – with the Punjabi and Kumaoni versions – the deaths of the pundits brought the translation to an end.

He was often asked how he had contrived to acquire so many tongues, and would answer that 'none knew what they could do, till they tried.' He would also remark that having once thoroughly mastered Bengali, Hindi, Sanskrit, Marathi, Persian, Punjabi, and Dravidian Telugu, all else was comparatively simple. The back of his task was broken once these seven languages were his, especially considering that his knowledge of Sanskrit, the basis of so many others, was so thorough. Thereafter, it was 'as easy,' he said, 'to learn ten other cognates as one quite independent tongue.' He asserted that three-quarters of the words of most of the secondary dialects could be understood through Sanskrit, Bengali and Hindi, and sometimes even seven-eighths. Their word-roots were similar; it was just their very diverse word-endings that gave them a strange sound. Carey soon grew practised in detecting these differences, and the acquisition of a few hundred fresh words in each language was to him not labour but delight, like a botanist discovering fresh species. 'The first time I read a page of Gujarati,' he once wrote, 'the general meaning appeared so obvious that I scarcely needed to ask my pundit any questions.' However, he was not always so sanguine, and in 1813 he wrote:

> If I could learn languages faster, the work of translation would be more rapid. But some of the languages are very difficult, and differ so widely from others as to occasion me much hard labour. Every translation goes through my hands, except the Burmese and the Chinese.

He knew full well that his versions were only pioneer productions.

His Bengali Testaments he repeatedly revised, thrice the Old, eight times the New. With the issue of each fresh pioneer version, he communicated with Europeans in the new language area, begging them to submit it to the judgement of capable Indians, undertaking to supply for this purpose interleaved copies, and publishing only a small edition until these local amendments could be assessed. He was happy to have Alexander Lish, a Serampore Eurasian student, revise his Khasi version of *Matthew* a few months before his death.

Carey's New Testaments for Kashmir and for the Garhwali, who lived near the highly-sacred mountain sources of the Jumna and the Ganges, were completed years before they could be taken to those for whom they were produced. Indeed, Carey never lived to see the Kashmiri version reach its people.

In the shaping of the Pashto Scriptures he took peculiar delight, for Sir William Jones had ventured to say (unreliably as it turned out) that 'with greater probability than any other nation these Afghans could claim to have descended from Israel's lost tribes, because of the many Semitic words in which their language abounded.' And, certainly, Dr John Leyden's Afghan pundit (later Carey's too) insisted that 'his people, though not Jews, were sons of Israel.' It thrilled Carey to think that in giving them the New Testament and Pentateuch, he might be hastening the day when they should begin again to seek their fathers' God.

Most of Carey's versions have been further revised, and, as he wished, superseded. But in seven he had no successors – in the Awadhi, Bhatneri, Bikaneri, Harauti, Jaipuri, Lahnda and Mewari. The development of travel and the circulation of newspapers and of books have so submerged these minor vernaculars as to render unnecessary the continuance of these versions. Two of Carey's versions were reissued as late as 1884. Basle missionaries to Mangalore discovered in that year a mutilated copy of Carey's Konkani New Testament, and so approved of it that with just a few changes they republished *Mark* and *John* in a different script for the Kanarese. (This is particularly interesting as one of his several slanderers had charged him with receiving £500 from the Bible Society for this very Konkani version, saying that 'no such language was spoken'!) Dr G. A. Grierson, later the head of India's Linguistic Survey, revised and reprinted Carey's Maghadi New Testament in 1890, while magistrate of Gaya, in Bihar.

Some preposterous slanderers defamed Carey, even claiming that he and his colleagues put translations through the press without knowing the languages, but the absurdity of such statements was too obvious for them to have any effect.

The summary of his Biblical translations stands thus:

Bengali, Oriya, Hindi, Marathi, Sanskrit and Assamese – whole Bibles.
Punjabi New Testament and Old Testament up to *Ezekiel 26.*
Pashto and Kashmiri New Testament and Old Testament up to *2 Kings.*
Telugu and Konkani New Testament and Pentateuch.
Nineteen other languages – New Testaments.
Five other languages – one or more Gospels.

Carey was given the opportunity, the power and the joy of rendering God's Word, or precious portions thereof, into thirty-five languages to a very empire of peoples. After his death, Marshman was constrained to say: 'He has scarcely left a translation to be attempted on this side of India.' And Carey knew that, though the living messenger was important to preach the Word, the Book itself, in the mother tongue of the people, was a permanent missionary, and also essential to the people of God 'for doctrine, for reproof, for correction, for instruction in righteousness', that they might be entire, and wholly equipped for 'all good works'.

Carey's Biblical Translations

Year of publication	New Testament	Pentateuch	Histories	Prophets	Hagiographa
1801	Bengali				
1802		Bengali			
1803					Bengali
1807				Bengali	
1808	Sanskrit				
1809	Oriya		Bengali		
1811	Hindi	Sanskrit		Oriya	Oriya
	Marathi				
1812	*THE YEAR OF THE FIRE*				
1813		Hindi			
		Marathi			
1814			Oriya		
1815	Punjabi	Oriya	Sanskrit		
	Balochi (Matt. Mk. Lk.)				
	R. Jaipuri (Matt.)				
1816	R. Mewari (Matt.)		Marathi		Hindi
1818	Telugu	Punjabi	Hindi	Sanskrit	Marathi
	M. Konkani			Hindi	Sanskrit
	Pashto				
1819	Assamese		Punjabi	Marathi	
	Lahnda				
1820	Gujarati				
	R. Bikaneri				
	H. Awadhi (Matt. Mk.)				
1821	Kashmiri	Telugu			Punjabi
	P. Nepali	M. Konkani			
	H. Bagheli				
	H. Kanouji				
	R. Marwari				

Year of public- ation	New Testament	Pentateuch	Histories	Prophets	Hagio- grapha
1822	R. Harauti	Assamese			
1823	Kanarese				
1824	Bhatneri	Pashto			
	H. Braj Bhasha				
1825	P. Kumaoni (to Col.)				
	Sindhi (Matt.)				
1826	P. Dogri				
	B. Maghadi			Punjabi	
	R. Malvi			(to Ezek.)	
1827	P. Garhwali	Kashmiri			
	Manipuri				
	P. Palpa				
1831	Khasi				
1832			Pashto & Kashmiri (to 2 Kings)		
1833			Assamese	Assamese	Assamese

NOTES

B. = Bihari; H., Hindi; M., Marathi; P., Pahari; R., Rajasthani.
The Pashto *Matthew* and *Mark* had been done under the superintendence of Dr Leydon.

Appendix
The Garden Grower

Many plants to be found in Bengal today came of seeds first bird-borne or wind-sown from Carey's garden.

PROF BRUHL, Calcutta University.

No person can be more passionately fond of natural history than Dr Carey. His aviary contains many birds never described nor named, till he possessed them. He has a pretty good collection of minerals and shells. His botanic garden is large, with four tanks of water, some of them, perhaps, 150 ft. sq. The principal one is opposite the garden gate, and we descend into it by a wide flight of steps. It is overshadowed by some noble trees, which in bloom make a delightful appearance. Here we now baptise.

LAWSON to Jonathan Dyer, 5 December, 1814.

SHEFFIELD
30 March, 1822

Dear Dr Carey,

Will you accept the following fancy piece from the hand of a stranger, who could not help writing it after the perusal of a letter from yourself to Mr Cooper of Wentworth, which casually fell into my hands, and in which you mention with a simplicity that delighted and affected me exceedingly, the beautiful circumstances of a daisy being unexpectedly borne into India of English earth transported thither. I have probably wronged your feelings in attempting to imagine what they were at this apparition. I am sure I have not done justice to my own in the imperfect expression of them, whilst assuming your character with so little ability to maintain it. But he who can cherish from year to year a succession of seedling daisies in India amidst all the labours of a missionary, speaking with tongues unacquired by inspiration, but surely assisted by God's Spirit, must have a kind heart, and will accept this poor offering from the West, from one whose parents were missionaries, and who would fain now and then give a cup of cold water to such disciples.

I am, with sincere respect,

Your friend,

JAMES MONTGOMERY

CAREY'S DAISY IN INDIA

Thrice welcome, little English flower!
My mother-country's white and red,
In rose or lily, till this hour,
Never to me such beauty spread:
Transplanted from thine island-bed,
A treasure in a grain of earth,
Strange as a spirit from the dead,
Thine embryo sprang to birth.

Thrice welcome, little English flower!
Whose tribes, beneath our natal skies,
Shut close their leaves while vapours lower;
But, when the sun's gay beams arise,
With unabashed but modest eyes,
Follow his motion to the west,
Nor cease to gaze till daylight dies,
Then fold themselves to rest.

Thrice welcome, little English flower!
To this resplendent hemisphere,
Where Flora's giant offspring tower
In gorgeous liveries all the year:
Thou, only thou, art little here,
Like worth unfriended and unknown,
Yet to my British heart more dear
Than all the torrid zone.

Thrice welcome, little English flower!
Of early scenes beloved by me,
While happy in my father's bower,
Thou shalt the blithe memorial be;
The fairy sports of infancy,
Youth's golden age and manhood's prime.
Home, country, kindred, friends, with thee,
I find in this far clime.

Thrice welcome, little English flower!
I'll rear thee with a trembling hand:
Oh, for the April sun and shower,
The sweet May dews of that fair land,
Where daisies, thick as starlight, stand
In every walk! that here may shoot
Thy scions, and thy buds expand
A hundred from one root.

Thrice welcome, little English flower!
To me the pledge of hope unseen:
When sorrow would my soul o'erpower,
For joys that were, or might have been,
I'll call to mind, how, fresh and green,
I saw thee waking from the dust;
Then turn to Heaven with brow serene,
And place in God my trust.

JAMES MONTGOMERY

Appendix
The Garden Grower

To KNOW AND GROW PLANTS was with Carey a vocation and a passion. He studied and wrought with the Word of God and also the works of God. The Scriptures were divine seed, and he rejoiced to be among the first to bring this supreme and vital seed to India's many peoples. But he also brought to them the seeds of finer and more varied grains, roots, flowers and fruits than they had ever been acquainted with, and taught them to grow and develop these for their service and delight.

'I have always,' he told Fuller, 'had a strong turn for natural history, and especially for botany, and know nothing fitter to relax the mind after close application.'

In his first Mudnabati letter, we remember, he sent home 'for instruments of husbandry, and a yearly assortment of all garden and flowering seeds, and also of fruit, field and forest trees, for the lasting advantage of what I now call my own country.' As soon as he could afford them he also sent for the monthly *Curtis's Botanical Magazine*, with its remarkable colour prints.

Very early in these Mudnabati years he corresponded with Dr Roxburgh, and they reciprocated gifts. Carey sent him, after his second excursion to Bhutan, twenty-four plant kinds, including a new species of sal tree, which Roxburgh called 'careya'. He reported on the hyacinths, narcissi, irises, amaryllids and tulips he had grown from his first English consignments. He begged seeds of nutmeg, coffee and cloves. 'My land is poor, but I am preparing special soil for them.' (The rotted stalks from the indigo vats made the best of manures.) He asked the exact botanical names of 117 plants, and gave their Bengali ones. 'I am ashamed of so large a request, but botanists are communicative.' He offered him samples of all, save one. Later, he sent Roxburgh forty other plant kinds and fruits, among which were a cheeralo, from the only such tree near Mudnabati, a very bitter febrifuge, a kind of Venus's looking-glass, yams from Bhutan, a fruit that intoxicated fish, and a very lovely convolvulus. He begged twenty special plant kinds, and again asked the botanical names of many pressed specimens he forwarded. (Alas! a third of Roxburgh's recent gifts perished on the long river voyage, and birds destroyed the black pepper.) He told of success with Patna wheat, less dark than the local, and had interested several Europeans in the culture of Roxburgh's nutmegs, all open sowing of which had failed. But he had succeeded in getting some to thrive in boxes of earth and sharp sand under a jack tree. When pressed to move to Serampore, he wrote of the pleasure he would find in being near to him and the Botanic: 'I have a thousand questions to ask.' Amongst the many treasures he took to him are 'a natural bark that looked burnt', and a rare fruit from a fearsome jungle.

The most valuable of his letters to Roxburgh contains a list of the 427 species of plants he had growing in his new Serampore garden in June 1800, within six months of his getting there, although those months must have been thronged with a thousand and one other urgencies. Carey had brought them, of course, from Mudnabati, from his garden which had astonished Ward, and which he had described as 'the best private one in Bengal'. Carey sent the list to Roxburgh, not to boast, but so that he might select anything he desired. Carey at the same time requested 66 other species! 'My desires are unbounded. I cannot expect half, but shall be grateful for any, especially the lilac tribes, next to fruit-trees and plants of utility.' He thanked him for the Cape seeds, and for mesembryanthemums and geraniums, which now adorned his verandah. 'I suffer none to water them but myself.' Carey speaks in these letters of his progress with nectarines, peaches, Malda mangoes; plants sent to him from Bhutan and the Sundarbans, and the Cape, and jute growing 'twelve feet high in Serampore'.

A little later in an illustrated paper before the Asiatic Society on the agriculture of Dinajpur, Carey described the district's soils and modes of tillage, and the remediable poverty of its cereals and of its roots and fruits and stock. He spoke particularly of the need to cultivate pulse, cucumber, sugar cane and capsicum, along with other plants. He made the earliest known plea in India for forestation, and Smith says 'his own park at Serampore was a practical model of what could be done in this line.' He named particularly teak, mahogany, the redwood of the Andaman Islands, satinwood, and Himalayan sissoo (prized in ship-yards).

He often distressed his colleagues by working in his garden with only a straw hat to protect his head from the heat, and Marshman got Roxburgh to remonstrate with him for this folly, but he only answered with a teasing evasion, 'What does Marshman know about a garden? He only appreciates it, as an ox does grass.'

While Dr Roxburgh was in England with his health broken, Carey edited and published his friend's *Hortus Bengalensis,* and after his death, his *Flora Indica* in three volumes, saving for Roxburgh's name and for the scientific world the valuable harvest of his lifelong labour. Roxburgh had added to the Botanic 2,200 species besides more than 800 species of trees. For 80 of these he acknowledges his debt to Carey, and for a further 30 to Felix. In his introduction to this *Hortus Bengalensis* Carey shows how vain, even to cultured Indians, all this botanic ardour seemed, numbering, as they did, only 500 plants in their fullest *Materia Medica,* nor ever conceiving the possible improvement of cereals, herbs, vegetables, fruits, spices, dyes, drugs and timbers.

How the publication of the *Flora Indica* stimulated the experts, the following from the superintendent of the Liverpool Botanic illustrates: 'Although we consider ourselves rich in scitamineous plants, so that we believe our collection surpasses all others in Europe, yet from the *Flora Indica,* which our kind friend Dr Carey has sent us, we see we are considerably short. We, therefore, beg your further favours. We have packed all the accompanying seeds,' he adds, 'in peat earth, as Dr Carey advises.'

To every possible helper Carey would send his appeals, to his home folk, of course, first. Nor did they fail to make response. His nephew Jesse writes, 'I am sending the seeds from Cottesbrooke. They appear to me a poor collection – not much more than what we call weeds. But you ask for them.' 'Hannah *[14]* and Carey *[8]* have gone to Pury Feast,' writes their Aunt Mary, 'to get you some bluebells, as there are none of that kind here. David *[17]* and Carey have sent you another parcel of seeds. Let us know if they are what you want.' As soon as this David emigrated to South Africa, his uncle rejoiced in a new rich source of supply.

William Byfield, a Pury gardener, Carey's 'cuson', would send (his spelling) – 'blubils, kings fingers, jonkils, tilips, snapdragons' – and mahogany saplings. 'Please send word if you want any urbs of any surt. I try to collect for you all seeds that I think will be yousful.'

He sued the help of every likely correspondent. To Fuller he would write for 'seeds and stones of English fruits, packed in dry sand, to arrive between September and December'. To Sutcliff: 'Do send me a few tulips, daffodils, snowdrops, lilies, etc. Only they must not be put into the hold. Send roots in a net or basket, to be hung up anywhere out of the reach of the salt water. Your cowslips and field daisies will be great acquisitions here.' And again: 'Were you to give a boy a penny a day to gather seeds of cowslips, violets, daisies, crowfoots, etc, and to dig up the roots of bluebells, after they have flowered, you might fill me a box each quarter. My American friends are twenty times more communicative in this respect than my English. Do try to mend a little.'

To a friend he wrote, 'Tell Captain Hague not to forget, on his return, his promise to furnish my garden with American flora.'

Of William, at Sadamahal, he begged:

> certain red-flowering plants that grow as high as one's knees, and the grasshopper with the saddle on his back, and the bird, whose large crest opens as it settles, and the noisy kite-khokora, which I think is an eagle. Send me every sort of bird which is not common here, with their Bengali names. Let me have them alive. When you have a good boat-load, send them under the charge of a careful person, and I will pay the cost. Spare no pains to send me seeds and roots. You can insert a pinch of seed in every letter.

To Jabez, on the eve of his embarking for Amboyna, he gave these solicitous instructions:

Be sure to send me every possible vegetable production. Plant tubers and bulbs in a box so thickly as to touch one another, or hang them dry in a well-covered basket in an airy part of the ship. Send, if you can, two or three hundred of each sort. I shall be glad of the smallest as well as the largest common plants. Think none insignificant. Plant the small in boxes, and always keep some well rooted and ready; if too recently planted, they die on the way. Just before dispatching them, sow very thickly amongst them seeds of trees, fruits and shrubs, covered with a finger's thickness of fresh soil. They should be watered a little on the voyage. You must often send the same thing, as it will be ten to one that they arrive alive. Do send abundant seeds of every sort, perfectly ripe and dry, in named paper packets, in a box or basket, secured from the rats; and, if possible, cite the due soil. Parasitical plants, such as you have seen me tie on trees, need only be stripped where they grow, and hung in baskets in any airy part of the ship, or even at the maintop. All boxes of plants must have strips of wood over them, to keep out the rats. Nothing must be put in the hold.

Send me as many live birds as possible; also small quadrupeds, monkeys, etc. Beetles, lizards, frogs, serpents may be put in a small keg of rum. I have much confidence in you to add greatly to my stock of natural productions. But you must persevere in both collecting and sending.

And Jabez faithfully complied, despatching by almost every opportunity seeds, bulbs, nuts, shells, saplings, curios, etc. We read of his sending cages of brilliant parakeets – 'four blackheaded, like the one mother has', 'two red and black striped', 'one very uncommon with a blue breast', and 'one that can almost speak'; wild green pigeons, white cockatoos and a black one; birds of paradise, living, and their skins; 'Loo', a cassowary, 'an old friend', and cassowary eggs, with flowers cut thereon; a species of kangaroo; boxes of lovely shells – 'two very thin, scarce and elegant'; cases and sacks of plants – 'plants from walls and trees', 'wild plants I have never seen in Bengal', wild onions and ginger, etc; sheets of fibre from the inner rind of a tree, used as clothing by the Alfoors and as shrouds for their dead; leaves that would erase writing and smooth wood; Alfoor spears and shields, etc.

Carey was specially pleased when his Fort William students, or perhaps Marshman's Serampore boarders, entered into his hobby and sent him gifts from afar – as Edward Gardiner kept doing from Nepal, and W. B. Martin from Amboyna, and David Scott from Assam, and several others. 'I have lately received,' he told Jabez, 'a parcel of seeds

from Moore, who, you may remember, was a big boy in Dr Marshman's school, when the printing office was burnt. They all bid fair to
grow. He is in the Malay Islands.' One of his most constant donors was
Matthew Smith, the septuagenarian superintendent of the Botanic in
Sylhet. We read of gifts of creepers and cowslips, plums and plumbago,
parasites and polypodia, sages and sassafras, crab-apple stocks for
apples and pears, etc. Indeed, from every boatload he dispatched to
Calcutta's Garden he requested that 'his most worthy friend' at Serampore should have a goodly share.

With a wistful eagerness Carey dealt with all arrivals. To Mr Cooper
of Wentworth, Lord Milton's gardener, he wrote:

> That I might be sure to lose nothing of your valuable present, I shook
> the bag over a patch of earth in a shady place. On visiting this a few days
> after, I found springing up to my inexpressible delight a *Bellis perennis*
> of our English pastures. I know not that I ever enjoyed, since leaving
> Europe, a simple pleasure so exquisite as the sight of *this English daisy*
> afforded me – not having seen one for upwards of thirty years, and
> never expecting to see one again.

A similar pleasure he tasted when, from seeds Johns brought him
from Olney, a little wild geranium flowered.

About this same time Carey was brought into fortunate touch with
another great private Yorkshire garden, that of the Hon and Rev William Herbert, the son of the first Earl of Caernarvon. After a brief
parliamentary career he had been ordained at thirty-six, and was in
due course called to the Deanery of Manchester. His chief recreation
was the growing of rare plants, and he made his Spofforth conservatories a treasury of plants from all parts of the world, and one of the best
botanic laboratories, devoted especially to the culture of bulbous
plants and to experiments in hybridisation. Carey and he collaborated
for fifteen years. Carey had sent the Dean a plant of the Amaryllidaceae
family (named '*careyanum*' by the recipient). In 1843, the latter wrote:

> This beautiful Indian plant was brought to light by Dr Carey, late of
> Serampore. I never saw him, but fifteen years' correspondence has
> accustomed me to look upon him as a dearly-valued friend. His life was
> devoted to the diffusion of the Gospel. Horticulture, natural history and
> botany afforded the brief recreation he allowed himself from his daily
> toil. His favourite plants were the Amaryllidaceae family, and to him we

are indebted for our knowledge of many of them. I have had the pleasure of naming after one of the best and most indefatigable and amiable of men this beautiful Indian *Amaryllis*, which was brought to light by himself.

Other rarities, which he owed to Carey and propagated at Spofforth, are the tall Rangoon *Crinum* (lily), with its thick columnar stem and its broad, upright leaves; the lily *Hedychium carneum*, with its flesh-coloured fragrant blooms; and the orchid *Dendrobium*, which Carey told him 'was cultivated in Calcutta by tying it on a tree, and conveying water to it by a string through a small aperture in a vessel above; and that, so treated, it would hang down six feet, covered with flowers after the fall of the leaves, and be one of the loveliest things in the vegetable kingdom.'

But Carey was also in constant communication through these years with one of Britain's most progressive *public* gardens, the Botanic of Liverpool, which had been founded as early as 1802 by a very remarkable man, William Roscoe. He and Carey were soon in correspondence, and by 1820, Carey had so aided his researches and enriched Liverpool's Garden that he was elected to its honorary membership. In his longest extant letter, discovered in September 1933, amongst the Roscoe papers, Carey acknowledges this honour. He modestly describes himself 'as rather a collector of plants than a botanist'; he attributes to Roscoe's article in the *Linnaean Transactions*, Vol. viii, his own increased interest in the *Canna* (Indian shot) and the Scitamineae (bananas, gingers, arrowroot, etc); he confesses that Roscoe's data had in two or three instances corrected his own previous misconceptions; but, on the other hand, he declares himself in doubt on several points of Roscoe's recent classification of several species of the genera *Curcuma* and *Zingiber* (the plants yielding turmeric and ginger), and gives his reasons. He hopes on Lady Hastings' return from Central India, and Dr Wallich's from his twelve months' botanising in Nepal, to send Roscoe some new species. But he is hopeful, also, of supplies from Sumatra, and even from Borneo, through the liberality of Sir Stamford Raffles. He intends to engage some Arakanese converts in botanical quests around Chittagong. He will this season send to Liverpool four species of the Scitamineae, in order that all doubts concerning them may be settled. (Roscoe notes in pencil in the margin that 'they have arrived and are all living.') He begs for any additions, which Roscoe can spare him, to his own 'monandrous' plants, and 'for all kinds of grasses and mosses'. He reports the formation of India's Agricultural and Horticultural Society, and then thus closes: 'I ought to apologise for the freedom with which I have written, but I doubt not you will forgive it.'

In a letter of January 1826, he thanks him for a further pair of his costly and noble volumes on the *'Monandrian'* plants, and reports 'an immense addition to our knowledge of the vegetable kingdom through the recent researches of his indefatigable friend Dr Wallich in Nepal, in Oudh and Rohilcund, and in the Moluccas.' 'He has great reason to be thankful to God,' he says, 'for the restoration of his own health, which is now nearly as perfect as it ever was, and for a large share of domestic happiness, and the still higher pleasure of seeing means for the betterment of the moral condition of the people of Hindustan vigorously employed, and attended with success far exceeding his most sanguine hopes.'

By the following May two other handsome *'Monandrian'* volumes excite his thanks. He also sends, preserved in spirits, the four species of Curcuma, which Roscoe has specially desired, and promises him still others. Lest any should be discoloured on arrival, he adds his draughtsman's drawings and colourings of the bracts of each kind. He again reports that Dr Wallich is bringing to Calcutta – though this time from the forests of Arakan, which defeated Burma had ceded to Britain – 'an immense cargo of living plants and of dried specimens, including new species of both *Crina [the lily]* and *Curcuma [the turmeric]'*, the favourite genera of both Roscoe and Carey. He will be sure to share these with his Liverpool friend. He begs that all seeds sent to him should be packed in peat earth.

How faithfully he had served the Liverpool Garden may be seen from their 1825 report, with its grateful reference to 'the immense number of East India plants, which assiduous friends there had transmitted to them', 'amongst whom none have conferred on us such signal and long-continued favours as the Rev Dr Carey of Serampore and Dr Wallich, the superintendent of Calcutta's Botanic. These may be truly said to have vied with each other in the joint and friendly interest they have taken in supplying us with every valuable and curious plant, which that country, so rich in its vegetable productions, could afford.'

Liverpool was fortunate also to have the enthusiastic service of John Shepherd, who proved himself a masterly cultivator, experimenter and administrator. Botanists from near and far sought the companionship of this horticultural genius. For at least twenty years Carey and he were in constant correspondence, stimulating and serving each other.

The abundance of treasure which Carey kept sending to John Shepherd for his garden, he repaid not only in kind, but by being the skilled and punctual transmitter of Carey's gifts to other British botanists – Liverpool's port being especially convenient for such transmission. One of the chief recipients of these contributions was Dr W. J. Hooker, the Regius Professor of Botany in Glasgow University. How long Carey and he had been in touch with each other we cannot determine, but Carey's seven letters to him found in 1933 in the library of Kew Gardens are obviously those of an established friendship. In three, Carey acknowledges costly gifts of the professor's: his *Musci Exotici* (exotic mosses), two volumes; his *Exotic Flora*, four volumes; and the first instalment of his *Illustrations of Indian Botany*. With six, Carey himself sends dried plants for the Glasgow Herbarium, or 'mosses and lichens', which have been sent to him from New South Wales, as 'the most likely step to make them available for the advancement of knowledge, as in India it is almost impossible to preserve specimens from the ravages of insects. As the box is not quite full, I have added some samples from my own garden.' He sends his gifts, as always, through 'my friend Mr J. Shepherd of Liverpool's Botanic'. 'I have but a small hope of there being much that is new to you; but I persevere in sending because there may probably be something which you have not seen before.' 'My people are great bunglers in preparing them; still, they are amongst the best to be found amongst the natives of this country.' One of these gifts, as Dr Hooker tells us in *Curtis*, was *Justicia speciosa*, very brilliantly purple-flowered, 'one of the greatest ornaments of the forest in the interior of Bengal'. Once Carey asks for a gift:

Should you at any time be able to send me some seeds and some bulbs of large fleshy roots, packed, or rather mixed, with peat earth, twice or thrice as much earth as seeds, you would greatly oblige me. I particularly desire to get seeds of *Geranium, Erodium, Pelargonium, Solidago, Helianthus, Buphthalmum* and other 'syngenesious' plants. [*Geranium, heron's bill, pelargonium, golden rod, sunflower and ox-eye.*]

He tells the professor of 'the magnificent collection of dried and living plants his very esteemed friend Dr Wallich is taking to England, which will suffice to employ all the European botanists for some years in arranging, describing and publishing.' He rejoices that 'the herbarium of Indian plants so long accumulating at India House has been delivered to Dr Wallich for distribution.' He answers a perplexed enquiry of the professor touching the 'Serampore controversy'. He reports Dr Marshman's safe return from his long furlough, and his bringing the charter for their college. He dares to think that in a certain botanical article the professor has mistaken the leaves of *Anona squamosa* for those of *Anona reticulata* (both fruit-trees bearing custard-apples). He affirms *Anona* to be of Indian, not, as generally declared, of West Indian, origin, and to be derived from *nona*, the Indian name of the fruit, and often occurring in India's classics. He also gives the Indian derivation of *Nelumbium*, the sacred lotus – *neel*, blue, and *umbra*, water. On 9 December, 1829, he tells in a joyous postscript that that very week *sati* had been abolished. On 16 June, 1830, he writes:

> Your correspondent, Lady Dalhousie, has paid me a visit, and I dined with her one evening at Lord Bentinck's. She had been examining a great many plants, and had ascertained many of them. We have had a great deal of talk about plants, and a little about you, all much to your honour. She is going soon with Lord Dalhousie to Himalaya, where I doubt not she will discover many valuable plants.

Professor Hooker dedicated the 1833 volume of *Curtis* to her as 'having rendered essential service to botany by her extensive collections'.

In June 1830, Carey tells the professor of the abolition of the Fort William College professorships, but of his own £500 a year pension. Then he writes:

> It is gratifying to see the great accession to your stock of plants in England from the west coast of America and from South America. We have received a few, which, in general, succeed with us. The plants we have not yet succeeded in preserving through the rains are from the Cape and from New South Wales. But I have seen so many obstacles overcome in the culture of plants, and so many new species introduced since 1793, the year I arrived here, that I do not despair of seeing the greatest difficulties surmounted.

A year later, on 30 January, 1832, he says:

As relates to myself, I am an invalid. During the last twelve months I have had ten or twelve attacks of fever and other complaints, and am now only recovering from five weeks of a serious illness. This has unfitted me for writing, and, indeed, for any kind of exertion. I do not expect my time here will be long, nor am I anxious about the period of my departure. I am now more than seventy years of age, thirty-nine of which have been passed in this country.

The last entry in *Curtis* linking Carey, Hooker and John Shepherd is in 1830, when Dr Hooker was its editor:

Jonesia asoca [now known as Saraca linnaeus, one of the Leguminosae] – I was favoured with the specimen here figured of this highly beautiful, fragrant and interesting plant by Mr John Shepherd of the Liverpool Garden, whither its seeds had been sent (packed in mould) by the Rev Dr Carey of Serampore. So skilful had been the mode of treatment pursued that it flowered in great perfection when only 4 ft. high.

'Notwithstanding Dr Carey's extreme and even morbid repugnance to letter writing,' says J. C. Marshman, 'he maintained an extensive correspondence with the most eminent botanists in Europe and America. His own botanical garden, which covered five acres, was stocked with the richest variety of plants from all parts of the world, and in point of scientific importance, was second only to the Government botanical garden, superintended by his friend Dr Wallich.'

This Dr Nathaniel Wallich, whose name we have met again and again, had been the Danish surgeon at Serampore, until he was appointed to succeed Dr Roxburgh as the Curator of Calcutta's Botanic. He was deeply beloved in the Mission circle. Dr Hooker calls him in *Curtis* 'that most enlightened and most liberal of botanists'. Carey and he were for so long such botanical comrades that the present writer felt sure of finding Carey letters in Calcutta's Botanic library, when once I knew that there was a wide shelf full of bound volumes there of Dr Wallich's correspondence with botanists from all over the world. He found *more than two hundred such Carey letters indexed*, and strangely separate from nearly all the rest; but the letters themselves were most tantalisingly missing. A few had evidently been personal – 'the loss of our little girl', 'the death of our child', 'Carey's 66th birthday', etc; but most were doubtless botanic. In a few instances their purpose is indicated: 'vegetable fibre for paper', 'strychnos', 'capsicums', 'Indian botanical names', *'Flora Indica'*, 'coffee cultivation', etc. One is described as 'a most excellent letter'. Twenty-two, Wallich says, he gave to Dawson Turner, the father-in-law of Professor Hooker, and a specialist in British fuci (seaweeds).

In 1821 Carey was elected a corresponding member of Britain's Royal Horticultural Society, and, two years later, a fellow of the Linnaean Society on the recommendation of H. T. Colebrooke.

We have seen how first by flood and then by hurricane Carey's garden was in his later years twice ruined – his five acres for a whole week just a mud tank, and then his redwoods and mahoganies and deodars crashing across his conservatories. In each case, after his tears, he braced himself at once to restore, to rebuild and to replant. Once, an army of locusts filled his garden. Frail as he was, just convalescing from strong fever, he fought for his plants, 'as active in their defence,' one of his colleagues said, 'as a commander in the day of battle.'

We have found him from boyhood and throughout his life almost as keen about birds as about plants – witness his entreaties to his sons to send him every live bird possible, which could not be found near Serampore. So the following entry in Ward's diary is no surprise:

Carey is making great *aviaries* adjoining his house, *with trees planted and growing within them.* He is collecting all kinds of birds there.

And Lawson told Mr Dyer: 'Carey's aviary contains many birds, never described till he possessed them.' At the end of 1811 Carey himself told Ryland:

I have for a long time been describing the birds of Asia, and have completed about half of those that are known. I shall, perhaps, publish them in a series of papers in *Asiatic Researches.* I have but little time for such pursuits, though a strong natural inclination. But nothing can be done without books, birds, correspondents in different countries, and the society of learned men. These I have in good measure, yet the work proceeds very slowly.

I love to think of his aviaries as completing his garden, with all their denizens' multiformity and colour, their gaiety and song. What a refreshment Carey found there amid the stress of his labours! How it all helped to keep him cheerful and sane!

For many years, as Carey told Lady Hastings in 1820, the formation of an agri-horticultural society for India had occupied a chief place in his mind, but he had always considered himself too unimportant to propose it with effect. But, under her deep interest and encouragement, he that year ventured to submit the proposal to a number of Calcutta and provincial friends. In the prospectus which he issued he laments that:

> in one of the finest countries in the world the state of agriculture and horticulture is so abject and degraded, and the people's food so poor, and their comforts so meagre. India seems to have almost everything to learn about the clearing of jungles, the tillage of wastes, the draining of marshes, the banking of river courses, the irrigation of large areas, the mixing of composts and manures, the rotation of crops, the betterment of tools and of transport, the breeding of stocks, the cultivation of new vegetables and herbs, the planting of orchards, the budding, grafting and pruning of fruit trees, and the forestation of timbers. Their only orchards are clumps of mangoes crowded together without judgement. The recent introduction of the potato and the strawberry suggest what might be done. Many British farms have quadrupled their produce, since they pooled their information and experience through agricultural societies.

Thirty-two wrote approving, and promising to join, so he called a meeting in the Calcutta Town Hall that September, a hot month, when the city was almost forsaken of its sahibs. Only seven people attended – Raya Vidyanath Raya, Ram Komal Sen (a Fort William colleague of Carey's), Charles Trower (one of his former students), H. Howell, H. Wood, Dr Marshman, and himself. The society was almost stillborn, yet on the strength of the approving letters they went forward, with Carey as secretary. Their trouble was the lack of land for experimentation, but at their second anniversary, the Governor-General, their willing patron, announced that a considerable portion of land just transferred to the Botanic was to be theirs. Of the plantation committee then formed Carey had to be the first secretary.

A hundred poundsworth of grafted fruit-trees were secured from England. Experiments were initiated in the culture of coffee, cotton, tobacco, sugar cane, cereals, etc, and prizes also were offered for the private growing of these and of other products. Carey's own young gardener, Halidhar, once won a medal with Rs 40 for his cabbages. Later, in 1827, land in Alipore was leased and given to the society for horticultural developments, and again the chief direction fell to Carey.

The following is part of his letter to the members of his committee, to incite their further suggestions:

> In all cultivation the command of water is of the first importance, and the common mode of watering being not only very expensive but highly objectionable (on account of the violence with which the water is poured, and also from its neglect in the hottest season of the year and its excess at other times), I recommend a reservoir near the tank, into which water may be pumped up. The bottom of the reservoir should be so raised above the level of the garden that by pukka drains communicating with every part of the ground, water may be conveyed in any required quantity to any part, according to need.
>
> Manures and composts of various kinds are of the utmost necessity. A plan should, therefore, be made for securing large quantities of cow or other dung, sweepings of Calcutta streets, rotten leaves, scourings of ditches, drains, etc. Nor should burnt clay, lately much recommended, be neglected. All these should be kept ready, variously mixed.
>
> In this country seedlings need protection in the rainy season, yet should have all the free air possible consistent therewith. Cabbages, cauliflowers, celery, and many other productions must be sown in the rains to secure a crop. The methods hitherto followed are in general unsightly and irregular. I recommend that effectual shelter, so arranged as to be ornamental, be provided. Perhaps the frames, which I have been desired to undertake, may answer the purpose.
>
> The practice of driving nails into walls for the training of fruit-trees is highly objectionable, as it breaks the walls (which should always be plastered) and thereby makes them of disagreeable appearance, and furnishes lodging places for insects. I therefore urge that hooks, or the newly-invented nails of this form [a sketch is inserted] be built into the walls in rows eight or nine inches above each other, and a foot asunder in the rows.

At the society's third show he could say that they were experimenting with grafts from English apple trees, from Seville and Mozambique oranges, from the best mulberries and peaches, from Cape figs, Canton lychees, Manilla guavas, and with the choicest pineapples and vines; also with the growth of arrowroot and celery, tobacco and cotton, and with the pruning of mangoes. Their vegetable display, he said, would not discredit any climate or horticulture in the world, though most of the vegetables were a few years back unknown to most Indian gardeners.

Of his own Serampore garden his son Jonathan writes:

No one was allowed to interfere in the arrangements of this his favourite retreat; and it was here he enjoyed his most pleasant moments of secret meditation and devotion. His arrangements were on the Linnaean system, and to disturb a bed or border was to touch the apple of his eye. It formed the best and rarest botanical collection of plants in the East, to whose extension, by his correspondence with eminent persons in Europe and other parts of the world, his attention was constantly directed; and in return, he supplied his correspondents with rare collections from the East. It was painful to observe with what distress my father quitted this scene of his enjoyments, when extreme weakness, during his last illness, prevented his walking there. Often he was drawn thither in a chair placed on a board with four wheels.

In order to prevent irregularity in his gardeners' attendance, he was latterly particular in paying their wages with his own hands. When at last confined to the house, he would send for them into the room where he lay, and converse with them about the plants; and near his couch, against the wall, he placed *the picture of a beautiful shrub,* upon which he gazed with delight.

The story is doubtless authentic that, not many days before he died, when asked the reason of some apparent distress, he answered, 'Oh, when I'm gone, Brother Marshman will let the cows into my garden!' But it must have been good-humoured teasing or a passing forgetfulness, for Dr Johann Voight, Marshman's surgeon son-in-law, had already undertaken its care, and counted the preservation of its order, beauty and wealth a very sacred stewardship, as his *Hortus Suburbanus Calcuttensis* demonstrates.

We fittingly close this appendix with the last 'Carey' entries in Dr Wallich's index to his correspondence, to which I have already made reference – though Carey would protest their fond extravagance:

20 October, 1833 – Mrs Grace Carey, with lock of his hair.
27 January, 1834 – Carey to Mrs Wallich – the ebbing of his precious life manifested in his handwriting.
31 March 1834 – The last lines I ever had – I believe, any one ever had – from incomparably the best, the greatest man India ever possessed – *take him all in all.*

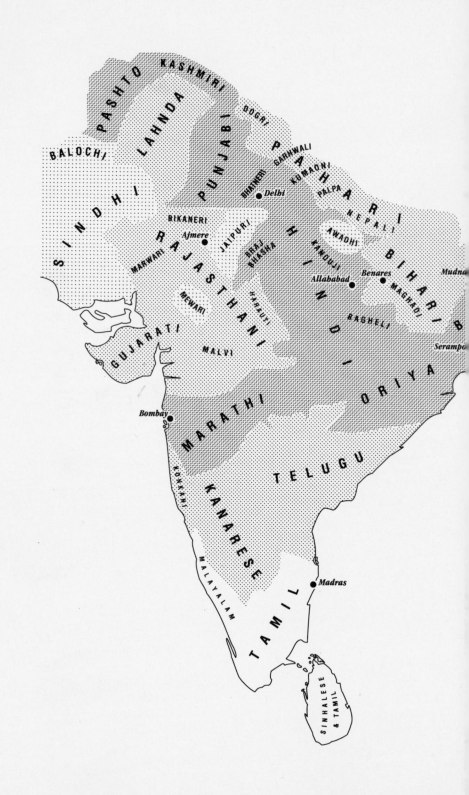